Transactions of the Royal Historical Society

SIXTH SERIES

XIV

CAMBRIDGE
UNIVERSITY PRESS

Published by the Press Syndicate of the University of Cambridge
The Edinburgh Building, Cambridge CB2 2RU, United Kingdom
40 West 20th Street, New York, NY 10011–4211, USA
477 Williamstown Road, Port Melbourne, VIC 3207, Australia
Ruiz de Alarcón 13, 28014 Madrid, Spain

A catalogue record for this book is available from the British Library

First published 2004

ISBN 0 521 84995 0 hardback

SUBSCRIPTIONS. The serial publications of the Royal Historical Society,
Royal Historical Society Transactions (ISSN 0080–4401) and Camden Fifth Series
(ISSN 0960–1163) volumes may be purchased together on annual subscription.
The 2004 subscription price (which includes print and electronic access) is £71
(US$114 in the USA, Canada and Mexico) and includes Camden Fifth Series,
volumes 24 and 25 (published in July and December) and Transactions Sixth
Series, volume 14 (published in December). Japanese prices are available from
Kinokuniya Company Ltd, PO Box 55, Chitose, Tokyo 156, Japan. EU subscribers
(outside the UK) who are not registered for VAT should add VAT at their country's
rate. VAT registered subscribers should provide their VAT registration number.

Subscription orders, which must be accompanied by payment, may be sent to
a bookseller, subscription agent or direct to the publisher: Cambridge University
Press, The Edinburgh Building, Shaftesbury Road, Cambridge CB2 2RU, UK; or in
the USA, Canada and Mexico; Cambridge University Press, Journals Fulfillment
Department, 100 Brook Hill Drive, West Nyack, New York 10994–2133, USA.
Prices include delivery by air.

SINGLE VOLUMES AND BACK VOLUMES. A list of Royal Historical Society
volumes available from Cambridge University Press may be obtained from the
Humanities Marketing Department at the address above.

Printed and bound in the United Kingdom at the University Press, Cambridge

CONTENTS

Transactions of the RHS 14 (2004), pp. 1–24 © 2004 Royal Historical Society
DOI: 10.1017/S0080440104000052   Printed in the United Kingdom

TRANSACTIONS OF THE
ROYAL HISTORICAL SOCIETY

PRESIDENTIAL ADDRESS

By Janet L. Nelson

ENGLAND AND THE CONTINENT IN THE NINTH CENTURY: III, RIGHTS AND RITUALS

READ 21 NOVEMBER 2003

ABSTRACT. This essay aims to show that in England and on the Continent, ninth-century individuals and groups in a wide variety of social milieux from peasants to substantial landowners, and including women, had a strong sense of rights to status and property that were rational in something like the modern sense while surrounded by rituals that seem very un-modern. Un-modern, too, seem the terms on which rights were held, and the forms and contexts in which rights were negotiated and renegotiated between local holders, lords and kings. With reference to material from Wessex and from various parts of the Carolingian Empire, it is suggested that the linkage of rights and rituals was symptomatic of sophisticated cultures with apt ways of managing conflict and creating consensus in localities and in kingdoms. The so-called decimation of King Æthelwulf is discussed as a meaningful case in point.

'Rights' is not a term often used in modern discussions of earlier medieval social practice or political thought. When Latin or Old English equivalents crop up in prescriptive or descriptive sources, they seem to refer, more often than not, to authority exercised by rulers and lords, and, by an understandable transfer of meaning, to the dues owed to them by inferiors.[1] Rights are only meaningful in social reality when viewed in relation to power; and the Middle Ages was a very inegalitarian world. Yet if ideas of the natural rights of rational men took philosophical shape only in the fourteenth century, already in the ninth there were ideas of rights, individual as well as collective, pertaining to persons of relatively low status as well as to *potentes*, men of power, and relating particularly

---

[1] R. Van Caenegem, 'Government, Law and Society', in *The Cambridge History of Medieval Political Thought*, ed. J. H. Burns (Cambridge, 1988), 174–210, at 179.

to property. One aim of this third of my four lectures to the Society is to repair an omission of the previous two by saying more about the less powerful. More positively, I also want to consider some ninth-century innovations as responses less to external threats than to the challenges of managing internal change – challenges that are coming to be recognised as comparable in England and in Francia.[2] Finally, I hope to show that rights and rituals, subjects usually put in separate intellectual boxes and hence considered by different types of historians, were closely connected in the minds of those ninth-century people we can know of through written records.[3] In insisting on this connection, I take a leaf out of Maitland's book: 'We cannot find [in Anglo-Saxon England] . . . a law which deals only with property and neglects religion.'[4]

I begin, though, with words, recalling at the outset pertinent health-warnings issued by Susan Reynolds: that the rationality we should attribute to medieval people 'can't be identified with the exact and consistent use of words which happened later to acquire peculiar legal significance'; and that 'words were used outside the law' to represent 'notions or concepts [that] may have been wider and more various than the legal records suggest'.[5] It is wise, then, to be wary of the words used by individuals or groups, by institutions and by kings in the ninth century to express what we can, without anachronism, call rights. For Anglo-Saxons, *riht*, just like *right* in modern English, had the general sense of what is right (as in 'do right') and a secondary sense of 'justifiable claim, on legal or moral grounds, to have or obtain something, or to act in a certain way' – but the second is very much less well documented than the first in OE texts, and not at all in the ninth century. Such searches, though made very much easier nowadays by large electronic data-bases and dictionaries, are complicated by a disciplinary divide between OE scholars in English department-boxes and Latin-users in History ones. The legal term *bocriht* is a rarity in the corpus, depicted by a probably early eleventh-century author (Archbishop Wulfstan?) as the hallmark of the thegn, a property right conferred by charter (*boc*) as reward for, and conditional on, service.[6] The consequences of, as distinct from the

² S. Reynolds, *Fiefs and Vassals: The Medieval Evidence Reinterpreted* (Oxford, 1994); R. Faith, *The English Peasantry and the Growth of Lordship* (1997), 59; P. Wormald, *The Making of English Law: King Alfred to the Twelfth Century* (Oxford, 1999), 478–83, also ch. 2 *passim* (65 n. 186 has large implications).

³ Cf. M. Bloch, *The Historian's Craft* (Manchester, 1954), 151.

⁴ F. W. Maitland, *Domesday Book and Beyond* (first publ. Cambridge, 1897; repr. with introduction by E. Miller, 1965), 403.

⁵ S. Reynolds, *Kingdoms and Communities in Western Europe 900–1300*, 2nd edn (Oxford, 1997), 65.

⁶ *Rectitudines Singularum Personarum*, ed. F. Liebermann, *Die Gesetze der Angelsachsen* (3 vols., Halle, 1903–60), I, 1, 444. P. Harvey, '*Rectitudines Singularum Personarum* and *Gerefa*', *English Historical Review*, 108 (1993), 1–22, shows that 1, 1, with its distinctively Scandinavian use of

qualifications for, receiving land by charter have been inferred from the later ninth-century will of Ealdorman Alfred. The ealdorman begins by associating his inheritance (*erfe*) and *bocland*, but later, in the specific context of bequests to his son, he leaves *folcland* 'if the king will grant him [the son] the *folcland* with the *bocland*'. The king's approval was no foregone conclusion: 'if he [the king] will not so allow', the ealdorman provides for one or another of the estates already earmarked for his wife and daughter to pass instead to his son. The *boc*, hence land owned by a *boc* as distinct from *folcland*, seems to confer a rather strong form of right over property, namely the right to bequeath away from kin. Yet the will as a whole, like other wills of high-status persons, is addressed to the king for approval.[7] The peculiarities of Ealdorman Alfred's dispositions, indicating that the wife he names here was not his first, suggest that to generalise principles from this case would be unwise. The claims of stepmothers and half-siblings always tended to create particular tensions within families.[8] Rights over land could in practice be qualified, not just by the formal reservation of certain royal interests but by changing conceptions of what those interests were (and it was a wise man who thought it worth saying that kings change their minds).[9] The interests and expectations of kin could be equally constraining if a charter explicitly reserved them.[10] We might call those interests and expectations 'rights': ninth-century OE texts, while they do not use *riht* in this context, use other expressions from which rights can (and could) be inferred.[11] But these Anglo-Saxon rights were less clear-cut, more conditioned by circumstance, with greater propensity to link law and religion, than people brought up on modern legal definitions tend to expect.

---

lagu for 'right' ('Ðegenlagu is, þæt he sy his bocrihte wyrðe') unlike the rest of this text is probably a Wulfstanian addition; cf. Wormald, *Making*, 387–9.

[7] Will of Ealdorman Alfred, ed. W. de G. Birch, *Cartularium Anglo-Saxonicum* (4 vols., 1885–99) [hereafter cited as B], II (1887), no. 558, pp. 195–7, and listed by P. Sawyer, *Anglo-Saxon Charters: An Annotated List and Bibliography*, Royal Historical Society Guides and Handbooks (1968), revised S. Kelly, *The Electronic Sawyer*, http://www.trin.cam.ac.uk/chartwww, no. 1508 [hereafter S]; trans. D. Whitelock, *English Historical Documents*, 2nd edn [hereafter EHD I] (1989), no. 97, p. 538. Reynolds, *Fiefs and Vassals*, 329 n. 25, points out a charter of 946 in which an inheritance (*yrfe*) includes *laenland*, loaned or leased land, as well.

[8] B. Kasten, 'Stepmothers in Frankish Legal Life', in *Law, Laity and Solidarities: Essays in Honour of Susan Reynolds*, ed. P. Stafford, J. L. Nelson and J. Martindale (Manchester, 2001), 47–67, at 49, 53; cf. J. S. Loengard, 'English Dower in the Year 1200', in *Women of the Medieval World: Essays in Honor of J. H. Mundy*, ed. J. Kirshner and S. F. Wemple (Oxford, 1985), 215–55, esp. 243–4.

[9] Maitland, *Domesday Book*, 351.

[10] Alfred, Laws, c. 41, ed. and trans. F. L. Attenborough, *The Laws of the Earliest English Kings* (Cambridge, 1922), 82–3.

[11] Even later as well, the word is rare in that sense: see *The Toronto Dictionary of Old English Corpus*, http://etext.lib.virginia.edu/oec.html.

The normal language of Anglo-Saxon charters was Latin, the language of law and religion. A West Saxon royal charter late in the long ninth century (actually 904) shows the importance of other kinds of rights, stakes and sets of interests. When Edward the Elder granted the *libertas* of the monastery at Taunton (Somerset) *in sempiterno graphio* ('in an eternal writing'), as the perpetual property of the bishop's church of Winchester and its community (*familia*), at the same time he reserved the army-service, fortress-work and bridge-work owed to the king, and also 'conceded to Christ that the bishop's men, noble and non-noble, resident in that countryside (*in praefato rure degentes*), should have in all dignity the very same right (*hoc idem ius*) that the men of the king have who live on royal estates'.[12] Here, at last, we find a word that looks as if it corresponds to a more or less familiar notion of right. But what was this *ius*, or these *iura*? The next passage in the charter explains: 'all judgements (*judicia*) of secular matters are to be exercised for the use of the bishops in just the same way that judgements about matters of royal business are dealt with'. *Judicia* means regular court-meetings, thrice a year, with the profits of justice going to the court-holder, in this case henceforth to be the bishop. *Libertas* meant immunity, that is, freedom at the king's command from all royal demands for dues and hospitality, except for the three reserved services.[13] The bishop's *homines*, those *in rure degentes*, will henceforward owe attendance at his court to participate in delivering justice, but their own cases will also be judged there. Local expertise conferred special qualifications to judge and special expectations of being judged justly. Customary knowledge was intimately linked with residence and with property in ways that transcended, at Taunton anyway, differences of social status (though the distinction between noble and non-noble may be formulaic). Shared judicial experience as well as participation, no doubt often burdensome, in the court's procedures and findings had symbolic value. In its local social setting – *in rure* – a court was a major public event. The bishop's royally delegated authority was on display, and so too were the identity and status of attenders. At court, the relationship between the bishop and 'his' *homines* was ritually re-enacted and reinforced. The bishop

---

[12] S 373, B 612.
[13] See for England, N. P. Brooks, 'The Development of Military Obligations in Eighth- and Ninth-Century England', in *England before the Conquest: Studies in Primary Sources Presented to Dorothy Whitelock*, ed. P. Clemoes and K. Hughes (Cambridge, 1971), 69–84; and Wormald, *Making*, 108; and for Francia, J. L. Nelson, 'Dispute Settlement in Carolingian West Francia', in *The Settlement of Disputes in Early Medieval Europe*, ed. W. Davies and P. Fouracre (Cambridge, 1986), 45–64, at 56, 62 (repr. in Nelson, *The Frankish World* (1995), 51–74, at 62, 69); P. Fouracre, 'Eternal Light and Earthly Needs: Practical Aspects of the Development of Frankish Immunities', in *Property and Power in the Early Middle Ages*, ed. W. Davies and P. Fouracre (Cambridge, 1995), 53–81; and B. Rosenwein, *Negotiating Space: Power, Restraint, and Privileges of Immunity in Early Medieval Europe* (Ithaca, NY, 1999), 99–134.

was now their lord, not just a collector of judicial profits but responsible for supporting and defending his men and their property-rights against any challenger. Though lordship might involve tenurial dependence, at Taunton later tenth-century evidence suggests that the bond between bishop and men was the more flexible one of patronage and protection, and that if the bishop turned exploiter rather than protector, his men looked to the king.[14] In King Edward's charter, Christ had been named as recipient, hence guarantor, of terms that cut two ways. *Iura* therefore had an experiential dimension for the charter's indirect beneficiaries. As for us, these rights lead beyond etymology to rituals of power and faith.

On the ninth-century Continent, some vernacular words for 'right' were derived from late Roman Latin *directum*, 'straight', used of a line, or a road (cf. Vulgate, *directio*, Ps. 44: 6, 118: 7, *directe* Sap. 5: 22), thence early medieval *directum*, *drectum*, *drictum*, meaning 'the law', 'what is lawful'. In ninth-century Frankish usage, *drictum* could refer generally to rights of lordship, as, famously, in Charlemagne's requirement following his coronation as emperor that all men over the age of twelve should swear a new oath of fidelity: 'I shall henceforth be faithful to my lord Charles the pious emperor . . . as a man ought to be to his lord *per drictum*.'[15] This was not to say that fidelity to lord and emperor were the same, but it was to clarify by way of analogy. In 841, the Strasbourg oaths bilingually invoke a brother's obligation 'to help his brother as a man ought in right' (*si cum om per dreit son fradra salvar dist*, and *so haldih tesan minan bruodher, soso man mit rehtu sinan bruodher scal*).[16] In a court-case at Autun in 819, nine 'true witnesses' swore that a man claiming to be legally free was *lege et dricto* in fact a *servus*.[17] *Drictum* and *dreit*, like *rehtu* (compare OE *riht*), seem more often to have the very broad sense of rightfulness than the more particular sense of right.

Justitia gets us further than *drictum*. The standard medieval Latin dictionary distinguishes twenty-four distinct meanings of *justitia*, most of them to be encountered in the ninth century.[18] It was commonly used in narrative sources and in capitularies to denote 'the whole of a person's or a corporate body's rights, his or her right' (meaning 14), also 'a particular right' (meaning 15), also 'a particular property right' (meaning 16). True,

---

[14] S 806. See B. Yorke, *Wessex in the Early Middle Ages* (1995), 213–14.

[15] Monumenta Germaniae Historica Capitularia regum Francorum [hereafter MGH Capit.], ed. A. Boretius and V. Krause (2 vols., Hannover, 1883–97), I, no. 34, c. 19, p. 101.

[16] Nithard, *Historiarum Libri IV*, ed. E. Müller, Monumenta Germaniae Historica Scriptores rerum Germanicarum in usum scholarum [hererafter MGH SRG] (Hannover, 1907), III, 5, p. 36.

[17] *Receuil des Chartes de l'Abbaye de Saint-Benoît-sur-Loire*, ed. M. Prou and A. Vidier (2 vols., Paris and Orleans 1900–32), I, no. 16, p. 37. For the context, see Wormald, *Making*, 76–9; and cf. Nelson, 'Dispute Settlement', 47.

[18] J. F. Niermeyer, *Mediae Latinitatis Lexicon Minus* (Leiden, 1997), s.v., 569–73.

it also meant 'the Augustinian idea of order and harmony', 'the Law', 'a particular body of law', 'the administration of justice', 'a law-suit', 'a judgement', 'the actualisation of Law as viewed from the standpoint of the individual' (meanings 1–6, 9). Other meanings have more to do with 'rights to dues', or 'a due', or 'fines' (meanings 17, 18, 19). Obviously the linkages between these senses were significant in referring the particular to the general, the concrete to the abstract and most important of all, the practical to the ethical. The twenty-four distinct meanings are the work of the modern lexicographer. In ninth-century usage, there was much overlap. Still, it is worth stressing that *iustitia* did sometimes have the sense of individual or institutional right. To the author(s) of the Royal Frankish Annals, a literary production of the only slightly elongated ninth century, the Franks' attacks on Italy in 755 and 756, and on Aquitaine in 760 were driven by pursuit of 'the *iustitia* of St Peter', of 'the *iustitiae* of the churches'.[19] Tassilo of Bavaria in 794 renounced *omnis iustitia et res proprietatis* in the duchy of Bavaria for himself and for his children.[20] Other capitularies require that royal officers (*missi*) hold enquiries 'concerning our [i.e. Charlemagne's] *iustitiae*, and the *iustitiae* of churches, widows, orphans, wards and others', and, shifting from meaning 1, 2 or 3 to meaning 14 or perhaps 15 in a single clause, that '*iustitia* be done concerning the *iustitiae* of churches, widows and orphans'.[21] Confirming the implied connection between rights and property is a grant made by a Bavarian husband to his wife *ad iustitiam et proprietatem*.[22] Echoing both narrower and grander meanings of *iustitia* is a charter of Charles the Fat sub-king of Alemannia to Beretheida, *fidelissima nostra*, on account of her faithfulness and the zeal of her service (*propter fidelitatem et obsequii illius instantiam*), granting lands *in proprietatem* with full powers of alienation and sale, as *lex et iustitia* allow to be held *de proprietate*.[23] *Proprietas* again is associated with *iustitia* here; and the background is of Roman legal tradition transmitted, notably, through formularies.[24]

To be free entailed rights to the integrity of your body. In 861, Charles the Bald, king of the West Franks, decreed that a free man found guilty of rejecting the king's coinage, if the pennies were found to be pure and

[19] *Annales regni Francorum* 755, 756, 760, ed. F. Kurze, MGH SRG (Hannover, 1895), 12, 14, 18. These annals were probably compiled in the early 790s.

[20] MGH Capit. I, no. 28, c. 3, p. 74.

[21] MGH Capit. I, no. 34, c. 19, p. 101 (cf. no. 35, c. 59, p. 104; no. 44, c. 2, p. 122; no. 69, c. 3, p. 158; no. 85, c. 2, p. 184); no. 90, c. 1, p. 190.

[22] *Die Traditionen des Hochstifts Freising, Quellen und Erörterungen zur bayerischen Geschichte*, ed. T. Bitterauf (Munich, 1905), no. 392, p. 333.

[23] MGH Diplomata regum Germaniae ex stirpe Karolinorum, Die Urkunden Karls III, ed. P. Kehr (Berlin, 1936–7), no. 2 (15 Apr. 877), p. 4.

[24] E. Levy, *West Roman Vulgar Law: The Law of Property* (Philadelphia, 1951); Nelson, 'Dispute Settlement', 46, 57 with further references.

of good weight, had to pay a fine of 30 *solidi*, 'half the Frankish bann', i.e. half the normal fine for a criminal offence; as for *coloni* and *servi* found guilty of the same offence in towns or markets, the king's officer had discretion to consider the person's age, physical state and sex – *quia et feminae barcaniare solent* ('because women too are often involved in petty trading') – and to have the guilty beaten either with heavy blows, later specified as *cum grosso fuste*, 'with a big truncheon', or with *minutae virgae*, 'switches'.[25] The clear differentiation of legal rights was there. Bodily punishment was for the unfree, though the death penalty was prescribed in England and Francia for traitors or rebels or perpetrators of violent crime, regardless of legal status, from the late eighth century onwards.[26] For men who had presumed to make sworn associations and then done evil, Charlemagne prescribed that 'the ring-leaders are to be executed, while those who aided them are to be flogged, one by another, and to have their noses slit, one by another', a type of public dishonouring particularly awful for persons of free status.[27] Some crimes were so serious as to justify denying normal legal rights.

Rights of the free to bodily integrity were linked with their immunity from labour services. A large-scale landlord could wield the sledgehammer of public justice to secure legal confirmation of a single peasant's unfreedom. Patrick Wormald has considered a number of such cases from the early and mid-ninth century.[28] They show a mix of aristocratic, ecclesiastical and royal interests in asserting lordly rights to the full, and before a local constituency of those whom one capitulary calls *homines bonae generis*,[29] but the fact that lordly claims were contested in court shows the passion with which peasants asserted what they believed (or claimed) were *their* rights.

When peasants speak in the surviving sources, they use various terms for individual and collective rights: *ius*; *lex*; *consuetudo*. Even unfree peasants could attempt to defend such rights in courts of law. The *servi* of Berndorf in Bavaria had been transferred in an exchange by the bishop of Regensburg to the lordship of a neighbouring abbot, who treated them so badly that the *servi* appealed repeatedly to the bishop. The oppressive abbot refused to make amends; so the bishop, unable to

---

[25] MGH Capit. II, no. 271, p. 302; cf. no. 273, c. 18, p. 317. For the free man, the catch was of course, that he might well have to sell himself and or his offspring into slavery in order to clear the fine.

[26] Legatine Synod (786), c. xii, ed. E. Dümmler, MGH Epistolae IV, p. 24; Alfred, Laws, c. 4 (5), ed. and trans. Attenborough, *Laws*, 64–5; MGH Capit. I, no. 20, c. 23, p. 51, no. 26, cc. 11, 12, 13, p. 69; Capit. II, no. 273, c. 25, p. 321.

[27] Thionville, 805, MGH Capit. I, no. 44, c. 10, p. 124.

[28] Wormald, *Making*, 76–80 (discussing six cases from Burgundy, one from Rheims involving a little group of people, and one from St-Gall).

[29] MGH Capit. I , no. 77, c. 12, p. 171.

tolerate the injury done to his *servi*, finally in 829 came to Berndorf with his companions and retainers to meet the abbot, and they agreed to reverse the exchange. These peasants made their case successfully.[30] Only the year before, far to the west within the empire of Louis the Pious, four named peasants together with an unspecified number of their peers (*pares*) travelled some 70 km from Antoigné in Touraine to Chasseneuil in Poitou to protest before the king of Aquitaine that their lord, the monastery of Cormery, a daughter-house of St-Martin Tours, had violated the *lex* of their predecessors by imposing 'more in rent and renders than they ought to pay *per drictum*'. The monastery's representatives counter-claimed that the peasants had in fact been paying the same dues and renders 'for thirty years', and they produced a *descriptio*, an estate-survey, made 'in the 34th year of Charlemagne's reign', i.e. 801–2, when Alcuin was abbot (796–804) in which the due rents and renders of each manse (peasant-holding) were specified, and some of those present had affirmed on oath (*cum iuramento*) that these were their dues. Under questioning, the peasants acknowledged that the survey was 'true and good' and they 'could not deny' that the dues they had actually paid since then had been those specified in the document. The peasants lost. But it looks if they had timed their claim to get it in before the thirty years' rule might nullify it and before living memory lapsed: in other words, they were not only well aware of their ancestral rights and the way the monastery had tampered with them, but they had also monitored the passing of twenty-seven intervening years. As it turned out, they had left it too late.[31]

In 861, the village of Mitry not far from Paris was divided. Twenty-three *homines*, together with eighteen women, of whom ten brought their children, travelled the 60 km to the palace of Compiègne to plead before the tribunal of Charles the Bald that they were not *servi* but *coloni* of the monastery of St-Denis. They claimed that the monastery 'wanted unjustly to bend them down into an inferior service by force (*per vim in inferiorem servitium*)'. The monks' estate-manager and the *maior* of Mitry also presented themselves along with twenty-three *idonei coloni*, to argue that *ista familia* were indeed *servi* and had 'done more than *coloni* would have done in right and law, as is obvious (*et plus per drictum et per legem quem coloni, sicut manifestum est, fecissent*)'.[32] The tribunal found against the plaintiff *familia*:

---

[30] *Die Traditionen des Hochstifts Regensburg und des Klosters S. Emmeram: Quellen und Erörterungen zur bayerischen Geschichte*, ed. J. Widemann (Munich, 1943), no. 25, pp. 31–2. On Bavarian *servi*, I am indebted to unpublished work by Carl I. Hammer, which I gratefully acknowledge here.

[31] L. Levillain, *Receuil des actes de Pépin I et Pépin II, rois d'Aquitaine (814–848)* (Paris, 1926), no. 12, pp. 46–7; see Nelson, 'Dispute Settlement', 48–51, 246–7 (repr. Nelson, *Frankish World*, 54–6, 71–2).

[32] G. Tessier, *Receuil des Chartes de Charles II le Chauve* (3 vols., Paris, 1943–55), II, no. 228, pp. 8–9; see Nelson, 'Dispute Settlement', 51–2 (repr. Nelson, *Frankish World*, 57–9).

of the governor's in *Fidelio*, participants' memories of a *placitum* no doubt retained the drama of cathartic ritual.

Ninth-century rights were not eighteenth-century-style rights of man, universal and egalitarian, though gendered men-only. Medieval rights were specific to particular persons and particular ranks, hence, as you will have observed, including some women. They were concrete, firmly linked with personal status, with property and inheritance, and with specific acts of recognition by the powerful. And yet, as Alain Boureau recently wrote à propos the thirteenth century: 'arguments over privilege played an important role [in developing the idea of a law that was common] for it was through [these arguments] that ideas of ... liberty and equality came to be clarified – ideas too often falsely alleged to have been unthinkable in the Middle Ages'.[39] Privileges were rights confined to the individual or institutional recipient. But they could be extended.

Lawyers created an age of privilege in the thirteenth century that ended only with the end of the ancien regime. Creating new rights was nothing new. Innovation after all is a Gospel message. Christianisation extended in the long ninth century both into new territories, Saxony for instance, and within its old heartlands into new social areas through the application of the law of Christian marriage. Not only did the parity of the marriage-bond transcend the difference between slave and free, but once the bond was tied, separation was canonically impossible. True, lords might try to prevent serfs from marrying outside the lordship, or to charge them for so doing. But that backhandedly shows lords' respect for the solidity of marriage once made. J.-P. Devroey has persuasively argued that ecclesiastical reinforcement of married relationships among the peasantry was a major factor in bringing about a significant decline in slavery in the ninth century.[40] These new rights were in principle universal and for both women and men. In practice lordly interests intruded. Presumably it was the fact that marriages made by peasant migrants inland from the lower Seine valley in the early 860s lacked lords' permission that made the West Frankish king Charles the Bald and assembled aristocrats at Pîtres in 864 declare such unions null and void.[41] That nobles prized the right to inherit

[39] A. Boureau, 'Privilege in Medieval Societies from the Twelfth to the Fourteenth Centuries, or: How the Exception Proves the Rule', in *The Medieval World*, ed. P. Linehan and J. L. Nelson (2001), 621–34, at 623.

[40] J.-P. Devroey, 'Men and Women in Early Medieval Serfdom: The Ninth-Century North Frankish Evidence', *Past and Present*, 166 (2000), 3–30, and *idem*, 'Femmes au miroir des polyptyques: une approche aux rapports du couple dans l'exploitation rurale dépendante entre Seine et Rhin au IXe siècle', in *Femmes et pouvoirs des femmes à Byzance et en occident (Vie-XIe siècles)*, ed. S. Lebecq, A. Dierkens, R. Le Jan and J.-M. Sansterre (Lille, 1999), 227–49. See further the key contribution of P. Toubert, 'La théorie du mariage chez les moralistes carolingiens', in *Il matrimonio nella società altomedievale*, Settimane di Studio del Centro di Studi sull'Alto Medioevo (2 vols., Spoleto, 1977), I, 233–82.

[41] Edict of Pîtres c. 31, MGH Capit. II, p. 324.

and to transmit inheritances is too obvious a point to need stressing. But peasants could have these rights too; and this was explicitly stated in West Frankish capitularies of the 860s, as in a reference to 'inheritances, that is, the holdings that the *coloni* hold'.[42] By the names they chose for their children, peasant parents expressed their strong consciousness of all that was entailed in inheritance, including rights.[43] Social status at all levels was hereditary. Legal status, for free and unfree, passed from mother to offspring, and it looks as if some unfree men took opportunities for social advancement by peasant hypergamy; but maternal descent could be important at higher social levels too.[44]

In ninth-century Wessex, King Alfred created new rights at least in theory (though their effectiveness in practice is impossible to assess) when he gave all free men but not *esne* and *esnewyrhtan* (these sound a bit like Italian *aldii*) thirty-six days' holiday a year at a series of great Christian festivals. *Esne* and *esnewyrhtan* ('slaves' and 'unfree workers' in the standard translation) instead were to get four days a years (the four Wednesdays in the Ember Weeks) 'to sell to whomsoever they pleased anything of what anyone has given them in God's name [that is, alms], or of what they can earn in any of their spare time'.[45] Were all of these workers men? Or could we guess that in England as in Francia women too often traded *in civitatibus et mercatis*? In the countryside, peasants' rights were limited and bound by customary dues, but those dues were not static. Though southern England is poorly documented by comparison with the Francia of the polyptychs, there is some evidence that the extensive lordships of the pre-ninth-century period were starting to be split into small estates, while lordly alterations to the distribution of peasant labour on those small estates show 'a spectrum of [peasant] dependence and independence'.[46] Boon works, etymologically derived from OE *ben*, prayer, and for which later arrangements are very detailed and varied, could have arisen, Ros Faith suggests, out of circumstances 'in which lords had had to bargain

---

[42] Edict of Pîtres (864), c. 30, MGH Capit. II, p. 323: 'hereditates, id est mansa quae [coloni] tenent'; cf. 'mansi hereditarii', Capitulary of Pîtres (869), c. 12, MGH Capit. II, p. 337. In the 864 reference, the object was to reduce the difficulties caused to landlords (including the king and churches) caused by peasant sales of their land, 'et hac occasione sic destructae fiunt villae'.

[43] H.-W. Goetz, 'Zur Namengebung bäuerlicher Schichten im Frühmittelalter: Untersuchungen und Berechnungen anhand des Polypychon von Saint-Germain-des-Prés', *Francia*, 15 (1987), 852–77.

[44] Peasants: see E. Coleman, 'Medieval Marriage Characteristics: A Neglected Factor in the History of Medieval Serfdom', *Journal of Interdisciplinary History*, 2 (1971/2), 205–19; nobles: K. Leyser, 'Maternal Kin in Medieval Germany', *Past and Present*, 49 (1970), 126–32.

[45] Alfred, Laws, c. 43, ed. and trans. Attenborough, *Laws*, 84–7; see *Alfred the Great: Asser's Life of King Alfred and Other Contemporary Sources*, ed. and trans. S. Keynes and M. Lapidge (Harmondsworth, 1983), 170, with nn. 31, 32 at p. 310.

[46] Faith, *English Peasantry*, 173.

for labour', and evolved 'over a long period of time and as result of a long series of bargains'; the emergence of villages and common fields, whether seen in terms of communities or of 'shares', involved the creation of rights.[47] Smaller-scale lords were multiplying, and so were their needs for an increasingly abundant supply of peasant labour. Who depended on whom?

In eleventh-century Francia, the practice of self-donation by serfs, as at Marmoutier in the Touraine, was previously interpreted as evidence of rural crisis and a more violent imposition of servitude. But Dominique Barthélemy argues for *des flexibilités du droit* and notes the significance of the self-donation of serf couples, hence of serf-marriage *de plein droit* as the vehicle of presumptive inheritance-rights. The public rituals whereby serfs sustained their lords also gave the serfs themselves a way of asserting their own value.[48] Self-donation in the Touraine is attested in eighth-century formulae.[49] Polyptychs quite independently suggest something similar for the ninth century. The warm scholarly discussion over arrangements documented in the survey of the monastery of St-Bertin will be half-predictable to historians who have followed the debate in the 1990s over whether the fall of the Roman Empire should or should not be allowed to have taken place.[50] In the red corner, bloody but unbowed from earlier combats, and ably supported by Elisabeth Magnou-Nortier, is Jean Durliat, arguing that St-Bertin functioned in the ninth century as a tax-farmer on behalf of the state, that the peasant-holdings (*mansi*) in the St-Bertin survey were tax-units, and the *servi* were tax-payers.[51] In the blue corner, a new contestant, Etienne Renard, suggests that some *mancipia* (usually translated 'slaves') may have been free men with military obligations, supported by the abbey but liable to royal summons.[52] There they are, with fixed duties that give every appearance of having been recently and specifically agreed. These were not mere human tools. Other *mancipia* worked for holders of little estates within the abbey's

---

[47] *Ibid.*, 176, also 112, 145–7, 149–52; cf. Reynolds, *Kingdoms and Communities*, 110–11, on tenth-century Latium.

[48] D. Barthélemy, *La mutation de l'an mil* (Paris, 1997), 89–90, 135–6.

[49] *Formulae Turonenses*, no. 43, ed. K. Zeumer, MGH Formulae Merowingici et Karolini Aevi (Hannover, 1886), 158.

[50] C. Wickham, 'La chute de Rome n'aura pas lieu', *Le Moyen Age*, 99 (1993), 107–26 (English translation, 'The Fall of Rome Will not Take Place', in *Debating the Middle Ages*, ed. L. K. Little and B. Rosenwein (Oxford, 1998), 45–57), offers a wry, incisive critique of Durliat (see next note). Cf. E. Magnou-Nortier, 'La chute de Rome a-t-elle eu lieu?', *Bibliothèque de l'Ecole des Chartes*, 152 (1994), 5.

[51] J. Durliat, *Les finances publiques de Dioclétien aux Carolingiens (284–888)*, Beiheft der *Francia* Band 21 (Sigmaringen, 1990), esp. 198–9; Magnou-Nortier, 'Le grand domaine: des maîtres, des doctrines, des questions', *Francia*, 15 (1987), 659–700.

[52] E. Renard, 'Lectures et relectures d'un polyptyque carolingien (Saint-Bertin, 844–859)', *Revue d'Histoire Ecclésiastique*, 94 (1999), 373–435.

big estate, originating in precarial grants (*precaria* from *preces*, prayer), and some of these *mancipia* owed very little indeed: a pennyworth of wax, six setiers of honey, two days' work a year. These could be called men with rights: men who had rather a good deal. This is truer still of *prebendarii*, who had specialist administrative jobs for the abbey. Far from antique survivals, the varied arrangements indicated in this text, and its inventive use of terminology, constitute 'un ensemble d'éléments en continuelle recomposition'. Far from static, 'la photo est floue'.[53] Nor is this just a matter of flexible management of the dependent workforce. The *breves* bear the imprints of renegotiations of the abbey's relationships with patrons and clients, as well as with the king. The obverse is that while giving property, even giving themselves and their families, to churches, lesser landowners at the same time kept property, adjusting the terms over time as required, and also kept, however legally labelled, a certain social status. This could form the stuff of arguments: it remained the stuff of rights, likewise 'en continuelle recomposition'.

Linking things usually kept asunder, Jesus told the parable of the unjust steward who reduced at a stroke of the pen what debtors owed to his lord. 'Make to yourselves friends of the mammon of unrighteousness that, when ye fail, they may receive you into everlasting habitations . . . If therefore ye have not been faithful in the unrighteous mammon, who will commit to your trust the true riches?' (Luke 16: 9–11). In 847, the West Saxon king Æthelwulf responded to those words, perhaps with a smile, in a charter granting lands to himself:

> If a man intent on good works expends as much as he can on generosity in almsgiving and applying those alms to the needs of those who are near to him, 'let him make for himself', as the Saviour said, 'friends of the mammon of unrighteousness who will receive him into eternal dwellings'. Therefore I King Æthelwulf with the consent and leave of my bishops and great men have booked to myself twenty manses so that I may enjoy them and leave them after my death to whomsoever I please in perpetuity.

And the charter goes on: 'These are the lands which his senators conceded to Æthelwulf.'[54] King Æthelwulf of Wessex is one of the great underrated among Anglo-Saxons. To take a rather crude measure: he was allowed just 2,500 words in the *Oxford Dictionary of National Biography* compared with Edward II's 15,000 or Elizabeth's 35,000.[55] A subtler measure would be the pious guile by which the king, with his leading men's consent, made a large tract of frontier-land free of dues normally owed to the ruler and also free of the rights of kin, so that he himself could bequeath estates as

[53] Renard, 'Lectures et relectures', 385–404, 406–25, with the quoted phrases at 427.

[54] S 298/B 451. See Maitland, *Domesday Book*, 293. Cf. Isidore, *Synonyma*, ed. J.-P. Migne, *Patrologia Latina* 83, cols. 865–6, for gifts as the antidote to wealth, and the comments of Rosenwein, *Negotiating Space*, 150–1.

[55] See 'Æthelwulf, King of Wessex', by J. L. Nelson, *Oxford Dictionary of National Biography*, forthcoming.

gifts. Here I want to establish his credentials in the ninth-century creation of rights and deployment of rituals by looking at what historians tend to refer to as the problem of Æthelwulf's decimation.[56] This had nothing to do with punishing every tenth man, or even with tithing (though Moses' rules as in Deuteronomy 14: 22–9 might have inspired it). Here is how the *Anglo-Saxon Chronicle* describes it: 'in this year [855] . . . King Æthelwulf granted the tenth part of his land over all his kingdom by charter for the glory of God and his own eternal salvation' (*gebocude Eþelwulf cyning teoþan dæl his londes ofer al his rice*).[57] This sounds clear enough, once we discount subsequent confusion between 'his land' and 'his kingdom': he gives '*his* land', that is, his personal lands, not the royal lands. He gives them so that they can be free for the beneficiaries to grant away if they so wish. He gives them, at the same time, as alms for God and for his own salvation.

And the problem? In part, it is of the sort that modernists have sometimes thought wearisomely typical of medievalists: a problem of diplomatic, in the technical sense of charter-forms and formalities. The problem has to be resolved, because charters, unlike the *Chronicle*, spell out context and meaning. The particular charters in question are mostly post-Conquest copies, and copies of Anglo-Saxon charters in monastic cartularies are often forged or interpolated. Initiates in what Nicholas Brooks calls 'the arcane mystery of charter scholarship' use mysterious S and B numbers.[58] They express their judgements on charters in special code, as on the purported records of Æthelwulf's decimation: 'these texts come from chartularies of the lowest possible character';[59] one is 'of disreputable appearance';[60] another, 'a rather pathetic example';[61] yet another, 'written by a scribe who was not an Englishman'.[62] Two are from the archives of the Old Minster Winchester, and Maitland in an inimitable footnote queried 'if anything that comes from Winchester is not suspected'.[63] I think Simon Keynes has cracked the decimation problem and I salute the learning he wears so lightly and dispenses so generously. Visit his anything but arcane website![64] The decimation happened in

---

[56] N. P. Brooks, 'Anglo-Saxon Charters', *Anglo-Saxon England*, 3 (1974), 211–34, reprinted with a new 'Postscript', in N. P. Brooks, *Anglo-Saxon Myths* (2000), 181–202, with 'Postscript' at 202–15, discussing the decimation charters at 202–3.

[57] *The Anglo-Saxon Chronicle: A Collaborative Edition*, general eds. D. Dumville and S. D. Keynes, III: *MS 'A'*, ed. J. M. Bately (Woodbridge, 1986), 45, trans. G. N. Garmonsway (1975), 66.

[58] Brooks, *Anglo-Saxon Myths*, 203. For S and B numbers see above, p. 3 n. 7.

[59] W. H. Stevenson, *Asser's Life of King Alfred* (Oxford, 1904), 187.

[60] Keynes, 'The West Saxon Charters of King Æthelwulf and his Sons', *English Historical Review*, 109 (1994), 1109–49, at 1121 n. 3, on S 308.

[61] *The Charters of Abingdon Abbey*, ed. S. Kelly, Part I (Oxford, 2000), 66, on S 302.

[62] Stevenson, *Asser's Life of King Alfred*, 187, on B 469 (S 308).

[63] Maitland, *Domesday Book*, 574 n. 1.

[64] http://www.trin.cam.ac.uk/users/sdk13/sdk13home.html.

two distinct phases, one in Wessex in 854, the second in Kent in 855, underlining the point that these remained separate kingdoms. Yet the texts of the charters belong to a single tradition, and wherever the royal court moved to, a small group of scribes permanently or semi-permanently attached to the court produced documents with similarities of form and substance, hence within the tradition. Each charter says, roughly:

> the Almighty has told us that good deeds here on earth allow us to gain heavenly reward. Therefore I, King Æthelwulf, at this holy feast of Easter, for the remedy of my soul and for the well-being of the kingdom and people assigned to me by God, have made the healthful decision together with my bishops, ealdormen and all my nobles to give a tenth part of [my] lands throughout our kingdom not only to holy churches but also to our *ministri* established in [the kingdom]. We have granted it to be held in perpetual liberty, in such a way that this gift should remain fixed and immutable and absolved from all royal service and from the servitude of all secular men.

It has been assumed that the object of giving *bocland* to laymen was to enable them to pass on the land to a church.[65] This is a reasonable enough assumption, though the timing of the future transfer was open, and it might well have involved the layman's retention of a life interest (or three lives' interest) or something resembling a benefice. There, already, are several possible scenarios. Here is another, different again: a bishop might be expected to pass on land to *advenae* and *peregrini* of suitable *dignitas*, and only in the absence of such *digni* and until such time as *advenae* again frequented *ista patria*, to use it 'for the reviving of the poor' (*ad pauperum refocillationem*).[66] Were these *advenae* foreign scholars? Or were they fighting men from kingdoms other than Wessex? These possibilities evoke Frankish parallels and a world in motion.

The following liturgical services are specified:

> Every Saturday, the community shall sing fifty psalms; a priest shall say two masses for King Æthelwulf and a third for the bishops and ealdormen: for the king while he lives, 'Deus qui iustificas impium' and for the bishops and ealdormen, 'Praetende domine.' For the king when he is dead, a special mass; for bishops and ealdormen [when dead?], collectively. We have done all this that the Almighty may be kind to us and those who come after us.

Keynes thoughtfully noted parallels for the two identified votive masses in the Leofric Missal, the relevant section of which is very probably late ninth century.[67] But earlier parallels noted in Nicholas Orchard's fine new edition of the Leofric Missal are Frankish, and one of these could well point to the monastery of Corbie in the early 850s, whence monastic votive masses could readily have got into a bishop's book via Odo, successively

---

[65] Whitelock, *EHD* I, no. 89, p. 525: 'it would appear that what the king did was to grant land to his thegns so that they could leave it freely to religious houses'.

[66] S 307/B 474.

[67] Keynes, 'The West Saxon Charters', 1121 n. 1. See now *The Leofric Missal*, ed. N. Orchard, Henry Bradshaw Society, vols. CXIII and CXIV (2 vols., 2002), 80, 105, 141.

abbot of Corbie (851–61/2) and bishop of Beauvais (861/2–881).[68] The opening prayer for the king is taken from a mass 'for a faithful friend' which indicates use for a monastic patron:

> *Deus qui iustificas impium*... God, you who justify the wicked and wish not the death of sinners, we humbly pray your majesty that you will protect kindly with heavenly help, and preserve with your constant protection, this your servant [.N.] who trusts in your mercy, that he may continually serve you and be separated from you by no temptations.[69]

The other prayers of this mass are also overwhelmingly concerned with purification from sin.[70] There is a striking contrast with the prayers in the mass for the bishops and ealdormen, which are conventional upbeat statements of 'give and it shall be given':

> *Praetende domine*... Stretch forth O Lord the right hand of heavenly help to your faithful ones, all the bishops, priests, abbots, monks, canons, and kings and governors and all our kinsfolk and those who have commended themselves to our prayers and given their alms, and to all the rest of the faithful of both sexes, so that they may seek you with their whole heart and be worthy to gain what they worthily request.[71]

The distinctive characteristic of the mass *pro rege vivente* strengthens the idea explicit in the one surviving example of the Kentish charters[72] that the decimation was associated with a notable act of personal and penitential devotion on Æthelwulf's part: namely, his visit to Rome in 855. He was the first Anglo-Saxon king for well over a century to make this journey, and the last before Cnut nearly two centuries later. The association of the leading *fideles* and their alms with the projected benefits has a political dimension, clearly suggested by the context in which the charters were issued: an assembly. At the same time, the grants of *bocland* to thegns signify largesse more closely targeted at the key agents of government in the royal household and in the localities.

The proportion of grants to laymen in the decimation charters is striking, three out of seven. Hunsige and Wiferth (854), and Dunn (855).[73] In Dunn's case, the giving-on of the *bocland* to a church is clear from a vernacular addition to the effect that the thegn wishes that after his death his wife should have a life interest, and that the land should then pass to St Andrew's Rochester. The proems of all these mention gift-giving in religious terms: *bona acta* merit perpetual felicity. The dispositive clauses are even more explicit: the king grants *pro meae remedio animae* and for the prosperity of 'the realm and people committed to me by God'. This

[68] *Leofric Missal*, ed. Orchard, I, 25–6, 57–60.
[69] *Ibid.*, II, no. 2087, pp. 347–8.
[70] *Ibid.*, nos. 2088–91, p. 348.
[71] *Ibid.*, nos. 2114–17, pp. 351–2.
[72] S 315/B 486, trans. Whitelock, *EHD* I, no. 89, p. 525; cf. Keynes, 'The West Saxon Charters', 1120 n. 4.
[73] S 304/B 468; S 308/B 469; S 315/B 486.

theme appears as early as 840 in one of Æthelwulf's charters, in which he granted a generous fifteen hides to a deacon (apparently a member of his own household) 'for the redemption of my one and only soul and for the remission of my crimes and for the stability of my kingdom' (*pro unicae animae meae redemptione et criminum meorum remissione et pro stabilitate regni mei*).[74] Those first two phrases are not conventional in charters. Æthelwulf was personally devout. As significant, he was very publicly binding certain chosen thegns to himself and into this project. The decimation charters granting to churches are formally very closely similar to the grants to laymen. All this takes us to the heart of ninth-century political sociology.

There are Frankish parallels: for instance, a number of grants by Charles the Bald to faithful men who were not themselves great magnates, that is, they were equivalent to thegns rather than ealdormen. In the period of Charles's reign that coincided with Æthelwulf's, i.e. 840–58, 25 out of Charles's 199 charters were such grants. A number of them were requested by the patrons of the *fideles* thus associating magnates as objects of these royal gifts. All the grants open with praise for the royal custom (*consuetudo*) of gift-giving to *fideles*. Most of these grants ended up in the hands of churches (otherwise no record would have survived) but in some cases demonstrably, and in others very probably, the transfer of ownership to churches occurred long after the beneficiary's death. Out of the twenty-five cases, only two were grants passed on to churches by beneficiaries themselves,[75] while a third was given by the beneficiary's widow,[76] and, more speculatively, a fourth granted to a *vassallus* of the abbot of St-Denis.[77]

Two other Frankish parallels are worth mentioning. Charlemagne's will made in 811 solemnly provided gifts of alms from his own resources, 'as is done among Christians', and hence clarified for his heirs what movables would come to them. Charlemagne associated the secular church, specifically the great archbishoprics, in this institutionalised charity.[78] In context, and by implication, given the representative thirty *amici et ministri*, fifteen lay as well as fifteen ecclesiastical, who attested it, the will was also an act of association and negotiation between the ruler and

---

[74] S 290, ed. M. O'Donovan, *The Charters of Sherborne* (Oxford, 1988), no. 3, pp. 5–8, with commentary at 8–11; see further, Keynes, 'The West Saxon Charters', 1114–15.

[75] *Receuil des Chartes de Charles II le Chauve*, ed. G. Tessier [hereafter T] (3 vols., Paris, 1943–55), I, nos. 28, 64. Cf. also T 5, 10, 11, 15, 16, 17, 19, 24, 35, 69, 84, 90, 94, 95, 96, 98, 118, 120, 145, 151, 164, 168, 185. There are very few such grants to laymen in Charles's reign from 859 onwards. For a comparative context, see Rosenwein, *Negotiating Space*, ch. 7, 'a gift-giving king'.

[76] T 24.

[77] T 5.

[78] Einhard, *Vita Karoli Magni* c. 33, ed. O. Holder-Egger, MGH SRG (Hannover, 1911), p. 38.

those other *christiani* who were his faithful ones. Here, as Matthew Innes put it, 'no cleavage between the personal and the public is possible'.[79] The experience of life at Charlemagne's court was designed to locate individual Christians' acts within a social dimension.[80] A second parallel to Æthelwulf's decimation plans comes in Charles the Bald's decree in 877 that

> if any one of our faithful men after our death should be inspired by love of God and of us and wish to withdraw from the world, he should be able to hand over, as he wishes, his *honores* to a son or a kinsman capable of benefiting the state, and if he wishes to live in peace on his own property let no one dare to put any obstacle in his way except that he must perform military service when summoned to the host.[81]

Charles apparently foresaw that some of his faithful ones, perhaps those of his own age, and men to whom he had shown generosity, might wish to live out their days praying for his soul in a quasi-monastic retirement that was not wholly removed from obligations to the state.[82] But, unlike Æthelwulf, Charles promulgated no large-scale realm-wide donation on a single great occasion; neither did the king give lavishly himself, nor did he arrange for vicarious giving on the part of his faithful men. A collective bond between king and *ministri* is not replicated in the West Frankish (or Italian) sources.

The pendant to Susan Reynolds's true saying that 'no ruler who wanted to tap the resources of the Frankish kingdom effectively could afford to ignore the enormous wealth of the church'[83] is that relationships between ruler and aristocrats could and can only be understood in a context including churches as players, partners, stake-holders and facilitators. This is as true, though less easy to demonstrate, for ninth-century Anglo-Saxons as for their Frankish contemporaries. Institutional form and structure, and mastery of the written word, should not make us see the church in any kingdom as a monolith. Rather these traits gave churches room to manoeuvre between mammon and virtue, wealth and charity. In practice, the rights of churches were negotiable, as, I have suggested, were everyone else's, but where churches were involved the paradoxes of this negotiability emerge with exceptional clarity, thanks to the written evidence. To say that there is no cleavage between public and private is putting it mildly: kings, bishops, monastic communities and laymen were interwoven in a web of charity and intercession for king and kingdom,

---

[79] M. Innes, 'Charlemagne's Will: Politics, Inheritance and Ideology in the Early Ninth Century', *English Historical Review*, 112 (1997), 833–55, at 855.

[80] Nelson, 'Was Charlemagne's Court a Courtly Society?', in *Court Culture in the Early Middle Ages*, ed. C. Cubitt (Turnhout, 2003), 39–57.

[81] MGH Capit II, no. 281, c. 10, p. 358.

[82] See Rosenwein, *Negotiating Space*, 149, on an Italian royal grant of immunity of 911 which 'treated the tranquillity [of a royal *iudex* and his *familia* within their castle] as an act of piety'.

[83] Reynolds, *Fiefs and Vassals*, 89.

for king and people, for churches' 'friends', in which church property – including churches themselves as property – was the subject and object of negotiation.

In Æthelwulf's decimation grants, exchange was not just about reciprocity: rights over land and people were given but also kept, values were metonymic (adjuncts substituted for things themselves), action was often vicarious and supernatural power was an active participant. In short, the people involved were thinking and acting not legalistically but ritualistically.[84] The king understood the difference between personal and regnal property just as his Frankish counterparts did: in his will, drawn up in 856, Æthelwulf divided his kingdom one way, his personal property in quite another.[85] Yet in giving away his personal property he sought the well-being of not just himself but of his followers, and sought, too, a dividend that was realm-wide, regnal. The thinking behind the decimation was paralleled in Francia. Nevertheless the formal documents breathed a different spirit. The Frankish ones invoked secular custom, Æthelwulf's religious duty. The context for Æthelwulf's action, decisive, and systematic, and above all public, was provided by ritual: Æthelwulf's oxygen of publicity.

The place of his 854 assembly was Wilton, identified in the decimation charters as 'our palace'. This is doubly new: new because Wilton acquired a new prominence in Æthelwulf's reign,[86] new because unprecedented in West Saxon ninth-century diplomatic, and clearly a borrowing from the standard Frankish form 'actum in X palatio nostro' ('enacted in our palace of such-and-such'). Only in the decimation charters of 854 does Wilton appear as *palatium* rather than *villa regalis*. I think it is tempting to see here the influence of a man known to have been working in Æthelwulf's writing-office in (perhaps) 843, and still influential at his court in 852, the Frankish notary Felix;[87] and tempting, further, to suggest he had some direct input into the management of the decimation project and the stage-management of its unveiling. By this date, Æthelwulf's court was in contact with Charles the Bald's; and the ground-work had been laid, knowingly or otherwise, for Æthelwulf's visit in 855.[88] Wilton was

[84] F. Theuws, 'Introduction: Rituals in Transforming Societies', in *Rituals of Power from Late Antiquity to the Early Middle Ages*, ed. F. Theuws and J. L. Nelson (Leiden, 2000), 1–13.

[85] Asser, *De rebus gestis Ælfredi* c. 16, ed. Stevenson, 14–15; *Alfred*, ed. and trans. Keynes and Lapidge, 72–3, 236–7.

[86] Wilton evidently gave its name to Wiltshire. In S 300 (850), Æthelwulf at Wilton granted a large estate in Kent to a Kentish *princeps* (Keynes, 'The West Saxon Charters', 125 n. 71) in the presence of a mixed assemblage of West Saxons and Kentishmen, including the king's eldest son, the sub-king of Kent.

[87] Lupus of Ferrières, *Epistulae* nos. 13, 14, ed. P. K. Marshall (Leipzig, 1984), 21–3.

[88] See Nelson, 'The Franks and the English in the Ninth Century Reconsidered', in *The Preservation and Transmission of Anglo-Saxon Culture*, ed. P. Szarmach and J. T. Rosenthal (Kalamazoo, MI, 1997), 141–58, at 143–8.

perhaps being developed as a major royal residence.[89] Like Aachen in Charlemagne's reign, it had the advantage of not being an episcopal see. It was also well inland, hence less vulnerable to raids.

The assembly at Wilton in 854 took place on a special day: Easter Sunday (22 April). This was one of the 'great feasts at which a full court would be assembled'.[90] 'Full court' is a relative term. Several hundred of the elite attended some Frankish assemblies. The '700-strong entourage worthy of a travelling medieval monarch' that accompanied G. W. Bush to London in 2003[91] included people whom no Frankish or Anglo-Saxon notary would have seen fit to name. The attesters listed in the Wilton charters in 854 probably included king's thegns of the regular 'entourage' – there were fifteen of those, and one priest – but also great men who had come for the occasion: the two West Saxon bishops of Sherborne and Winchester, six ealdormen (called *duces* in Latin), including the king's two elder surviving sons and perhaps his mother's brother, two abbots and the two younger princes Æthelred and Alfred who must then have been aged perhaps seven and five.[92] This was a royal family-gathering as well as an aristocratic assembly with the intimacy of a rather small kingdom. Æthelwulf's one surviving gift-ring, adorned with a motif of two peacocks flanking a tree of life – still to be seen in the British Museum – may stand for dozens lost. The ritual aspects of such a gathering were shared with those of other, larger, polities.

On Easter Saturdays, Louis the Pious, whom Notker praised as 'keen on alms-giving' (*elemosinis intentus*), had made a distribution of precious objects and clothes to 'all those with official posts in the palace and serving in the royal court each according to his dignity' (*cuncti in palatio ministrantes et in curte regia servientes iuxta singulorum personas*). This was the setting for one of Notker's seriously funny stories that depended on audience-recognition of a cluster of associations: Easter, baptism, renewal, royal mimesis of Christ, gift-giving, new clothes.[93] The model of Louis's Aachen ritual might well have been the Palm Sunday gift-giving ritual of Constantinople, though

---

[89] It seems no coincidence that one of the four encounters of Alfred's army with Vikings in 871 occurred at Wilton. There is no reference to Wilton in Alfred's reign, perhaps because it had suffered severely in 871? Evidence for a nunnery there that was 'not just a "royal" foundation, but one closely connected with leading aristocratic families of the shire' in the late ninth and early tenth centuries is discussed by B. Yorke, *Nunneries and the Anglo-Saxon Royal Houses* (2003), 83; cf. S. Foot, *Veiled Women* (2 vols., 2000), 221–31, esp. 226.

[90] *Charters of Sherborne*, ed. O'Donovan, 9.

[91] *The Guardian*, 19 Nov. 2003.

[92] Nelson, 'Reconstructing a Royal Family: Reflections on Alfred from Asser Chapter 2', in *People and Places in Northern Europe, 500–1600: Essays in Honour of Peter Hayes Sawyer*, ed. I. Wood and N. Lund (Woodbridge, 1991), 47–66, at 57–8.

[93] Notker, *Gesta Karoli* II, 21, ed. H. F. Haefele, MGH SRG (Munich, 1980), 91–2. See Nelson, *The Frankish World*, 85–6, and M. Innes, ' "He Never Allowed his White Teeth to be Bared in Laughter": The Politics of Humour in the Carolingian Renaissance', in *Humour,*

the earliest description is Liutprand's tenth-century one.[94] But it may not be too far-fetched to surmise Easter gift-giving already practised by ninth-century West Saxon kings. In Alfred's reign, Eastertide was the appropriate time for an annual ritual of gift-giving to 'the men who serve me (*þam mannum þe me folgiað*)... 200 lb to be given and divided between them'.[95] Why should this not have begun in his father's reign? If it had, at Æthelwulf's Easter-court in 854, the instruments of the king's charitable giving included a further addition: the decimation charters themselves, not brought by beneficiaries for royal approval, but produced, as Simon Keynes persuasively argues, by royal notaries in the king's household – his *hired*.

Rituals, then, helped constitute rights, and so complemented them, as the decimation charters turn out to show. Rituals are well documented in the ninth century: indeed many of the most interesting are *first* documented then in any detail. Royal gift-giving in institutionalised form is a case in point. I briefly touched on oath-swearings and marriage. Had time allowed, I would have said more about them, especially about marriage, for the first recorded full marriage-rite is that of Æthelwulf and his Carolingian bride Judith in 856: a rite which was also the first queenly consecration.[96] I would have said more about royal consecrations in both Francia and England: for the ninth century is the period of their liturgical formation, with continuities from 856 to 1953. I would have said more about assembly-rituals, for Tim Reuter's model of assembly politics, formed of ninth-century materials, includes rituals as critical working parts. You could also say such politics were oiled by rituals, ranging from formal reception and permission to depart, to reciprocity and submission, and punishment: Charles the Bald's assembly at Pîtres in 864 has examples of all these,[97] and his and Æthelwulf's reigns have much more evidence than modern historians of ritual have recognised, partly because Germans tend to make tenth-century Germany a starting-point as well as a focus.[98]

History and Politics in Late Antiquity and the Early Middle Ages, ed. G. Halsall (Cambridge, 2002), 131–56, at 149–50.

[94] Liudprand, *Antapodosis* VI, 10, ed. J. Becker, *Liudprandi Opera*, MGH SRG (Hannover, 1915), 157–8.

[95] Will of Alfred, S 1507/B 553, in *Alfred*, ed. and trans. Keynes and Lapidge, 177.

[96] Nelson, 'Early Medieval Rites of Queen-Making and the Making of Medieval Queenship,' in *Queens and Queenship in Medieval Europe*, ed. A. Duggan (Woodbridge, 1997), 301–15.

[97] Edict of Pîtres (864), MGH Capit. II, no. 273, pp. 310–28; *Annales Bertiniani* 864, ed. F. Grat, J. Vielliard and S. Clémencet (Paris, 1964), 113–14; *The Annals of St-Bertin*, trans. J. L. Nelson (Manchester, 1991), 118–19.

[98] G. Althoff, *Spielregeln der Politik im Mittelalter: Kommunikation in Frieden und Fehde* (Darmstadt, 1997). On this and earlier German scholarship on royal ritual, see the appreciative, judicious critique of J. Barrow, 'Playing by the Rules: Conflict-Management in Tenth- and Eleventh-Century Germany', *Early Medieval Europe*, 11 (2002), 389–96. It is perhaps only partly fair to

But I want to use my remaining time to defend rituals as invaluable sources for historians of the ninth century. Defence has to be undertaken because a young French, now American, historian, Philippe Buc, has recently argued that earlier medievalists' enthusiasm for rituals has got out of hand, betrays methodological naivety and has entrenched serious misunderstandings. He has highlighted three dangers: one, rituals were manipulated in performance, subverted in contemporary interpretation, so that the question of what they meant at the time becomes meaningless; second, accounts of rituals were authorial constructs in clever narratives so that they are decontextualised from a world of 'more prosaic components'; third, rituals risk being misread by us historians in functionalist terms prescribed by social scientific models derived from medieval theology: 'the social-scientific "reading" of texts [is] generated by a culture from which the social sciences themselves descend'.[99] 'Is [that] reading... *eo ipso* invalid?' Buc asks, in what medievalists are trained to recognise as a question expecting the answer yes. Circular arguments are never good. But *is* this argument circular? Must we stop thinking we can think about rituals? Have modern medievalists misread medieval writers as functionalists *avant la lettre*? I think not. And actually, I have come to the conclusion that Buc thinks not. Intent on jolting us out of imbibing anthropological texts of a certain vintage, and into more careful and critical readings of medieval texts, Buc admits in the end that 'ceremonial practices' (shall we just call them rituals?) were 'extremely important in reality'.[100]

In pursuit of reality, let us return, just for a moment, to Wilton 22 April 854. We did not get there by way of clever authorial constructs. We risked no postmodernist Black Hole. Simply, there were those charters, and those prayer-texts to be read in the context of very prosaic writings about rights. The sense of an ambient culture was not superimposed but arose out of that material. The event at Wilton was an assembly, its purpose to hold together groupings that were still fragile: the two kingdoms and two elites of Kent and Wessex, the ecclesiastical and secular powers of those

---

include within the German historiographical tradition Karl Leyser's illuminating 'Ritual, Ceremony, and Gesture: Ottonian Germany', in Leyser, *Communication and Power in Medieval Europe: The Carolingian and Ottonian Centuries*, ed. T. Reuter (2 vols., 1994), 181–213.

[99] P. Buc, *The Dangers of Ritual: Between Early Medieval Texts and Social Scientific Theory* (Princeton, NJ, 2002), where the first two criticisms are well represented in Part I, ch. 2, on the ninth century, pp. 51–87. The first quoted phrase comes from p. 9, the second from p. 237. For percipient critiques of Buc's book which nevertheless acknowledge its interest and timeliness, see G. Koziol, 'The Dangers of Polemic: Is Ritual still an Interesting Topic of Historical Study?', *Early Medieval Europe*, 11 (2002), 367–88, and A. Walsham, 'The Dangers of Ritual', *Past and Present*, 180 (2003), 277–87 (dealing especially with the third of Buc's criticisms). Cf. also the review by Nelson in *Speculum*, 78 (2003), 847–51.

[100] Buc, *Dangers*, 256.

kingdoms, the shire leaders and their followings in what had, not long ago, been politically distinct regions, the king and his thegns in the various localities, last but not least the members of the royal family. The culture that bound was one of cult, the celebration of Easter and its associated gift-giving, gift-keeping and giving while keeping – and gifts that included prayer along with property.[101] The bonds that held were personal: between the king, his kin and those who served them. In the circumstances of 854, the king needed to reinforce loyalties that his imminent departure for Rome would put to the test and which would, in the event, be tested to near-destruction, but in the end prove the strengths of the arrangements Æthelwulf put together for his kingdom. Without Æthelwulf, no Alfred.

Assemblies were always more than ritual events: but they were important political institutions because they were *also* ritual events. Rooted in the prosaic, but linking it with the transcendent, rituals stuck in hearts and minds and memories. They turned political experiments into political habits, individual hopes into collective expectations. They provided a context for political negotiation to replace confrontation, allowing fences to be mended even after violent struggles. They provided the public stage on which kings and faithful men interacted and agendas were articulated, and recorded. Establishing common behavioural forms, they linked the regnal with the local. Because Anglo-Saxons and Franks shared far more than divided them, and, crucially, had religious and political cultures in common, the ninth-century narratives and capitularies that preserve so much about Frankish assemblies at local as well as regnal levels can be used as magnifying-glasses for Anglo-Saxon materials, allowing us to see Wilton as Aachen or Pîtres writ small. And small is where I began, in another sense, with peasant negotiators and individual battles for status. A continuum makes an ugly plural; but plural continuums are what we get by working sideways as well as back. If rights can be inferred from rituals, rights certainly need to be *referred to* rituals, and vice versa. The ending affirms the beginning.

---

[101] A mobile court could have a degree of stability of personnel across space as well as time: the same group that had been at Wilton on 22 April was apparently still together some days later at the royal residence of Edington, some 30 km north; *Charters of Sherborne*, ed. O'Donovan, 9; Keynes, 'The West Saxon Charters', 1122–3. As Hincmar of Rheims said in a letter (November 858) intended for two Carolingian kings and their courts, MGH Concilia III, ed. W. Hartmann (Hanover 1984), no. 41, c. v, p. 412: 'The palace of the king is so called on account of the rational human beings who dwell therein, not on account of walls or courtyards that are insensible things.'

Transactions of the RHS 14 (2004), pp. 25–46 © 2004 Royal Historical Society
DOI: 10.1017/S0080440104000064   Printed in the United Kingdom

THE LEGACY OF THE NINETEENTH-CENTURY BOURGEOIS FAMILY AND THE WOOL MERCHANT'S SON

By Leonore Davidoff

READ 14 FEBRUARY 2003 AT THE UNIVERSITY OF GREENWICH

ABSTRACT. Changes in familial relations have influenced historical scholarship. The family is now seen more in terms of relationships that have to be activated to be meaningful. This study first looks at general features of the European nineteenth-century bourgeois family and its context, in particular the dramatic fall in the marital birth rate. Sigmund Freud's family is then taken as a case study. Turning attention from the usual psychoanalytic focus, it is possible to tease out those relationships in which Freud was actually embedded, particularly with his siblings and siblings-in-law. The consequences of neglecting these features are highlighted.

Introduction

After many years of eclipse, the last decade has witnessed a renewed interest in the family and kinship. Anthropologists in the West have begun to apply their skills and techniques to these topics within their own societies.[1] Sociologists of the family as well as social psychologists have begun to incorporate issues around gender, age, 'race', ethnicity – and power – into what had been a low-status and rather sterile field.[2] Why this has happened is complicated. Undoubtedly some of the interest stems from the radical political movements since the 1960s. Feminism, the rights of gays and lesbians, racial and ethnic minorities and the nationalisms emerging in former colonial societies have opened narrowly defined, static boundaries of familial and kin relations.

Above all, changes in family life itself in the last part of the twentieth century – co-habitation, high divorce rates, women's massive entry into the work force, continued low birth rates, increased longevity and the impact of reproductive technologies – all have brought into question beliefs about the family and its natural foundations. There are now

---

[1] Jeanette Edwards and Marilyn Strathern, 'Including Our Own', in *Cultures of Relatedness: New Approaches to the Study of Kinship*, ed. Janet Carsten (Cambridge, 2000).
[2] *The New Family?*, ed. Elizabeth B. Silva and Carol Smart (1999).

suggestions for re-conceptualising family as a process,[3] as a web of lived relationships or as categories and roles that have to be activated to be meaningful.[4] Meanwhile, and somewhat paradoxically, recent increased knowledge of genetics has stressed the physicality of kinship ties, a position reinforced by the claims of the now fashionable neo-evolutionists.[5]

The history of the family and kinship has not gone untouched by these shifts. In any case, over the past half-century, the work of historians has been instrumental in demonstrating variability as well as change in family forms. Historical insights have also contributed to the understanding that ideas about family are embedded in the economic, social and cultural patterns of a period.

Here I want to look at nineteenth-century Western, particularly bourgeois, family and kinship relations and the way they have formed our thinking for many decades into the following century. For self-conscious emphasis on *family* and *domesticity* was a central component of economic, social and cultural class identity.[6] Therefore first I will consider some common general features of the bourgeois pattern and will then take one family as a case study. It should be stressed that the following argument is at a general level, more in the nature of a composite Weberian 'ideal type' than a specific historical portrait.

The bourgeois family (and its many local variants) became dominant in the middle and upper strata of Western culture at the same time as an emphasis on *the individual* and *individualism*, associated with the liberal state, the modern economy and the formation of classes. However, in the extensive literature on the relationship of individual to society, the family is often by-passed or taken for granted. One of the fundamental reasons for this hiatus is the unspoken gender implication of these concepts. The core element of individualism lies in an abstract realm of reason, honouring mind over body and emotions. It has been understood as something crafted, wrested from the vagaries of Nature and of everyday life, above all an integral part of a type of masculinity.

Keep in mind that the division between a natural realm and civilised society was itself a product of Western culture elaborated from the eighteenth century onwards.[7] Within this dual framework, the family unit is seen to be natural, the building block of society, yet outside of 'the social'. For family has been regarded as a feminine domain. Men's relationship to

[3] David H. J. Morgan, *Family Connections: An Introduction to Family Studies* (Cambridge, 1996).

[4] L. Davidoff, M. Doolittle, J. Fink and K. Holden, *The Family Story: Blood, Contract and Intimacy 1830–1960* (1998).

[5] Andrew Brown, *The Darwin Wars: The Scientific Battle for the Soul of Man* (2000).

[6] Mary Jo Maynes, 'Class Cultures and Images of Proper Family Life', in *Family Life in the Long Nineteenth Century*, ed. David Kertzer and Marzio Barbagli (New Haven, 2002), 195.

[7] *Languages of Nature: Critical Essays on Science and Literature*, ed. Ludmilla Jordanova (1986).

the family, despite nineteenth-century patriarchal assumptions and legal definitions, remains unstable and problematic. The categories 'woman' and 'child' are defined through their relationships; the category 'man' theoretically floats free.[8] These unexamined assumptions are illustrated in a general text on the history of the family, in use until recently, which unselfconsciously uses the expression: 'the individual – his wife and family'.[9]

Bearing in mind this confusion, I turn first to an examination of the basic elements of the nineteenth-century bourgeois family and kinship. These general features are the context for the case study that follows. The large bourgeois family, in horizontal or lateral as well as vertical relationships, in extensive kin networks, played a central role in people's lives far beyond our late twentieth-century imagination. Looking at one family in detail can prod that imagination but out of the hundreds of thousands of such families why have I chosen this particular one, although granted it exemplifies so many of the common features?

Because this was the family of the man, Sigmund Freud, who has had more influence on conceptualising family dynamics for at least the following hundred years than any other single person. While lip service has often been paid to the fact that Freud was a 'product of his time' and reams written about his psychic familial formations, there has been a neglect of his actual familial and kinship situation. Part of the reason for this is that it is exceptionally difficult to construct a full biography because he deliberately covered his tracks, being insistent that his legacy would be through his written work, disciples and students (including his daughter, Anna, who here appears more in the guise of the typical unmarried daughter at home).[10] And to this day, Freud's Archive has continued to deny access to crucial personal papers.

For many years, this secrecy did not unduly trouble the psychoanalytic community for the focus of Freud biography has been on those aspects of his life seen as directly relevant to his internal, psychic life and to psychoanalytic theory and practice, in particular the elements of the Oedipal triangle of father, mother and child. Furthermore, in keeping with the general emphasis on great men, the viewpoint has been from Freud himself with a penumbra of kin and non-scientific friends in secondary place. Relationships between Freud and these others, much less among themselves, remain almost blank so that the material presented

---

[8] These issues continue to be debated around the concept of 'social capital' as an integrating factor in contemporary society. See R. Edwards, J. Franklin and J. Holland, *Families and Social Capital: Exploring the Issues*, Families and Social Capital ESRC Research Group Working Papers No. 1 (2003).

[9] James Casey, *The History of the Family* (Oxford, 1989), 15.

[10] Peter Gay, *Freud, Jews and Other Germans: Masters and Victims in Modernist Culture* (Oxford, 1978), 39.

here has had to be patched together from passing references and, by default, has continued to take Freud as the central figure.

Taking the Freud family as an illustrative case of the European bourgeoisie raises the issue of different cultures and their role in familial and kinship interaction.[11] In the case of Freud's cultural background, emphasis has been given to the specificity of his Jewish heritage, and its secular development in this period. This is compounded by the fact that in Germany, by the 1870s, 85 per cent of Jews were middle class, predominantly urban, and there is no reason to believe that Vienna was very different.[12] But by disentangling economic and demographic features from culture and ethnicity, by 'leaching out' such variations and concentrating on kinship relationships as lived, it is possible to highlight features common to wide strata of the period even while recognising the artificiality of such an exercise.[13]

Common features of the nineteenth-century bourgeois family

1. Before the late eighteenth century, except for court, church and some municipal governing bodies, few of these societies had much infrastructure for the exercise of trade, manufacture or fee-paid professionals except for the remnants of medieval guilds (more extensive in some places than others). Thus *family* and *kin* were the central forms for economic and political as well as social interaction. Those groups at the forefront of commercial and professional development were often members of tightly knit religious and ethnic communities that extended their kinship networks.

2. In many cases members of these strata often tended to be both geographically and socially mobile – 'incomers' to local towns and cities where they depended heavily on kin to build networks of support.

3. Families as the basis of economic activity were extended through the informal mechanism of male partnership, mainly of father and son, brothers or uncle, nephew and in-laws.

[11] Considerable attention has been paid to middle-class or bourgeois culture, see, for example, John Gillis, *A World of their Own Making: Myth, Ritual and the Quest for Family Values* (Oxford, 1996).

[12] Marion Kaplan, *The Making of the Jewish Middle Class: Women, Family and Identity in Imperial Germany: 1871–1918* (Oxford, 1991), ix.

[13] For example Steven Beller disputes Carl Schorske's emphasis on Freud's Jewish heritage, seeing him rather as a member of an educated subset of the liberal bourgeoisie, Steven Beller, *Vienna and the Jews 1867–1938* (Cambridge, 1989); for English Anglican and Non-Conformist cultural influences as well as similar economic and demographic features see Leonore Davidoff and Catherine Hall, *Family Fortunes: Men and Women of the English Middle Class 1780–1850* (2002); Noel Annan, 'The Intellectual Aristocracy', in *Studies in Social History*, ed. J. Plumb (1955).

4. Women, although not formal partners, were a key resource in these 'establishments':

   a) as sources of capital and skill through dowries and maintaining social contacts, particularly through marriage partners
   b) through producing the 'personnel' of sons, nephews, apprentices
   c) through their own labour, often carried on behind the scenes
   d) their activities as homemakers and consumers were vital for the households standard of living
   e) through these many activities maintaining the status and credit-worthiness of the family and enterprise in the community.

Characteristics of bourgeois family and kin

1. These groups practised carefully controlled, 'free choice' marriage, usually within their religious and/or ethnic communities. This helped to bring in and preserve capital as well as skills and contacts. With some groups, such as the Quakers and Jews, their community could move far beyond local or even national boundaries.

2. These factors also produced a trend towards marriage among kin including between first cousins. There was also a widespread minority pattern of brother–sister from one family marrying sister–brother from another or sister–sister marrying brother–brother resulting in double in-laws, double aunts and uncles–nieces and nephews and double grandparents–grandchildren.

3. Given the necessity to build up capital and/or professional training (for males), and unlike working-class marriages, for these couples age at marriage was relatively late, for example, as late as the early thirties for men and around the mid-twenties for women.[14] In most cases the groom was older than his bride, sometimes considerably so, a pattern that would be reinforced by widowers marrying a younger woman, often to care for their motherless children.

4. Despite late marriage, large numbers of children followed – an average of around seven although ten to fifteen was not unusual with birth intervals of around fourteen to twenty months, indicating that a birth control strategy was not followed or, at least, not effectively.

5. This resulted in 'long families' with elderly parents for the younger children. There was a range of ages that resulted in an *intermediate generation* between parents and younger children. This was made up in two ways: since there was twenty years or more between oldest and youngest siblings the elder became caretakers and playmates of the

---

[14] In England, for example, this was considerably later than for the population as a whole at this period. See E. A. Wrigley and R. S. Schofield, *The Population History of England: A Reconstruction* (1981), 255.

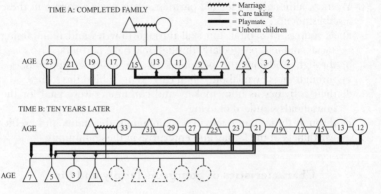

Figure 1   The intermediate generation: siblings in 'long families' and younger siblings of parents.

younger members of the family. When these elders married and had children themselves, the younger siblings would have grown into their teens and were recruited as caretakers and playmates for their small nephews and nieces. These teenagers and young adults were often resident in the homes of their elder brothers and sisters, the boys as apprentices or more informally as extra hands in the enterprise and the girls as mothers' helpers and companions. Large families such as these generally resulted in much sibling interaction on several dimensions:

a) instrumental as caretakers, disciplinarians
b) as significant 'role models', especially in terms of gender
c) as key actors in friendships and courtship
d) as business partners *and* in-laws.

6. Aunts and uncles had important roles as substitute parents and mentors, in turn producing the cousins who acted as playmates, friends, potential marriage partners and as a source of social, material and cultural contacts.

7. These households were enlarged by mainly residential servants, who worked for both the family and enterprise. In many cases those recruited as servants had some kinship links with the employing family.

Changes in family and kinship patterns

1. Depending on the economic and cultural situation in a particular society, as the nineteenth century progressed the development of a

more effective infrastructure such as banking mechanisms effected – and was effected by – family and kin relations. For example the introduction of limited liability facilitated the separation of the family's residence and place of work. The interior of this domestic space was distributed in a similar way whether in the English house (including farm houses) or continental urban flat.

2. There was less emphasis on family-trained personnel and a slow shift to externally recruited management although this only was complete with the introduction of large public companies in the mid-twentieth century. The use of family, kin and friendship networks gradually lost its manifest advantages and became negatively redefined as *nepotism*.

3. There was less need for wives and daughters to be directly involved in the enterprise while the status of the family was ever more associated with women's domestic role and separation from the labour market reflected in the growth of residential suburbs. Conversely men were more removed from domestic affairs with a more stringent association of masculinity with extra-familial and public affairs.

4. The above elements were associated with higher expectations and the ensuing costs of a bourgeois lifestyle, particularly the education of sons and to a much lesser extent some educational provision for daughters.

5. These developments were closely connected with gradual but steady fall in the marital birth rate to three or four children and by the inter-war period to around two. However, the means to accomplish this were not fully in place until technically sophisticated methods replaced late marriage, abstinence and withdrawal (coitus interruptus)

6. These changes were associated with an intense interest in sexuality and the creation of 'sexology' towards the end of the nineteenth century. This was further fuelled by the rise of science and medicine (as well as the status of their practitioners) in the interpretation of sexual behaviour increasingly removed from religious definitions of morality. This was part of a more general turning from the power of religious ideas and institutions. As religion lost its saliency, the *ideal* of family love and duty became even more central to a moral order, especially as an 'a-moral' free market became more dominant in the economic and political spheres.

A case study: the Freud family

Jacob Freud was a wool merchant, one of five brothers, born around 1815 in Galacia, a rural backwater of eastern Europe. The family were traders in various goods but especially wool, his brother Joseph spending some time in prison over suspected currency counterfeiting. Jacob married

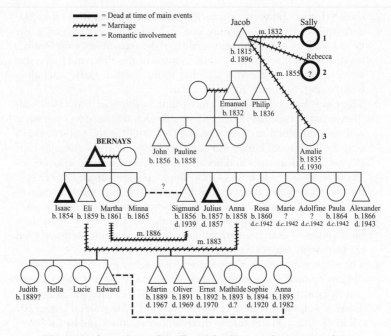

Figure 2   Genealogy of the Freud family over three generations.

young and had two sons but shortly afterwards his wife died. It is believed that he married again, briefly, but, if so, this second wife was also dead within a year. At age forty he then married a young woman of nineteen and they began married life in the small town of Freiberg in Moravia, living in a room over a blacksmith's forge.

Meanwhile the two sons of the first marriage had grown up, the elder, Emanuel, now married with a small son and daughter of his own, the younger son of an age with his new stepmother. The two families together migrated to the town of Leipzig in Germany where they lived close by each other, sharing domestic arrangements including a general servant-cum-nursemaid.

In 1856, between the birth of Jacob's grandson, John, and granddaughter, Pauline, his young bride produced a son, Sigismund. As the first-born, her 'golden boy Ziggy', his mother adored him. For several years in the gardens and meadows of Freiberg, the three children played together daily. Note that Sigismund was uncle to a nephew a little less than a year his senior who he later described as his closest playmate and best enemy.[15] They enjoyed romping in the open fields with Philip, the second, still unmarried, son of the first marriage; a young uncle to his elder brother's two children and half-brother to the wool merchant's little Ziggy.

When Sigismund was just under a year old, another son, Julius, was born, but at eight months the common scourge of infant death struck, and the new baby was dead. We can speculate that the couple was not using birth control, or at least not successfully and hypothesise that the young mother was either not breast feeding or only for a short time because a year later a daughter, Anna, was born.

By 1859 the two families separated, the sons of the first marriage leaving for Manchester to try their luck in the burgeoning textile trades. Middle-aged Jacob and young Amalie with their three-and-a-half-year-old son and one-year-old daughter left for the rapidly expanding regional capital, Vienna. There they settled with others like themselves in an area that had become a Jewish quarter, for by the 1880s, Vienna's approximately 40,000 Jews included many immigrants from the countryside.[16] Here the Freuds lived a somewhat hand to mouth existence, having to stretch their erratic income to cover the successive births of four more daughters, Rosa, Marie (Mitzi), Adolfine (Dolfi), Paula and finally, another son, Alexander, just ten years younger than his only brother.

The young mother now became a stout matriarchal figure devoted to keeping the family as respectably as possible. The education and training of the children depended much on the particular circumstances of the family at the moment and followed appropriate gender patterns: education for the boys; some sort of marriage settlement for the girls. While Sigmund (no longer Sigismund) was sent to an academic school and given further support for his scientific studies, when it came to Alexander's turn, resources only stretched to an informal apprenticeship with his eldest sister, Anna's, future husband leading to a mixed career in commerce and politics.

In this family, undoubtedly, Sigmund, as the eldest male child, had the lion's share of attention as well as resources. In the rather cramped quarters of the flat, he alone had a small bedroom/study to himself. As a studious schoolboy he was excused from strict appearance at meal times and allowed to eat alone in his room if he wished. When Anna – in keeping with coveted respectable bourgeois refinements – began to learn the piano, he objected to the noise which put a stop to the lessons,[17] for in

---

[15] Freud did not discuss his ambivalent relationship to John directly but it appears in his 'Interpretation of Dreams'. Helen W. Powers, *Freud: His Life and Mind: A Biography* (1949), 20.

[16] Marsha Rozenblit, *The Jews of Vienna: Assimilation and Identity: 1867–1914* (Albany, NY, 1983), 5.

[17] Paul Ferris, *Dr. Freud: A Life* (1997), 22.

Plate 1   Children of Jacob and Amalie Freud, c. 1867. From *Sigmund Freud: His Life in Pictures and Words,* ed. Ernst Freud, Lucie Freud and Ilse Grubrich-Simitis (1978), 50–9.

spite of his youth, 'Sigmund's word and wish were respected by everyone in the family.'[18] Indeed, at the age of ten it was he who had the naming of the last child and only other boy and Sigmund chose that of his favourite hero, Alexander the Great.

Despite limited material resources, neither the mother nor later any of the daughters seem to have worked for wages. Somehow the family managed to employ at least the intermittent help of a domestic servant and, now and again, some sort of family holiday. Although the father took

---

[18] Anna Freud Bernays, 'My Brother, Sigmund Freud', in *Freud As We Knew Him,* ed. Hendrick M. Ruitenbeck (Detroit, 1973), 140.

Plate 2   Jacob and Amalie Freud with assorted children and friends, c. 1867.
From *Sigmund Freud: His Life in Pictures and Words*, ed. Ernst Freud, Lucie Freud
and Ilse Grubrich-Simitis (1978), 80–1.

part in the growing secularisation of the later nineteenth century, a muted
religious observance was still followed by the mother and children.

As he grew up, Sigmund was drawn to the natural sciences despite
the school's classical curriculum. But despite differences of ability and
interests, it was taken for granted that all the girls would have a domestic
training with minimal education. Indeed, from an early age their elder
brother considered it his duty to act as a 'window on the world' for his
younger sisters, explaining the meaning of public affairs going on around
them.[19] For example when he was eighteen and Anna fifteen he told her
that Balzac and Dumas were not suitable reading, but she read them
anyway, keeping them hidden among the linens where a young man was
not likely to look.[20]

He also overlooked his sisters' social behaviour. When he was twenty,
Rosa, who was sixteen, had been performing on the zither while on an
early visit away from home and he warned her against being puffed up

[19] Martin Freud, *Glory Reflected: Sigmund Freud – Man and Father* (1957), 20.
[20] Bernays, 'My Brother', 142.

by slight social success, telling her that unscrupulous people over-praised young girls to the detriment of their later character.[21] His younger sister, Paula, also remarked how he could show severity if he found them erring. He had caught her spending money on sweets when she was not supposed to, a snub that fifty years later she had neither forgotten nor forgiven.[22]

As the Freud children grew into their teens and twenties they became more integrated into the social life of the city, although still living at home. Sigmund's father held to more traditional ideas about his son's future. In keeping with the pattern of close kin marriages, Jacob sent the nineteen-year-old Sigmund to Manchester for a visit with his eldest half-brother, Emanuel, with the idea of marrying him to Emanuel's daughter Pauline, but nothing came of this scheme.[23]

In the coffee houses and meeting places of Vienna, Sigmund had become part of a group of like-minded friends, young men who met to discuss scientific, political and cultural matters. Anna, Rosa and Mitzi, too, made friends with other young women, although mainly within a domestic setting. They had become intimate with the family of a well-off widow's two daughters and a son, Martha, Minna and Eli Bernays, the latter also part of the informal coffee house gatherings. It was during a casual visit of Martha to his sisters, that Sigmund's attention was caught. (Note, too, that Sigmund's first childish love had been with a friend of Anna's.)[24]

He was soon deeply in love and determined to marry Martha despite her mother's coolness on the grounds of his family's social position, his poor financial situation and his secular beliefs. Five years passed in which Sigmund and Martha's courtship blew hot and cold. He longed ceaselessly for his 'little girl', so called in his letters although she was only five years his junior. At this juncture of his life he exhibited all the romantic expect-ations and bourgeois aspirations of his period and class. Although valuing Martha's ability to be his intellectual confidante during their courtship days, he held typical bourgeois ideas about appropriate gender behaviours. In response to the 'absurd ideas of J. S. Mill' and anxious about Martha's seeming lack of 'yielding docility' he wrote: 'Am I to think of my delicate, sweet girl as a competitor? . . . I will make every effort to get her out of the competitive role into the quiet, undisturbed activity of my home.'[25]

And the young scientist had firm ideas about what that home would be. In their extensive correspondence he outlined in detail the furnishings

[21] Ernest Jones, *Sigmund Freud: Life and Work* (3 vols., 1953), I, 23.
[22] Freud, *Glory Reflected*, 20.
[23] Jones, *Sigmund Freud*, I, 23.
[24] Ronald Clark, *Freud: The Man and the Cause* (1980), 26.
[25] Kaplan, *The Making of the Jewish Middle Class*, 42.

and comforts of their future 'little world of happiness in a pair of rooms, some tables, beds, easy chairs, rugs, glasses and china . . . decent linens, hats with artificial flowers, big bunches of keys'.[26] Predictably the actuality of the ensuing marriage transformed his 'sweet girl' into the essence of a hausfrau, obedient to her husband's scientific and secularised wishes to the point of giving up the religious observance so dear to her.

As friendship between the two families of young people continued, his eldest sister, Anna, clinched the intimacy by becoming engaged to Eli Bernays, the brother of Sigmund's fiancée; a typical brother–sister, sister–brother set of marriages. (Note too that Sigmund's friends and fellow physicians, Oscar Rie and Wilhelm Fliess, had married sisters.) But the situation of the two couples was not equal. While Eli was on the way to becoming a prosperous businessman, Sigmund was faced with a dilemma. His wish to marry his beloved meant being able to support her (and the children which were sure to follow) but his scientific position was such as to bring in only a tiny income which was sustainable if he continued living at home but impossible for a married man. The problem was partially solved by his decision to set up a private medical practice.[27]

Ultimately it was funds from Martha's dowry plus a gift from an aunt and loans from his friends that finally allowed the marriage to take place in June 1887 when he was thirty-one, his dearly won bride twenty-six. The fact that Eli and Anna, although engaged later than Sigmund and Martha, had been able to marry the year before compounded Sigmund's envy and dislike, already roused by Eli's having borrowing from his sister Martha's marriage portion.

From then on, building up a medical practice enough to sustain not one, but several households became a priority for Sigmund, for the elderly merchant father had died by the time the children of his third marriage had reached full adulthood. Three out of the four remaining Freud sisters were married off, one to a distant cousin, thus retaining the Freud name, the others to respectable bourgeois husbands from the city.

During his prolonged courtship, a medical friend who was negotiating to found a sanatorium for mental cases proposed that Sigmund be installed there as a married man and employ his sister-in-law Minna Bernays and his own sister, Dolfi, in the domestic sphere and, in time, some patients would marry them.[28] But despite such continued efforts to settle Dolfi, she remained unmarried, having nursed their father until he died, staying on as companion to the ageing mother and acting as devoted aunt to her siblings' children.

[26] Gay, *Freud, Jews and Other Germans*, 61.
[27] Jewish physicians in Vienna were mostly in private practice as it was difficult for them to get hospital appointments. Rozenblit, *The Jews of Vienna*.
[28] Jones, *Sigmund Freud*, I, 156.

Sigmund, as eldest son, believed it was his duty to support this mother–sister household. His sense of his masculine role is indicated in his directions to his younger brother, Alexander, 'who together with me carries the responsibility for two old people and so many women and children'.[29] Sigmund continued to visit his mother every Sunday throughout his adult life. He took it as given that he would help out his other sisters at times of difficulty. For example Marie (Mitzi), on marriage had settled in the same block of flats as her brother and, shortly after the move, when suddenly widowed and left with two small boys to bring up, her brother stepped in to help support this household as well as that of sister Paula, when later she, too, lost her husband.

Jacob Freud had been fifty years old when his youngest son, Alexander, was born and a frail elderly man during the boy's formative years. It seemed natural for his elder brother to look after the younger's upbringing but, unlike the case of Sigmund's sisters, for Alexander it was to guide him into an income-earning profession and the intricacies of masculine pursuits. Alexander took part in the coffee house discussion groups and lived for some time in the Bernays household also guided by Eli, Anna's fiancé (and which also included Martha, Sigmund's fiancée). Every year at holiday time, Sigmund and Alexander would set out on a trip of strenuous walking as well as sightseeing which would last for some weeks and would take them to some part of the Mediterranean seaboard.[30] Alexander vividly remembered Sigmund early on instructing him in a sense of masculine familial responsibility:

> When I was a boy of six my brother was sixteen. He said to me 'Look, our family is like a book. You and I are the first and the last of the children, so we are like the strong covers that have to support the weak girls who were born after me and before you.'[31]

As an adult, Alexander took these lessons to heart, helping Sigmund with funds to support their mother and sisters. The quality of Alexander's relationship with his older brother veered between identification with Sigmund and efforts to differentiate himself, an ambivalence that echoes a general pattern.[32] When Alexander was approaching thirty, Sigmund had urged Fliess to psychoanalyse his 'little brother' who, he felt, was neurotic and escaping his influence too much, noting that Alexander 'does move in different circles of people and ideas'.[33] According to one of

---

[29] Jeffrey Masson, *The Complete Letters of Sigmund Freud to Wilhelm Fliess: 1887–1904* (Cambridge, MA, 1985), 135.

[30] *Sigmund Freud: His Life in Pictures and Words*, ed. Ernst Freud, Lucie Freud and Ilse Grubrich-Simitis (1978), 149.

[31] *Ibid.*, 59.

[32] Francine Klagsbrun, *Mixed Feelings: Love, Hate, Rivalry and Reconciliation Among Brothers and Sisters* (New York, 1992).

[33] Masson, *The Complete Letters*, 135.

Sigmund's sons, the two brothers, although so close in many ways, could not have been more different in their outlook on life: for example, while Alexander greatly enjoyed music, Sigmund, by his own admission, had no interest in it.[34]

Once Sigmund and Martha were married, a pattern was set for the new family; and the birth of six children followed in regular and rapid sequence. This time, we know from written evidence that, despite – or possibly because of – his medical training, Freud did not approve of conscious contraception being practised.[35] Once again, the short birth intervals also indicate that the babies were not being breast fed by their mother, or at least not for very long periods.[36] Nevertheless, the whole subject generated much tension. Sigmund's struggles with sexuality and the need for 'restraint' are hinted at in letters and other documents, although little is known of Martha's views. At the age of forty-four Sigmund wrote to Fliess: 'I have done with begetting children.' Yet somewhat ambiguous unpublished jottings into his fifties indicates that intercourse had occasionally taken place and clearly this was a subject of much soul searching at this time.[37]

The experience of the Freud family fits well with the little we know of English couples in the late nineteenth and early twentieth centuries as discussed by Simon Szreter. A relatively long period of courtship, filled by some men with casual liaisons with lower-class women (a practice doubtful but not inconceivable in this particular family) would be followed by unrestrained sexual intercourse until the requisite number of babies was born, then the couple would turn to abstinence and/or withdrawal or both, these efforts made more ineffectual by the misunderstanding about the menstrual cycle.[38]

Unfortunately the separation between the histories of sexuality, usually seen as a cultural phenomenon, and of reproduction, the province of historical demographers, has made this difficult subject even more intractable. As Angus McLaren has pointed out, in the very decades in which Freud and the 'sexologists' were sketching out their theories, the European middle classes were radically reducing their fertility, the reduction especially evident among medics and clergymen some of whom were among the most vociferous to publicly rail against the practice of family limitation. As McLaren queried: 'why this artificial reduction in

---

[34] Freud, *Glory Reflected*, 17.

[35] David Feldman, *Marital Relations, Birth Control and Abortion in Jewish Law* (New York, 1975), 96.

[36] One son, Martin, claims he had been wet nursed, Freud, *Glory Reflected*; the last child, Anna, was bottle fed, Lisa Appignanesi and John Forrester, *Freud's Women* (1992), 273.

[37] Ferris, *Dr. Freud*, 176; see also Angus McLaren, *The Trials of Masculinity and Policing Sexual Boundaries 1870–1930* (Chicago, 1999), 143–8.

[38] Simon Szreter, *Fertility, Class and Gender in Britain 1860–1940* (Cambridge, 1996), 558.

family size – this truly momentous demographic transition – has not been more closely linked to cultural focus on sexuality remains unclear'.[39]

Sigmund Freud's close involvement with the Bernays, his likes and dislikes among his in-laws, also followed a pattern familiar within the Western bourgeoisie. In particular, much ambivalence, highly charged with emotion, coloured his feelings for Eli who had been a good friend but relations then changed to suspicion and hostility around the time of the double engagements. Their dealings seem to have first become strained over Eli's treatment of Alexander during the period of his tutelage in the Bernays household, but Sigmund also blamed Eli for at least part of his future mother-in-law's original hostility to his marriage and he once described Eli as his most dangerous rival during his prolonged courtship, quite aside from the financial irregularities connected to Martha's dowry. So strong were his feelings that he refused to attend Eli and Anna's wedding. Even years later the suspicious attitude continued for Freud thought of him as 'a bankrupt, philanderer and draft evader'.[40] But since Eli was so firmly part of the Freud extended family, some interaction, no matter how grudging, was inevitable.

Relations between them were eased when the Bernays left for New York in the 1890s. Despite the tensions between the two families, typically the emigrant branch left their teenage daughter, Lucie, in Vienna to live for several years with her 'double' aunt Martha, uncle Sigmund and clutch of cousins. Reciprocating later, one of Sigmund's Americanised 'double' nephews, Edward Bernays – his sister's son *and* son of his wife's brother – proved an ally in furthering his European Uncle Sigmund's professional visits to the New World. Later still, during Edward's visits to Vienna, young Anna is reputed to have fallen in love with her double cousin, although nothing came of this brief romance.[41] Another of Anna and Eli's daughters, Hella, also had holidays with her European cousins. After one such spent with their mutual Aunt Rosa, one of Sigmund and Martha's sons recalled that Hella, 'having a Bernays for a father and a Freud for a mother, was really more a sister than a cousin to me'.[42]

Even more complicated was Sigmund's relationship with Martha's sister, Minna. Such brother and sister-in law connection seems to have had special resonance in this period. It was a classic theme in the bourgeois scenario, partly because a man's unmarried sister-in-law might spend a good deal of time in his household and was potentially the most logical caretaker for his children in the event of his wife's early death. In England,

[39] Angus McLaren, 'Contraception and its Discontents: Sigmund Freud and Birth Control', *Journal of Social History*, 12 (1997), 513 .

[40] Ferris, *Dr. Freud*, 257.

[41] Appignanesi; and Forrester, *Freud's Women*, 20.

[42] Freud, *Glory Reflected*, 56 n. 13.

for example, where the issue aroused much controversy, from 1837 to 1907, marriage to a deceased wife's sister had been legally prohibited.[43]

In the Freud–Bernays case, Minna was four years younger than her sister and a rather different temperament with widespread interests and intellectual curiosity. Around the time of Sigmund and Anna Freud's courtships with the Bernays, Minna, too, had been engaged to a young man, Ignaz Schönberg, part of the coffee house discussion circle and a particularly close friend of Sigmund. But her tragedy, like so many others, was to witness the death of her fiancé through tuberculosis before the wedding could take place. The prospective bride was left a daughter at home, whose social and emotional life now centred on Sigmund and Martha's household. To the doctor she had become an important ally, his 'Treasure' as he wrote in one of the frequent letters they exchanged.[44]

When later on as some of Sigmund's wilder flights of scientific speculation were being ridiculed, she, almost alone, took him seriously and he described her to a colleague as 'my closest confidante'.[45] As more children were born to the young couple in rapid succession, Minna came for long visits, acting as the helpful maiden aunt. In 1895, just after the sixth child's birth, she moved in permanently as an invaluable factotum in the household, caring for and disciplining the children, sharing domestic duties with her sister, as well as companion to her brother-in-law.

Minna remained with the family during holidays spent in the mountains and often accompanied her brother-in-law on his travels when the unadventurous Martha returned to town with the children. As Sigmund had written to his future sister-in-law at the time of his engagement: 'I count a sincere, warm, unequivocal friendship with you. Not only because you are her only sister . . . I believe that there is in our own natures enough reason to expect joy and profit from faithful companionship.'[46]

Inevitably, such a characteristically close and intense relationship between brother and sister-in-law provokes speculation about what was then regarded as a potentially incestuous as well as adulterous liaison.[47] It has also been suggested by recent commentators that this pattern may partly be a form of displacement by a sister-in-law for incestuous feelings

---

[43] Although the issue generated a heated public debate, until recently it has tended to be treated more as a joke as in Gilbert and Sullivan's 'the annual blister' of deceased wife's sister used as the fairy queen's curse in 'Iolanthe'. See N. Anderson, 'The "Marriage with a Deceased Wife's Sister" Bill Controversy: Incest Anxiety and the Defence of Family Purity in Victorian Britain', *Journal of British Studies*, 21 (1982).

[44] Peter Gay, *Freud: A Life for our Time* (1988), 76.

[45] Masson, *The Complete Letters*, 71.

[46] *Sigmund Freud*, ed. Ernst Freud *et al.*, 99.

[47] Peter Swales, 'Freud, Minna Bernays and the Conquest of Rome: New Light on the Origins of Psychoanalysis', *New American Review* (Spring/Summer 1982).

Plate 3   Sigmund, Martha, Minna and five of the six children (note that Minna is dressed plainly, almost as a nanny/governess). From *Sigmund Freud: His Life in Pictures and Words*, ed. Ernst Freud, Lucie Freud and Ilse Grubrich-Simitis (1978), 150–1.

for an actual sister,[48] a supposition that is strengthened by the dominant theme of sibling incest in pornography of this period.[49]

In many respects, the young family repeated the pattern experienced in Jacob and Amalie's generation; in other ways they were more 'modern', more fully integrated into urban life. The six children, close in age, were brought up at the centre of a web of kinship, holidaying with myriad cousins, drawing on the resources of aunts and uncles and more distant kinsmen.

Alexander, the unmarried uncle, ten years junior to their father, would not only go off with Sigmund and his three nephews for the strenuous mountain walking that would not be attempted by the women but was also the children's regular companion. He was the jolly playful uncle compared to the kindly but more distant father. For, although, like many professional men, Sigmund's consulting rooms were an extension of the family's living space and he had his mid-day meal at home, work always came first. While in scientific writings as well as in his conception of

[48] Prophecy Coles, *The Importance of Sibling Relationships in Psychoanalysis* (2003).

[49] James B. Twitchell, *Forbidden Partners: The Incest Taboo in Modern Culture* (New York, 1987).

himself, Freud mixed family affairs with professional concerns, as with many of his bourgeois contemporaries, his behaviour seems to have been more compartmentalised.[50]

As they grew up, the six children were launched with professional careers for the three sons and suitable marriages for two of the daughters. None of the latter appeared to have taken advantage of the new educational and career opportunities slowly opening for women. The youngest girl, Anna, however, remained unmarried and living at home with her parents, just as her Aunt Dolfi had done before her.

The advent of the First World War made family and kin networks even more crucial with funds and food parcels from the Manchester Freuds and New York Bernays staving off the worst effects of inflation and shortages. After the war, the Freud sons continued to be sent off to work with kinsmen; the daughters for long visits to learn the ways of other households. Sigmund as father, brother and uncle, and now clearly head of the family, was the centre of advice and decision making for his extended kin including his widowed sisters and their children. Throughout the following decades and despite the flourishing practice and scientific interests which kept Papa so occupied, he continued to act, in his own words, as a 'human post box for getting and retailing news'.[51]

The Freud family and its legacy

The connection between the 'enterprise' which Sigmund Freud founded and nineteenth-century family establishments is strong. Indeed it has been noted how psychoanalysis was 'a profession whose social organisation was familial'.[52] This familial conception may go some way to illuminating the paradox of Freud's attitudes to women. On the one hand was his conventional concept of marriage and reluctance to see any of his daughters, much less his sisters, have formal training or enter the labour market. Yet not only was the preponderance of his patients female, but he encouraged women (many of them ex-patients) as analysts.

Freud as father figure, wrestling with the inevitable pulling away of his scientific 'sons', has been well documented. His ambivalence, swinging between love and hate and his inability to maintain more egalitarian relationships with male colleagues – most notoriously his break with Jung but also with Wilhelm Fliess – has been cast back to his competitive relationship to his 'nephew' John, in his first three years. And it is true that Freud himself gave a special place to his youthful playmate and their mutual teasing of John's younger sister, Pauline. Yet until now, his real life

---

[50] Lydia Flem, *Freud the Man* (New York, 2003), 3; see John Tosh, *Man's Place: Masculinity and the Middle-Class Home in Victorian England* (New Haven, 1999).

[51] Clark, *Freud*, 195.

[52] Appignanesi and Forrester, *Freud's Women*, 7.

relationships with his full siblings have seldom entered the psychoanalytic canon.

One of the strands in the general revaluation of Freud in the past few decades has been the 'exposé' of his relationship with Minna. Whether this was ever incestuous in a physical sense, there is no doubt that within his own family, Freud experienced and encouraged the split between his well-named spouse, Martha, and his more 'masculine' intellectual sparring partner and travelling companion, Minna. Significantly, Freud scholars have focused on the erotic elements of their relationship while overlooking Minna's intellectual support and input to the development of his thought. For example Peter Gay cites Fliess as Freud's *only* confidante during the years when he was struggling with the foundation of psychoanalysis.[53]

More recently attention has turned to the reaction of the eighteen-month-old Sigmund to the birth and death of his baby brother, Julius,[54] whose existence is not even mentioned in Ernest Jones three-volume study of Freud. Juliet Mitchell's recent book on hysteria does give a central role to the sibling relationship, noting that 'feelings for siblings and peers cast their shadow over relations with parents', thus reversing the usually understood order.[55]

But even she, who extensively investigates the Sigmund/Julius constellation, devotes only a few sentences to his eldest sister, Anna.[56] Freud noted that even a year-old child could have jealous feelings about a new baby which has been taken to refer to Julius, yet he claims he had no memory of the birth of the next baby, Anna. By all accounts his relationship to Anna seems to have been consistently cool if not negative. He said that he had never had 'any special relationship' with her as he had with his other sisters, particularly Rosa, 'and her marriage to Eli B. has not exactly improved it'.[57] Yet the virulence of Sigmund's feelings towards Anna's husband, Eli, who had been in many ways a stand in for Martha's dead father as well as being her only surviving brother, indicates a complicated ambivalence. For example, although Sigmund's youngest child was ostensibly called Anna after the daughter of an old friend and teacher, the name must have been a powerful reminder of this sister.[58]

As Lynn Segal has commented, 'psychoanalysis, for all its remarkable achievements, has failed to focus on the historical conjuncture framing its

---

[53] Gay, *Freud, Jews and Other Germans*, 82.

[54] James W. Hamilton, 'Some Comments about Freud's Conceptualization of the Death Instinct', *International Review of Psychoanalysis*, 3 (1971), 151.

[55] Juliet Mitchell, *Mad Men and Medusas: Reclaiming Hysteria and the Effects of Sibling Relations on the Human Condition* (2000), 23.

[56] *Ibid.*, 76.

[57] Masson, *The Complete Letters*, 406.

[58] Flem, *Freud the Man*, 73. Against Jewish tradition, all Sigmund's children were named for living people, the naming obviously his choice, not Martha's.

intricate accounts of psychic life and familial dynamics'.[59] (It is particularly poignant but not widely known that the historical conjuncture of the late 1930s prevented Freud, the masterful elder brother, from saving his sisters who had remained in Austria – Rosa, Mitzi, Dolfi, Paula – and their descendants from the Nazi death camps.)[60]

These limitations have left unanswered some fundamental questions: Why did Freud, as so many of his contemporaries, in his writing, at best give slight weight to the sibling relationship, constantly casting it in relation to the Father and Mother? Why were siblings, aunts, uncles, nephews, nieces, cousins and servants not seen as a central part of family interaction in their own right and left aside as only part of 'objective reality', thus not part of the psyche's internalised social relationships?[61] Why have these elements continued to be ignored through the twentieth century?

The 'psychic life and family dynamics' of Freud's time and place were centrally concerned with the creation of a self in terms of masculine individualism, supposedly free from attachment to others but actually based on intense relationships of super and subordination, dependency and exploitation as well as mutual interaction.[62] Freud himself, in his few but influential references to the topic, saw sibling relationships in terms of rivalry, even deadly hatred, a view that has only recently begun to be modified in psychological circles.[63]

In contrast, the idea and language of brotherhood (and sisterhood) imply an egalitarian experience, if only symbolically. Siblings have provided a model for particular structures: monastic orders, Freemasonry, utopian communities, the labour movement. Now, at the start of the twenty-first century's more democratic political and social climate, perhaps it is understandable that there has been a turning away from a hierarchical model that constantly privileges the vertical relation of parent and child.

Feminist thinkers and activists have contributed much to the evaluation of power in unequal relationships.[64] While power is one of the universal characteristics of human society, the way it is understood as well as used is

[59] Lynn Segal, *Why Feminism* (1999), 138.

[60] Giovanni Costigan, *Sigmund Freud: A Short Biography* (1967), 2.

[61] Eloise Moor Agger, 'Psychoanalytic Perspectives on Sibling Relationships', *Psychoanalytic Inquiry*, 8 (1988), 7.

[62] Leonore Davidoff, 'Regarding Some "Old Husband's Tales": Public and Private in Feminist History', in *Worlds Between: Historical Perspectives on Gender and Class* (Cambridge, 1995).

[63] See especially the chapter on Melanie Klein in Coles, *The Importance of Sibling Relationships*; Juliet Mitchell, *Siblings: Sex and Violence* (Cambridge, 2003).

[64] In relation to psychoanalysis see Judith M. Hughes, *Reshaping the Psychoanalytic Domain* (Berkeley, 1989).

extremely variable. In one of the most illuminating discussions of power in personal relationships, the feminist psychoanalyst Jessica Benjamin pleads that 'the issue is not how we become free of the other, but how we actively engage and make ourselves known in relationship to the other'.[65] Freud's remarkable insights into the psychic creation of 'the other' inevitably were framed by his time and place in history. The task of this historical excursion has been to uncover something of that time and place.

---

[65] Jessica Benjamin, *The Bonds of Love: Psychoanalysis, Feminism and the Problem of Domination* (New York, 1988), 18.

All plates by permission of A. W. Freud *et al.* and Paterson Marsh Ltd.

Transactions of the RHS 14 (2004), pp. 47–71 © 2004 Royal Historical Society
DOI: 10.1017/S0080440104000076   Printed in the United Kingdom

PRISTINA LIBERTAS: LIBERTY AND THE ANGLO-SAXONS REVISITED*

By Julia Crick

READ 14 MARCH 2003

ABSTRACT. The association between liberty and the Anglo-Saxons has been rendered mythical by later retellings, both in the Middle Ages and afterwards. This later history notwithstanding, it is argued here that liberty occupied a significant place in the early English documentary record. Originally part of the cultural and linguistic inheritance from late antiquity, the notion of liberty was deployed by English churchmen in defence of monastic freedom from the eighth century onwards, creating an archival legacy which was rewritten and imitated in later centuries, becoming fixed in institutional memory as fiscal and legal freedoms bestowed on the populations of monasteries and towns by pre-Conquest kings.

Liberty and the Anglo-Saxons once co-existed in happy equilibrium. As long as later Englishmen pictured the England of the Anglo-Saxons as the fount of the ancient constitution or cradle of the English nation they projected on to this apparently formative period their aspirations, liberty among them;[1] from at least the seventeenth century to the twentieth historians, politicians and polemicists sought and found liberty in the pre-Conquest past. The traces of their sentimental quest are unmistakable. Stubbs celebrated the Anglo-Saxon chronicle (in almost Ossianic terms) as 'The song of the people emulous of ancient glories, girding itself up for a strong and united effort after liberty.'[2] Edward Freeman, on a lecture

---

* Versions of this essay were presented at seminars in Cambridge and Oxford in November 2000 and June 2002. Its final form owes much to questions, comments and advice offered by members of the audience at all three public readings. In addition I owe particular thanks to Jonathan Barry, Rosamond Faith, Nicholas Orme and Susan Reynolds who guided me on specific points, and to Sarah Hamilton, Bruce O'Brien, Julia Smith and Alexandra Walsham, who generously read drafts, shared expertise and provided strategic advice.

[1] Hugh A. MacDougall, *Racial Myth in English History: Trojans, Teutons and Anglo-Saxons* (Montreal, 1982); Simon Keynes, 'The Cult of King Alfred the Great', *Anglo-Saxon England*, 28 (1999), 225–356, and below, n. 5. Liberty has been discussed by Eric Gerald Stanley, *Imagining the Anglo-Saxon Past: The Search for Anglo-Saxon Paganism and Anglo-Saxon Trial by Jury* (Cambridge, 2000), 113–22; see also James Campbell, *The Anglo-Saxon State* (2000), 12.

[2] William Stubbs, *The Constitutional History of England in its Origin and Development*, 6th edn (3 vols., Oxford, 1903), I, 233.

tour of New England in 1881, invited his audience to view William 'the Great' as 'a friend disguised in the garb of an enemy' who by the Norman Conquest had ensured not the destruction but the preservation 'of English law, of English freedom, of all that makes England England'.[3] More than two centuries earlier Thomas Hedley, addressing parliament in June 1610, had defended the 'ancient freedom and liberty of the subjects of England' a status confirmed in Magna Carta but of much greater antiquity, rooted in 'the ancient laws and liberties of the kingdom' before the Norman Conquest.[4] In the rhetoric of liberty we may detect something of the spirit which once fired the passion for Anglo-Saxon studies.

The Anglo-Saxon liberties to which Stubbs, Freeman and earlier Hedley appealed of course vanish on inspection. Hedley and the common lawyers divined in the pre-Conquest past freedoms derived from ancient law;[5] Freeman and Stubbs pursued a romantic quality intrinsic to the national character since the inception of the English as an island nation.[6] Such rhetoric died with racial Anglo-Saxonism, alongside faith in the concrete manifestations of the spirit of liberty explored by its historians: the notion of free Englishmen and the village commonwealth,[7] the proto-democratic credentials ascribed to the king's witan.[8] Liberty has been

---

[3] Edward A. Freeman, *Lectures to American Audiences*, I: *The English People in its Three Homes*; II: *The Practical Bearings of General European History* (Philadelphia, 1882), 153. On this text see now William M. Aird, 'Edward A. Freeman in America and "The English People in their Three Homes"', *Haskins Society Journal*, forthcoming.

[4] 'For I do not take Magna Carta to be a new grant or statute, but a restoring or confirming of the ancient laws and liberties of the kingdom, which by the conquest before had been much impeached or obscured': *Proceedings in Parliament 1610*, ed. Elizabeth Read Foster (1966), II, 190; cited by Paul Christianson, *Discourse on History, Law and Governance in the Public Career of John Selden, 1610–1635* (Toronto, 1996), 31.

[5] J. G. A. Pocock, *The Ancient Constitution and the Feudal Law: A Study in English Historical Thought in the Seventeenth Century* (Cambridge, 1957); William Klein, 'The Ancient Constitution Revisited', in *Political Discourse in Early Modern Britain*, ed. Nicholas Phillipson and Quentin Skinner (Cambridge, 1993), 23–44; Richard Tuck, 'The Ancient Law of Freedom: John Selden and the Civil War', in *Reactions to the English Civil War 1642–1649*, ed. John Morrill (1982), 137–61; Paul Christianson, 'Ancient Constitutions in the Age of Sir Edward Coke and John Selden', in *The Roots of Liberty: Magna Carta, Ancient Constitution, and the Anglo-American Tradition of Rule of Law*, ed. Ellis Sandoz (1993), 89–146.

[6] See further MacDougall, *Racial Myth*, 89–103, esp. 96–102.

[7] Analysed by J. W. Burrow, ' "The Village Community" and the Uses of History in Late Nineteenth-Century England', in *Historical Perspectives: Studies in English Thought and Society in Honour of J.H. Plumb*, ed. Neil McKendrick (1974), 255–84.

[8] For a late endorsement of this view from a highly authoritative hand see F. Liebermann, *The National Assembly in the Anglo-Saxon Period* (Halle, 1913). On Anglo-Saxonism see MacDougall, *Racial Myth*; Allen J. Frantzen, *Desire for Origins: New Language, Old English, and Teaching the Tradition* (1990), esp. 27–61; Allen J. Frantzen and John D. Niles, 'Introduction: Anglo-Saxonism and Medievalism', *Anglo-Saxonism and the Construction of Social Identity* (Gainesville, 1997), 1–14.

effectively eliminated from the vocabulary of Anglo-Saxon studies.[9] But alongside these relatively familiar expressions of national sentiment, now long gone, there lies a much earlier, medieval tradition, an ascription to pre-Conquest origins of freedoms of a different sort. Strictly speaking the connection between this and later manifestations remains entirely superficial – this earlier kind of liberty belongs to a cultural and conceptual universe remote from those of later constructions of personal and constitutional liberty.[10] It embraces privilege licensed by kings, a right claimed for institutions, an abstraction of a sort but more circumscribed and concrete in nature than the freedoms later claimed. But Anglo-Saxon liberty in its medieval guise resembles the later manifestations of liberty claims in one particular: it appears to function as an origin myth, a sought-after quality anachronistically attributed pre-Conquest origins. It is this rhetorical and historical tradition which I wish to explore.

Some years ago Sir James Holt traced the seventeenth-century theory of English constitutional liberties to Magna Carta and before, to what he described as 'an earlier antiquarian movement in the late twelfth century' when 'monks were developing a new interest in the English past to replace the wary hostility with which they had regarded the traditions of the conquered English hitherto'.[11] In so doing he challenged a point of origin embedded in the historical literature and beckoned students of liberty further back into the Middle Ages.[12] He also argued for strong connections between the Ancient Constitutionalists of the seventeenth century and medieval texts, suggesting that the medieval textual authority used by Coke contained a 'parent myth' of pre-Conquest constitutional origins.[13] In locating a tradition of Anglo-Saxon liberties in the twelfth century Sir James pursued the constitutional not the institutional tradition to be explored in this essay. Nevertheless, his study prefigures the present one

---

[9] Although, for a dissenting voice, as Bruce O'Brien has reminded me, see Campbell, *The Anglo-Saxon State*, xxix.

[10] On the problems of translating notions of freedom from the classical to the medieval 'thought-world' see Brian Tierney, 'Freedom and the Medieval Church', in *The Origins of Modern Freedom in the West*, ed. R. W. Davis (Stanford, 1995), 65.

[11] J. C. Holt, 'The Origins of the Constitutional Tradition in England', in *Magna Carta and Medieval Government* (1985), 1–22, at 8.

[12] On the notion of Magna Carta as a point of origin see Sir Herbert Butterfield, *Magna Carta in the Historiography of the Sixteenth and Seventeenth Centuries*, Stenton Lecture 1968 (Reading, 1969); Anne Pallister, *Magna Carta: The Heritage of Liberty* (Oxford, 1971); *Magna Carta and the Idea of Liberty*, ed. James C. Holt (1972); Christopher W. Brooks, 'The Place of Magna Carta and the Ancient Constitution in Sixteenth-Century English Legal Thought', in *The Roots of Liberty: Magna Carta, Ancient Constitution, and the Anglo-American Tradition of Rule of Law*, ed. Ellis Sandoz (1993), 57–88.

[13] 'What mattered in the seventeenth century was not so much that Coke regarded the common law as ancient, but that he buttressed his view with tales and texts which already embodied the myth in a parent myth of their own': Holt, 'The Origins of the Constitutional Tradition', 17.

in two respects. It connected seventeenth-century antiquarian tradition with that of the twelfth;[14] it highlighted the importance of written and documentary tradition in the medieval construction of pre-Conquest liberty. The existence of rival constructions should occasion no surprise. The pairing of Anglo-Saxons and liberty has proved susceptible to invention and reinvention over many centuries. In looking beyond the constitutional tradition of Anglo-Saxon liberty to institutional claims, however, a more radical periodisation emerges: pre-Conquest evidence comes into contention. This present study will suggest that the rhetoric of liberty, although dormant for long periods, never went away at all, or at least not very far.[15]

The pristine liberty of my title, an original freedom ('pristina libertas') derived from Anglo-Saxon antiquity, belongs to polemic not only of the seventeenth century, but of the twelfth.[16] The liberty in question concerned not the nature of royal prerogative and parliamentary redress as it might have done in a later age, but a grant of fiscal freedom allegedly made on the eve of the Norman Conquest in which Edward the Confessor restored to Westminster Abbey its original liberty previously renewed in the tenth century by his grandfather, King Edgar, Archbishop Dunstan and later by his father, Æthelred.[17] The justice of the claims need not concern us here – for the purposes of the present argument I shall adopt a deliberately agnostic stance towards the question of the substance of claims to special privilege – but in appealing to ancient royal concessions as protection from current burdens the monk of Westminster who created the document in the twelfth century worked within a paradigm well rehearsed by his contemporaries. Henry I had publicly invoked pre-Conquest precedent when, in his coronation charter, he declared a return to the laws of Edward the Confessor.[18] Virtually from the time of the Conquest English monastic writers had claimed pre-Conquest freedom of a very specific sort, that their institutions should enjoy special freedom from interference – *libertas* – because of privileges granted by Anglo-Saxon kings, sometimes long dead. Such liberty sanctioned freedom from

[14] For other examples of the same linkage see Stanley, *Imagining the Anglo-Saxon Past*, 132–5, and Bruce R. O'Brien, *God's Peace and King's Peace: The Laws of Edward the Confessor* (Philadelphia, 1999), 123–6.

[15] For a brief discussion of liberty on either side of the Middle Ages see Quentin Skinner, *Liberty before Liberalism* (Cambridge, 1998).

[16] The term 'pristine liberty' was employed, for example, by John Hall in 1700: quoted by Skinner, *Liberty before Liberalism*, 20.

[17] 'Resolutum est coram me, et recitatum de terribili loco, qui uulgo ab incolis Westmynster nuncupatur, qualiter auus meus Eadgarus et Dunstanus archiepiscopus et postea Ethelredus pater meus renouauit suam pristinam libertatem.' *Anglo-Saxon Charters: An Annotated List and Bibliography*, ed. P. H. Sawyer (1968) [hereafter S], no. 1040.

[18] On which see O'Brien, *God's Peace*, and Patrick Wormald, *The Making of English Law: King Alfred to the Twelfth Century*, I: *Legislation and its Limits* (Oxford, 1999), 400–1.

certain forms of jurisdiction or taxation and in their most developed form the zones thus created, sometimes known as liberties, became islands of private jurisdiction, free from interference by the king's or bishop's men. These semi-autonomous zones had no direct pre-Conquest precursors; indeed the specific rights by which they were defined had no meaning in a pre-Conquest context, but many special freedoms were defended using alleged Anglo-Saxon precedent, none the less. Thus, in the twelfth century many religious foundations claimed special liberties bestowed in Anglo-Saxon antiquity, documenting their case using the diplomas of pre-Conquest kings, the charters of founders and benefactors, improved or even created for the purpose. The monks of Ely appealed to King Edgar (957–75), those of Bury St Edmunds to Edward the Confessor (1042–66), while the community of Evesham sought more ancient authority in Bishop Ecgwine of Worcester (693 × 717).[19]

This pattern, the ascription of institutional freedoms to Anglo-Saxon origins, has acquired such familiarity as to have become almost banal, reproduced with drab predictability throughout the monastic record. Those who have drawn attention to it in recent years have done so often to stress its inauthenticity. The climate of production hardly suggests otherwise. Medieval Europe supplies many examples of collective retrospection in the wake of conquest, rights claimed in conquered territory said to derive from 'those days', the time before conquest.[20] In England in particular, monastic writers bristled with defiant nostalgia for the pre-Conquest past on behalf of their own institutions and the English in general; Richard of Ely, for example, writing in the mid-twelfth century, described the fenlanders' heroic resistance to William the Conqueror in terms of defence of their homeland and their fathers' freedom (*libertas*).[21] One might speculate further that this ancient trope of lost freedom, otherwise expressed as absence of oppression, finds unlikely reinforcement

---

[19] On these examples and others see Julia Crick, 'Liberty and Fraternity: Creating and Defending the Liberty of St Albans', in *Expectations of the Law in the Middle Ages*, ed. Anthony Musson (Woodbridge, 2001), 91–103, esp. 95–6. See also below, nn. 28, 29. See also Nigel Berry, 'St Aldhelm, William of Malmesbury and the Liberty of Malmesbury Abbey', *Reading Medieval Studies*, 16 (1990), 15–38.

[20] Robert Bartlett, *The Making of Europe: Conquest, Colonization and Cultural Change 950–1350* (Harmondsworth, 1993), 93–5. See also M. T. Clanchy, 'Remembering the Past and the Good Old Law', *History*, 55 (1970), 165–76; Paul Brand, ' "Time out of Mind": The Knowledge and Use of the Eleventh- and Twelfth-Century Past in Thirteenth-Century Litigation', *Anglo-Norman Studies*, 16 (1993 [1994]), 37–54.

[21] 'in defensionem patriae et paternae libertatis': *Lestorie des Engles solum la translacion Maistre Geffrei Gaimar*, ed. T. D. Hardy and C. T. Martin (Rolls Series 1888–9), I, 374 (*Gesta Herwardi*, attributed to Richard of Ely). On resentment more widely see, for example, M. T. Clanchy, *England and its Rulers 1066–1272*, 2nd edn (Oxford, 1998), 31–4.

in some modern historiography of Norman government.[22] Whatever the cause, we may report as a fact a pronounced historiographical trend: post-Conquest presumption of pre-Conquest liberty has registered in recent printed discussion primarily as an artefact of immediate circumstances, a 'camouflage for direct economic and social interests', a construction of 'a sort of Christian citizenship'.[23] In short, it has been possible to conclude that 'the manufacture of so many fraudulently ancient liberties implies that something in the post-conquest climate was creating a new demand for them'.[24]

We have indeed come to understand much of what drove the appeal to ancient liberties after the Norman Conquest – the need for defence against secular and ecclesiastical predators, the imperative to define and delineate rights and privileges, the whiff of legalism in the monastery.[25] But by treating the evidence of this medieval hope as inert or transparently inauthentic, we are missing something. The rhetoric of liberty is a history not simply of absence, of relative lack of lordship, but of something more concrete. Scant attention has been paid to the process of construction, to the repeated invocation of ancient *libertas* as a hedge against encroachment, to its deployment as a defence in time of need. This body of so-called bogus material attests the existence of a historical paradigm of some tenacity, significant in the number of occasions on which it was invoked and also in their chronological range; from at least the eleventh to the seventeenth century groups defended rights by appealing to liberties rooted in the pre-Conquest past. Like the grandest medieval historical myths, therefore, like Arthur's imperial exploits, or the Trojan foundation of the French nation, Anglo-Saxon liberty outlived the Middle Ages. Like post-medieval historical ideas, furthermore, ours can claim to have enjoyed 'social circulation':[26] the notion escaped its original confines to be perpetuated in a variety of forms, narrative and documentary, and it enjoyed a currency among illiterate as well as literate. The story of Anglo-Saxon liberty as an institutional construct thus merits consideration as a cultural phenomenon of some significance.

[22] Although for trenchant opposition to this line of argument see Campbell, *The Anglo-Saxon State*.

[23] Alain Boureau, 'How Law Came to the Monks: The Use of Law in English Society at the Beginning of the Thirteenth Century', *Past and Present*, 167 (2000), 29–74, esp. 70–2.

[24] Patrick Wormald, 'Frederic William Maitland and the Earliest English Law', *Law and History Review*, 16 (1998), 1–25, reprinted in his *Legal Culture in the Early Medieval West: Law as Text, Image and Experience* (1999), 45–69, at 51.

[25] Above, nn. 23–4.

[26] The term was coined in a post-medieval context: Daniel Woolf, *The Social Circulation of the Past: English Historical Culture 1500–1730* (Oxford, 2003), 9.

Medieval liberty

The evidence for the medieval trope of pre-Conquest liberty spills out of the familiar narratives and records of later medieval monasticism.[27] Individual incidents are well known, indeed notorious, but the collective evidence has not, to my knowledge, ever been assembled and I shall not attempt to do more than outline some examples here. More than forty medieval English houses kept in their archives documents in which pre-Conquest donors, usually kings, purportedly bestowed liberties on the institution concerned or certain of its estates. This reservoir of documentation, much of it spurious, could be drawn on as needs dictated. In 1275 when the abbot of Glastonbury needed to defend his claim to return of writs, he invoked charters from the time of Ine, king of Wessex (688–726).[28] A decade later, in 1287, the abbot of St Albans defended the same privilege in the name of Offa of Mercia (757–96).[29] Thus thirteenth-century abbots invoked precedents established by the rulers of long-defunct polities to defend rights not formulated until after the Norman Conquest: the incongruities speak for themselves. As late as 1415, or so it has been argued, a monk of Crowland cited forged Anglo-Saxon charters in order to defend his monastery against nearby Spalding in a dispute about fishing rights.[30] These charters appear in the chronicle of pseudo-Ingulph and are laden with references to *libertates*.[31] Later still, in 1486, the abbot of Abingdon's claims to *libertas* at his estate at Culham were contested during a trial for high treason after the defendant, Humphrey Stafford, had attempted to elude arrest by sheltering there.

---

[27] Roger of Wendover, *Chronice sive Flores historiarum*, ed. H. O. Coxe (1841–4), I, 258–62, II, 161–4; *Chronicon Abbatiae de Evesham*, ed. W. D. Macray (Rolls Series 1863); *Memorials of St. Edmund's Abbey*, ed. Thomas Arnold (Rolls Series 1890–6), I, 60–7 (Hermann, *Miracula*, chs. 25–9); *Willelmi Malmesbiriensis monachi De Gestis Pontificum Anglorum*, ed. N. E. S. A. Hamilton (Rolls Series 1870), 378–81 (William of Malmesbury, *Gesta pontificum*, V, 225–6, discussed by Berry, 'St Aldhelm'). For further examples and discussion see David Knowles, 'Essays in Monastic History, IV – The Growth of Exemption', Downside Review, 50 (1932), 201–31, although some of his judgements have been superseded by subsequent work. See Patrick Wormald, below, n. 49.

[28] Helen Cam, *Law-Finders and Law-Makers in Medieval England: Collected Studies in Legal and Constitutional History* (New York, 1963), 41 n. 2. For references and discussion see Crick, 'Liberty', 95–6.

[29] Cited by Brand, ' "Time out of Mind" ', 38–9. For examples of appeal to alleged pre-Conquest precedent by tenants see Rosamond Faith, 'The "Great Rumour" of 1377 and Peasant Ideology', in *The English Rising of 1381*, ed. R. H. Hilton and T. H. Aston (Cambridge, 1984), 43–73, esp. 56–8.

[30] Daniel Williams, 'The Crowland Chronicle, 616–1500', in *England in the Fifteenth Century: Proceedings of the 1986 Harlaxton Symposium*, ed. Daniel Williams (Woodbridge, 1987), 371–90 at 375. On the sources of the compilation see David Roffe, 'The Historia Croylandensis: A Plea for Reassessment', *English Historical Review*, 110 (1995), 93–108.

[31] Æthelbald's charter freed the monks from all secular burdens on the estates given which were granted 'cum omnibus libertatibus et liberis consuetudinibus': S 82.

The abbot defended his right to offer sanctuary using a charter purporting to be a grant made by Coenwulf, king of Mercia, in 821. The charter, in fact a twelfth-century forgery, was not enough to save Stafford: he was executed.[32]

What this stock of supposed pre-Conquest material sometimes lacked in efficacy it made up for in versatility. Indeed, the symbolic and monetary value of Anglo-Saxon liberty attracted imitators, not just among religious houses. Towns, too, adopted the paradigm.[33] One of the most famous examples of appropriated claims to Anglo-Saxon liberty comes from the Peasants' Revolt.[34] When the mob marched on the abbey of St Albans on the morning of Saturday 15 June 1381, they reportedly demanded the release of documents, in particular those concerning their freedoms, *libertates*. The abbot allegedly complied, handing over rolls and charters from the monastery's archives which the rebels burned in the marketplace immediately outside the abbey's gates. According to Walsingham, the house historian, the crowd was still not satisfied. They demanded a certain ancient charter concerning the liberties of the townsmen, which was decorated with blue and gold capitals.[35] When the abbot proved unable to produce it they stormed the monastery and began looting. The ancient charter which had eluded the abbot so is commonly referred to as a charter of Offa and Walsingham records that the townsmen claimed that the liberties which they sought had been bestowed on them by King Offa.[36] Given that forged privileges of Offa had secured exceptional privileges for the monastic community, not least the formal delineation of their liberty extracted from the papal curia, this is a request of some interest. In rhetorical terms at least, the townsmen fought or were obliged to fight on their oppressor's ground. They voiced their desires and aspirations in terms laid down by their opponents in writing and championed by them for centuries. For town and monastery Offa was the originator of liberties, whatever mixed messages were thereby encoded.[37]

---

[32] S 184. *Charters of Abingdon Abbey, Part 1*, ed. S. E. Kelly, Anglo-Saxon Charters VII (Oxford, 2000), xlv and 48.

[33] On the connection between the legal claims of towns and monasteries in the post-Conquest period see O'Brien, *God's Peace*, 112–13.

[34] See, for example, Faith, 'The "Great Rumour"', 64–5; Steven Justice, *Writing and Rebellion: England in 1381* (1994).

[35] *Thomae Walsingham Historia Anglicana*, ed. Henry Thomas Riley (Rolls Series 1863–4), 475.

[36] *Gesta abbatum Monasterii Sancti Albani*, ed. Henry Thomas Riley (Rolls Series 1867–9), III, 365.

[37] Note that Offa was seen to have liberated the institution and to have guaranteed the liberation of the people. For discussion of tenants' use of archival material see Faith, 'The "Great Rumour"'. On comparable instances of rhetorical appropriation see J. G. A. Pocock, 'The Concept of a Language and the *métier d'historien*: Some Considerations on Practice',

Wherever credible, then, monasteries and towns claimed and sometimes won liberties rooted in the pre-Conquest past. Established by the
early twelfth century, the pattern continued as long as the monasteries
survived. Even after the Reformation altered or expunged the institutions
for which the notion had been developed, Anglo-Saxon liberty lived on.
A charter purporting to be a grant of 'perpetual liberty' made by King
Cnut in 1019 to the abbot and brethren of St Mary's Exeter in 1019
was presented for royal confirmation four times in the sixteenth century,
twice after the reformation of the cathedral, and was copied a further four
times in the post-medieval centuries.[38] At a time when medieval records
were being scoured in the pursuit of civic dignity, privilege and title to
former monastic property, an ancient document such as this, freeing the
monastery and its property from royal and secular exaction, certainly
deserved notice.[39] Towns continued to invoke Anglo-Saxon liberties by
charter later still. Since at least the fourteenth century, the burgesses of
Malmesbury had been in possession of an undated charter purporting
to demonstrate that King Athelstan (925–39) had restored to their tenth-
century predecessors free customs originally granted by his father, Edward
the Elder.[40] After the Middle Ages, interested parties, presumably the
citizens of Malmesbury, sought and obtained royal confirmation on a
number of occasions, the last under James I, at a time when Malmesbury
was in dispute with its neighbours.[41] Other forged pre-Conquest charters
staking claims to liberties attracted a comparable surge in interest after
Dissolution.[42] Not only could the stock be replenished, new uses could be
found for it.

---

in *The Languages of Political Theory in Early-Modern Europe*, ed. Anthony Pagden (Cambridge,
1987), 19–38, at 24.

[38] S 954. *Charters of Exeter*, ed. C. Insley, Anglo-Saxon Charters (Oxford, forthcoming),
no. 24, MSS J, L, M, N, O, R, S, W, X.

[39] 'hanc cartulam concedo . . . ad perpetuam libertatem, ut liberum permaneat ipsum
monasterium cum omnibus prediis illi concessis, et cum omnibus rebus ad eum rite
pertinentibus . . . ab omni regali et seculari grauedine maiora aut minora . . . nisi sola
expeditione et pontis constructione'. On the search for medieval precedent for the status of
towns see Robert Tittler, *The Reformation and the Towns in England: Politics and Political Culture,
c. 1540–1640* (Oxford, 1998), 281–3.

[40] 'quod habeant et teneant semper omnes functiones et liberas consuetudines suas sicut
tenuerunt tempore regis Eduuardi patris mei': S 454. *Charters of Malmesbury Abbey*, ed. S. E.
Kelly, Anglo-Saxon Charters (Oxford, forthcoming), no. 36.

[41] Confirmation Rolls 2 James I, pt 2, no. 14. The dispute is mentioned by Tittler, *The
Reformation and the Towns*, 205.

[42] Alleged (spurious) pre-Conquest grants of liberty were much copied after the Middle
Ages: twelve of a total of forty-two copies of Edgar's grant of liberties to Ely (S 779) date
from the sixteenth century or later, likewise twelve of twenty-three copies of Edgar's grant
to Thorney (S 792), and eight of thirty-two copies of Cnut's grant to Bury in which he is
made to renew King Edmund's original gift of liberty (S 980). On the early modern copying
of forged pre-Conquest charters see Julia Crick, 'The Art of the Unprinted: Transcription

Across the Conquest

Anglo-Saxon liberty, then, was deeply rooted in the historical consciousness of English institutions in the later Middle Ages and beyond.
Monasteries and towns cultivated fond memories of Anglo-Saxon kings
who, as founders and patrons, dished out grants of *libertas*, a commodity
ill-defined and thus unencumbered by historical baggage, of enduring
value in fending off new threats. They kept in their archives testimony to
this effect, overwhelmingly forged, which they had validated periodically
by royal confirmation. This deference to pre-Conquest founders and
patrons suggests the cultivation of historical memory of some vigour,
but what kind of phenomenon was this? Through what channels did it
develop? Clearly it was perpetuated by competition and imitation, much
like national origin stories: once the Franks had staked a claim to Trojan
origins, their rivals followed suit.[43] Arguably the notion of Anglo-Saxon
liberty outgrew its original boundaries and escaped into rumour and oral
tradition, as reportedly it did at St Albans.[44] But studies of national origin
stories stress the careful cultivation of such traditions: they grow from
seeds deliberately planted.[45] It could certainly be argued that examples of
claims to Anglo-Saxon liberty emanating from monastic, and sometimes
also urban, communities had no connection with pre-Conquest tradition.
Did they, like later constructions of Anglo-Saxon liberty, rest on little more
than wishful thinking?

There are a number of reasons why one might believe this. Mayke
de Jong recently alluded to the search for an authoritative past inherent
within Christianity, particularly medieval Christianity.[46] Parallel to this
notion, and perhaps illustrative of it, is the tendency of the members
of institutions in the Middle Ages and later to seek the oldest possible
precedent for any privilege sought. We have become attuned to the allure
exercised in the remote past in the Middle Ages, the unseemly races
for antiquity pursued in particular by those charged with protecting the
dignity and upholding the claims of nations, which brought Egyptians to
Scotland and Joseph of Arimathea to Somerset.[47] For an institution such

---

and English Antiquity in the Age of Print', in *The Uses of Script and Print, 1300–1700*, ed. Julia
Crick and Alexandra Walsham (Cambridge, 2004), 116–34.

[43] Susan Reynolds, 'Medieval *Origines gentium* and the Community of the Realm', *History*,
68 (1983), 375–90.

[44] Compare Justice's account of the effects of writing in mobilising the St Albans rebels:
Writing and Rebellion, 13–66. Also Faith, 'The "Great Rumour"'.

[45] R. R. Davies, 'The Peoples of Britain and Ireland, 1100–1400: I Identities and Peoples',
ante, sixth series, 4 (1994), 2.

[46] Mayke de Jong, 'Religion', in *The Early Middle Ages: Europe 400–1000*, ed. Rosamond
McKitterick (Oxford, 2001), 132.

[47] For example, Bruce Webster, 'John of Fordun and the Independent Identity of the Scots',
in *Medieval Europeans: Studies in Ethnic Identity and National Perspectives in Medieval Europe*, ed.

claims had to be narrowly focused and to abide by certain rules: they had to pass muster among contemporaries. Association with a founder suggests that the rights claimed are intrinsic to the institution: it never existed without them. We have seen this kind of logic displayed in the competing claims of town and abbey connected with Offa, hailed by both sides as the founder of their liberties. Thus it might be natural for post-Conquest historians to seek to press back to the time of foundation the closest fought and most dearly held claims of an institution. For many monasteries this meant Anglo-Saxon kings.

A second reason for thinking post-Conquest claims to Anglo-Saxon liberty manufactured has already been mentioned: the charters which make the case most eloquently are, without exception, forged. In recent years, Patrick Wormald has been emphatic on this point: 'It is not just that those who postulate extensive pre-Conquest immunities must depend on dubious texts. The very prevalence of such fabrications may say something about the urgency that the issue was assuming in the post-Conquest world.'[48] He ruled out the existence of any authentic evidence for extensive grants of liberty before the Conquest, with the possible exception of a single writ, and cited cautionary tales of scholars misled by spurious charters.[49]

There is a third reason for scepticism about pre-Conquest antecedents to later claims to liberty in England. Liberties in their twelfth-century form, as designated zones immune from outside interference, are indeed a post-Conquest phenomenon. *Libertas ecclesiae* was a slogan of the reforming papacy of the eleventh century and a formidable amount of scholarship, from the 1930s to the present day, has elucidated the connection between the rhetoric of liberty and the so-called investiture dispute.[50] Thus the term was not invented in its territorial sense before the Conquest.

Alfred P. Smyth (Basingstoke, 1998), 85–102; Charles T. Wood, 'Fraud and its Consequences: Savaric of Bath and the Reform of Glastonbury', in *The Archaeology and History of Glastonbury Abbey: Essays in Honour of the Ninetieth Birthday of C. A. Ralegh Radford*, ed. Lesley Abrams and James P. Carley (Woodbridge, 1991), 273–83.

[48] As n. 24.

[49] Patrick Wormald, 'Lordship and Justice in the Early English Kingdom: Oswaldslow Revisited', in *Property and Power in the Early Middle Ages*, ed. Wendy Davies and Paul Fouracre (Cambridge, 1995), 114–36, 128–9, reprinted in his *Legal Culture*, 326.

[50] Hans Hirsch, 'The Constitutional History of the Reformed Monasteries during the Investiture Contest', in *Medieval Germany 911–1250: Essays by German Historians*, ed. and trans. G. Barraclough (2 vols., Oxford, 1938), II, 131–73; Gerd Tellenbach, *Libertas, Kirche und Weltordnung im Zeitalter des Investiturstreites* (Stuttgart, 1936) (*Church, State and Christian Society at the Time of the Investiture Contest*, trans. R. F. Bennett (Oxford 1940), 1–37); Rudolf Schieffer, 'Freiheit der Kirche: vom 9. zum 11. Jahrhundert', *Die Abendländische Freiheit vom 10 zum 14 Jahrhundert*, ed. J. Fried (Sigmaringen, 1991), 49–66. See also H. E. J. Cowdrey, *The Cluniacs and the Gregorian Reform* (Oxford, 1970), 3–43, and his *Pope Gregory VII, 1073–8* (Oxford, 1998), 536–9 (I owe this last reference to Dr Hamilton).

I have no quibble with any of these arguments. The post-Conquest history of Anglo-Saxon liberty is indeed a history of impossible expectation – no historical precedent could support all or indeed any of the claims which succeeding generations chose to base on the notion of Anglo-Saxon liberty. It is a little heralded fact, however, that the forged claims to extravagant exemptions made by post-Conquest draftsmen present only one side of the story. Critics have been overzealous in their attempt to extirpate *libertas* from the pre-Conquest record. They have given inadequate attention to the fact that *libertas*, before its militant reinvention in the eleventh century at the hands of Gregorian reformers, had an earlier history. From the letters of Paul, through the writings of the church fathers, *libertas* had a secure place in Christian rhetoric[51] and, although lodged in the body of texts inherited from the late Empire, the rhetoric of liberty escaped into active use, deployed in Carolingian synods of the ninth century, known and used by contemporary English draftsmen, and only later seized upon by post-Conquest forgers. *Libertas* before the end of the first millennium did not mean what later monastic propagandists took it to mean – full-scale exemption from episcopal and perhaps royal interference. It had a life of its own and its presence in the documentary record of England before the Norman Conquest puts a different complexion on the received view both of pre-Conquest diplomatic and the use and nature of Anglo-Saxon precedent in the later Middle Ages.

The remainder of this essay is concerned with the use and meaning of *libertas* before the Norman Conquest. I shall base my arguments on a distinct subset of pre-Conquest documents defined not by authenticity but by date: all survive in pre-Conquest form. This necessarily excludes a substantial body of evidence believed to be authentic but surviving only in later copy but the sacrifice is necessary in order to be clear about the nature of pre-Conquest tradition.

Before the Conquest

Michael Clanchy once memorably likened an early medieval archive to an old lady's handbag, filled with objects of diverse character and significance, each betokening something important to the owner.[52] If so, a continental churchman inspecting the archives of certain pre-Conquest monasteries after the Norman Conquest might well have been struck by

[51] Willy Szaivert, 'Die Entstehung und Entwicklung der Klosterexemtion bis zum Ausgang des 11. Jahrhunderts', *Mitteilingen des Institutes für Österreicheische Geschichtsforschung*, 59 (1951), 265–98.
[52] M. T. Clanchy, *From Memory to Written Record: England 1066–1307*, 2nd edn (Oxford, 1993), 156. His analogy captured the physical diversity of archives, objects as well as texts, but the same heterogeneity applies to the texts themselves.

the wealth and also the eccentricity of the old lady in question. He would have found written title to estates and privilege, perhaps of considerable value; he might have been disappointed not to find claims to exemption (*immunitas*) as seen on the Continent[53] (*immunitas* is a phrase all but confined to post-Conquest forgery, indeed almost symptomatic of it); but he might instead have found claims of a less defined but more ideological sort, claims to liberty. Such claims appear to have been relatively rare in continental diplomatic. Benoît-Michel Tock, in a preliminary survey of the language of French and Belgian charters published in 1997, compiled frequency-tables of the use of diplomatic terms. *Libertas* hardly registers before the eleventh century.[54] But look across the channel and liberty is emblazoned across the English written record of the ninth, tenth and early eleventh centuries, not just in post-Conquest forgeries but in documents certainly copied before the Norman Conquest. Some 15 per cent of original pre-Conquest charters deployed the rhetoric of liberty in some form and the percentage rises further if we extend the field to authentic and spurious charters which survive as pre-Conquest copies.[55]

Moreover, this body of documentation offered rich pickings to scavengers in search of documentary proof of the status of the churches of newly conquered England: grants of liberty, privileges of liberty, grants of liberty made by earlier benefactors, and not just liberty but ecclesiastical liberty, *ecclesiastica libertas*, *libertas ecclesiarum*, even the Gregorian formulation *libertas ecclesiae*. The abbey of Abingdon, for example, possessed a privilege of liberty, *libertatis privilegium*, whose surviving record, copied at or near 993 when King Æthelred had granted the charter, includes no fewer than fifteen references to *libertas*, including one to 'the liberty of the sacred monastery of Abingdon': *sacri Æbbandunensis coenobii libertatem*.[56] Worcester, too, possessed riches.[57] No fewer than thirty-nine charters surviving in pre-Conquest form, a significant fraction of the pre-Conquest archive, in which the elusive *libertas* is associated with Anglo-Saxon donations, most notably in the early eleventh-century cartulary associated with Wulfstan, bishop of Worcester 1002–16, archbishop of York 1002–23. Here again

---

[53] Emile Lesne, *Histoire de la propriété ecclésiastique en France*, I (Paris, 1910), 260–78; E. Magnou-Nortier, 'Etude sur le privilège d'immunité du ive au ixe siècle', *Revue Mabillon*, 60 (1984), 465–512; Barbara H. Rosenwein, *Negotiating Space: Power, Restraint, and Privileges of Immunity in Early Medieval Europe* (Manchester, 1999).

[54] Benoît-Michel Tock, 'Les mutations du vocabulaire latin des chartes au xie siècle', *Bibliothèque de l'Ecole des Chartes*, 155 (1997), 119–48.

[55] See Appendix, tables 1 and 2.

[56] S 876, *Charters of Abingdon Abbey, Part 2*, ed. S. E. Kelly, Anglo-Saxon Charters VIII (Oxford, 2001), no. 124. Discussed by Alan Thacker, 'Æthelwold and Abingdon', *Bishop Æthelwold: His Career and Influence*, ed. Barbara Yorke (Woodbridge, 1988), 43–64, at 53–4.

[57] On the Worcester charters see most recently Francesca Tinti, 'From Episcopal Conception to Monastic Compilation: Hemming's Cartulary in Context', *Early Medieval Europe*, 11.3 (2002), 233–61.

we find rhetoric pregnant with significance for later readers: a 'privilege of liberty' dated 781 in which Offa, the great king of Mercia, is recorded as giving land to St Peter's Worcester 'for the use of ecclesiastical liberty', alongside other eighth-century gifts for the use of ecclesiastical liberty *in usus/ius ecclesiasticae libertatis*.[58] With raw material like this post-Conquest churchmen hardly faced an imaginative leap in claiming for their churches pristine liberty: in confecting statements of ancient privilege they were defining and extending rights licensed in part by the pre-Conquest record.

Proof of the connection comes from the reuse of pre-Conquest documents – their copying, expansion, improvement.[59] This is not the place to attempt to demonstrate the process in detail, except to note one fact. Of the six English monasteries founded before the Norman Conquest which acquired exceptional legal privilege in the twelfth century, a process intimately connected with the fabrication of pre-Conquest documentation, all but one laid claim to early documents which deploy the rhetoric of liberty.[60] Two possessed charters which made mention of *liberty*, a further two possessed tenth- and eleventh-century single sheets which described early grants of *libertas* made by King Offa, and the fifth possessed an apparently authentic charter mentioning *libertas* for which no early copy survives.[61]

This raises a series of further questions: when, where and how did the term liberty enter the documentary record? Furthermore, given that later monastic draftsmen and historians often misconstrued the notion of liberty in the pre-Conquest period, what did *libertas* in its pre-Conquest guise actually mean? We will begin with the second question. *Libertas*, as used in these pre-Conquest charters, appears not to convey a single meaning, let alone a precise one. Aesthetic and rhetorical judgements as much as technical considerations appear often to have lain behind its deployment. The word occurs in relatively unstructured documents – dispute settlements, exchanges, leases initiated by bishops as well as kings, synodal agreements, even private charters, in places where draftsmen had

---

[58] S 120: 'priuilegium libertatis,' 'ad utilitatem ecclesiasticae libertatis'. See also S 59, 139, 173, 190.

[59] For an example see Simon Keynes, 'The Reconstruction of a Burnt Cottonian Manuscript: The Case of Cotton MS. Otho A. I', *British Library Journal*, 22.2 (1996), 113–60, at 145 nn. 30–1 . See also Crick, 'Liberty', and *Charters of St Albans*, ed. J. Crick, Anglo-Saxon Charters (Oxford, forthcoming), nos. 1–3.

[60] Christopher Cheney listed as 'totally exempt from episcopal jurisdiction', St Augustine's, Canterbury, Westminster, Bury St Edmunds, St Albans, Evesham and Malmesbury: *Episcopal Visitation of Monasteries in the Thirteenth Century*, 2nd edn (Manchester, 1983), 39.

[61] St Augustine's Canterbury S 20 (s. xiii copy of extant s. ix single sheet preserved at Christ Church); Evesham S 495 s. x; Westminster S 670, S 1450 s. x; St Albans S 916 s. xi; Malmesbury S 363 s. xii.

more freedom of expression than in the more disciplined framework of a royal charter.[62] Furthermore, when it occurs in Anglo-Saxon charters, *libertas* is a term used very informally indeed, apparently with no precise technical or diplomatic terms of reference.[63] It is used in two particular contexts: either to describe a bundle of rights granted in a charter or to denote the charter itself. *Libertas* in this second sense occurs reasonably regularly in ninth- and tenth-century originals.[64] Liberty has come to stand for little more than a grant.[65] The first meaning – liberty as a bundle of rights – is less straightforward.[66] The nature of the *libertas* thereby conceded is rarely explained, except in general terms, but to judge from context it takes one of two sorts. *Libertas* can mean an active right, freedom to do something, usually to bequeath.[67] More commonly, however, liberty worked negatively. In the rhetoric of the Peasants' Revolt liberty came to represent a negation of the usual burdens and expectations attached to the possession of land.[68] Half a millennium earlier, it seems, liberty served a similar purpose, it denoted freedom from normal worldly dues and royal exaction, all that is, except for the rights reserved to the king, the so-called common burdens of bridgework, army duty and fortress work.[69] To a beneficiary before the Norman Conquest, therefore,

[62] See further Crick, 'Liberty', 97–8.

[63] It can appear in almost any part of a charter in the granting clause, in the statement of powers, in the immunity clause, in the anathema, in the royal attestation, in endorsements.

[64] In three mid-ninth-century single sheets surviving as apparent originals, a *libertas* is confirmed or written, whether so described in the attestations, endorsement or in the main text of the charter (Appendix: table 1, S 190, 1270, 338). For example, in a grant to Worcester of 836 Wiglaf, king of Mercia is made to declare 'hanc libertatem scripsi et scribere precipi [*sic*]' and the contemporary endorsement describes the document as 'ðes friodom' (S 1270).

[65] Much like the usage of *immunitas* on the Continent: Rosenwein, *Negotiating Space*, 3.

[66] In a private charter of 875 (S 1203), copied by Christ Church scribe, the lay donor is made to grant land to Wighelm in return for 120 mancuses of gold 'cum eadem libertate quam Ælfredus rex Occidentalium Saxonum necnon æt Cantwariorum mihi in ius proprium . . . donauit'.

[67] Thus S 40 'Potestas quoque ipsi datur ut in libertate terram habeat quamdiu uiuat et postea cuicumque hominum uoluerit in aeternam libertatem derelinquat' or S 890 'in eadem libertate relinquiendi licentiam habeat'.

[68] '[*Libertas*] did metaphorical duty for abolition of all the oppressions under which the countryside labored', Justice, *Writing and Rebellion*, 45 also 36.

[69] For example, 'Sit autem predictum rus perpetuali libertate liber ab omni mundiali censu et regali coactione excepto communi labere expeditione pontis arcisue coedificatione' S 470 (AD 940). On the nature of these burdens see N. P. Brooks, 'The Development of Military Obligations in Eighth- and Ninth-Century England', *England before the Conquest: Studies in Primary Sources Presented to Dorothy Whitelock*, ed. Peter Clemoes and Kathleen Hughes (Cambridge, 1971), 69–84, reprinted in his *Communities and Warfare 700–1400* (2000), 32–47; Richard P. Abels, *Lordship and Military Obligation in Anglo-Saxon England* (1988), 43–57; Rosamond Faith, *The English Peasantry and the Growth of Lordship* (Leicester, 1997), 94–9. Exemption from the common burdens and/or general statements of freedom from royal dues occurs very commonly in single sheets mentioning *libertas*.

a grant of *libertas* had a familiar function; it suspended a designated area of land from normal expectations, from royal obligations, from anticipated routes of transmission.[70] The details of the process elude description, the burdens from which the lucky recipient has been spared are never dwelt on and perhaps varied over time (the beauty of the unwritten), but in all circumstances, the outcome was plain enough. Thus *libertas* is a precious commodity. When land changed hands owners were permitted to ensure that it passed with any special freedom granted in the past.[71] *Libertas* thus represents the Latinising of a peculiarly home-grown practice, the releasing of land from unwritten obligations. *Libertas* is effectively the quality bestowed when land is booked.[72]

Further demonstration of the ease with which *libertas* can be situated within the vocabularies of English draftsmen before the Norman Conquest comes from consideration of related terms. Far from being an anachronism or foreign intrusion, *libertas* fits comfortably into pre-Conquest diplomatic as part of a vocabulary of the freeing of land whose other components have attracted relatively little notice. Latin cognates of *libertas* serve as verbs, adjectives and adverbs to describe grants,[73] and a penumbra of vernacular terms can be identified. In his recent study of slavery in early medieval England, David Pelteret identified from a range of sources, narrative and documentary, twenty-three words, mostly vernacular, which describe the giving of land in terms of subjection and liberation.[74] Some of the compounds which he lists, such as *sundor-freodom* (a special right over land) and *freolsboc* (which he translates as 'a land charter granting superiority over land, with freedom from the jurisdiction of others'), fall outside the limits of the present study: they do not occur in documents surviving in pre-Conquest form. Certain of his terms do, however. *Freo-dom* and *freols*, for example, surely direct OE equivalents of *libertas*, mirror Latin usage strikingly closely and are attested in documents copied in the ninth, tenth and eleventh centuries.[75] *Freodom* has six meanings in Pelteret's list.[76] The first, which can be summarised as personal freedom, is the liberty associated with the Anglo-Saxons by post-medieval writers. The last two provide direct translations of *libertas*

[70] For examples of the range of possible obligations on land see Faith, *The English Peasantry*, 89–105.

[71] S 40, 1264, 890. Above, nn. 66–7.

[72] On this term see, for example, Susan Reynolds, 'Bookland, Folkland and Fiefs', *Anglo-Norman Studies*, 14 (1991 [1992]), 211–27, esp. 216–17.

[73] *Libero, liber, libere*. For their use in early documents see, for example, S 31 (copied before 800) and S 41 (AD 805–7).

[74] David A. E. Pelteret, *Slavery in Early Mediaeval England from the Reign of Alfred until the Twelfth Century* (Woodbridge, 1995), 47–8, 276–8, 283–4, 303–4.

[75] Listed below, Appendix, table 3.

[76] Pelteret, *Slavery*, 276–8.

as it is used in pre-Conquest Latin charters: 'freedom to exercise rights without being subject to the control of another', 'a charter granting rights over property'.[77] *Freols*, another term employed in documents copied before the Norman Conquest, shows a range of meanings extending in identical fashion from the general to the particular, from personal and fiscal freedom to the document itself.[78]

Pelteret's discussion helps us round a conceptual difficulty. Liberty is not a word bandied about by many of the current generation of Anglo-Saxon historians – reciprocity, conspicuous consumption, slavery, certainly, but not liberty. Liberty, after all, is a very classical notion. As an abstraction its origins are Greek (*eleutheria*). As a working concept, it is Roman, developed within a state with a territorial mentality: boundaries, controls, law. It appears in this sense in the New Testament, especially in the letters of Paul which supply a quarter of all references to the word in the Vulgate concordance;[79] indeed, the Christian notion of freedom links the antique to the Anglo-Saxon particularly fruitfully. For the church fathers, as for other citizens of the Roman Empire, freedom did not operate in a vacuum; freedom could only be understood in relation to something else. Thus freedom and service are often paired.[80] Understood in relation to slavery, so much more familiar an aspect of the Anglo-Saxon social and political landscape, liberty looks less like an exile from an alien cultural environment, and more like a term assimilable to a post-Roman milieu. By focusing not on liberty, but slavery (the same servitude–freedom pairing as in Christian writing), we gain a fresh light on *libertas*. Draftsmen in Anglo-Saxon England in the years around AD 800 described the conveyance of land in written form in all its complexity using a metaphor drawn from Christian tradition: freedom. Modern historians have adopted a different vocabulary for the granting of land by charter. Following a parallel metaphor used by certain Anglo-Saxon draftsmen at approximately the same date, they describe the charter in terms of literate record: the book.[81]

This brings us to the final question about the arrival of the rhetoric of freedom in the apparently alien environment of pre-Conquest England. How did it get there? As I have already suggested, there is a case for regarding the appearance of *libertas* as a rhetorical strategy, a word chosen

[77] Definitions 2–3 concern spiritual freedom; the fourth entails 'Freedom from dues payable to an overlord': *ibid.*, 276–7.

[78] Pelteret, *Slavery*, 282–3.

[79] Seven of twenty-six references.

[80] Tellenbach, *Church, State and Christian Society*, 2–10.

[81] Eric John identified the first reference to the charter as book in a document of AD 798 (S 153): *Orbis Britanniae and Other Studies* (Leicester, 1966), 74. On the etymology of the term see D. H. Green, *Medieval Listening and Reading: The Primary Reception of German Literature 800–1300* (Cambridge, 1994), 37.

by certain draftsmen to express something for which draftsmen elsewhere found a different word or words. In these circumstances the time and place of the deployment of the language of liberty become significant. We have touched on two important episodes in this history already. Numerous references to liberty adorn the Worcester cartulary, a collection compiled and copied in the early eleventh century and associated with Archbishop Wulfstan, homilist and canonist. A generation before, strong statements about ecclesiastical liberty had issued from the newly reformed Benedictine abbey of Abingdon, an institution invigorated by contact with the motors of ecclesiastical reform on the Continent and under the direction of Bishop Æthelwold, a man portrayed by his tenth-century biographer granting privileges of liberty in gold letters.[82] Both at Worcester and at Abingdon these reformers were inspired by proximity to sites of particular religious authority where *libertas*-rhetoric was deployed, one historical, the other contemporary: Wulfstan through his exposure to canonical texts, Æthelwold through contact with Cluniac monasticism and the return to canonical values.[83] The *libertas*-tradition latent in Christian writing periodically manifested itself.

Another such episode predates the examples just examined by early two centuries. The rhetoric of liberty begins to flow from the pens of English draftsmen in strength from the turn of the ninth century but starting as a trickle in the middle of the eighth. The circumstances are instructive. Like the Frankish empire of Charles Martel, created in the second quarter of the eighth century using monastic lands and the control of ecclesiastical appointments, the Mercian hegemony constructed at approximately the same time across the channel was built on very selective respect for ecclesiastical power. Offa's creation of a third archiepiscopal see, at Lichfield, in 787 is the boldest example, which allowed him to override and ultimately to stifle the archbishop of Canterbury, at least for a while, but there are plenty of other manifestations of open competition between ecclesiastical privilege and royal prerogative, from the synod of Gumley in 749 to Archbishop Wulfred's war with Coenwulf of Mercia and his successors over domination of the Kentish monasteries, fought in the 810s and 820s.[84] It is perhaps not surprising to witness the deployment of the language of liberty by the church in these circumstances. According

---

[82] *Wulfstan of Winchester: The Life of St Æthelwold*, ch. 21, ed. Michael Lapidge and Michael Winterbottom (Oxford, 1991), 36–7. Cited by Kelly, *Charters of Abingdon*, xli.

[83] For Æthelwold's Cluniac context see Patrick Wormald, 'Æthelwold and his Continental Counterparts: Contact, Comparison, Contrast', in *Bishop Æthelwold: His Career and Influence*, ed. Barbara Yorke (Woodbridge, 1988), 13–42. See also Crick, 'Liberty', 100–1.

[84] See Nicholas Brooks, *The Early History of the Church of Canterbury: Christ Church from 597 to 1066* (Leicester, 1984), 132–43; Simon D. Keynes, *The Councils of Clofesho*, 11th Brixworth Lecture (Leicester, 1994); Catherine Cubitt, *Anglo-Saxon Church Councils c. 650–c. 850* (Leicester, 1995), 218–22.

to the manuscript-evidence, the earliest datable reference to *libertas* in the Anglo-Saxon written record comes from the synod of Gumley.[85] The first significant concentration of documents deploying the rhetoric of liberty come from the pontificate of Wulfred.

Archbishop of Canterbury for nearly thirty years, from 805 to 832, Wulfred presided over the see of Canterbury during the reigns of four Mercian kings and subsequently survived the transition from Mercian to West Saxon control. Nicholas Brooks tells us that his wheelings and dealings transformed the landed wealth of the church at Canterbury, but he is perhaps best remembered for his ability to fight three successive Mercian kings in a series of acrimonious disputes over royal domination of the Kentish church which lasted fifteen years, caused him to be deprived of his office at some point before 822 and was only settled in 826.[86] A great deal of evidence points to a connection between Wulfred and the language of liberty. More charters mentioning *libertas* may be associated with him than with any other figure. He was donor, beneficiary, his scribes copied them, he has even been credited with copying one and forging another.[87] The rhetoric of *libertas* is even deployed in a number of forgeries linked with Wulfred on the grounds that they 'seem to bear on [his] claim to the lordship of Reculver and Minster-in-Thanet', in other words the dispute which caused strife with successive Mercian kings between 817 and 826.[88] The occurrences of *libertas* in these charters concern little more abstract than the granting of land, but it is significant that this archbishop's draftsmen should have begun to describe bookland in these terms.

Wulfred inhabited an environment in which liberty was being actively deployed. His Carolingian counterparts took measures to protect clerical and episcopal *libertas* in a series of important synods in the second quarter of the ninth century: Council of Paris 829, Aachen 836, Quierzy 858.[89] Already, by 803, similar notions had reached Canterbury. Æðelheard, Wulfred's predecessor, exhorted the monasteries 'which have once been

---

[85] S 92. On the manuscript see Keynes, 'The Reconstruction', and Cubitt, *Anglo-Saxon Church Councils*, 266–7.

[86] Brooks, *The Early History*, 134, 180–3.

[87] See below, Appendix, tables 1–2. As donor and beneficiary: S 40, 41, 1264, 169, 177, 168, 1266, 1436, 188. S 90 (copy), S 22 (forgery); see below, n. 88.

[88] Brooks, *The Early History*, 191. Brooks, without reference to the *libertas* connection, linked three charters with Wulfred on quite different grounds: two privileges concocted, so Brooks suggested, at Christ Church during Wulfred's pontificate (S 22, 90) and records of synods of Clofesho of 824 and 825, one of which (S 1436) contains references to grants of *libertas*: *The Early History*, 191–7. Below, Appendix, tables 1–2.

[89] *Concilia aevi Karolini I. II*, ed. A. Werminghoff, Monumenta Germaniae Historica [hereafter MGH] Concilia II (Hannover, 1908), 669, 680, 721; *Die Konzilien der karolingingischen Teilreiche 843–859*, ed. Wilfried Hartman, MGH Concilia III, Concilia aevi Karolini DCCXLIII–DCCCLIX (Hannover, 1984), 413. See also the discussion by Schieffer, 'Freiheit der Kirche', 60.

dedicated to Christ, the Lord, by faithful men in perpetual liberty *perpetuam in libertatem*' to reject lay lordship and look to the monastic life.[90] He made the plea at a synod at Clofesho acting on the authority of a 'mandate' of Leo III which he had brought back from Rome, shortly after the restoration of his own metropolitan authority by the same pope.[91] Comparable claims had been made at Worcester half a century earlier. There, as at Canterbury, *libertas* first occurs in charters which appear to offer a response to the aggression of Mercian kings, although the word is not used in the Æthelheardian sense to defend monasteries in general, but rather the privileges exercised on their estates. Brooks noted a series of eighth- and ninth-century charters in which the bishops of Worcester took monasteries directly into their own lordship, five of which include references to *libertas*.[92] Such charters would have served to preempt royal control.

The first evidence for the use of the language of liberty in Anglo-Saxon charters comes from the Mercian supremacy, but less clear is the precise nature of the source. Continental tradition does not supply an immediate explanation: neither the Rule of Chrodegang, nor that of Benedict, nor Carolingian diplomatic provide direct analogies for the Anglo-Saxon use of *libertas*.[93] That draftsmen operating in eighth-century England encountered and deployed the word need occasion no surprise, however. The central texts of Christianity, the New Testament, the patristic and canonical writings of the church in the former Roman Empire offered a natural medium for the flow of Roman ideas to the remote West. Any number of channels might have served, each of them accessible directly or through intermediate sources throughout the pre-Conquest period. Augustine, Gregory, Jerome, Cassian and other late antique writers used the term *libertas* freely and their writings stocked the libraries of early England.[94] Texts known at the Canterbury school as early as the late seventh century include at least one which deployed the

---

[90] The apparently contemporary single sheet S 1431b; see Brooks, *Early History*, 179 and n. 16 (his translation).

[91] Papal influence is palpable, too, in the Carolingian councils: *Concilia aevi Karolini I. II*, ed. Werminghoff, 605.

[92] Brooks, *Early History*, 179–80 and n. 17: S 1255, 1257, 139, 207, 172, 146, 1187.

[93] *Libertas*, where it occurs in Carolingian charters, usually means personal freedom, manumission. It occasionally denotes the freedom of monastic houses but it pertains to the community rather than its estates. Thus the *libertates* mentioned have a meaning closer to the post-Conquest: see Wilhelm Schwarz, 'Jurisdicio und Condicio: eine Untersuching zu den Privilegia libertatis der Klöster', *Zeitschrift der Savigny-Stiftung für Rechtsgeschichte*, K. A. 76 (1959), 34–98.

[94] The *Patrologia Latina* database reveals multiple examples of use of *libertas*, particularly by patristic writers (Jerome, Ambrose, Augustine, Gregory, Orosius especially) and later by Carolingian authors (Rhabanus Maurus, Smaragdus). John Cassian used the term with some frequency, but usually in the Pauline sense of *libertas arbitrii* – free will.

rhetoric extensively.[95] *Libertas* occasionally appears in the canons, most particularly those of the Council of Carthage of 525.[96] Potentially, at least, the papacy operated as channel for the passing of Roman terminology and concepts to the unRoman parts of the West. The term *libertas* could be synonymous with papal privilege in Old English and Latin, and contact with the papacy often preceded or was identified with the rhetoric of liberty.[97] Proximity to *Romanitas* brought exposure to notions of liberty.

Conclusions

The pre-modern story of Anglo-Saxon liberty as presented here divides into three: the pre-Conquest, the closely post-Conquest and the post-Reformation. Modern commentators attempting to understand property transfer in England before the Norman Conquest will recognise the divisions; they necessarily find their vision clouded by the copying and rewriting to which the pre-Conquest documentary record was subjected at these times. Indeed, it was in an effort to dispel some of the cloud that the tradition of pre-Conquest liberty was rejected altogether. As is well recognised, *libertas* constituted a goal to which forgers aspired in the middle period. *Libertas*, to them, carried expectations of well-defined freedoms. New life was breathed into the medieval traditions after the Middle Ages, by institutional heirs seeking precedent for rights apparently sanctioned by ancient charter. Just as constitutional rights were pressed back to English antiquity, institutional claims followed a similar trajectory; the textual re-mnants of the middle period could be pressed into service again. But post-Conquest and post-Reformation invocation of pre-Conquest precedent cannot be understood without reference to the first period, when an earlier rhetorical tradition flourished, different from what followed in scope and aim, but not unconnected with it. As we have seen, *libertas* already belonged in the written record before the Norman Conquest, a fact de-monstrated by the physical evidence, authentic and inauthentic texts sur-viving in pre-Conquest form, and by the existence of an entire vocabulary of liberation associated with the granting of land by charter. Its presence there serves to remind us of well-known facts: the inescapable hold which late antique thought and writing exercised over nascent English Latinity and learning, and the hybridity and eclecticism of the English legal

---

[95] Michael Lapidge, 'The School of Theodore and Hadrian', *Anglo-Saxon England*, 15 (1986), 45–72, at 54–5. Orosius's *Historiae aduersum paganos* is the text in question.

[96] *Concilia Africae A. 345–A.525*, ed. C. Munier, Corpus Christianorum Series Latina CCLIX (Turnhout, 1974), 255–82, for example, 255–6, 274, 276, 279–80; see also Council of Carthage of AD 345–8, *ibid.*, 3–10. I have not been able to plot a definitive connection between these canons and any of the main outbreaks of *libertas*-rhetoric before the Conquest.

[97] See, for example, Pelteret, *Slavery*, 303–4; Brooks, 133–4; Wilhelm Levison, *England and the Continent in the Eighth Century* (Oxford, 1946), 18–33; also above, nn. 90–1.

tradition, a body of learning indebted to the canons and to Christian thought in general, and hardly yet launched as a technical discourse.[98]

This brings us to another constant in this discussion: the written word. In the same way that the tradition of English constitutional liberties hangs on a chain of textual authority, however tenuously, leading back to Magna Carta and before, the notion of institutional liberties was authorised by the written record.[99] The monastic researchers with whom some of this essay has been concerned, the draftsmen and historians responsible for the wholesale adaptation of the written record after the Norman Conquest did not conjure the rhetoric of monastic liberty out of thin air.[100] They elaborated, interpreted and extended a form of discourse deployed in the written record which they had inherited. We should not be surprised at the wilfulness of their interpretation. Brian Tierney noticed a certain 'creative misunderstanding' in medieval jurists' attempts to interpret notions of freedom which they found in texts from late antiquity, from an environment so alien to the one which they knew that much was lost in the process of translation across time.[101] Adaptation of textual authority is a marked feature of the story of Anglo-Saxon liberty. Liberty was invoked partly because it was licensed by written authority, whether that authority resided in the prescriptive texts of the Christian religion, as used by English churchmen in the eighth and ninth centuries, or whether it was contained in archival material rewritten after the Conquest or rediscovered after the Reformation.[102] Behind the so-called 'bogus' charters stands not a perversion of the written record but an *inuentio* in the medieval sense: a finding. This was no crude anachronism and blindness to the past but a movement *ad fontes*, an appropriation of the written record certainly, and one undertaken in a polemical spirit, but a return to the past of the sort which perhaps inspired the adoption of the *libertas* rhetoric in the first place and which, in later centuries, would lead other churchmen to seek to recreate the Anglo-Saxon past in the spirit of reformation.

---

[98] Wormald, *The Making of English Law*, I, esp. 416–29. Note, too, the comments of Martin Brett, 'Theodore and the Latin Canon Law', *Archbishop Theodore: Commemorative Studies on his Life and Influence* (Cambridge, 1995), 120–40, at 137. On the underlying intellectual problems see Vivien Law, *The History of Linguistics in Europe from Plato to 1600* (Cambridge, 2003), 124–6.

[99] Above, nn. 4, 11.

[100] On the process of reinvention of the written record after the Conquest see Bruce O'Brien, 'Forgery and the Literacy of the Early Common Law', *Albion*, 27.1 (1995), 1–18. On 'exemplifications' from Domesday Book see Faith, 'The "Great Rumour"' and on the search for precedent in the Middle Ages see Susan Reynolds, 'Magna Carta 1297 and the Legal Use of Literacy', *Historical Research*, 62 (1989), 233–44 at 235.

[101] See above, n. 10.

[102] This history thus does not obey generalisations about medieval communication suggested by some early modernists: see, for example, Woolf, *Social Circulation*, 11, Adam Fox 'Custom, Memory and the Authority of Writing', in *The Experience of Authority in Early Modern England*, ed. Paul Griffiths, Adam Fox and Steve Hindle (Basingstoke, 1996), 89–116 at 110.

APPENDIX: THE LANGUAGE OF LIBERTY IN CHARTERS
BEFORE THE NORMAN CONQUEST

Table 1 *Charters surviving in arguably contemporary form which make reference to* libertas.

Date of transaction	Reference	Archive	Additional comments
749	S 92	Worcester	Grant of privileges to Mercian churches
770	S 59	Worcester	
785	S 123	Christ Church, Canterbury	
793 × 796	S 139	Worcester	
801	S 1186a	Christ Church, Canterbury	
803	S 1431b	Christ Church, Canterbury	Synod of Clofesho
805	S 1259	Christ Church, Canterbury	Restoration secured by Æthelheard
805	S 40	Christ Church, Canterbury	Archbishop Wulfred as beneficiary
805 × 807	S 41	Christ Church, Canterbury	Archbishop Wulfred
811	S 168	Christ Church, Canterbury	Archbishop Wulfred as beneficiary
811	S 1264	Christ Church, Canterbury	Archbishop Wulfred as grantor
812	S 169	Christ Church, Canterbury	Archbishop Wulfred as beneficiary
814	S 173	Worcester	
814	S 177	Christ Church, Canterbury	Archbishop Wulfred as beneficiary
824	S 1266	Christ Church, Canterbury	Archbishop Wulfred as grantor
825 [827]	S 1436	Christ Church, Canterbury	Archbishop Wulfred as party
831	S 188	Christ Church, Canterbury	Archbishop Wulfred as party
836	S 190	Worcester	
838	S 1438	Christ Church, Canterbury	Dispute settlement
840 × 852	S 1270	?Hereford	
843	S 293	Christ Church, Canterbury	
845	S 1194	Christ Church, Canterbury	
867	S 338	Christ Church, Canterbury	
875	S 1203	Christ Church, Canterbury	
901	S 221	Much Wenlock	
903	S 367	Christ Church, Canterbury	
940	S 470	New Minster, Winchester	
944	S 497	Christ Church, Canterbury	
944	S 495	Evesham	
947	S 528	Christ Church, Canterbury	
960	S 687	Abingdon	
966	S 745	New Minster, Winchester	
974	S 795	Exeter	
987	S 864	Rochester	
995	S 884	Muchelney	
997	S 890	Exeter	
998	S 892	Coventry	
1007	S 916	St Albans	*Libertas* associated with King Offa
1019	S 956	New Minster, Winchester	
1024	S 961	Abbotsbury	
1031	S 971	Exeter	
1042	S 994	Old Minster, Winchester	
1044	S 1003	Exeter	

Table 2 *Charters surviving as pre-Conquest copies which make reference to* libertas.

Date of copy	Date of transaction	Reference	Archive	Additional comments
s. ix	699	S 20	Christ Church, Canterbury	Privilege to Kentish churches
s. ix[1]	742	S 90	Christ Church, Canterbury	Privilege to Kentish churches
s. x[2]	955	S 671	Rochester	
s. x	951 (?for 959)	S 1450	Westminster	Liberty associated with Offa
s. x	951	S 670	Westminster	Liberty associated with Offa
s. x/xi	956	S 587	Abingdon	
s. x/xi	680 (?for 685)	S 230	Christ Church, Canterbury	Spurious
s. x/xi	993	S 876	Abingdon	
s. x/xi	933	S 421	Exeter	
s. xi[1]	699 × 716	S 22	Christ Church, Canterbury	Privilege to Kentish churches
s. xi[1]	680	S 52	Worcester	Worcester cartulary
s. xi[1]	699 × 704	S 64	Worcester	Worcester cartulary
s. xi[1]	765	S 107	Worcester	Worcester cartulary
s. xi[1]	718 (?for 727)	S 84	Worcester	Worcester cartulary
s. xi[1]	766	S 192	Worcester	Worcester cartulary
s. xi[1]	774	S 1255	Worcester	Worcester cartulary
s. xi[1]	777 × 779	S 147	Worcester	Worcester cartulary
s. xi[1]	780	S 116	Worcester	Worcester cartulary
s. xi[1]	781	S 120	Worcester	Worcester cartulary
s. xi[1]	781	S 121	Worcester	Worcester cartulary
s. xi[1]	781	S 1257	Worcester	Worcester cartulary
s. xi[1]	793 × 796	S 146	Worcester	Worcester cartulary
s. xi[1]	794	S 137	Worcester	Worcester cartulary
s. xi[1]	799 (?for 802)	S 154	Worcester	Worcester cartulary
s. xi[1]	804	S 1187	Worcester	Worcester cartulary
s. xi[1]	814 (for 813)	S 172	Worcester	Worcester cartulary
s. xi[1]	816	S 180	Worcester	Worcester cartulary
s. xi[1]	840	S 192	Worcester	Worcester cartulary
s. xi[1]	841 (for 840)	S 193	Worcester	Worcester cartulary
s. xi[1]	841	S 194	Worcester	Worcester cartulary
s. xi[1]	841 (for 840)	S 196	Worcester	Worcester cartulary
s. xi[1]	845 (for 844)	S 198	Worcester	Worcester cartulary
s. xi[1]	849	S 199	Worcester	Worcester cartulary
s. xi[1]	855	S 206	Worcester	Worcester cartulary
s. xi[1]	855	S 207	Worcester	Worcester cartulary
s. xi[1]	857	S 208	Worcester	Worcester cartulary
s. xi[1]	864	S 210	Worcester	Worcester cartulary
s. xi[1]	875	S 215	Worcester	Worcester cartulary
s. xi[1]	880 [887]	S 217	Worcester	Worcester cartulary
s. xi[1]	889	S 346	Worcester	Worcester cartulary
s. xi[1]	929	S 401	Worcester	Worcester cartulary
s. xi[1]	929	S 402	Worcester	Worcester cartulary
s. xi[1]	934	S 428	Worcester	Worcester cartulary
s. xi[1]	962	S 1298	Worcester	Worcester cartulary
? s. xi[1]	900	S 360	New Minster, Winchester	Imitative script
? s. xi[1]	938	S 443	Old Minster, Winchester	Imitative script
? s. xi[1]	948	S 540	Old Minster, Winchester	Imitative script

Table 3 *Charters surviving in pre-Conquest form employing vernacular terms for* libertas.

Date of copy	Date of transaction	Reference	Archive	Vernacular term
s. ix	836	S 190	Christ Church, Canterbury	Friodom
s. ix *med.*	845 × 853	S 1510	Christ Church, Canterbury	Friodom
s. ix	888 (?for 868)	S 1204	Christ Church, Canterbury	Friols
s. x	958	S 1506	Christ Church, Canterbury	Freodom
s. xi[1]	873 × 888	S 1507	New Minster, Winchester	Freols
s. xi[1]	781	S 1257	Worcester	Freols
s. xi[1]	After 822–3	S 1432	Worcester	Freodom
s. xi[1]	883	S 218	Worcester	Freodom

Transactions of the RHS 14 (2004), pp. 73–92 © 2004 Royal Historical Society
DOI: 10.1017/S0080440104000088   Printed in the United Kingdom

DISTANCE AND DISTURBANCE: TRAVEL, EXPLORATION AND KNOWLEDGE IN THE NINETEENTH CENTURY*

By Felix Driver

READ 2 MAY 2003 AT OXFORD BROOKES UNIVERSITY

ABSTRACT. How should information about distant places be collected? How should it be made available to the reading public? And how far could it be trusted? Such questions were posed by the expansion of exploration and travel during the eighteenth and nineteenth centuries. According to the leading scientific authorities, the making of accurate observations, the use of precise instruments, the methodical collection of specimens and the writing of narratives provided the principal means by which knowledge itself could travel. Yet the relationship between metropolitan science, travel writing and field observation remained fraught with difficulty. This essay considers a variety of ways in which the experience of disturbance shaped the culture of exploration during the nineteenth century, focusing in particular on writing, collecting and sketching.

In the annals of exploration and discovery, there are many strange and wonderful tales, but few quite so singular as the case of 'Hollowayphobia' narrated by the traveller and novelist Winwood Reade in his *African Sketch-Book*, published in 1873. This is the story of a nervous middle-aged Englishman, Archibald Potter, who develops a phobia about the advertisements for Holloway's pills which he sees prominently displayed around the public spaces of Victorian London. The name 'Holloway', we are told, bore down on him

> every hour of the day, in every newspaper he read, in every omnibus he entered, at every railway station, on every boarding ... He looked down as he walked and found it written on the paving stones; he shut himself up at home, and it came to him as a prospectus by post, and dropped out of the books which were brought from the circulating library.

The very word made his flesh creep. Increasingly distressed, he flees abroad and eventually reaches the shores of Africa where he hopes

* I am grateful to Luciana Martins, Beryl Hartley, Sandip Hazareesingh, Simon Naylor and Catherine Hall for comments on various versions of this essay. The latter part draws on research conducted with Luciana Martins for an AHRB research project on 'Knowing the tropics: British visions of the tropical world, 1750–1850.'

to escape the tyranny of the commodity sign. But on landing in Sierra Leone, he is alarmed to come across a crimson poster 'with *Holloway's Pills* upon it, in letters of gigantic stature'; in Angola he finds respite, but his nerves are shattered by the discovery of the remains of yet another poster recycled to wrap a long-awaited parcel of boots. So on he travels further and further into the heart of Africa, finally settling in a remote forest village. But here he discovers the final horror. That distinctive Holloway's poster, seemingly the ultimate mark of modernity, has been transformed by the locals into a 'fetish': 'the beautiful crimson colour, the great black stripes, the crisp rustling of the paper, which they supposed to be the voice of the demon from within, [had] powerfully affected their imagination'. Enraged and disorientated, the traveller rips the poster to shreds, only narrowly avoiding a violent death in the ensuing struggle. He dejectedly makes his way back to England, and continues to suffer: even the most innocuous of greetings – 'Hollo! old fellow, how are you?' – sends him into convulsions. Eventually, and somewhat miraculously, he is cured of his ailment – unlikely as it may seem – by actually taking a course of the pills.[1]

I

Reade's curious tale provides a useful prologue to an essay on the theme of travel, exploration and disturbance. At the level of form, for example, it raises some important questions about the genre of travel writing. What was this story doing within the pages of a book which was supposed to represent the fruits of its author's exploring expeditions to West Africa? Winwood Reade, novelist and would-be explorer, had indeed travelled to both Angola and Sierra Leone during the 1860s.[2] On his second expedition, sponsored by the trader Andrew Swanzy, he had been loaned equipment by the Royal Geographical Society; he had sent botanical specimens to Kew, and ethnological information to Darwin, and he had tried, at least, to collect insects for the naturalist Henry Walter Bates. His aspirations as a novelist having met with failure at the hands of unforgiving critics, he had turned to the worlds of anthropology, natural history and medicine in his quest to become a 'man of science', a disciple of Huxley and Darwin. But Reade's style in the *African Sketch-Book* was thoroughly writerly, conspicuously blurring the frontiers between exploration narrative and romantic fiction. The accompanying illustrations picture Reade himself as the principal subject

---

[1] William Winwood Reade, *The African Sketch-Book* (2 vols., 1873), I, 169–201.
[2] Felix Driver, 'Becoming an Explorer: The Martyrdom of Winwood Reade', in *Geography Militant: Cultures of Exploration and Empire* (Oxford, 2001), 90–116; J. D. Hargreaves, 'Winwood Reade and the Discovery of Africa', *African Affairs*, 56 (1957), 306–16.

Figure 1 W. Winwood Reade, 'By Ox and Hammock', from *The African Sketch-Book* (2 vols., 1873), 1.

of the story, a latter-day Mungo Park in search of the sources of the Niger (Figure 1).

I have found the idea of a 'culture of exploration' useful as a means of highlighting the ways in which ideas, images and practices of exploration traversed the realms of public culture during the long nineteenth century. It is not that boundaries do not exist between, say, scientific exploration and adventurous travel, the sober and the sensational, or the analytical and the aesthetic. It is just that these boundaries are always in the process of construction: far from taking them for granted, the task of the historian is to highlight their unsettled nature. Throughout the nineteenth century, as in our own time, the idea of exploration was freighted with a variety of meanings, associated variously with science, literature, religion, commerce and empire. The business of the scientific explorer was not always, or easily, distinguished from that of the literary flaneur, the missionary, the trader or the imperial pioneer. True, Winwood Reade was in many ways a marginal figure, whose brief and unsparkling career as a writer was cut short by his death at the age of thirty-six: shortly before the end, he wrote despondently to a friend that 'After all my African fevers and dysenteries safely got over I am to die of consumption like the heroine in a novel.'[3] Yet for all Reade's sense of failure, his negotiation of the dual

---

[3] West Sussex Records Office, Maxse Papers, 203: Winwood Reade to Frederick Maxse, 3 Mar. 1875.

spheres of fiction and travel writing tells us something important about the wider cultures which he attempted to negotiate. The hostile response of the literary establishment to Reade as a writer anticipates the response of the geographical establishment to Henry Morton Stanley as an explorer. In both cases, 'sensationalism' was the key term, a charge that crystallised deep anxieties about social change, culture and civilisation.[4]

The moment of Reade's death in 1875 marked, I think, a significant shift in the history of this culture of exploration, signalled by the arrival of more recognisably modern figures like Stanley on the public stage. Reade himself – like Joseph Conrad after him – was captivated by the romance of navigation and exploration in an earlier era – that of Cook and Humboldt – when the dominion of natural science was extended over the blank spaces of the globe.[5] In this context, we should note that historians have come increasingly to appreciate the aesthetic and indeed literary dimensions of what has come to be known as 'Humboldtian science', a research programme more usually associated with the use of new instruments, a commitment to fieldwork, analytical precision, measurement and above all mapping in the study of magnetic, geodetic, climatic, biogeographical and geological variations across the globe. As Michael Dettelbach has argued, Humboldt's work as a whole can be seen as constituting an aesthetic project, an effort to define a scientific sensibility for a new age, synthesising subjective experience and universal law.[6] As far as the grander goal of philosophical synthesis is concerned, the project may have been doomed: yet we should not underestimate the continuing significance of writing in the form of the travel narrative for the culture of scientific exploration.

Consider, for example, the career of one of Humboldt's many British admirers: Basil Hall, naval officer, Fellow of the Royal Society and one of the founders of the Royal Geographical Society in 1830. Hall was a prominent representative of an influential group of 'scientific servicemen', actively engaged in the pursuit of scientific investigations in the early decades of the nineteenth century.[7] His exemplary scientific credentials were confirmed by the astronomer John Herschel in his

[4] Felix Driver, 'Henry Morton Stanley and his Critics', *Past and Present*, 133 (1991), 134–66; W. Hughes, *The Maniac in the Cellar: Sensation Novels of the 1860s* (Princeton, 1980).

[5] Compare, for example, Reade, 'Heroes of Central Africa', *Atlantic Monthly*, 19 (1867), 625–35, or 'African Martyrology', *Belgravia*, 1 (1867), 46–53, with Joseph Conrad, 'Geography and some explorers', in *Last Essays*, ed. R. Curle (1926), 1–31.

[6] Michael Dettelbach, 'Global Physics and Aesthetic Empire: Humboldt's Physical Portrait of the Tropics', in *Visions of Empire: Voyages, Botany and Representations of Nature*, ed. David P. Miller and Peter H. Reill (Cambridge, 1996), 258–92. On the question of Humboldtian travel narrative, see Nigel Leask, *Curiosity and the Aesthetics of Travel Writing* (Oxford, 2002), 281–98.

[7] David Miller, 'The Revival of the Physical Sciences in Britain, 1815–1840', *Osiris*, new series 2 (1986), 107–34.

Preliminary Discourse on the Study of Natural Philosophy (1830), a widely quoted defence of contemporary scientific epistemology. In a passage praising Hall's accurate navigation of an 8,000 mile track from the west coast of Mexico round Cape Horn to Rio de Janeiro, Herschel portrayed the feat as a kind of travelling experiment in which a hypothesis based on observations at sea was tested against the experience of arriving safely at port. 'It is needless to remark', Herschel noted, 'how essentially the authority of a commanding officer over his crew may be strengthened by the occurrence of such incidents, indicative of a degree of knowledge and consequent power beyond their reach.'[8] Herschel's example was well chosen, insofar as it emphasised the practical utility of scientific observation and, more subtly, the virtues of a social hierarchy based on skill rather than birth. Yet it was also partial, for a naval captain's authority over his crew was not equivalent to the reputation of a scientific observer amongst his peers: and the credibility of observations in the field (or at sea) depended on more than mathematical skill or reliable instruments. The authority of the explorer, in fact, depended substantially on the writing of a narrative of travel, either first or second hand. Ironically, in fact, Basil Hall himself would later become much better known – perhaps in a sense more authoritative – as a writer of popular travel literature, including nine volumes published in the 1830s under the title *Fragments of Voyages and Travels*. Alas, this work was Hall's undoing: as one biographer recalls, 'constant literary exertion weakened his brain, and he lost his reason'.[9]

Basil Hall's descent into madness brings me back to the disturbing case of 'Hollowayphobia' with which I opened this essay. The idea of madness – or simply bewilderment – is a common theme within the literature of travel and exploration, and it serves a variety of purposes, most notably in naming the sense of disorientation which always threatened the unwary traveller.[10] But Reade does not present the case of Hollowayphobia as a by-product of exploring the unfamiliar or encountering the exotic: on the contrary, it is a symptom of an ever-more global modernity. In this tale – part parable, part parody – the spell of the commodity sign is transformed into a curse, as its victim finds himself confronted with an all-too-literal rendering of what Marx had called (just a year or two before) 'commodity fetishism'. We might pause here to reflect on the

---

[8] John Herschel, *Preliminary Discourse on the Study of Natural Philosophy* (1830), 29. Herschel's notion of the ship as an instrument, and its captain as a heroic experimenter, was not in itself new: see Richard Sorrenson, 'The Ship as a Scientific Instrument in the Eighteenth Century', in *Science in the Field*, ed. H. Kuklick and R. Kohler (Chicago, 1996), 221–36.

[9] Basil Hall, *Fragments of Voyages and Travels* (3 series, 9 vols., Edinburgh, 1832–3). The quote is from a biographical preface to one of many abridged editions: *Voyages and Travels* (1895).

[10] Johannes Fabian, *Out of our Minds: Reason and Madness in the Exploration of Central Africa* (Berkeley, 2000); Jonathan Lamb, *Preserving the Self in the South Seas, 1680–1840* (Chicago, 2001).

global reach of the Holloway marketing machine during this period. The veneration of the humble pill as an agent of globalisation could reach staggering heights, as in one effusive newspaper advertisement: 'In the wilds of Tartary, the Siberian desert, the celestial empire, yea in the very mountains of the moon, are the praises of the great pillular deity Holloway sung, and his name blessed in every known and unknown tongue as the "mighty healer".'[11] Beside this, you might well think, Marx's remarks about commodity fetishism look pretty tame.

It hardly needs to be said that Reade's fanciful reading of the power of the commodity sign is far from Marx's highly worked metaphorical critique of the alienation of labour under capitalism. Still, the case of 'Hollowayphobia' points towards broader questions about not only the culture of the commodity in late Victorian Britain, but also the psychic and cultural aspects of urban modernity.[12] At the heart of the narrative is the theme of disturbance: first irritation, then flight, finally derangement. It presents us with a story about an unsettled life, apparently dreamed up while Reade himself was travelling through West Africa in search of a reputation for himself as a writer and traveller. It also reflects a relatively pervasive critique of the modern which one finds in various influential strands of late Victorian popular anthropology and adventure fiction.[13] Never mind that such a critique was in many ways itself irredeemably modern, the fact that images of Holloway's pills were circulating even at the frontiers of the known world was in this perspective a matter for anxiety rather than celebration: a world of cultural difference was being contaminated by the world market. Or as the anthropologist Lévi-Strauss was to put it years later in *Tristes Tropiques*, an anti-travel narrative if ever there was one: 'The first thing we see as we travel round the world is our own filth, thrown into the face of mankind.'[14] While Winwood Reade would not have subscribed to such a bleak diagnosis of what is now called globalisation, his tale does remind us that travel writing could provide a vehicle for unsettling accounts of modernity.

The fact that 'Hollowayphobia' takes the form of an escape from the metropolis rather than a journey in search of knowledge or power appears to reverse the standard narrative of exploration as a quest. Yet reflections on the vices of 'over-civilisation' are often to be found within late Victorian narratives of exploration, so much so indeed that they

[11] A. Harrison-Barbet, *Thomas Holloway: Victorian Philanthropist* (Egham, 1994), 75.

[12] Thomas Richards, *The Commodity Culture of Victorian England: Advertising and Spectacle, 1851–1914* (Stanford, 1990). The haunting power of advertising in the modern metropolis provided the opening theme in an essay by Charles Dickens on 'Bill Sticking', published in *Household Words* in March 1851, which may have influenced Reade's rendition of his tale.

[13] Andrea White, *Joseph Conrad and the Adventure Tradition: Constructing and Deconstructing the Imperial Subject* (Cambridge, 1993).

[14] Claude Lévi-Strauss, *Tristes Tropiques* (1973 edn), 43.

seem almost a requirement of the genre. Ironically too, given the subject of Reade's tale, the figure of the resourceful explorer was often credited in such narratives with almost occult powers when it came to exploiting modern technology to gain the confidence of indigenous peoples. Hence Samuel Baker's comments on the demonstration effects of Holloway's pills:

> These are most useful to an explorer, as, possessing unmistakeable purgative properties, they create an undeniable effect upon the patient, which satisfies him of their value. They are also extremely convenient, as they may be carried by the pound in a tin box, and served out in infinitesimal doses from one to ten at a time, according to the age of the patients.[15]

Ultimately, though, perhaps what really matters about Reade's tale is not simply its form or its content, but its setting. The Holloway posters on London railway stations and street corners are expected, if disturbing to a sensitive soul like Archibald Potter. Sighted in various parts of Africa, their power in the mind's eye of Victorian readers becomes immeasurably more sinister. The image of Africa as the Dark Continent was coming to dominance at precisely the time this tale was published. In Reade's narratives, as in many other contemporary works, Africa functioned as a stage on which the desires and fears of white civilisation could be played out.[16] At the same time, as we have seen, the tale complicates the familiar colonial story of European civilisation and African barbarism. In this context, it should be noted that Reade had already gained notoriety during the 1860s for his outspoken criticisms of Christian missions and his partial defence of polygamy in West Africa, sentiments which proved too much even for the Anthropological Society of London. These positions reflected his association with Richard Burton and the acolytes of the infamous Cannibal Club: here a politics of difference, if a conservative one, was at work.[17]

Reade's best-known work – *The Martyrdom of Man* (1872) – was later acclaimed by radicals and conservatives alike. The book, which became a best-seller years after Reade's death, combined an unorthodox, Africa-centred narrative of world history with a bald attack on Christianity. It was subsequently to be lauded by figures as various in their politics as Cecil Rhodes (who once said 'It made me what I am'), Sidney Webb, Harry Johnston and George Orwell.[18] In the preface to his seminal essay

---

[15] Samuel Baker, *The Nile Tributaries of Abyssinia* (1867).

[16] Patrick Brantlinger, 'Victorians and Africans: The Genealogy of the Myth of the Dark Continent', *Critical Inquiry*, 12 (1985), 166–203.

[17] Ronald Rainger, 'Race, Politics and Science: The Anthropological Society of London', *Victorian Studies* (1978), 51–70.

[18] Cecil Rhodes read the book as an Oxford undergraduate: R. Rotberg, *The Founder: Cecil Rhodes and the Pursuit of Power* (Oxford, 1988), 100.

on *The World and Africa*, published in 1947, the African-American critic W. E. B. Du Bois reflected that 'One always turns back to Winwood Reade's *The Martyrdom of Man* for renewal of faith.'[19] How different were these reactions to those in Reade's own lifetime: Gladstone attacked the book as blasphemous, Darwin (who drew liberally on Reade's travel reports in *The Descent of Man*) winced at its unrestrained assault on the established church, while most reviewers either condemned or ignored it. One of the reasons for the posthumous success of the book (and likewise its fall from favour after the mid-twentieth century) lies in its lyrical style as much as its full-blooded faith in a progressive and a rather un-Darwinian evolutionary model: the book presented a poetic portrait of human history, claimed by H. G. Wells as a prime inspiration for his *Outline of History*. Quite how and why Reade came to write this remarkable work, and to what effect, is a story which I have tried to tell elsewhere.[20] Suffice it to say that *The Martyrdom of Man* is one of those enormously popular Victorian books which today have almost entirely sunk without trace. Marx's version of world history did rather better.

II

Reade's meditation upon distance and disturbance draws us towards wider questions about the language of space and place, and the role such geographical imaginaries play in our understanding of exploration and travel. While the main focus of this essay is on exploration and travel, it is worth pausing to consider the parallels with recent work in the field of imperial history.[21] In this context, the spatial language of imperialism – of metropole and colony, centre and periphery – has proved remarkably resilient, even when historians have tried to escape from its grasp. Within an imperial perspective, of course, the destiny of the colony is inevitably seen in relation to the mother-country, though the degree of its autonomy may be open to question. In the case of the British empire, it was the prospect and then the reality of decolonisation during the twentieth century that heralded the emergence of another view, as a new generation of historians questioned the primacy of the metropole in shaping the pattern of imperial policy: in this sense, it was suggested, what happened in the 'periphery' may have shaped policies

[19] William E. B. Dubois, *The World and Africa: An Inquiry into the Part which Africa has Played in World History* (New York, 1947), x.

[20] Driver, *Geography Militant*, 106–13.

[21] See especially Antoinette Burton, 'Rules of Thumb: British History and "Imperial Culture" in Nineteenth- and Twentieth-Century Britain', *Women's History Review*, 3 (1994), 483–99; Anne Stoler and Frederick Cooper, 'Between Metropole and Colony: Rethinking a Research Agenda', in *Tensions of Empire: Colonial Cultures in a Bourgeois World*, ed. Cooper and Stoler (Berkeley, 1997).

and practices in London, as much as vice versa. While this perspective offered a necessary corrective to the world-view of previous generations, more needed to be done than simply shifting the weights on the imperial scales. Recent work in the field of imperial history has thus eschewed the language of 'centrality' and 'peripherality' altogether, in favour of more nuanced accounts of the interrelations between different sites in and beyond empire: between, for example, Jamaica and Birmingham, the Cape and New Zealand or the City of London and Rio de Janeiro.[22] As well as paying more attention to the complex dynamics of colonised societies, historians have begun to map the fractured nature of imperial projects on to the material and imaginative landscapes of the metropolis itself.[23] Effectively, the very notion of a 'centre' – the 'official mind' at the heart of empire, as it were – has been put on the analyst's couch: what we now have to consider is not one mind, or one centre, but many.

In accounts of the modern history of exploration, as in that of empire, the spatial language of centre and periphery – as in the terms home and abroad, the cabinet and the field, the metropolis and the frontier – has long held sway. In this context, the empirical knowledge of explorers and navigators is often portrayed as a counterpoint to the theoretical speculations of metropolitan theorists. Seen in this perspective, eighteenth-century voyages of exploration provided a vastly greater bank of field data for natural philosophers, transforming speculative assumptions about the way the world ought to be into accurate knowledge of the way the world actually was. Yet this account, which rests essentially on the movement from the cabinet to the field, greatly simplifies the complex and highly charged nature of debates over exploration, which threw into relief precisely the spatial contexts in which new knowledge was being generated. On the one hand, voyagers like Cook and La Pérouse certainly did write contemptuously of 'armchair geographers' speculating in the comfort of their metropolitan salons and clubs. The same criticisms were to be directed at the geographical establishment throughout the nineteenth century: one disenchanted critic of the Royal Geographical Society thus complained in 1846 that 'a few cunning mapmakers and closet geographers' were conspiring to discredit 'discoveries opposed to their theories and vain speculations'.[24] On the other hand,

[22] See for example Catherine Hall, *Colonial Subjects: Metropole and Colony in the English Imagination, 1830–1867* (Cambridge, 2002); Alan Lester, 'British Settler Discourse and the Circuits of Empire', *History Workshop Journal*, 54 (2002), 25–48; Luciana Martins and Mauricio Abreu, 'Paradoxes of Modernity: Imperial Rio de Janeiro, 1808–1821', *Geoforum*, 32 (2001), 533–50.
[23] Antoinette Burton, *At the Heart of the Empire: Indians and the Colonial Encounter in Late-Victorian London* (Berkeley, 1998); *Imperial Cities: Landscape, Display and Identity*, ed. Felix Driver and David Gilbert (Manchester, 1999).
[24] Hugh Robert Mill, *Record of the Royal Geographical Society* (1930), 56.

the claims of returning explorers were often greeted with incredulity at home, especially if (like Henry Morton Stanley) they lacked the credentials of the gentlemanly man of science.[25] Such disputes are not merely colourful episodes in an otherwise straightforward history of enlightenment: as Dorinda Outram has argued, they raise wider questions about the epistemology and authority of observation in the field.[26] From the perspective of the sedentary natural philosopher, scientific mastery depended less on the bodily experience of movement into new spaces, than on the observer's very capacity to reflect on knowledge gathered at a distance. In this view, the cabinet is the place where the raw material of nature is imaginatively synthesised, patiently transformed into true knowledge. This tension between the speculative knowledges of the cabinet and the mobile knowledge of the field remained in evidence throughout the nineteenth century. For geography, as for many other field sciences during this period, the question was how to be both in and out of the closet.

The increased emphasis on observation in the field raised fundamental questions about how the explorer's knowledge itself could travel across space. How should information about distant places be gathered? By what means could it be made available to metropolitan science? How could its credibility be guaranteed? Given that the field was necessarily a more open and more diverse space than that of the study or the laboratory, there had to be ways of ensuring that claims to the production of new knowledge could be trusted. According to the metropolitan scientific academies and societies of the day, one of the prime ways of ensuring that observations could be relied upon was through the requirement that travellers record information precisely and methodically: most commonly, through the use of authorised instruments, techniques of observation and inscription. A whole methodology of observation was designed to ensure that reliable and unvarnished information could be collected, stored and eventually transmitted back to the centre. Effectively, this process represented the extension of the space of the cabinet into the field, in the interests of metropolitan 'centres of calculation'.[27]

[25] Driver, 'Henry Morton Stanley'; Stuart McCook, '"It May Be Truth, but It Is Not Evidence": Paul du Chaillu and the Legitimation of Evidence in the Field Sciences', in *Science in the Field*, ed. Kuklick and Kohler, 177–97.

[26] Dorinda Outram, 'On Being Perseus: New Knowledge, Dislocation and Enlightenment Exploration', in *Geography and Enlightenment*, ed. David Livingstone and Charles Withers (Chicago, 1999), 281–294, and 'New Spaces in Natural History', in *Cultures of Natural History*, ed. Nicholas Jardine, James Secord and Emma Spary (Cambridge, 1996), 249–65.

[27] David Miller, 'Joseph Banks, Empire and "Centers of Calculation" in Late Hanoverian London', in *Visions of Empire: Voyages, Botany and Representations of Nature*, ed. David Miller and Peter Reill (Cambridge, 1996), 21–37.

A striking example of this model of observation is represented in William Burchell's portrait of his wagon, a sort of mobile laboratory in which he travelled as a naturalist across southern Africa in 1810–15.[28] This small sketch, now in the possession of the Oxford Museum of Natural History, finds room for all kinds of instruments – compass, telescope, thermometer, weighing scales, writing and drawing materials, maps, specimen cases, plant press, rifle and pistols – as well as botanical and zoological specimens, a library of works of natural history (fifty volumes in all), charts, maps, ethnographic portraits, flag, hammock and a flute. Burchell's mobile home, adapted from the standard Cape ox-wagon, itself functioned as an instrument, the rotations of its wheels providing a means of calculating the distances travelled each day. As an instrument, the wagon was not merely designed to serve the needs of metropolitan science, its disarticulated construction was also well adapted to the uneven terrain: global functions calibrated to local conditions. Of course, like any savant's cabinet, the space of the wagon was not actually as self-sufficient as it appeared. Burchell depended throughout his travels on the labours of numerous servants, the health of his oxen, and his constant negotiations with Boer farmers and black Africans alike. Traces of some of these transactions may be detected in the presence of porcelain beads amongst the baggage of the travelling naturalist. (Burchell carefully noted in his published narrative that the black, white and blue were more sought after than the red or transparent).[29] Yet the sketch itself presents a contained view, looking in, not out: it is an interior space, the cabinet transposed to the field.

The task of collecting, sketching, cataloguing and describing nature's forms demanded a variety of different sorts of skill, as well as considerable resources of time and money. William Burchell, for example, relied heavily on family income to sustain himself during his travels in South Africa and Brazil, and devoted decades of his life to the task of comprehending his collections. It took him a full three years to unpack and re-arrange the 49,000 botanical specimens gathered in his five-year journey through Brazil, and he spent four more years re-labelling them.[30] His skills as an observer of nature were not merely cognitive or conceptual: he was also an accomplished draughtsman, as is evident from the drawings which survive in the archives at Kew and elsewhere. One notable example is his sketch of a hermit crab from St Helena, where he spent five years between 1805 and 1810 (Figure 2). The depth and detail of the colouring in this image bears witness to Burchell's commitment to visual precision in the depiction of the forms of nature. As Luciana Martins and I have

[28] The image is discussed in Driver, *Geography Militant*, 17–19.
[29] Burchell, *Travels in the Interior of Southern Africa* (2 vols., 1822–4), I, 119, II, 400.
[30] Edward Poulton, *William John Burchell* (1907), 54–5.

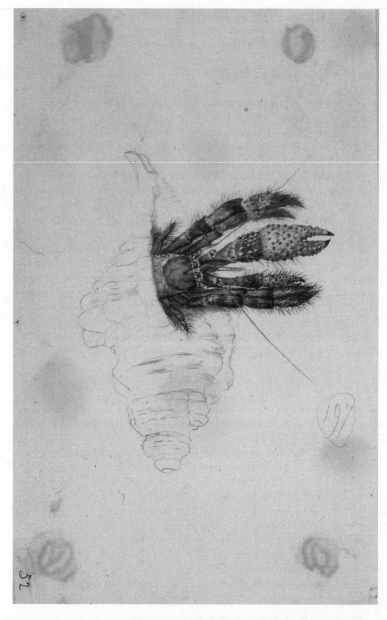

Figure 2   William J. Burchell, 'Hermit Crab', n.d., St Helena plants, 52. By permission of the Director and the Board of Trustees of the Royal Botanic Gardens, Kew.

argued elsewhere, such drawings are not simply accurate illustrations or representations: they also constitute material evidence in themselves, specimens by proxy.[31]

Burchell's attempt to make a permanent record of his observations in the field, through both the preservation of specimens and the creation of proxies, exemplifies a wider process through which knowledge was being transmitted from the field to the centres of metropolitan science. It is important to note, however, that the means and methods of observation in the field were by no means self-evident. For reports from the field to be credible from the perspective of the scientific establishment, travellers had to learn not only *what* to look for, but also *how* to observe: and this meant following rules – or what might well in this context be called 'observances'. Hence the burgeoning discourse on field observation during the first half of the nineteenth century, including manuals for surveyors, instructions to naval officers and field guides for zoologists, entomologists, botanists, geologists and geographers. The common thread within this instructional literature was the belief that, as William Herschel had put it, 'seeing is . . . an art which must be learnt'.[32] The proper conduct of observation – in sketching or in collecting, for example – required training not only of the eyes, but also of the hands, the feet, and indeed of the whole body of the observer. It was a matter of both appropriate equipment and correct comportment, a disciplining of the senses: there was certainly much more to observing than just looking. Yet the precise manner in which field observations were to be carried out was still a matter for debate, as the fraught history of many of these publications indicates. On my reading, for example, the Royal Geographical Society's celebrated manual, *Hints to Travellers*, appears less as a coherent assertion of a geographical way of seeing, than a fragile attempt to resolve some fundamental dilemmas about the means and status of observation in the field.[33]

III

One of the main inspirations for *Hints to Travellers*, first published in 1854, were the instructions which had long been issued to naval officers conducting surveying expeditions and voyages of exploration. This is in itself unsurprising given the substantial maritime contribution to the development of natural science generally, and the field of geographical knowledge in particular, during the eighteenth and nineteenth centuries.

---

[31] Luciana Martins and Felix Driver, 'The Struggle for Luxuriance: William J. Burchell Collects Tropical Nature', in *Tropical Views and Visions*, ed. Felix Driver and Luciana Martins (Chicago, in press).

[32] William Herschel, cited in Greg Dening, *Readings/Writings* (Melbourne, 1998), 8.

[33] 'Hints to Travellers', ed. Robert Fitzroy and Henry Raper, *Journal of the Royal Geographical Society*, 24 (1854), 328–58; Driver, *Geography Militant*, 49–67.

In the British context, the Royal Navy provided logistical support to major scientific expeditions: indeed many of the most *avant-garde* scientific programmes of the day – from terrestrial magnetism to astronomy – were unimaginable without it. Key Admiralty officials like John Barrow and Francis Beaufort played a notable role in the founding of the Royal Geographical Society, as they did also in discussions over exploration at the Royal Society and the British Association for the Advancement of Science. These institutional and individual connections matter a great deal to the development of the field sciences during this period, as many historians have pointed out.[34] In the present context, though, my focus is on the connections between the practices of maritime observation and the developing epistemology of observation in the field. The log-book and the sketch-book of the navigator, just as much as those of the naturalist, provided the means of apprehending the experience of travel through unfamiliar territory; they were mobile tools of knowledge, designed to register observations in a standard and consistent manner. Their contents tell us much about contemporary practices of field observation, and what happened to them in the process of circulation through the maritime world.

Figure 3 shows a page from a log-book kept by midshipman John Septimus Roe on a voyage from England to New South Wales in 1817.[35] The page contains routine observations made on departure from the harbour at Rio de Janeiro, a common port of call for British ships during this period, including a sketch of the fort at Santa Cruz and a topographic profile of the Sugar Loaf and adjacent coastal features. While they have been considerably re-worked, the basic form of these drawings reflects a routine feature of maritime observation. The ability to render in graphic form the dimensions, detail and colour of coastal landscapes was after all an essential aspect of the surveyor's task.[36] The coastal view was an integral component of maritime charts and log-books, part of a common visual code rendering the maritime world intelligible to navigators. In some respects, then, these images represent a way of seeing the maritime world from the point of view of the British coastal surveyor, part of a much wider network, coordinated from the Admiralty, through which the naval empire was secured. More particularly, in this

[34] Miller, 'Revival of the Physical Sciences'; Janet Browne, 'Biogeography and Empire', in *Cultures of Natural History*, ed. Jardine *et al.*, 305–21.

[35] Roe's log-book images are discussed at length in Felix Driver and Luciana Martins, 'John Septimus Roe and the Art of Navigation, c. 1815–1830', *History Workshop Journal*, 54 (2002), 144–61. The summary here draws on Driver, 'Imagining the Tropics: Views and Visions of the Tropical World', *Singapore Journal of Tropical Geography*, 25 (2004), 10–11.

[36] Andrew David, 'Coastal Views', in *The Charts and Coastal Views of Captain Cook's Voyages: The Voyage of the Endeavour 1768–1771* (1988), xxxviii–xli; Luciana Martins, 'Navigating in Tropical Waters: British Maritime Views of Rio de Janeiro', *Imago Mundi*, 50 (1998), 141–55.

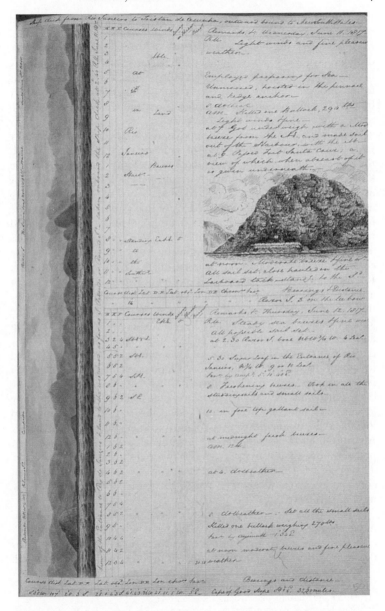

Figure 3   John Septimus Roe, observations at Rio de Janeiro, June 1817, from the log-book of the Dick. By permission of the Battye Library, Perth.

instance, they reflect Roe's prior training in the arts of drawing and mapping at Christ's Hospital school, and the subsequent development of his technique at sea, which is evidenced in his surviving correspondence during this period.[37] The log-book itself, of course, had a key role to play in both the practice of navigation and the politics of naval discipline. Its format in a sense mirrored the strict spatial organisation of the ship: every little bit of information had its proper place, the entries so designed to make optimum use of the available space.

Seen in this way, the log-book appears as a local version of Admiralty writ. But there are other ways of reading these images, in which the experience of disturbance comes more clearly into view. For one thing, such log-books could express more personal aspirations, insofar as drawing – like writing – offered a means of self-advancement to aspiring midshipmen and officers. Many of Roe's surviving log-books are immaculately produced, including ornate frontispieces clearly designed to impress his superiors and his relatives. The cultivation of his skills as a draughtsman needs to be seen in the wider context of the intense competition for naval posts in the post-1815 era. For six years from 1817, Roe worked under the supervision of Phillip Parker King, undertaking a coastal survey of Australia. King had been specifically instructed by the Admiralty to supervise Roe's drawing and colour-washing on the journey out to Australia.[38] The physical labour of drawing, mapping and sketching is painfully visible in Roe's correspondence to his family during this period. Throughout his early naval career, he never ceased to lament the effect of constant observation, sketching and drawing on his overworked eyes. In December 1818, writing from Port Jackson, he complained that 'My sight has been so much impaired by constantly looking out, since my being employed in this service, that I now find it difficult to distinguish objects plainly without the aid of a glass.'[39] Apart from his books and drawing instruments, it seems that Roe's most precious possession was the eye-water made up to his mother's recipe. The intensity of the tropical sun, as well as the countless hours spent confined in candle-lit cabins preparing his charts, would strain even the most imperial eye.

The sketches of the naval surveyor, then, take on a rather different meaning when seen in the context of the field, or on board ship. In Roe's case, they appear as both laborious experiments in a way of seeing and as the far-from-certain means of an attempt to secure a place in the world.

[37] Driver and Martins, 'John Septimus Roe', 146–53.
[38] State Library of Western Australia, John Septimus Roe Papers: J. S. Roe to J. Roe, 21 Apr. 1817; M. Hordern, *King of the Australian Coast: The Work of Phillip Parker King in the Mermaid and Bathurst, 1817–1822* (Melbourne, 1997), 24, 26.
[39] Roe Papers, J. S. Roe to J. Roe, 7 Dec. 1818.

Of necessity, naval survey had imperial functions: but its power was far from guaranteed in advance. In this context, it is also worth considering what happens when disturbance becomes catastrophe: as in the case of shipwreck, for example, when global networks of maritime knowledge and power are momentarily shattered. The fragility of the human condition, and specifically the limits to worldly knowledge and power, are of course recurring themes in accounts of maritime disaster across the ages. Here I am more particularly concerned with the challenge posed by such events to the project of charting the world, and the role of text and image in rendering them knowable. If a maritime voyage could be conceived as a sort of travelling experiment, as we have seen in the writing of John Herschel, then the loss of its principal instrument – the ship itself – clearly demanded an explanation. And in the naval context, perhaps above all others, narratives of cause and effect were closely connected to the attribution of responsibility and blame.

On 4 December 1830, the forty-six-gun frigate *Thetis* sailed out of the harbour of Rio de Janeiro bound for England with a large quantity of bullion on board.[40] The next day, on a calm but foggy night, the vessel smashed full-sail into the cliffs of Cabo Frio Island, with the loss of 28 of the 300 men on board. The wreck puzzled many commentators, as the island was a well-known landmark and sailing conditions had been unexceptional. While the ship's captain attributed the disaster to 'the wonderful and extraordinary nature of the current', unmarked on any chart, the subsequent and inevitable court martial blamed him for relying solely on dead reckoning and making insufficient allowance for the effect of strong southerly winds on sea-currents.[41] But these were not the only explanations canvassed. A matter of weeks after the court's verdict, Professor Peter Barlow, an authority on terrestrial magnetism, read a paper at the Royal Society arguing that the effects of 'local attraction' on the ship's compass caused by the increasing use of iron in naval construction would be sufficient to account for the loss.[42] Subsequently, further accounts of the drawn-out salvage operations were read at the Royal Society, particular attention being paid to design of a number of diving bells, air pumps and a large derrick. Numerous charts of the site, and drawings of the wreck itself based on underwater sketches made in

[40] The following summary is drawn from a longer study: Felix Driver and Luciana Martins, 'Shipwreck and Salvage in the Tropics: The Case of H. M. S. Thetis, 1830–1854' (unpublished paper, 2003).

[41] Public Record Office, Court Martial Papers, 'Narrative of the Loss of H.M.S. Thetis', by Captain Samuel Burgess, 15 Mar. 1831, and 'Court Martial Judgement', 21 Mar. 1831, ADM 1/5476.

[42] Peter Barlow, 'On the Errors in the Course of Vessels Occasioned by Local Attraction; with Some Remarks on the Recent Loss of His Majesty's Ship Thetis', *Philosophical Transactions*, 121 (1831), 215–21.

Figure 4   'The Remains of His Majesty's Late Ship, Thetis, Wrecked at Cape Frio, 4 December 1830, Sketched from the Diving Bell 23 November 1831', *Nautical Magazine* (1832), 126.

diving bells, accompanied progress reports despatched to the Admiralty and the Royal Society, and some found their way into the press (Figure 4). And at least one marine artist was tempted to join the imaginative plunder: John Christian Schetky produced two paintings in oils, under the title 'Salvage of Stores and Treasures from H.M.S. Thetis at Cape Frio' (1833), now held at the National Maritime Museum. One depicts the orderly efforts of the salvage team, ant-like creatures working with derrick and bell, dwarfed by spectacular cliffs; the other appeals to the sublime forces of nature as a stormy sea rages beneath the suspension cables.

Accounting for such a loss was an essential, if contested, part of making maritime knowledge. To rectify the disturbance represented by the wreck of a ship, various different kinds of imaginative work were required. The loss and salvage of the *Thetis* yielded a treasure trove of images, in the form of sketches, maps, charts, diagrams and paintings, as well as a wealth of narratives which steadily multiplied in the weeks and months following the event. The story-telling did not stop here, as legal disputes over the salvaged treasure continued for a quarter of a century. From the perspectives of science, government and commerce, a moment of catastrophic failure had first to be represented, and then accounted for. If the experiment of navigation had failed, in this case catastrophically, the sources of error had to be rendered intelligible, whether they were human (the failure to keep proper observations) or physical (the effects of local attraction): and in either case, there were lessons to be learned. The Admiralty, for its part, initially treated this like every other shipwreck as a disciplinary matter. The purpose of the court martial was to measure individual culpability through examination and combination of all the available evidence, including competing narratives of the event and visual sketches of the site. The same narratives and images were subsequently enrolled in drawn-out legal proceedings over the division of the spoils from the salvage, though here the case turned on questions of credit rather than culpability. Shipwreck narratives and imagery in other contexts could represent maritime catastrophe in the poetic registers of heroism, tragedy or retribution. With the *Thetis*, however, much more was invested in the story of its salvage than that of its loss.

IV

In recent years, historians have drawn attention to the sheer ambition of the naturalists, navigators and explorers of the age of enlightenment, who extended the reach of British power and knowledge across every continent.[43] They brought into existence vast collections of information, and great empires of learning, presided over by influential figures such as Joseph Banks, Roderick Murchison and Joseph Hooker. Theirs was an essentially imperial vision, in which the explorer's role was to fill in the blanks: as keepers of the imperial archive, they would do the rest. Yet these same archives reveal evidence of something more, beyond both imperial ambition and planetary consciousness: in a word, evidence of disturbance. Jonathan Lamb, referring to eighteenth-century voyages of discovery, expresses it thus:

> The commanders of these expeditions may have been committed to large and comprehensive views, and believed devoutly in systems of classification and cadastral measurement; but their data proved intractable, their experiments prone to failure, and they became periodically distracted, behaving unlike themselves owing to the stress of isolation, disease, fear – and occasionally exquisite pleasure.[44]

In this essay, I have highlighted some of the diverse meanings of disturbance for nineteenth-century travellers. The fictional Archibald Potter was thus brought to life in 1873 by Winwood Reade in order to dramatise the curative effects of travel on metropolitan disturbance: in this case it was proximity and not distance which was truly unsettling. Reade attempted to make his own reputation as a scientific explorer, in the wake of his better-known contemporaries, but he found only disappointment. Sixty years earlier, William Burchell had gone to incredible lengths to minimise the disturbing effects of travel, carrying with him instruments

---

[43] *Visions of Empire*, ed. Miller and Reill; Robert Stafford, *Scientist of Empire: Sir Roderick Murchison, Scientific Exploration and Victorian Imperialism* (Cambridge, 1989); Matthew Edney, *Mapping an Empire: The Geographical Construction of British India, 1765–1843* (Chicago, 1997); Richard Drayton, *Nature's Government: Science, Imperial Britain, and the 'Improvement' of the World* (New Haven, 2000).

[44] Lamb, *Preserving the Self*.

of every description, as well as the latest authorities in the form of books, as protections against the wild. His wagon, remember, was especially built in order to minimise the stresses and strains of the journey: it was designed, quite literally, as a mobile shock-absorber. But in the end, Burchell succeeded only too well as a collector, and failed as a philosopher: overwhelmed by his vast collections, he lost his reason. In 1863, after decades of unpacking, labelling and re-packing his specimens, he ended his own life. The verdict of the jury was 'suicide during temporary insanity'.[45]

In comparison with Burchell, John Septimus Roe was a lowly figure in the ranks of science, without a private income to support him. His route through the establishment was arduous but ultimately successful, and following his retirement from the Navy he went on to become surveyor general of Western Australia, a post he held until 1870. One measure of disturbance for Roe was his estimate of the physical effects of his labours on behalf of the imperial state. Clearly the business of survey came at a cost: as he recorded impassively in his letter of resignation, 'whilst actively employed in the Public service the sight in one eye has been completely destroyed, that of the other eye very much damaged, the head has twice been severely injured, as also the left hand, and incurable hernia has been contracted whilst forcing [sic] almost impenetrable country'.[46] If Roe's sense of disturbance was absorbed into his own body, the loss of a ship was a matter which demanded a quite different sort of response. The multiple accounts of the wreck and salvage of the *Thetis* provide some measure of the different ways in which institutions and individuals attempted to absorb and to exploit the shock of disturbance through the telling of stories and the making of images.

Each of these examples draws our attention to the ways in which the traveller's knowledge itself travels and what this entails, from the labour of observation to the mobilisation of trust. The imperial eye sees in this process a more or less coherent network through which information circulates before finally becoming translated into settled knowledge. But there are other stories, presented here through the figure of disturbance, in which knowledge is anything but settled. To put this another way, as far as the traveller is concerned, the jury is always out.

---

[45] Poulton, *Burchell*, 55–6.
[46] Driver and Martins, 'John Septimus Roe', 159.

Transactions of the RHS 14 (2004), pp. 93–116 © 2004 Royal Historical Society
DOI: 10.1017/S008044010400009x   Printed in the United Kingdom

THE LITERARY CRITIC AND THE VILLAGE LABOURER: 'CULTURE' IN TWENTIETH-CENTURY BRITAIN

The Prothero Lecture

By Stefan Collini

READ 2 JULY 2003

ABSTRACT. Debates about the concept of 'culture' in Britain are usually related to the perceived rise of 'mass society' in the early decades of the twentieth century. This essay re-situates such debates in relation to the development, from the 1870s onwards, of an ethically driven interpretation of changes in English society in the late eighteenth century. Through an examination of the later work of the Hammonds and of its reception in the late 1940s and early 1950s, this essay brings out how Raymond Williams's enormously influential *Culture and Society* ties the understanding of the concept of 'culture' to the emergence of this 'new civilisation'.

'The severance of the English peasant from the soil is an economic change which most people deplore.' It may seem no more than a fitting acknowledgement of the occasion that I should begin this Prothero lecture with an apt quotation from Prothero, but here I must warn you that things are not all as they seem. To begin with, my Prothero is the wrong Prothero. My opening quotation is not from Sir George Prothero, past president of this society after whom this lecture is named, and of whom, as Roy Foster memorably told us a few years ago, Yeats said 'I never look at old Prothero for five minutes without a desire to cut his throat',[1] but from his younger brother, R. E. Prothero, better known (if now known at all) as Lord Ernle, author of *English Farming, Past and Present*, an authoritative history that was first published in 1913 and in revised editions over the next twenty-five years. It has to be said that the Protheros may have contributed to any confusion posterity has had over their identities: that they should each have edited the *Quarterly Review* is already a trap for the unwary, one compounded by the fact that it was the elder brother

---

[1] R. F. Foster, 'Yeats at War: Poetic Strategies and Political Reconstruction from the Easter Rising to the Free State', *Transactions of the Royal Historical Society*, 11 (2001), 125.

who succeeded the younger.[2] In any event, my quotation is the opening sentence of the 'wrong' Prothero's review in the *Times Literary Supplement* of *The Village Labourer*, the celebrated work by J. L. and Barbara Hammond first published in 1911. The Hammonds certainly deplored the severance of the English peasant from the soil, and their hugely influential book and its successors (I shall return to the question of their impact) amounted to a fierce indictment of the selfishness and rapacity of the governing classes for their part in bringing about that severance. But although Prothero's opening words may at first suggest some sympathy with the Hammonds' argument, his review was in fact largely critical of it, as one might have expected from a historian who also served as a Tory MP and the duke of Bedford's land agent. Prothero (writing anonymously, of course, as was the *TLS* custom at the time) itemised several ways in which he believed the Hammonds had simplified or distorted the evidence to present an exaggeratedly dark picture of the impact of enclosures and associated changes during their chosen period. It was in keeping with his tone of severe and objective scholarship that Prothero should, in the quoted sentence, have confined himself to treating the fate of that emotive but elusive species 'the English peasant' simply as 'an economic change'.[3]

Let me now jump forwards across five decades to quote a sentence from a very different kind of writer addressing a quite different set of concerns.

> For many years literary education has tended to produce an enormous revulsion from a world dominated by industry and science ... and before we know where we are we are back in the never-never land of the organic society with those happy peasants, Dr Leavis, Richard Hoggart, Raymond Williams, and David Holbrook.

This passage is by the Cambridge literary critic Graham Hough, writing in 1963,[4] and in addressing that hardy perennial, 'the crisis in literary education', Hough's remark may seem to have nothing in common with Prothero's, other perhaps than its metaphor-induced suggestion that the few remaining English peasants had, following their severance from the soil, had to fall to and scratch a living by cultivating a spot of literary criticism. But metaphors have a constant tendency to exceed or escape their users' control, and Hough's lightly mocking phrase may have signalled a larger continuity than he intended. He was writing, as his earlier invocation of C. P. Snow had made explicit, in the context of the 'two cultures' debate, and it is relevant to my theme today to recall that

---

[2] For the elder Prothero, see C. W. Crawley, 'Sir George Prothero and his Circle', *Transaction of the Royal Historical Society*, 20 (1970), 101–28; for the younger, see *Dictionary of National Biography*.

[3] 'The Peasant and the Soil', *Times Literary Supplement*, 4 Jan. 1912, 3. Prothero's authorship is identified in the *Times Literary Supplement Centenary Archive Online, 1902–1990*.

[4] Graham Hough, 'Crisis in Literary Education', *Sunday Times*, 17 Mar. 1963, 26.

'culture', the central term in my title, first came to be used in its modern senses as a metaphorical extension of its earlier horticultural meaning. Indeed, nineteenth-century English commentators, in discussing the disappearance of peasant landholding in England, frequently used the phrase '*la petite culture*', drawn from the country thought by some observers to exhibit not just the economic but also the political and, as one might now say, 'cultural' benefits of continuing to have large numbers of legally secure peasant proprietors. That one discursive development in the course of the twentieth century could be said to involve the displacement of *la petite culture* not by high farming but by 'high culture' may point to more than just a neat trans-lingual pun.

For my purpose, Hough's remark possesses a further interest, namely his inclusion of the name of Raymond Williams in his roll-call of happy peasants. This is bound to seem anomalous to most modern literary scholars familiar with Williams's work, for he is known, above all through his later classic study *The Country and the City*, as a trenchant critic of precisely that kind of 'ruralist nostalgia' that he identified as a recurrent element in English cultural diagnosis and as underlying Leavis's cultural pessimism in particular, a position from which he distanced himself in the sharpest terms.[5] It is possible that Hough himself came to feel uneasy about including Williams in this company, since in an essay published in the following year he repeated this passage verbatim, but silently omitted Williams's name.[6] While this further thinning of the ranks of the English peasantry would no doubt meet with general critical approval now, I shall follow the clue offered by Hough's first thoughts and treat Williams as just the right literary critic to discuss in the light of that remark by the wrong Prothero. In other words, in this essay I want to explore the hinterland of ideas that lay behind and connected, sometimes in indirect and unobvious ways, my two opening quotations and the worlds of discourse that they represent. I want to do so as a way of contributing to the understanding of one of the central and recurring issues in twentieth-century British culture, namely disputes over the cloudy, vexed and morally charged category of 'culture' itself. My focus will be on the decades running from the 1910s to the 1960s, and if we need any reminding of the centrality of the question of culture to public debate in this period, especially as contributed to by literary critics, then a short list of familiar titles should suffice: *Mass Civilization and Minority Culture*, *Notes towards the Definition of Culture*, *Culture*

---

[5] Raymond Williams, *The Country and the City* (1973); see also Williams's subsequent comments in Raymond Williams, *Politics and Letters: Interviews with New Left Review* (1979), esp. 97–132, 303–23.

[6] Graham Hough, 'Crisis in Literary Education', in *Crisis in the Humanities*, ed. J. H. Plumb (Harmondsworth, 1964), 96.

and Society, *The Two Cultures* and so on.[7] I shall not offer to map all of this difficult and treacherous terrain here, but the element on which I want particularly to focus is the relation between understandings of the concept of 'culture' in the middle decades of the twentieth century and one, by then well-established but far from uncontested, interpretation of changes in economic life in England in the eighteenth and early nineteenth centuries.

John Maynard Keynes famously claimed that 'practical men, who believe themselves to be quite exempt from any intellectual influences, are usually the slaves of some defunct economist'.[8] I am tempted to try to parallel this dictum by suggesting that we shall find, in a similar way, that the literary critic writing as social critic also often turns out to be the slave of some defunct economic historian. That may be unduly provoking – at least to the literary critics; it probably seems the merest platitude to the economic historians. A slightly more inflected way of putting the point would be to say that literary critics, especially in their larger thematic ruminations, are often unwittingly presupposing a particular interpretation of relevant episodes or epochs of non-literary history, and I hope this essay may serve as a modest advertisement for bringing together material usually considered as the preserve of disciplines that, for all the talk of inter-disciplinary *glasnost*, can still show themselves to be touchily possessive about their intellectual property.

The most general framework in which to set my argument concerns a pervasive, but indistinct and rather under-characterised, feature of the thought and sensibility of a whole swathe of the English educated class in, roughly, the first half of the twentieth century. At its simplest, this feature involved the repeated insistence on the need to identify and make effective some alternative to the operation of economic logic understood in its purest, profit-maximising form. Such an alternative was being asked to provide, simultaneously, a set of motives, a determining force in social organisation and a criterion of value (three elements I have distinguished for analytical purposes, though they were not always so distinguished at the time). Hostility or aversion to the alleged dominance of the instrumentality of economic reason can, needless to say, take many forms; during this period, the search for alternatives was broadly ethical in character, though as so often with the sensibility of that particular stratum of English society it was hard to disentangle the ethical from the aesthetic.

<hr />

[7] By, respectively, F. R. Leavis (1930), T. S. Eliot (1948), Raymond Williams (1958) and, under the title 'The Two Cultures and the Scientific Revolution', C. P. Snow (1959). One might add to this list the first modern edition of Matthew Arnold's *Culture and Anarchy*, ed. J. Dover Wilson (1932).

[8] J. M. Keynes, *The General Theory of Employment, Interest, and Money* (1936), *Collected Writings of John Maynard Keynes* (30 vols., 1971–89), VII, 383.

Of course, described in these general terms there may seem to be nothing distinctive or period-specific about this concern, and certainly it is in many respects continuous with elements to be found in English thought both before and after the period in question, as well as elsewhere. But distinctiveness in these matters is often principally a matter of emphasis or proportion rather than of complete novelty. In the present case, I would suggest that the confluence of three strands marks the discourse I am dealing with. First, it understood economic rationality as the operation of systematic selfishness. Second, it saw this not just as one feature of the working of contemporary society, but as its determining and officially sanctioned principle. And third, this was not assumed to be a timeless feature of human life, but was seen, rather, as the defining characteristic of a particular, and recent, period – the emergence in England of a new kind of society in the late eighteenth and early nineteenth centuries. This discourse can be further isolated not just by these components of its content, but also by two features of its status or purchase. First, by the early decades of the twentieth century, it did not simply take the form of individual claims or arguments, but ramified widely, constituting a kind of shared moral vocabulary in the relevant circles. And, second, although, needless to say, not all sections of educated opinion exhibited an equal affinity for this discourse, it was certainly not confined to one stratum or profession, nor to one political sect, still less to a few prominent but idiosyncratic individuals.[9]

The roots of the *historical* assumptions underlying this discourse are, I would suggest, peculiarly tangled, even if, for convenience, one leaves aside their earliest appearances in French and German social thought of the early nineteenth century.[10] The proximate sources for many of the relevant ideas were to be found in the writings of the so-called 'historical

[9] I am mindful here of Peter Mandler's monitory remarks about the dangers of exaggerating the appeal of the broader complex of anti-modernist attitudes referred to as 'Englishness' in his 'Against "Englishness": English Culture and the Limits to Rural Nostalgia, 1870–1940', *Transactions of the Royal Historical Society*, 7 (1997), 155–75. However, whether or not Mandler is right to see such attitudes as confined, at least before 1914, to 'fairly marginal artistic groups' – 'self-consciously anti-Establishment' 'faddists' (170) – the discourse I am discussing was clearly more broadly distributed than that. Stewart Weaver understandably leans in the opposite direction when he writes: 'Far from being controversial, the catastrophic view of the age of industry was by 1925 if not commonplace, then conventional. The Hammonds' was the accepted wisdom.' Stewart A. Weaver, *The Hammonds: A Marriage in History* (Stanford, 1997), 195.

[10] There is now a large literature on the origins and early uses of the notion of 'the Industrial Revolution'; for helpful discussions, see D. C. Coleman, *Myth, History, and the Industrial Revolution* (1992); David Cannadine, 'The Present and the Past in the English Industrial Revolution, 1880–1980', *Past and Present*, 103 (1984), 131–72; Gareth Stedman Jones, 'National Bankruptcy and Social Revolution: European Observers on Britain, 1813–1844', in *Political Economy of British Historical Experience 1688–1914*, ed. Donald Winch and Patrick K. O'Brien (Oxford, 2002), 61–92.

economists' in the last three decades of the nineteenth century, though not only was that group more politically and methodologically diverse than is sometimes allowed, but some of them, such as William Cunningham or W. J. Ashley, ultimately emphasised the continuity of English economic and social history rather than any sudden rupture of it.[11] Nevertheless, partly as a result of a morally charged selective reading of Arnold Toynbee's influential lectures on *The Industrial Revolution in England*, first published in 1884, partly as a result of polemics against the alleged moral failings of orthodox political economy on the part of leading figures in the Christian Social Union such as Bishop Gore and Canon Scott Holland, partly as a result of the wide dissemination of the Ruskinian heterodoxies of the New Liberal publicist J. A. Hobson and above all as a result of that confluence of scholarly research, moral protest and political purpose to be found in the abundant historical writings of the Webbs, R. H. Tawney and the Hammonds, there was propounded in the early decades of the twentieth century a highly elaborated account of the Industrial Revolution not just as a social catastrophe for certain classes, but also – something that now tends to be neglected though it was an even stronger claim – as establishing a quite new form of civilisation, one driven by the narrow and unchecked pursuit of profit.

Needless to say, this interpretation was far from holding unchallenged sway even at the time: its central claims were disputed by several leading academic historians and economists – the names of Alfred Marshall and J. H. Clapham might stand in for many less influential figures here – and these claims have of course also come in for some pretty rough handling by later scholars.[12] It is no part of my purpose on this occasion to engage with this later scholarly literature; it is enough for now simply to note how the ethical impulse to subordinate the claims of economic logic to some 'higher' values drove a catastrophist interpretation of English history in which the nineteenth century figured as a 'new civilization' desperately in need of some modern equivalent for the practices and values that had supposedly been lost.

Obviously, this historical interpretation could readily be given a radical and reforming twist in contemporary debate, but, as I have suggested, it was far from being confined to such sectarian purposes. By the inter-war period, in particular, versions of this ethically framed narrative of temptation and fall were to be found right across the political spectrum.

[11] Stefan Collini, 'Particular Polities: Political Economy and the Historical Method', in Stefan Collini, Donald Winch and John Burrow, *That Noble Science of Politics: A Study in Nineteenth-Century Intellectual History* (Cambridge, 1983), 247–75; Gerard M. Koot, *English Historical Economists, 1870–1926* (Cambridge, 1987); Alon Kadish, *Historians, Economists, and Economic History* (1989).

[12] For a helpful overview see the 'Introduction' in *Political Economy of British Historical Experience*, ed. Winch and O'Brien.

We may hardly be surprised to discover that ardent ruralist, G. M. Trevelyan – recently described as 'without a doubt... the most popular and widely-read English historian of the first half of the twentieth century',[13] – beginning his *British History in the Nineteenth Century* (which, interestingly, covered the years 1782 to 1901) with a high-toned evocation of 'the quiet old England of the eighteenth century before the machines destroyed it', but we should also note that in his hugely successful *English Social History*, published during the Second World War, he constantly stigmatised the Industrial Revolution as a 'sudden catastrophe' and a 'tremendous social disaster', which had destroyed 'the harmonious fabric of English society', the way having been prepared by our old historiographical friends, the rising middle classes, who, in an oddly routine phrase, are described as 'often selfish enough'.[14] In similar vein, Sir Arthur Bryant – who has been comparably described as 'arguably the most widely read British historian of the post-war era'[15] and who was scarcely a spokesman for rancorous radicalism – looked back from the vantage-point of 1940 and saw the previous hundred years as having been dominated by 'selfishness'. 'Private profit-making', he intoned, summarising a view he expected would command wide assent,

> formerly regarded merely as a means to the acquisition of that modest ownership that makes virtuous and free men, became accepted as an end in itself... [M]an, who had once tried to model his life on the divine, came to take his orders from the lender of money and the chartered accountant.[16]

And to take just one example of the broader purchase of this interpretation, we find it structuring many of the contributions to the Church of England's Malvern conference in 1941 on 'The Life of the Church and the Order of Society', in ways that hint at, while also transcending, its Christian Social Union genealogy. This gathering was attended by 23 bishops, led by William Temple, archbishop of York, soon to be translated to Canterbury, and over 200 members of the clergy and laity (including T. S. Eliot), and the published version of the proceedings became an unexpected best-seller. In it, a succession of contributors lamented that 'it is the profit motive which has infected our existing civilization' and urged that 'the English are called upon to redress one of the greatest historical errors of humanity'.[17]

---

[13] Victor Feske, *From Belloc to Churchill: Private Scholars, Public Culture, and the Crisis of British Liberalism 1900–1939* (Chapel Hill, NC, 1996), 139.

[14] G. M. Trevelyan, *British History in the Nineteenth Century* (1922), 'Introduction'; idem, *English Social History* (1944), 463–4, 474, 123; see also David Cannadine, *G. M. Trevelyan: A Life in History* (1992), 107–9, 169–74.

[15] Feske, *Belloc to Churchill*, 238.

[16] Arthur Bryant, *English Saga (1840–1940)* (1940), 328–9.

[17] *Malvern, 1941: The Life of the Church and the Order of Society* (1941), 169 (Kenneth Ingram), 33 (W. G. Peck), 137 (V. A. Demant). On the success of the volume, and Eliot's involvement, see

This ethically driven interpretation of the special significance of social and economic change in Britain in the late eighteenth century is related in both obvious and unobvious ways to those debates about 'culture' which figured so prominently in British intellectual life from the inter-war period up to at least the 1960s. The literary scholars and others who have attended to these debates have by and large seen them in terms of responses to the advent of so-called 'mass society' in the years after 1918, a native form of 'Kulturkritik'.[18] This is clearly an important part of the story, one made more salient by the almost exclusive concentration in this body of scholarship on the writings of F. R. Leavis. But this scholarship itself usually relies on the understanding of the category of 'culture' most influentially expounded by Raymond Williams, and it is the historical assumptions underlying that understanding which I want to explore. Obviously, in the space available I shall have to be highly selective, so for illustrative purposes I shall focus on the work of the Hammonds themselves, albeit on some of the less familiar features of that work. This, as will become clear, is not principally an argument about 'influence' – though I do think that the impact of the Hammonds on literary critics and cultural commentators of Williams's generation has even now not been fully appreciated – but rather a matter of drawing attention to certain homologies of argument, certain shared frameworks, certain recurrent verbal and tonal patterns.

I

Modern scholarly discussion of the Hammonds' work has mainly focused on two issues: first, the relation of their 'Labourer' trilogy, published between 1911 and 1919, to the progressive politics of the first two or three decades of the twentieth century, and second, their place in the subsequent 'standard of living' debate about the Industrial Revolution.[19] In themselves, these emphases are justifiable, but they have had the effect

---

Stefan Collini, 'The European Modernist as Anglican Moralist: The Later Social Criticism of T. S. Eliot', in *Enlightenment, Passion, Modernity: Historical Essays in European Thought and Culture*, ed. Mark S. Micale and Robert L. Dietle (Stanford, 2000), 207–29, 438–44.

[18] For example, Chris Baldick, *The Social Mission of English Criticism 1848–1932* (Oxford, 1983); Terry Eagleton, *Literary Theory: An Introduction* (1983); and in particular Francis Mulhern, *Culture/Metaculture* (2000), on which see the (as yet unfinished) exchange in *New Left Review* [hereafter *NLR*]: Stefan Collini, 'Culture Talk', *NLR*, 7 (Jan.–Feb. 2001), 43–53; Francis Mulhern, 'Beyond Metaculture', *NLR*, 16 (July–Aug. 2002), 86–104; Collini, 'Defending Cultural Criticism', *NLR*, 18 (Nov.–Dec. 2002), 73–97; Mulhern, 'What Is Cultural Criticism?', *NLR*, 23 (Sept.–Oct. 2003), 35–49.

[19] See respectively Peter Clarke, *Liberals and Social Democrats* (Cambridge, 1978), and Malcolm I. Thomis, *The Town Labourer and the Industrial Revolution* (1974); the emphasis of the former is continued in Teresa Javurek, 'A New Liberal Descent: The "Labourer Trilogy" by Lawrence and Barbara Hammond', *Twentieth-Century British History*, 10 (1999), 375–403. The fullest and best account of the Hammonds is now Weaver, *The Hammonds*.

both of somewhat neglecting the Hammonds' later work and of assuming that their impact was greatest at the point where they (which is really to say Lawrence Hammond) were still actively involved in political journalism. I want instead to look at certain aspects of their later books, and also to draw attention to the impact their work had quite some time after its first publication, in the second half of the 1940s and early 1950s, the key years for the debate about 'culture' in England.

First, it is worth re-emphasising just what a morality tale the original 'Labourer' trilogy actually was. The response of two sympathetic readers of the first two volumes catches this most economically. Reviewing *The Village Labourer*, Graham Wallas compared it to *Uncle Tom's Cabin*, hoping that the Hammonds' book, too, 'may start a national movement of humiliation and amendment', a theme which R. H. Tawney's language echoed when he wrote to the authors following the publication of *The Town Labourer* saying that their achievement lay 'in destroying the historical assumptions on which our modern slavery is based'.[20] The governing classes' callous treatment of the poor in the years between 1760 and 1832 was the great wrong now crying out for acknowledgement and some form of redress. The Hammonds sought an explanation for the harshness of what they called the 'new civilization' created in these years in the triumph of a philosophy that justified the unfettered pursuit of profit, and the first victim of this new principle was the English peasant. In other words, they treated the enclosure movement and associated agricultural developments in the middle and later years of the eighteenth century as an integral part of the Industrial Revolution, which destroyed the previously effective moral and customary restraints on the pursuit of profit. 'The peasant with rights and a status, with a share in the fortunes and government of his village', they wrote, 'makes way for the labourer ... No class in the world has so beaten and crouching a history.'[21]

Lord Ernle (the 'wrong' Prothero, that is to say) had not been the only critic to find fault with the way in which the 'Labourer' volumes presented the facts of economic history as a tragedy in three acts. Sir John Clapham registered the most telling misgivings, culminating in the first volume of his *Economic History of England*, published in 1926, with its carefully documented corrections of the Hammonds' calculations about average wages.[22] In the course of a series of responses to Clapham and other critics in the later 1920s, the Hammonds in effect withdrew some

---

[20] Graham Wallas, 'The Village Labourer', *Nation*, 11 Nov. 1911, 248; R. H. Tawney to the Hammonds, 24 June 1917, quoted in Clarke, *Liberals and Social Democrats*, 189.

[21] J. L. and Barbara Hammond, *The Village Labourer, 1760–1832: A Study of the Government of England before the Reform Bill* (1911), 81.

[22] J. H. Clapham, *An Economic History of Modern Britain*, I (Cambridge, 1926); for this and other criticisms, and for the Hammonds' responses, see Weaver, *The Hammonds*, ch. 6, 'The Clapham Complex'.

of their more incautious assertions about the decline in the incomes and standard of living of the working class as a whole during the Industrial Revolution, but they by no means abandoned their attempt to characterise the peculiarly degraded quality of what they called the 'new civilization' that had come into being. When *The Age of the Chartists* was published in 1930, Trevelyan congratulated Lawrence Hammond on 'us[ing] the criticisms directed against your earlier work by Clapham ... to lead you not back but on to the discovery of another and larger truth'.[23] Since it is often assumed that the Hammonds were forced by such criticisms to abandon their 'catastrophist' case, it is worth pausing to ask what exactly Trevelyan, and indeed the Hammonds themselves, thought this 'other and larger truth' consisted in. To answer this, we need first to look at the strategy of their immediately preceding book, *The Rise of Modern Industry*.

'This book', they announce at the outset, 'is written for the general reader and not for the specialist. It is an attempt to put the Industrial Revolution in its place in history.'[24] At times, the book can, it has to be said, read like an attempt to 'put it in its place' in a more colloquial sense, too, but what the Hammonds were offering here was a much longer time-scale and much wider comparative framework than in their more celebrated 'Labourer' trilogy. Their opening historical survey of 'Commerce before the Industrial Revolution' makes a stab at isolating what is supposed to be distinctive about 'the industrial age', characterising the latter (cloudily and without analytical edge) as 'an age in which commerce and finance are no longer aspects, growing in importance yet still aspects of its life, but the basis on which a society depends' (23). One may note in passing that it was a recurring feature of that strain of ethical criticism of the 'organised selfishness' of industrial society that it struggled to identify the sense in which economic rationality was less of an operative force in all earlier periods. (Even Tawney was later to remark wryly upon the Hammonds' tendency 'to write at times as though the fall of man occurred in the reign of George III'.[25])

Having introduced the central section of the book on what they call 'The English Industrial Revolution' with a chapter entitled 'The Destruction of the Peasant Village', they move to a parallel chapter on 'The Destruction of Custom in Industry', concluding that in both cases 'the victory of capital was complete' (108). Their account of the industrial development of South Wales, a process creating an entirely new community unhampered by existing custom and tradition, brought

[23] Quoted in Feske, *Belloc to Churchill*, 131.

[24] J. L. and Barbara Hammond, *The Rise of Modern Industry* (1925), 'Preface'; all quotations are from the 8th edition (1951); hereafter page references will be given in the text.

[25] R. H. Tawney, 'J. L. Hammond, 1872–1949', *Proceedings of the British Academy*, 46 (1960), 276.

the structuring assumptions even more clearly into view: 'There the economic man was not a mere nightmare of the new textbooks; he was an omnipotent force in a world existing for a single purpose' (158). At this point, the book moves to its pivotal chapter, portentously entitled 'The Curse of Midas'. In laying his curse, Midas was assisted by that elite corps of assistant magicians, the political economists: 'The economist dismissed moral and religious impulses, finding in selfishness the driving power of industrial enterprise' (217). But then, in a revealing and in some ways unexpected shift, the Hammonds extend the familiar charge against political economy by suggesting 'Public beauty seemed to have been banished by the new science.' They point the moral, as they increasingly did in these later works, by means of a contrast with the Ancient World: 'The Greeks and the Romans put a great deal of beauty into their public buildings.' Earlier periods of English history, too, 'gave some place in common life to the satisfaction of the imagination and the senses'. But not so in the early nineteenth century: 'The Curse of Midas was on this society' (218–19, 228). No less revealing, I think, is the way in which they in effect compensate for the cloudiness of their analysis of the role of economic rationality in earlier periods by their rhetorical exaggeration of its supremacy in 'the machine age', as when they say of property-owners during the Industrial Revolution: 'In their surroundings there was nothing to compel them, or indeed to prompt them, to think of anything but making profit' (243). Or, as one might re-state such exaggeration in the idiom of the period in question: 'It is a truth universally acknowledged that a single man in possession of a good fortune must be in want of a higher return upon capital.'

How were any contrary and restraining values to be re-introduced into the self-seeking world of this 'new civilization'? Fortunately, help was, if not exactly at hand, at least only an education away. For, 'England, the first nation set down face to face with this task, was not left entirely to its own resources.' The English governing class, we are reminded, could draw upon the fruits of another and perennially valuable historical experience, since 'the best representatives of that class were steeped in the humanism of the classics' (252). Here, perhaps surprisingly, was a corrective to 'the reigning standard of profit' (254), a corrective that functioned more effectively than the all-too complaisant teaching of the churches in this dark period. The literature of Greece and Rome laid its restraining hand on the unchecked pursuit of gain by the unlikely means of Factory Acts, the Civil Service and trade union legislation. That the factory inspectors proved to be cultivated men was crucial, as the Hammonds made clear in the following remarkable passage:

> From this time [the establishment of inspection] the self-centred life of industry was explored and partly regulated by men for whom the world was older than the steam-engine: for whom Euripides and Shakespeare had lessons to teach mankind, not less

important than those taught by the eager merchant selling cotton piece goods on the Manchester Exchange. In this way the English people turned to their resources of culture and tradition, in order to bring a standard of conduct into this new world. (255–6)

The bald structure here is, implicitly, 'culture', drawing upon an 'older' world, versus 'economics', with a play upon 'self-centred' in relation to the latter which combines suggestions of selfishness and parochialism, in need, on both counts, of 'a standard of conduct'. The contrast is drawn in positively Arnoldian terms, including the characteristic unfairness of pitting that too-eager Manchester cotton merchant against Euripides and Shakespeare, joint captains of the world's cultural All-Stars. In this way, the longer perspectives of *The Rise of Modern Industry* provide, if not a happy ending, then at least a more upbeat sense of the corrective potential of a cultural inheritance.

Five years later in 1930 the Hammonds published a work whose full title was *The Age of the Chartists, 1832–1854: A Study of Discontent*, and then in 1934 they produced an abridgement of this book in the form of the slim volume entitled simply *The Bleak Age*, one of their best-known titles, though it is important to be aware that the 1947 Penguin edition involved not only some cutting and re-writing, but also the re-instatement of omitted chapters from *The Age of the Chartists*. These later books are sometimes simply seen as extensions of the 'Labourer' trilogy further into the nineteenth century, but in each of them the story of how unrestrained greed was tamed by the resources of culture became more and more prominent. Their distinctive character and strategy were surely signalled by the fact that in each version of this study of social conditions and popular unrest in England in the 1830s and 1840s, the first substantive chapter is devoted to the civilization of Greece and Rome, and also by the fact that in *The Bleak Age* their select list of 'Books for Further Reading' contains thirty titles, twelve of which are books dealing exclusively with the Ancient World.[26] Of course, the conjunction of the glory of Greece and the condition of England was hardly unknown to generations of classically educated readers throughout the nineteenth century, but the Hammonds used it to sketch a polemical characterisation of the 'new civilization' of England after the Industrial Revolution. The binary categories governing their account emerge ever more starkly:

Between the spirit of Athens and that of a goldfield, between a number of persons whose bond of union is their enjoyment of art, religion, beauty, and amusement, and the same number of persons whose bond of union is that each of them hopes to become a rich

---

[26] J. L. and Barbara Hammond, *The Bleak Age* (1934), 143; this bibliography was not reproduced in the 1947 Penguin edition. Hereafter, page references to *The Bleak Age* will be to the 1934 edition, followed by the 1947 edition.

man, there is a difference that affects the depths and not merely the surface of social life.[27]

There is a more than Arnoldian tendentiousness to this, of course: the leisured citizens of Athens, we notice, pass their days entirely in the enjoyment of culture (in these pictures of the Ancient World, women and slaves are always just off-camera), whereas the vast complexity of nineteenth-century English society is reduced to the metaphor of the goldfield, always a resonant allusion for two former 'pro-Boers' such as the Hammonds. Their discussion centred on the mitigation of the harsh reality of labour in the Ancient World by the public provision of amenity and beauty: in that epoch, 'the poor man ... could imagine, for the hour he passed beneath some noble portico ... that drudgery was only part of his life'.[28] By contrast, the 'drudgery' was not similarly mitigated in early nineteenth-century England, and this, it transpires, is their rather remarkable explanation for the emergence of Chartism. In the Hammonds' account, the Chartists were not primarily moved by economic or even political impulses: rather, Chartism expressed 'a revolt of the spirit' against the lack of such amenity in the 'new civilization' of industrial England.

Within that civilisation, they discerned, again in crisply binary fashion, 'two opposing philosophies'. On the one hand there was 'the school that simplified human nature' by looking to 'the incentive of gain as the moving power'; this philosophy was 'the most powerful influence on the mind of the age'.[29] As usual, no proper names are attached to this one-dimensional parody of political economy, and it is simply assumed to represent the actual operation of society in England in the first half of the nineteenth century. The other philosophy developed as a response to this reductive creed: 'All that Bentham had forgotten crowded into the pages of Shelley and Wordsworth, Coleridge and Southey, Carlyle and Dickens, Mill and Maurice, Peacock and Disraeli.'[30] Variants on this literary roll-call were to become increasingly familiar in the debates about culture in mid-twentieth-century Britain (not least to the many readers of Raymond Williams's work), as was the casual identification of Utilitarianism with classical political economy.[31]

---

[27] *Ibid.*, 140/224.

[28] *Ibid.*, 138/242; the whole paragraph in which this passage occurs was reproduced verbatim in the 1947 edition, but the words 'for the hour he passed beneath some noble portico' were omitted, though the passage still concludes that the poor man in the Ancient World remained 'a man among men, lost like his fellows in contemplation or enjoyment'.

[29] *Ibid.*, 82 (this passage was omitted in 1947).

[30] *Ibid.*, 135/241.

[31] See Donald Winch, 'Mr Gradgrind and Jerusalem', in *Economy, Polity, and Society: British Intellectual History 1750–1950*, ed. Stefan Collini, Richard Whatmore and Brian Young (Cambridge, 2000), 243–66.

Their characterisation of this other philosophy is worth quoting more fully:

> The fundamental philosophy underlying the humanist protest against the gospel of the Industrial Revolution – the idea that man was a complex character, and society a complex body, not to be left to the steam-engine and the railways for the satisfaction of instincts and tastes that had created and demanded, in other ages, art, culture, religion – this idea ... inspired in different forms the teaching of Wordsworth and Mill, Coleridge and Carlyle.[32]

Once again, the historical contrast which drives the argument is with those 'other ages' where man's complex needs had been met within the operating norms of his society, whereas in nineteenth-century England culture is assigned the task of 'protesting' against those norms as represented by the emotive synecdoche of 'the steam engine and the railways'. Functionally, ancient porticoes here played the same part as earlier invocations of the 'village community' of pre-enclosure England, little more than mnemonics for a world not driven by 'the incentive of gain'.

Portraying Chartism as a revolt of the spirit against the lack of those consoling forms of amenity or 'culture' that all previous societies, including the society of pre-industrial England, had known is, paradoxically, what enabled the Hammonds to give a more optimistic cast to what seems at first a story of unmitigated loss and defeat. Bleak as life in the 'treadmill cities' may have been in the middle of the nineteenth century, 'man's complex needs' still sought their satisfaction – and found it in such unlikely forms as the Ten Hours Act, the Public Health Act, Public Libraries and – particularly dear to the hearts of the fresh-air worshipping Hammonds – Commons Preservation. Through what they termed the 'growth of common enjoyment', something of what had been lost was being restored.[33] Even if 'the English peasant' of earlier ages had not usually passed many hours 'under noble porticoes', he had still known the solace of field and sky. What previous generations had experienced through the accessibility of 'nature' had had, in the middle and later decades of the nineteenth century, to be painfully reconstructed by the efforts of 'culture', where culture embraces both the teachings of Euripides and Shakespeare and forms of political and collective organisation, their common feature lying in the corrective they both provided to a society founded on the unrestrained pursuit of pecuniary gain.

---

[32] *Bleak Age*, 82 (this passage was omitted in 1947).
[33] See the even more positive and optimistic account in J. L. Hammond, *The Growth of Common Enjoyment* (L. T. Hobhouse Memorial Trust Lectures, no. 3) (Oxford, 1933).

II

As I have already suggested, the period of the Hammonds' greatest impact came some time after the publication of what are today their best-known works. It is true that at least the first two volumes of the 'Labourer' trilogy went through several reprintings in the 1920s, but this was a modest scale of success compared to the steeply rising graph of their sales in the 1940s. Consider, simply by way of illustration, the following details. It is indicative of the audience that *The Bleak Age* was thought capable of reaching at the end of the war that in 1944 the Stationery Office bought up much of the existing stock for what Longman's referred to as some sort of 'fighting services post-war educational scheme'.[34] In 1947 Penguin published a revised version of the book in an edition of 75,000 copies, and this edition was in turn reprinted the following year. Meanwhile, *The Rise of Modern Industry* enjoyed the peak of its success as a textbook in this period: its sixth edition came out in 1944, the seventh in 1947 and the eighth in 1951. As a consequence, the 'Labourer' volumes enjoyed a further lease of life, as Stewart Weaver has recently noted: 'Guild Books, a cooperative venture that aimed at competing with Penguin for the paperback trade, published a two-shilling edition of *The Village Labourer* in 1948 (50,000 copies); and Longman reprinted *The Town Labourer* (26,000 copies) in 1949.'[35] The reference to some sort of 'fighting services post-war educational scheme' indicates well enough the milieu in which the Hammonds' later work was making its mark, the milieu of the Army Bureau of Current Affairs, spreading out into the Workers' Education Association and the broader post-war expansion of adult education, an audience eager to understand the distinctive course of modern British history, to account for the great historic wrong done to the class from which so many of them were drawn and to find means through which an ethic of fairness and solidarity might curtail the ravages wrought by selfishness and exploitation.

It has often been remarked how the roots of that debate about 'culture' which particularly flourished in the 1950s and 1960s, as indeed of the later academic discipline known as 'Cultural Studies', are to be found in that adult education world of the immediately post-war years.[36] One adult education tutor who played a prominent part in both those developments was, of course, my other main witness, Raymond Williams. Thanks to John McIlroy's researches in the archives of the Oxford Extra-Mural Delegacy, we now know that Williams first gave a course entitled 'Culture and Environment' in the academic year 1946–7; the resonant title 'Culture

---

[34] Longman's to J. L. Hammond, 11 Oct. 1944, quoted in Weaver, *The Hammonds*, 255.

[35] Weaver, *The Hammonds*, 255–6.

[36] There is a large literature on this: for immediately relevant material, see Tom Steele, *The Emergence of Cultural Studies 1945–65* (1997); Lawrence Goldman, *Dons and Workers: Oxford and Adult Education since 1850* (Oxford, 1995).

:

and Society' appears as early as 1948–9.[37] An early article by Williams in the journal *Use of English* in 1950 discussed 'Books for teaching "Culture and Environment"', a theme he regarded as 'of fundamental importance, particularly to students and teachers of English'. What the teacher should aim at, he insisted, was to go beyond 'particular studies in cultural forms' to undertake a 'fuller cultural analysis of our kind of society'. Williams was, of course, here working in a vein pioneered by the Leavises and their *Scrutiny* associates, as he acknowledged, but he professed himself unhappy with the 'minority' emphasis of that work. 'In any case', he added, 'one ought to use books like those of J. L. and Barbara Hammond (*The Bleak Age*, which is excellent, as well as *The Town Labourer* and *The Village Labourer*).' The short bibliography recommends using the 1948 Penguin reprint of *The Bleak Age* and the Guild Books edition of *The Village Labourer*, published in the same year.[38] He drew on this latter edition in another practical article published two years later where he based an exercise for a writing-class on a passage from the chapter on 'The Last Labourers' Revolt'.[39]

The contemporary debate about 'culture' to which Williams addressed himself in these early courses was associated with the names of Clive Bell, F. R. Leavis and T. S. Eliot, writers whom he represented, perhaps not altogether adequately, as clinging to a notion of culture as the precious, time-less possession of a minority threatened by the democratisation of society in the twentieth century. Williams sought to relativise this defensive and superior notion by tracing a much longer and more complex genealogy for the idea of culture. His larger ambition was to extrapolate from the notion of culture as 'a whole way of life' to provide a more inclusive and enabling conception which would encompass forms of working-class organisation and solidarity. However, in so doing, he in effect tied the emergence of the concept of culture itself to the great rupture in English history which marked the arrival of a 'new civilization' at the end of the eighteenth century. In 1953 he contributed an essay to the recently founded Oxford-based journal *Essays in Criticism*, arguing that 'The idea of Culture . . . is an aspect of that larger and more deeply complex response which men of the nineteenth and twentieth centuries

[37] *Border Country: Raymond Williams in Adult Education*, ed. John McIlroy and Sally Westwood (Leicester, 1993), 289–90; see also R. Fieldhouse, 'Oxford and Adult Education', in *Raymond Williams: Politics, Education, Letters*, ed. W. J. Morgan and P. Preston (Basingstoke, 1993).

[38] Raymond Williams, 'Books for Teaching "Culture and Environment"', *Use of English*, 2 (1950), 177–8. It is worth remarking that the origins of the *Labourer* trilogy lay in a never-realised project by Lawrence Hammond to write a life of Cobbett (see J. L. and Barbara Hammond, '"A Socialist Fantasy": A Reply', *Quarterly Review*, 252 (1929), 290); three-quarters of a century later, Raymond Williams exhibited the same sense of genealogy in choosing Cobbett as his preferred 'Past Master' (Raymond Williams, *Cobbett* (Oxford, 1984)).

[39] Raymond Williams, 'Culture and Environment II', *Use of English*, 4 (1952), 183.

have made to the Industrial Revolution and its consequences.'[40] This 1953 essay was the germ of what is still perhaps Williams's most famous book, published in 1958, *Culture and Society*. Actually, that book's full title is *Culture and Society, 1780–1950*: the dates are now often omitted in references to it, but they signal something crucial to its argument – and to mine. From its opening sentences, the book is presented as an account of (and note the use of the first person plural) 'our responses in thought and feeling to the changes in English society since the late eighteenth century'. And in his conclusion he summarises the argument in similar terms: 'The history of the idea of culture is a record of our reactions, in thought and feeling, to the changed conditions of our common life . . . The working-out of the idea of culture is a slow reach again for control.'[41] At first reading, that use of 'again' can slip by almost unnoticed, though as one ponders the passage it comes to seem to be bearing a heavy historical load.

I shall not here dwell on the ways in which Williams's classic account actually provides an oddly selective and tendentious narrative if understood (as that book usually is understood) as a history of conceptions of 'culture' in Britain during the century and half he covers.[42] Instead, my focus is on the way in which the conception of the book expresses a particular historiographical perspective, one preoccupied with the question of the moral damage wrought by the arrival in the late eighteenth century of a 'new kind of society'. This is a matter of structure at least as much as of content: it was not that Williams and others who continued to work within that perspective in the middle of the twentieth century actually recommended some notional return to a pre-industrial form of society, but rather that their thinking about this issue was conditioned by a sometimes explicit but usually implicit assumption that, as a result of this unparalleled historical shift, the concept of 'culture' came into being to function as a counter to, or check upon, the operation of a uniquely ruthless economic logic. There is in fact very little direct discussion of social and economic developments in *Culture and Society*, and

---

[40] Raymond Williams, 'The Idea of Culture', *Essays in Criticism*, 3 (1953), 244. Of the disputed term 'Industrial Revolution', he wrote: 'The economic and social changes which the term indicates are real enough, and I do not subscribe to the tendency to play down their importance which has been evident in the work of some recent historians' (244). For Williams's close involvement with *Essays in Criticism* during this period, see Williams, *Politics and Letters*, 84–6.

[41] Raymond Williams, *Culture and Society, 1780–1950* ((1958) Harmondsworth, 1961), 11, 285; hereafter page references are given in the text.

[42] I attempted to support this criticism in the unpublished paper referred to in Winch, 'Mr Gradgrind', 249 n. 19: 'The Origins of Cultural Criticism: The Culture-and-Society Tradition Re-Visited'; this paper has not yet been revised for publication. The shortcomings of the historical account provided by Williams are noted, from a different perspective, in the excellent recent study by Philip Connell, *Romanticism, Economics, and the Question of 'Culture'* (Oxford, 2001), esp. 1–12, 276–84.

none at all of the nature of society in pre-industrial England. As later commentators have frequently remarked, the book stays very close to 'the words on the page' of the works by his chosen authors in ways that bespeak Williams's early training in Cambridge English. Nonetheless, the selection and interpretation of the writers who make up what has ever since been referred to as 'the culture-and-society' tradition is driven by a fundamentally historical argument. The traditional and customary checks on profit-maximising having been destroyed by the Industrial Revolution understood as a moral catastrophe, the need had ever since been to find a replacement in what Williams, following T. S. Eliot, called 'culture as a whole way of life' (229–30). Previously unnecessary as a separate category, 'culture' now served a remedial or corrective function. Unless one reconstructs the logic of Williams's argument in this way, it is very hard to see how he could propose forms of working-class social organization such as 'the trade unions, the cooperative movement, or a political party' as central to the expanded concept of 'culture', as he does in his long concluding chapter (285–324). But the equivalence of function between, say, deliberately wrought objects of beauty and, say, the Factory Acts, where both are seen as expressing some alternative ideal to the pursuit of profit, was the merest commonplace to the Hammonds and their many thousands of readers.

McIlroy is simply summarising the conventional wisdom in English studies, echoed in countless primers and textbooks, when he writes that *Culture and Society* 'was and remains a major achievement in its reconstitution of a lost or suppressed tradition of opposition to the organisation of society since the industrial revolution'.[43] But there are assumptions at work here which have become so familiar that we are in danger of ceasing to notice their oddity. Williams's book, it is said, recovers a 'lost or suppressed tradition of opposition'. Really? Burke, Wordsworth, Carlyle, Mill, Newman, Ruskin, Arnold – these are hardly 'lost and suppressed' figures in the nineteenth century any more than are Lawrence, Eliot, Orwell and company in the twentieth. The claim only makes sense, insofar as it does, on the assumption that there has been one clearly dominant form of 'the organisation of society since the Industrial Revolution', and, no less remarkably, one which has also been pretty unchanging during that long period, one which excluded the very diverse preoccupations of those influential and widely admired writers. But that, I think, *is* the premise of Williams's book, as it had been the premise of that tradition of discourse which saw economic developments in late eighteenth-century England as marking a great ethical divide. As Williams himself summarises this part of his argument, the emergence of the concept of 'culture' expresses 'the recognition of the practical

---

[43] McIlroy, *Border Country*, 305.

separation of certain moral and intellectual activities from the driven impetus of a new kind of society' (17). With that premise in place, he can go in search of various precursors for the still-continuing attempts to find an alternative to that system in England (as he, like most of his contemporaries, at this point unselfconsciously referred to the country in which he lived); that is why it is a narrative of '*our* responses'.

Another way to bring out the structuring force of this historical interpretation in Williams's book is to ask why it begins where it does. After all, the relevant modern sense of the actual *word* 'culture' only came into currency in the middle of the nineteenth century, and it does not in fact figure in the early chapters of the book.[44] It was, surely, the familiar historiographical interpretation of the ethical significance of the Industrial Revolution that led Williams to begin his story in 1780. This ethical framework is also evident in the assumption that there had been a need, since the Industrial Revolution, for a tradition of 'opposition to the organisation of society' in a way that was not true for earlier periods, which had therefore not needed to project their values and aspirations onto the corrective, oppositional, idea of 'culture'. As he put it at one point in *Culture and Society*: 'Over the England of 1821 there had, after all, to be some higher Court of Appeal' (64). Williams evidently reckoned, as his use of 'after all' begins to suggest, that his readers would find it self-evident why this need existed in 1821 but had not done so in 1721 or 1621 or any earlier years.

Although, as I indicated above, some of Williams's later work gave a sharply critical account of certain literary forms of twentieth-century nostalgia for pre-industrial society seen as part of a longer tradition of idealising the rural, it remained the case that *Culture and Society* did more than any other single volume to shape understandings of the category of 'culture' appealed to in modern academic literary scholarship, even when all reference to interpretations of *English* history has disappeared.[45] In the field-defining volume, *Re-Drawing the Boundaries* which appeared a decade ago under the auspices of the American Modern Language Association, the chapter on 'Cultural Criticism' explicitly founds that activity on the narrative provided by Williams's book. This, as Gerald Graff and Bruce Robbins summarise it, traces the development of an idea of 'culture' as '"a court of appeal" against the divisions and fragmentations of industrial society'. Placing the project of 'cultural criticism' at the

---

[44] Only in Chapter 6 do we reach the point (with Arnold's use of 'culture') 'which at last gives the tradition a single watchword and a name' (124).

[45] Williams himself may have been somewhat ambivalent about the enduring success of this book, given his own sense of having moved well beyond it in his later thinking: 'It is not a book I could conceive myself writing now . . . It is a book most distant from me'; *Politics and Letters*, 107.

heart of contemporary literary study, Graff and Robbins see that activity as founded on what they call 'a concept of culture that is presumed to be "critical", an antidote for a dissociated and disembodied social actuality.'[46] Or as Robbins re-states the point elsewhere: modern literary studies are, following Williams, working with 'a concept of "culture" that is "critical" – set against social actuality – *by its very definition*'.[47] This may indeed accurately reflect the self-understanding of many modern literary scholars, but building this function into the *definition* of culture surely ties it too closely to this one, highly disputable, account of its origin. A further danger this then brings in its train is that of implying that only 'industrial society' has such 'divisions and fragmentations', and that the very concept of 'culture' had been unnecessary before, since in earlier periods the 'wholeness' it allegedly posits had been part of 'social actuality'. Lurking behind the self-conscious radicalism of such accounts is the shadow of a much older historiographical interpretation of the significance of 'the Industrial Revolution in England', a framework which, when made explicit, may now appear both dated and parochial.

III

In his recent study, *Culture: The Anthropologists' Account*, Adam Kuper observes that 'Culture is always defined in opposition to something else.'[48] In the work of early twentieth-century anthropologists that 'something else' was most often race, biology or evolutionism; for others it has been by turns the social system, or the functional or workaday world, or the superficial or inauthentic or, particularly in the tradition I have been examining, all those activities we group under the heading of 'the economic'. Certainly, in any fuller account of conceptions of 'culture' during this period one would need to attend to the usage (or, in practice, usages) that emerged from mid-nineteenth-century German social thought and then were elaborated in the work of German and American anthropologists in the 1890s and 1900s, especially through the writings of Franz Boas and his pupils, before coming to pervade the social sciences and to spill out into general educated discourse in the 1920s and 1930s.[49] The hallmark of the anthropological sense

[46] Gerald Graff and Bruce Robbins, 'Cultural Criticism', in *Re-Drawing the Boundaries: The Transformation of English and American Literary Studies*, ed. Stephen Greenblatt and Giles Gunn (New York, 1992), 422, 433.

[47] Bruce Robbins, *Secular Vocations: Intellectuals, Professionalism, Culture* (1993), 60 (italics in the original).

[48] Adam Kuper: *Culture: The Anthropologists' Account* (Cambridge, MA, 1999), 14.

[49] These developments are charted in considerable detail in the work of George Stocking; see especially *Race, Culture, and Evolution: Essays in the History of Anthropology* (New York, 1968), and *After Tylor: British Social Anthropology 1888–1951* (1996).

is the use of 'cultures' in the plural, those patterns of practices and beliefs that are supposed to define the quiddity of various social groups. 1911, the year of the Hammonds' *Village Labourer*, also saw one minor landmark in this development when W. H. R. Rivers gave his presidential address to the anthropological section of the British Association for the Advancement of Science on 'The ethnological analysis of culture', in which he argued against a single evolutionary scheme through which 'lower' races developed into 'higher', and in favour of the close observation and unhierarchical classification of 'cultures' in the plural.[50]

However, these different senses soon began to infect each other, and usage of the term has rarely been exact. For a pertinent example of such crossover, one has only to recall how frequently the Leavises invoked the model of anthropology in their early studies of 'mass civilisation': Queenie Leavis's first book, *Fiction and the Reading Public*, had, in its PhD form, been subtitled 'A Study in Social Anthropology',[51] and it is a noticeable (and otherwise curious) fact that the one discipline other than literary criticism that was heavily colonised by Leavisites was anthropology, a discipline that could be seen, after all, as also exploring those societies which, like Shakespeare's or Bunyan's England but unlike the England of 'the machine age', had a living 'culture'.[52] But of course, the Leavises were only trading on the anthropological sense, not using it in any pure form. For, in the anthropological sense, no group is without its distinctive 'culture', whereas the Leavises represented the city-dwellers of the nineteenth and twentieth centuries as having 'lost' their culture, a strongly normative sense of the term that re-affirmed in their own distinctive idiom the close relationship between the 'minority culture' now defended by literary criticism and 'the living culture' of pre-industrial England.[53] In practice, the broader intellectual diffusion of the anthropological sense of culture had in the first instance often subserved similar purposes. As Williams himself observed in *Culture and Society*:

> We have been given new illustrations of an alternative way of life. In common thinking, the medieval town and the eighteenth-century village have been replaced, as examples, by various kinds of recent simple societies. These can re-assure us that the version of life that industrialism has forced on us is neither universal nor permanent. (229)

[50] W. H. R. Rivers, 'The Ethnological Analysis of Culture', in *Psychology and Ethnology*, ed. G. E. Smith (1926), 120–40.

[51] Q. D. Leavis, *Fiction and the Reading Public* (1932); for the subtitle of the PhD version, see Ian McKillop, *F. R. Leavis: A Life in Criticism* (1995), 130.

[52] There seems to be no proper scholarly account of this interesting aspect of (in particular) immediately post-Second World War academic and intellectual life in Britain; my own understanding of it owes most to a correspondence with Professor D. F. Pocock, one of the early migrants from literature to anthropology.

[53] E.g.: 'The English people did once have a culture'; 'This culture the progress of the nineteenth century destroyed' and so on; F. R. Leavis and Denys Thompson, *Culture and Environment: The Training of Critical Awareness* (1933), 2–3; F. R. Leavis, *For Continuity* (1933), 165.

I have already indicated why Graham Hough's first thoughts about including Raymond Williams in his list of 'happy peasants' may not have been wholly wrong, and we may now return to the second of my opening quotations, since the episode in which it occurred brought several of my themes together in a particularly revealing way. Hough, it will be recalled, was addressing the debate around C. P. Snow's notion of 'the two cultures'. So great has been the volume of attention subsequently devoted to that notion, above all in its educational implications, that it is easy now to overlook how much of Snow's case, as well as of its immediate and often very heated reception, turned on the evaluation of the human consequences of the Industrial Revolution.[54] In his original lecture of 1959, Snow had charged most intellectuals, 'in particular literary intellectuals', with being 'natural Luddites' in their failure to understand and appreciate the benefits of the Industrial Revolution, and in preparing his 'The Two Cultures: A Second Look' four years later he solicited the help of leading eighteenth-century historians to bolster his case in the face of Leavis's notoriously swingeing dismissal of Snow and the 'technologico-Benthamite civilization' he represented.[55] As Snow put it in the published form of his response: 'It is important for the pre-industrial believers to confront the social historians', and he quoted J. H. Plumb on the delusions of historical nostalgia, and cited the researches of British and French demographic historians on the appalling facts of mortality in pre-industrial society.[56]

As part of these behind-the-scenes discussions, Snow's friend J. H. Plumb promised to summarise the latest historical work 'about the historical findings on the Industrial Revolution', and he then went on, in a passage that is particularly telling for the purposes of my argument:

> One would like to tackle Raymond Williams, Hoggart and Leavis as a group on this subject. These are the dangerous descendants of the craft Socialists – the Chestertons, Coles, ultimately Morrises, who wanted to turn their backs on industrialization and, as

[54] For this point, and a fuller account of the reception as a whole, see Stefan Collini, 'Introduction', in C. P. Snow, *The Two Cultures* (Cambridge, 1993), vii–lxxi.

[55] Snow, *Two Cultures*, 22. Leavis's 'Two Cultures? The Significance of C. P. Snow' had appeared in the *Spectator*, 9 Mar. 1962, and was re-printed in Leavis, *Nor Shall My Sword: Discourses on Pluralism, Compassion, and Social Hope* (1972). Snow's consultations with eighteenth-century historians can be documented from his correspondence in the HRHRC, Austin Texas; 'The Two Cultures: A Second Look' appeared in 1963 and is included in Snow, *Two Cultures*, 53–100.

[56] Snow, *Two Cultures*, 82–4. The passage he quotes from Plumb and describes as coming from 'one of his attacks on the teaching of a pretty-pretty past' was actually composed by Plumb, at Snow's request, expressly for inclusion in 'A Second Look'; see Snow to Plumb 3 Sept. 1963 (copy), Snow papers, HRHRC, Texas. The original of this letter is in the J. H. Plumb Papers, Cambridge University Library (I am grateful to David Cannadine for alerting me to the availability of these as-yet uncatalogued papers and to Bill Noblett of the CUL staff for assistance in consulting them).

most people do, tried to find an historical justification for that attitude and found it –
[?]uncertainly – in Barbara and J. L. Hammond.[57]

The politics of this speculative genealogy may strike some readers as
rather confused, since few people would now put the author of *Marxism
and Literature* and *The Country and the City* in the same camp as, say, the
author of the 'Father Brown' stories. But in terms of the controversy
to which Plumb was responding, his grouping possessed a certain logic,
albeit one informed by political antipathy, and it is certainly grist to my
case to find him making this link with the Hammonds and to note his
belief that, as late as 1962, their account of the Industrial Revolution was
still playing a part, perhaps even a 'dangerous' part, in contemporary
debate.

More generally, it is noticeable how by this date the catastrophist
interpretation of eighteenth-century English history was coming to seem
dated among historians, its waning ethical power now assumed to be
felt principally by the literary critics. Writing in the following year about
'the crisis in the humanities', Plumb again took aim at those responsible
for perpetuating hostility to the Industrial Revolution, declaring 'It runs
like dry rot through literary criticism.'[58] Plumb's surveyor's report on the
condition of literary criticism was ungenerous in several respects, not least
because the fungus he identifies had initially spread from the neighbouring
house of Clio. But it was true that what had once been a widely shared
perspective was now coming to be seen as in various ways sectarian.[59]
Another of the historians whose help Snow solicited in the early 1960s,
and who contributed to the argument of 'A Second Look', was Peter
Laslett, and a sentence from the opening chapter of his celebrated *The
World We Have Lost*, first published in 1965, struck a more contemporary
note and perhaps provided something of an epitaph for the tradition I
have been discussing. 'Our whole view of ourselves', wrote Laslett, 'is
altered if we cease to believe that we have lost some more humane, much
more natural pattern of relationships than industrial society can offer.'[60]

The assumptions underlying the tradition I have been discussing have
proved, I would suggest in conclusion, more a hindrance than a help in
trying to think about the complex knot of issues that the term 'culture'
now designates, especially that tradition's reliance on a rickety structure

[57] Plumb to Snow, 1 July 1962; Snow Papers, HRHRC, Texas.

[58] J. H. Plumb, 'The Historian's Dilemma', in *Crisis in the Humanities*, 42.

[59] In a fuller account, one would need to place the work of E. P. Thompson in relation to
the debates discussed here. The affinities between his *The Making of the English Working Class*
(1963) and the work of the Hammonds was widely remarked, though for many historians
this only indicated, by the mid-1960s, its dated and sectarian character. For some suggestive
observations on Thompson in relation to Leavis and Williams, see Winch, 'Mr Gradgrind
and Jerusalem', esp. 250–6, 264–6.

[60] Peter Laslett, *The World We Have Lost* ((1965), 2nd edn, 1971), 249.

which makes 'culture' oppositional to a 'society' driven by unchecked economic rationality, but integral to other, less ruthless forms of 'society'. Too much of the talk about 'culture' in mid-twentieth-century Britain was premised on assumptions of a moral Fall at an earlier point in history, and of culture as a kind of bandage for the wound, a legacy inherited from the earlier animating concern with the selfishness of the 'new kind of society'. This tradition did more than just make a useful working distinction between 'culture' and 'society': it erected a binary but asymmetrical divide in which the activity of the modern world is largely classed on the 'society' side and assumed to be governed by a narrow and implacable economic logic, while under 'culture' are grouped those disparate attempts to oppose or criticise this logic, whether in the name of art, solidarity, human flourishing or any similar kind of 'higher' ideal. As part of this pattern, the idea of 'the village community', having begun life in the political-legal world of the Victorian Whig historians as a way of establishing or contesting the legitimacy of political institutions and forms of property-holding, went on to figure in early twentieth-century social criticism as the antithesis to the unchecked economic egoism of industrial society – and then perhaps eked out the last days of its existence by haunting the Cambridge English Tripos.

Debates about 'culture' have moved on since the period on which this essay has focused: it is surely now less common for culture to be spoken of as an antidote to 'the selfishness system' and more common to find it accompanied by concerns about 'elitism', 'inclusiveness' and so on. But what I have been talking about is perhaps not entirely a world we have lost. It was, after all, not so long ago that one observer remarked that in the eyes of many Tories 'the Arts Council is the Labour party in a smock'.[61] Reflecting on the trajectory traced in this essay, one can see a teasing but appropriate uncertainty in whether the offending garment should be thought of as an artist's or a peasant's smock.

---

[61] Bernard Crick, 'Intellectuals and the British Labour Party', *Revue Française de Civilisation Brittanique*, 4 (1980), 18.

ELIZABETH I AND THE EXPANSION OF ENGLAND

A Conference held at the National Maritime Museum, Greenwich, 4–6 September 2003

Transactions of the RHS 14 (2004), pp. 119–22 © 2004 Royal Historical Society
DOI: 10.1017/S0080440104000246   Printed in the United Kingdom

INTRODUCTION

By Simon Adams

The four hundredth anniversary of the death of Elizabeth I and the accession of James I inspired a number of conferences, the majority seemingly devoted to the new Stuart Britain. The last queen of England received her commemoration in the exhibition *Elizabeth* held at the National Maritime Museum from May to September 2003.[1] The Museum and the Royal Historical Society also agreed to sponsor a conference to accompany the exhibition. Nigel Rigby, head of research, and Robert Blyth, curator of imperial and maritime history, organised both the mounting of the conference and the subsequent editing of the papers with the consummate professionalism that has become the National Maritime Museum's hallmark.

Fairly early on in the preparations it was agreed that the conference should close the exhibition, although an unfortunate previous booking on 7 September prevented the conference itself from concluding on Elizabeth's birthday. Given the location, a maritime emphasis was irresistible, and the title 'Expansion of England' was then shamelessly plundered from the second volume of A. L. Rowse's portrait of the Elizabethan Age. A more immediate text was Richard Hakluyt's proud if not bombastic claim in the dedication to the first edition of *The Principal Navigations, Voiages and Discoveries of the English Nation* that 'in this famous and peerless government of her most excellent majesty, her subjects . . . in searching the most opposite corners and quarters of the world . . . have excelled all the nations and peoples of the earth'.

The range of possible subjects encouraged the exploitation of a wide variety of scholarly expertise, the panel of speakers being selected jointly by the National Maritime Museum and the Royal Historical Society. To avoid yet another explosion of the myth of Elizabeth I, the conference was given a deliberately neutral stance with contributors encouraged to take whatever positions they chose.[2] David Starkey, guest curator of the exhibition, provided the opening address. As the conference proceeded it

---

[1] See the catalogue, *Elizabeth: The Exhibition at the National Maritime Museum*, ed. Susan Doran (2003).

[2] The 'Myth' was the subject of a conference held at St Mary's College, Strawberry Hill, in July 2002; see *The Myth of Elizabeth*, ed. Susan Doran and Thomas S. Freeman (Basingstoke, 2003).

became clear that despite its formal structure it was implicitly addressing two broad questions, and these in turn have shaped the present order of the papers. The first was how England's place in the world changed during the second half of the sixteenth century. The second was would this have occurred whoever had been on the throne?

The reality of the myth of an heroic age of maritime endeavour forms an initial sub-theme of its own. If the supreme artistic celebration of the Elizabethan Navy – the Armada Tapestries – was destroyed with the Old Palace of Westminster, the tapestries themselves are commemorated *in situ* in the House of Lords in John Singleton Copley's *Death of the Earl of Chatham*. Moreover, as Karen Hearn shows in her detailed study of a fanciful painting of the defeat of the Armada, the tapestries were merely the grandest of numerous depictions of the Armada battles privately commissioned in subsequent decades. Charles Knighton and Nicholas Rodger explore the naval heritage further. The scale of naval operations after 1660 effectively made the Elizabethans irrelevant as direct examples, yet men as knowledgeable as Samuel Pepys were still very conscious of living in their shadow. The heroic image of the Elizabethan Navy was further politicised by seventeenth- and eighteenth-century debates over naval policy. Haunting the gentlemen versus tarpaulins debate was the ghost of Drake, implicitly or explicitly the greatest of the tarpaulins.

But the myth rested on solid foundations, as two surveys of the technical aspects of maritime expansion reveal. The assessments of the growth of English navigational skills and map-making by Susan Rose and Peter Barber are clear evidence of the advances of 1603 on 1558. No less important was the contemporary interest in travel literature, which, William Sherman argues, reveals a Hakluyt appealing to an audience already in existence. Among the voyages Hakluyt celebrated (albeit in his second edition) was William Harborne's establishing of direct commercial contact with Constantinople in the 1580s. The late Susan Skilliter published much of the related correspondence between Elizabeth and the sultan Murad III, which is here reprised by Lisa Jardine. The Turkey trade also had its nuts and bolts aspect. The principal attraction of England to Murad III, like Ivan the Terrible and the sharif of Morocco, Mulay Ahmed, was ordnance, of which Elizabethan England was the chief manufacturer in Europe.[3]

If the reality of Elizabethan naval power – the best ships and guns in Europe – shaped the international perception of England, there was also an intellectual shift. Despite the perennial argument about England's peripheral place in Europe, Charles Giry-Deloison and Peter Lake reveal how the events of Elizabeth's reign were also European. If it is no surprise

---

[3] See Simon Adams, 'Britain, Europe and the World', in *The Shorter Oxford History of the British Isles: The Sixteenth Century 1485–1603*, ed. Patrick Collinson (Oxford, 2002), 205–7.

to find from Giry-Deloison's detailed survey of contemporary French printed literature on England that the fate of the Queen of Scots took centre stage, the volume of publications is still revealing. Much may have been propaganda, either public relations exercises by the Elizabethan government or the Catholic *ligue* retailing horror stories of the cruelties suffered by English Catholics, but the very existence of these propaganda campaigns was itself significant. Even that most apparently introverted subject, the English succession, had its wider resonance. As Peter Lake shows, the Stuart claim of indefeasible right to the English throne, whether argued by Mary or James VI, had an immediate impact in France, where the contemporary succession debate raised similar issues. If James VI's *True Lawe of Free Monarchies* has traditionally been seen as a rebuttal to George Buchanan, it was no less a response to Robert Persons's succession tracts. Fundamental to the wider defence of absolute monarchy was the freeing of the succession from regulation by an external power.

But did Elizabeth I herself matter? One important sub-theme illustrated by Maurice Howard as well as by Barber and Hearn is the lack of interest of this profoundly literary woman in the visual arts and her diffidence about her own image.[4] In the absence of active royal patronage – as found under Henry VIII or Charles I – propagation of the regime's image rested effectively in private hands. Yet at the same time it is one of the paradoxes of Elizabeth that she surrounded herself with men who were fascinated by the visual arts, as well as maps and geography. It was, after all, Sir Francis Walsingham to whom Hakluyt dedicated *The Principal Navigations* in 1589, not the queen.

On this level there are strong reasons for denying Elizabeth any personal role in an expansion of England in her reign. Indeed, David Armitage disputes whether the Elizabethans had any concept of empire at all. This was certainly true of her attitude towards the other inhabitants of the British Isles. Roger Mason argues that Elizabeth was almost completely unresponsive to the concept of Britain, which, with a few exceptions, caught Scottish imaginations rather than English. In a persuasive survey of contemporary Irish historical writing Hiram Morgan argues that Elizabeth failed decisively to rise to the challenge of being queen of Ireland. All three effectively give the Stuarts the credit – negative or positive – for the founding of a British Empire.

The argument that Elizabeth can claim no credit for the achievements of her reign was first popularised by J. A. Froude and has been sustained more recently by Wallace MacCaffrey and Christopher Haigh. But Elizabeth also made a virtue of her lack of ambition for territorial

---

[4] An exception can be made for the portrait miniature, of which Elizabeth was at least a collector.

expansion, as the editor argues in his account of her response to the two separate offers of sovereignty from the Netherlands. The reign opened and closed with the surrenders of foreign garrisons in Britain, the French at Leith in 1560 and the Spanish at Kinsale in 1602. In both cases the garrisons were supplied with passage back to their homelands. These were civilised gestures in which Elizabeth took great pride and were, whatever had occurred in the interval, how she wished to be remembered. Hakluyt's 'peerless government' thus unites myth and reality. The later sixteenth century saw the battle between the ancients and the moderns begin in earnest. By 1603 there was a wide perception that great personages of the age were the equals of those of the classical world, and in the case of Drake, for example, actually surpassed them. In the eyes of both domestic and international opinion, Elizabeth's place in that pantheon was assured.[5] Which brings us back full circle to the Apothecaries' Armada painting.

[5] For an excellent example of both the wider contemporary comparison between ancient and modern and Elizabeth's place in it, see the memoirs of Michel de Castelnau, sieur de Mauvissière, the French ambassador in England 1575–85, most conveniently published in *Collection complète des mémoires relatifs à l'histoire de France*, ed. C. B. Petitot, XXIII (Paris, 1823).

Transactions of the RHS 14 (2004), pp. 123–40 © 2004 Royal Historical Society
DOI: 10.1017/S0080440104000222   Printed in the United Kingdom

ELIZABETH I AND THE SPANISH ARMADA:
A PAINTING AND ITS AFTERLIFE*
By Karen Hearn

ABSTRACT. A well-known painting owned by the Worshipful Society of Apothecaries of London, *Elizabeth I and the Spanish Armada*, has long presumed to have been made in around 1588. By examining both internal and contextual evidence, however, this paper establishes that the work instead dates from during the reign of James I. It unpicks the multiple layers of events that are depicted simultaneously within the image, and suggests some of the diverse influences operating on the unidentified artist(s) and unknown patron. Finally, it examines the new purposes for which the work was to be appropriated in the mid-nineteenth century at the time of its presentation to the Apothecaries.

This paper focuses on a remarkable painting in the collection of the Worshipful Society of Apothecaries of London (Figure 1). It is usually known as 'Elizabeth I and the Spanish Armada', and during the twentieth century it was included in a number of exhibitions.[1] It has always been presumed to be roughly contemporary with the action depicted within it, and therefore has frequently been used in magazines and popular books as a useful illustration for any account of the Armada campaign. Mr John Nussey presented the painting to the Society of Apothecaries in 1846. Nussey was a leading member of that society, and significantly he was official Apothecary to the young Queen Victoria. It is still displayed at Apothecaries Hall in London.

---

* In 1996 I was asked by the Society to undertake research into this work and delivered my initial findings as the Society's Gideon de Laune lecture on 29 April 1997. I am extremely grateful to Professor Rodney H. Taylor for inviting me to embark on this project and to Major Charles O'Leary, Colonel Stringer, Dai Williams and Dee Cook of the Society for all their assistance.
[1] Oil on canvas, 121.3 × 284.5 cm (47 3/4 × 112 in); lent *inter alia* to *Armada 1588–1988* exhibition, National Maritime Museum [herafter NMM], Greenwich, 1988. *Armada* (official catalogue) [hereafter *Armada NMM*], ed. M. J. Rodriguez-Salgado and the staff of the NMM (1988), 261, no. 14. *Dynasties: Painting in Tudor and Jacobean England 1530–1630* (catalogue of the *Dynasties* exhibition, Tate Gallery, 1995–6), ed. Karen Hearn (1995), 89, no. 44.

Figure 1 *Elizabeth I and the Spanish Armada*, unknown artist(s), early seventeenth century; oil on canvas, 121.3 × 284.5 cm (47 3/4 × 112 in) (The Worshipful Society of Apothecaries of London).

One task was to untangle whatever facts could be recovered from the myths associated with it from the moment that it appeared.[2] A major tool has been the pragmatic methodology used by a museum art historian – that is, one who has the opportunity, and indeed the privilege, to engage with the physical nature of a work, both through technical examination in collaboration with conservators[3] and through access to the minute detail in the image itself. In the case of *Elizabeth I and the Spanish Armada*, evidence gathered in this way – and combined with an analysis of the historical context – affords scope for a reassessment of the date and commission of the painting.

The picture is, on a number of counts, an almost unique survival. It is unusual in its great width and horizontal format, although obviously this is appropriate to the subject matter. The content, too, is rare, although a small number of other – and quite diverse – images exist that relate to the Armada and are of roughly similar date. It bears neither texts nor inscriptions. Nor is there a signature (or even a monogram). The picture poses three fundamental questions. Who painted it?[4] For whom was it painted? And where was it located during the centuries prior to Mr Nussey's gift of it to the Society in the mid-nineteenth century? It must be stated from the outset that, unless further documentary evidence should appear, these questions cannot be answered.

An absence of really concrete information on three such basic questions is not unusual with paintings of the sixteenth and seventeenth centuries with British contexts. Moreover, most surviving pictures of the sixteenth and early seventeenth centuries of British origin are portraits, rather than narrative images like this. The first definite mention of this painting appears in the records of the Society of Apothecaries, and it reveals that from the start there were a host of misconceptions about it. The minutes for the Meeting of the Court Assistants on 4 August 1846 state that:

> A curious and ancient picture representing Queen Elizabeth reviewing the Fleet after the defeat of the Spanish Armada painted by Hilliard in 1577 (see Walpole's Anecdotes of Painting), was presented to the Society by Mr Nussey a Member of the Court, and having been cleaned and repaired by Order of the Master and Wardens was placed in the parlour of the Hall.

---

[2] A number of specialists very generously answered queries, including the late Janet Arnold, Dr Ron Brand, Dr Remmelt Daalder, Dr Ian Friel, George Keyes, the late Mr A. V. B. (Nick) Norman and Roger Quarm.

[3] I am grateful to my colleagues Rica Jones and Joyce Townsend at Tate, and to Elizabeth Hamilton-Eddy of the NMM.

[4] Comparison with securely identified paintings by the Netherlands-based artists Hendrick Vroom, Cornelis Claesz Van Wieringen, Abraham Willaerts and Andries van Eertveld, for instance, demonstrates that it is not by any of them.

In response it was resolved that 'thanks should be given to Mr Nussey for his donation'.[5]

One obvious error is that the date given here – 1577 – considerably antedates the actual year of the sailing of the Spanish Armada in 1588. In addition, the attribution of the picture to the Elizabethan portrait-miniaturist and medallist Nicholas Hilliard (1546/7–1618) cannot be supported. No other work by Hilliard of this size or type is known. His surviving works are almost all medals or portrait miniatures – tiny images, to be held in the hand.[6] The Apothecaries' picture is painted on canvas. This form of support came into use in England for serious paintings only very late in the sixteenth century. There, discrete pictures were for the most part still painted on prepared wooden – normally Baltic oak – panels. As Maurice Howard observes elsewhere in this volume, images were also painted directly on to wall surfaces, though very few of these now survive.

The writer and collector Horace Walpole observed in his book *Anecdotes of Painting in England* (first published in four volumes during the 1760s) that Charles I had owned a number of works by Nicholas Hilliard 'particularly a view of the Spanish Armada'.[7] The detailed written catalogue of Charles I's collection made in the 1630s by Charles's curator, Abraham van der Doort, shows, however, that this item was a considerably smaller work, listed as measuring only six inches high and thirteen and a half inches wide. As van der Doort noted: 'Item the Spanish fleete in liming [that is a term often used to mean miniature-painting] of: 88: in a black frame . . . Don by ould – Hilliard which your Majesty had of Sir James Paumer.'[8] The present whereabouts of that work appears to be unknown.[9]

---

[5] Worshipful Society of Apothecaries of London, Minutes of Meetings of Court Assistants, fol. 21.

[6] For Nicholas Hilliard's *œuvre*, see Katherine Coombs, *The Portrait Miniature in England* (1998), 28–44, and Karen Hearn, *Nicholas Hilliard* (forthcoming, 2005). The probable, but by no means certain, exceptions are two larger pictures of Queen Elizabeth I, dating from *c.* 1572–5, Walker Art Gallery, Liverpool, and National Portrait Gallery (on loan to Tate Britain). Similarities to Hilliard's miniature images of the queen suggest that these two may be by him also; both are on wooden panel rather than canvas.

[7] Horace Walpole, *Anecdotes of Painting in England*, ed. Ralph N. Wornum, rev. edn (4 vols., 1888), I, 173. Incidentally, it seems certain that this work did not belong to Horace Walpole himself; see Peter Hill, *Walpole's Art Collection* (Twickenham, 1997).

[8] 'Abraham van der Doort's Catalogue of the Collections of Charles I', ed. Oliver Millar (Walpole Society, XXXVII, 1960), 121. Sir James Palmer (1584–1657) was appointed a Gentleman of the Bedchamber in 1622; a close companion of the future Charles I, he was an amateur miniature portrait painter, thought to have received some training from Hilliard.

[9] Two surviving closely related miniature images of the Armada have sometimes been mentioned in this context. Both are painted in bodycolour on vellum, the medium and support generally used at this period for portrait miniatures. They are of similar but *not* identical dimensions to the limning in Charles I's inventory, but neither can be identified as the work of Nicholas Hilliard. The first, measuring 13.3 × 31.8 cm (5 1/4 × 12 1/2 in), is in the

I would now like to look at the Apothecaries' picture in the light of known facts about the Armada. The art historian necessarily relies on the accounts of maritime and political historians.[10] The purpose of the Armada was to provide a vanguard to ensure the safe crossing of 17,000 troops, under the command of the duke of Parma, as an invading force from the Netherlands to England. The fleet itself carried a further army of about 20,000. As the English had no idea where the Spaniards would try to land, thousands of men were brought to London to protect the queen. Seventeen thousand of these were grouped under the earl of Leicester at Tilbury to prevent an attack via the Thames. To prevent Spanish access, a boom, constructed of chains and ships' cables, was arranged across the river from Tilbury to Gravesend.

The Armada set sail on 22 July 1588, and was sighted on 29 July off Cornwall. It seems that there is still considerable doubt as to the exact locations of the Spanish and English fleets during this campaign. The clearest indications appear in the charts made afterwards by Robert Adams, surveyor of the queen's buildings. These were commissioned by the lord admiral, Charles, Lord Howard of Effingham, and were based on his account of the action.[11] Engravings were made by Augustine Ryther after Adams's charts to accompany an official history of the campaign, written by the Florentine Petruccio Ubaldini and published in 1590.[12] The engravings are notable for showing two successive actions in one frame – as does the Apothecaries' painting. Once an engraving had been made

---

National Maritime Museum, London (*Armada NMM*, 254, formerly in the collection of the earls of Rosebery); it bears a French inscription incorporating the arms of James I ('IR') as king of England, and is therefore thought to have been made *c.* 1603–10 for presentation to James. The second, previously on loan to the Rijksmuseum, Amsterdam, between 1975 and 1995, was recently sold at auction in London (Bonhams, 10 Dec. 2003), and is currently [June 2004] with the London art dealer, Rafael Valls Ltd. Measuring 14 × 35 cm (5 1/2 × 13 3/4 in), it bears an inscription in Dutch and is signed in monogram, bottom right, 'V / HE'. Like the Apothecaries' painting, these small pictures show Spanish, English and, indeed, Dutch vessels in combat, with a representation of a coastline including beacons and a small number of figures, although in this case on the right-hand side of the image. While very similar to each other in overall effect, the two differ greatly in detail; painted in a manner that suggests a Netherlandish origin, and perhaps from the same studio, they can be interpreted as an assertion of the Protestant Dutch role as England's ally in the defeat of the Spanish Armada.

[10] The following sources have been consulted: Garrett Mattingly, *Defeat of the Spanish Armada* (Harmondsworth, 1983); Colin Martin and Geoffrey Parker, *The Spanish Armada* (1988); and *Armada NMM*.

[11] In a full-length portrait painted by Daniel Mytens in 1620 (NMM), near the end of his life, Howard was depicted wearing the robes of the Order of the Garter; and although it was thirty-two years later, Howard chose to include Armada-related ships in the background of his portrait.

[12] *Expeditionis Hispanorum in Angliam vera description Anno Do: MDLXXXVIII* (1590), reproduced in *Armada NMM*, 243–8.

of something, its image (whether accurate or not) could become known surprisingly widely and rapidly – both nationally and internationally. As will be seen, the charts were also to form the basis for the designs of a set of tapestries about the Armada – likewise commissioned by Lord Howard. The engraving of Adams's chart of the events of 30–1 July shows ninety English ships, commanded by Howard, with Sir Francis Drake as vice admiral, awaiting the Spanish at Plymouth and emerging as the Armada advances in crescent formation. Alarm beacons were lit along the coast. There was a skirmish, but the Armada pressed forward.

By 6 August, the Armada had anchored at Calais, where it was awaiting the arrival of the duke of Parma and his army. In fact, Parma was not ready to join them. After dark on the night of 7 August, the English sent eight fireships towards the Spanish vessels. This action temporarily dispersed them, and caused them to lose irreplaceable hawsers and anchors, thus forcing them out of the harbour. The next morning, 8 August, the damaged Armada was driven into battle off Gravelines. Lasting into the evening, this was the longest and fiercest battle of the campaign and a number of Spanish ships were damaged or captured. The captain-general of the Armada, the duke of Medina Sidonia, was compelled to order his fleet to escape northwards, towards Scotland and round to Ireland. But the weather quickly deteriorated, with four nights of gales, and many Spanish vessels were wrecked on the British and Irish coasts. Most of the Spaniards who did reach the shore were murdered. The remnants of the Armada limped back to their home ports.

It was, in fact, some time before the English realised the extent of their success. Thus, when Queen Elizabeth made her celebrated visit to the camp at Tilbury, on 8 and 9 August, it was only after her arrival there that news would come that the Spanish forces had been scattered and the Armada was already on the run.[13] Indeed, at that time, and for some weeks to come, a Spanish invasion still seemed an imminent possibility.

So, looking at the Apothecaries' painting (Figure 1) with these events in mind, it is clear that it does not show one single scene, but rather that it combines various key elements of the Armada story – elements that had passed very quickly into legend. Moreover, although the prints after Adams's charts are the best visual evidence that survive, no artist is known to have been present at any of these encounters. In the Apothecaries' picture, the alarm beacons are shown flaming away along an exotic rocky landscape evidently meant to represent the English coast. In reality, they probably did not take this exact form – they were bonfires and braziers – but they were indeed lit, and the Spanish commented on seeing

---

[13] For a detailed account of the visit, see Miller Christy, 'Queen Elizabeth's Visit to Tilbury in 1588', *English Historical Review*, 34 (1919), 43–61. See also Susan Frye, 'The Myth of Elizabeth I at Tilbury', *Sixteenth Century Journal*, 23 (1992), 95–114.

them.[14] Eight years later, in 1596, a Venetian visitor, Francis Gradenigo, described the English early warning system: the hills near the coast were topped with 'braziers, filled with inflammable material which is fired by the sentinel if armed ships of the enemy are sighted'.[15]

To the right and centre of the picture is a sea battle, which must represent the action off Gravelines, as this was the only major engagement of the whole campaign. It was the first time there had been a battle at sea using broadside-firing guns, shooting from a distance, as the English did. Prior to then, fighting at sea had consisted of coming in close and grappling and boarding the enemy vessel – which was indeed what the Spanish were expecting to do. On the far right, an English galleon, which flies the Royal Standard and is thus likely to represent Lord Howard's *Ark Royal*, fires on a Spanish vessel, which flies a flag bearing a religious image. It has been suggested that this might be the *Nuestra Señora del Rosario* (Our Lady of the Rosary), which was specifically recorded as losing her foremast. This event had actually happened a few days earlier, in a collision with another Spanish ship, the *Santa Catalina*, and was unconnected with any English attack, although Drake had subsequently pursued and captured the *Rosario*. The ship to the left of this is a Spanish galleass. These vessels could move under both oar and sail, and the Armada included four of them. They seem to have made a strong impression on English commentators. It is just possible that it may represent the *San Lorenzo*, a galleass which was to run aground off Calais where it was then boarded and stripped by the English. The shape of its fighting top is very characteristically Spanish, and the striped awning, under which its commanding officers stand, is in the red and yellow colours of Spain. The next vessel along flies a red and yellow Spanish ensign, and has a magnificent decorated lantern. The artist has presented the mass of boats behind more schematically and they are hard to differentiate. The two small vessels by the shore to the front are English pinnaces. These were used to carry messages and to pick up survivors.

Many of the details of the boats in the painting are, it seems, comparatively accurate and convincingly observed – right down to the stitching and the rope loops on the billowing mainsails on the *Ark Royal*, for example.[16] This suggests that the artist used as his source good-quality engravings of ships. There are just a few places where points are incorrect, the principal example being one boat where details of the rigging and indeed the entire bowsprit are missing.

---

[14] David Cressy, *Bonfires and Bells: National Memory and the Protestant Calendar in Elizabethan and Stuart England* (1989), 112.

[15] Frank Kitchen, 'War Flame', *National Trust Magazine*, 53 (Spring 1988), 21–2.

[16] Dr Ian Friel, discussion with the author, 22 Apr. 1997.

Moving again to the left, we see Queen Elizabeth and various troops. This area is evidently intended to show her visit to the great camp mustered at Tilbury. Its inclusion here testifies to the tremendous public relations value of this event, and this factor had clearly been part of the strategy from the outset. The earl of Leicester had written on 27 July to invite her: '[By coming] you shall comfort not only these thousands but [also] many more that shall hear of yt.'[17] The camp was pitched a little away from the Thames, on the steep-sided hill on which stands West Tilbury church, and extended inland for some distance. On 8 August – which turned out to be the day of the battle of Gravelines – the queen left St James's Palace and travelled down the Thames by barge. On landing, she was met by an escort of 1,000 horse and 2,000 foot. The fullest accounts of the ceremonies are both written in verse, and were published in 1588, very soon after the events described. One is by Thomas Deloney who is unlikely to have actually been present, and the other by one James Aske, apparently a soldier, who was.[18]

The queen stayed overnight at nearby Arderne Hall and revisited the camp the following day, where she formally reviewed the troops. It is not known how she was dressed; James Aske merely reported that she was:

> Most bravely mounted on a stately steede
> With trunchion in her hand (not used thereto).[19]

However, the artist depicts her holding her sceptre and, to leave no room for doubt that this is the queen, wearing her crown. Her doublet appears to be of white silk with a gold pattern; her deep plum or mulberry coloured velvet skirt is decorated with two rows of braid round the hem.[20] Her white horse is caparisoned with enormous plumes. Deloney recounts that:

> The Sergeant Trumpet, with his mace,
> and nyne with trumpets after him,
> Bare headed, went before her Grace,
> in coates of scarlet color trim.
> The King of Heralds, tall and comely,
> was the next in order duely,
> With the famous Armes of England,
> wrought with rich imbroydered gold,

---

[17] The National Archives (Public Record Office), State Papers, 12/213/79–80, cited Christy, 'Queen Elizabeth's Visit to Tilbury in 1588', 46–7.

[18] Thomas Deloney, *The Queen's visiting of the Campe at Tilsburie, with her Entertainement there* (John Wolf for Edward White, 1588); James Aske, *Elizabetha Triumphans, with a Declaration of the Manner how her Excellency was entertained by her Souldyers into her Campe Royall, at Tilbury, in Essex* (Thomas Orwin, 1588), both cited by Christy, 'Queen Elizabeth's Visit to Tilbury in 1588'.

[19] Cited Christy, 'Queen Elizabeth's Visit to Tilbury in 1588', 53.

[20] As identified by Janet Arnold, personal communication, 1997. As Susan Frye, 'The Myth of Elizabeth I at Tilbury', points out, no reliable eye-witness account exists of what Elizabeth wore at Tilbury.

On finest velvet, blue and crimson,
that for silver can be sold.[21]

It is likely that the unknown artist may have taken some details from
one of these widely available written accounts. The queen then delivered
a speech. The earliest manuscript source for the best-known version is
described as 'late 16th century or early 17th century' in the British Library,
and inscribed 'Gathered by one that heard it.' It now appears that it was
taken down by Dr Lionel Sharpe, chaplain to the earl of Leicester and
present with him at Tilbury camp. The pivot of this speech is the sentence:
'I know I have the body butt of a weake and feble woman, butt I have
the harte and stomack of a king, and of a king of England too, and take
foule scorn that Parma or any prince of Europe should dare to invade
the borders of my realm.'[22] Like so much about the Armada, these words
have become a part of legend although Susan Frye does point out that
another Tilbury oration – with a different text – was to be reported in
a sermon by William Leigh, published in 1612.[23] What is not in doubt is
that Elizabeth delivered a highly effective and rousing speech.

The queen now returned in her barge to London. It had nevertheless
been an act of considerable personal courage for her to make the
Tilbury visit, and in years to come her presence there was retrospectively
presented as a major element in the defeat of the Spanish forces. Through
her mediation, it appeared, God had taken England under his special
protection, and the 'Protestant wind' that scattered the Armada was a
proof of this. The so-called deliverance of '88 became imprinted on the
national memory.

Let us now look at evidence from the physical, the material, nature of
the painting. As mentioned earlier, it is painted in oils on canvas or rather,
on three vertical pieces of fine tabby weave linen canvas sewn together.
Each piece is about 950 mm wide. It has been suggested that it may have
been made from English canvas because an English ell measured 1140 mm
wide, while a Flemish one was much narrower, at 690 mm.[24] When the
painting went to the National Maritime Museum to be conserved in 1979,
the Society of Apothecaries gave consent for samples of paint to be taken

---

[21] Christy, 'Queen Elizabeth's Visit to Tilbury in 1588', 54.

[22] It was recently stated that the speech that subsequently became so familiar did not
appear in print until 1623, and that it did so in a document of Protestant propaganda
connected with Sharp, and written specifically against the proposed marriage of the future
Charles I with a Catholic Spanish princess (see Frye, 'The Myth of Elizabeth I at Tilbury').
However, it seems now to be agreed that the earliest surviving manuscript version, British
Library Harleian MS 6798, fo. 87, is in the handwriting of Lionel Sharpe himself, and that
it does provide a reasonably authentic account of what the queen said (Felix Pryor, *Elizabeth
I: Her Life in Letters* (2003), 98–9, 140 n. 42).

[23] Frye, 'The Myth of Elizabeth I at Tilbury', 101–2.

[24] NMM, conservation department file.

for study in cross-section. An area of the sky, seen at ×250 magnification, revealed an orange-coloured ground (bottom layer), and this is evident over the surface of the whole painting. Above it is a pale blue grey layer that is the second ground layer with which the artist broadly blocked in main areas of the composition. Grey on top of russet is a construction found commonly among early seventeenth-century paintings, particularly of Netherlands-trained artists. Although, prior to the introduction of certain synthetic pigments in the eighteenth and nineteenth centuries, it can be hard to be very period-specific about paints, none of the pigments found was inconsistent with a date of painting prior to about 1700. These cross-sections also tell us that the overall impact of the picture would once have been quite different – its present quiet, even dull colours were originally strong and bright. Early paintings can undergo various forms of irreversible physical change over time that affects how they now appear. The paint sample from the sky white lead mixed with good quality smalt. Smalt is a translucent glassy blue pigment that tends to discolour with age.[25] The sky in the Apothecaries' picture would once have been very blue.

Although the painting is highly individual, differing artistic influences can be traced within it. These come from various directions. In terms of its genre, it actually unites two different kinds of subject matter – marine painting and landscape painting. Both of these, as practices, only developed their own individual existence during the sixteenth century. Before then, landscapes and seascapes had merely formed the backgrounds of religious pictures. The first artist in whose work these elements began to dominate significantly was Flemish – Joachim Patinir, who worked in Antwerp, and died in 1524. In his imaginary rocky landscapes, with their wide sweeping vistas, he reduced the figures in his religious pictures to tiny narrative elements.[26] The next influential figure was another Fleming, Pieter Brueghel.[27] Brueghel's works became known throughout Europe through the engravings made after them, and were thus extremely influential. The print of his *Large Alpine Landscape* of 1555–6 conveys a sense of the craggy drama of the Alps through which Brueghel had travelled on his way to Italy.[28] It represents a type of image that has recently been dubbed a 'cosmic panorama' in which a landscape is seen as a birds-eye view, stretching out before the spectator – as in the

[25] On smalt, see Rica Jones, 'The Methods and Materials of Three Tudor Artists: Bettes, Hilliard and Ketel', in *Dynasties*, ed. Hearn, 231–40.

[26] For Patinir's career, see *Dictionary of Art*, ed. Jane Turner (1996), XXIV, 259–62.

[27] For Brueghel's career, *ibid.*, IV, 894–910.

[28] For Brueghel's prints, see F. W. H. Hollstein, *Dutch and Flemish Etchings, Engravings and Woodcuts*, III (Amsterdam [1960]); *Large Alpine Landscape*, 1555–6, is repr. 260.

Armada picture.[29] Brueghel's prints of seascapes and sailing vessels were also much admired. The most spectacular is the large naval battle in the Strait of Messina of 1561, recording an attack on the southern Italian coast that Brueghel himself may have witnessed.[30]

There could also be an emblematic or moralising element to marine pictures, in which human life was equated to a sea voyage and, for instance, a rock emerging from the sea was a symbol of constancy. This parallel is explicitly seen in an English portrait of 1550, Hans Eworth's portrait of Sir John Luttrell (Courtauld Institute of Art), who had fought in the coastal battle of Pinkie-Musselburgh. Its inscription likens Luttrell to a rock amid the raging seas, steadfast and constant in his allegiance.[31] Perhaps this imagery may give a clue to the exotic, rocky depiction of the landscape in the Apothecaries' painting – so very un-English in appearance. Its rocks can be read as symbolic of England's steadfastness against attack. Meanwhile, in technical terms, it is the Flemish handling of these rocks that suggests a Flemish-trained artist may be responsible for at least that area of the picture.

This painting would have been a luxury item, but it was tapestries that were the most precious possessions of monarchs and aristocrats in northern Europe. They were immensely costly, and far more highly regarded than paintings – even though it was only the wealthy who would own and/or commission a painting like the Apothecaries' example. Shortly after the Armada campaign, Howard of Effingham commissioned the great set of tapestries mentioned earlier depicting the Armada, from a Dutch weaver, Francis Spierincx, probably the most admired tapestry maker in Europe.[32] Spierincx employed a Dutch artist, Hendrick Vroom, to draw ten large cartoons showing the daily incidents of the campaign. Vroom, who was born in Haarlem around 1566, was at this time developing ship painting into a distinct genre. He seems almost single-handedly to have created a market for such pictures. Indeed it is notable that marine painting emerged as a separate specialism, just at the time that the northern Netherlands were fighting to establish their status as an independent state.[33]

Vroom took Robert Adams's charts as his source. As previously mentioned, most of these depicted two consecutive actions on one chart,

[29] Walter S. Gibson, *Mirror of the Earth: The World Landscape in Sixteenth-Century Flemish Painting* (Princeton, 1989).

[30] Pieter Brueghel, *Naval Battle in the Strait of Messina, 1561*, repr. Hollstein, *Dutch and Flemish Etchings, Engravings and Woodcuts*, III 261.

[31] See *The Portrait of Sir John Luttrell: A Tudor Mystery* (Courtauld Institute of Art, 1999).

[32] *Armada NMM*, 248–51, nos. 14.12–14.21.

[33] See Remmelt Daalder, 'Maritime History in Paintings: Seascapes as Historical Sources', in *Praise of Ships and the Sea* (Museum Boijmans van Beuningen, Rotterdam, 1996–7, and Staatliche Museen zu Berlin, 1997), 37.

and Vroom followed this example. The print of Adams's chart of the battle off Gravelines can be compared with a print after Vroom's tapestry of the same event. Each tapestry had a broad ornamental border, containing portraits of the commanders of the English fleet, with that of Howard in the middle. These exceptional luxury items were a major statement about the importance of the Armada battles, and of Howard's leading role therein. Howard took delivery of the set in 1595, paying the colossal price of £1,582.[34] In 1616 he gave them to James I. In 1650 Oliver Cromwell had them moved to the House of Lords. They remained there until their destruction in the fire of 16 October 1834 – just twelve years before Mr Nussey presented his picture. Our principal knowledge of what they looked like comes from the engravings of them, which were published in 1739 by John Pine, although it is known that Pine altered some of the original elements.[35] The prominent display of these tapestries at the heart of British government can only have reinforced the idea that the deliverance from invasion, and victory over Catholic Spain, had safeguarded the British constitution. They can be glimpsed in the celebrated painting of 1779–80 by J. S. Copley of the death of the earl of Chatham. Chatham is shown collapsing in the House of Lords, on the walls of which the Armada tapestries are clearly visible.[36] Although the hangings have been destroyed, a further idea of their impact can be gained from a surviving tapestry, also designed by Vroom and made in 1598. This depicts another naval drama – the last fight of Sir Richard Grenville's ship *Revenge* in an engagement with the Spaniards in 1591.[37]

These tapestries were not the only representations of the Armada made for English consumption at the end of the sixteenth century. The subject appears in the background of some surviving portraits of the queen, the so-called 'Armada portraits'.[38] Moreover, a handful of Dutch seventeenth-century images of the Armada also exist, for it was of course an event of considerable importance for the Protestants in the United Provinces. One example, a painting now in the Tiroler Landesmuseum Ferdinandeum in Innsbruck, *The Seventh Day of the Battle of the Armada*, is by Hendrick Vroom himself. It is thought to have been painted in about 1600, because it may be the work referred to by Karel van Mander in 1604, who stated that it had been seen 'with surprise and warm approval' by William the

---

[34] See Margarita Russell, *Visions of the Sea* (Leiden, 1983), 121, where it is stated that Howard initially displayed them at his manor in Chelsea, before installing them in 1602 in his new London residence, Arundel House, in the Strand.

[35] *Ibid.*

[36] John Singleton Copley, *The Collapse of the Earl of Chatham in the House of Lords, 7 July 1778* (1779–80, oil on canvas, 228.6 × 307.3 cm: Tate Collection, N00100).

[37] Reproduced *Armada NMM*, 279, no. 16.23.

[38] Reproduced, *inter alia*, in Janet Arnold, *Queen Elizabeth's Wardrobe Unlock'd* (Leeds, 1988), 35.

Silent's heir, Count Maurits van Nassau.[39] It too is a composite image of a number of different events. The fireships can be seen in the middle distance, with the Dunkirk to Ostend coastline beyond. The battle in the foreground may again be that off Gravelines. However, comparing the two works also demonstrates how different Vroom's handling of paint is from that in the Apothecaries' picture.

How far, therefore, can the likely creation date of the Apothecaries' picture be established? One strategy for narrowing this down is to examine specific details in the light of specialised knowledge. Both the Royal Standard, flying on the *Ark Royal*, and the tabards worn by the heralds accompanying the queen, show the English royal arms as used up to Elizabeth's death in 1603. With the union with Scotland upon the accession of James I, a new form was introduced.[40] This is the type of detail that a painter who was working considerably later might get wrong. Moreover, Janet Arnold, the costume historian, offered the view that the tall hats seen here were fashionable from about 1600 to 1610, as were the hairstyles of the three men in red doublets.

While little is known about marine flags of this period, the ensign flying from the stern of the *Ark Royal* in the painting closely resembles that recorded elsewhere from the late sixteenth century up to 1630.[41] Dr Ian Friel has commented that a key element in dating the ships seen here is the absence of any bowsprit topmasts. This is an additional mast on the bowsprit, which was first documented in the 1590s and was in common use by 1610; he considered that one would definitely expect to see it in a picture of, say, 1620.[42] Along with the fact that it is painted on canvas rather than wooden panel, these details seem to date the Apothecaries' picture to the first decade or so of the seventeenth century, and thus in the reign of James I.

From the early seventeenth century come a disparate group of English images of the Armada – though none is as technically sophisticated as the present one. Many contemporaries saw the uncovering of the Gunpowder Plot in 1605 as further evidence of divine protection for Protestant England from Catholic attack, and writers and preachers of the day explicitly linked it with the defeat of the Armada. John Heywood's play *The Second Parte of, If You Know Not Me, You Know No Bodie* (1606) showcased 'the famous Victorie of Queen Elizabeth in the Yeare 1588' and concludes with Elizabeth at Tilbury receiving news from Sir Francis

---

[39] Reproduced *Armada NMM*, 252–3, no. 14.28. See the 'Life of Henrick Cornelissen Vroom, painter of Haarlem', in Karel van Mander, *The Lives of the Illustrious Netherlandish and German Painters: From the First Edition of the Schilder-boeck (1603–1604)*, ed. H. Miedema (Doornspijk, 1994), 406–13 (fos. 287r–288v).

[40] The late Mr A. V. B. Norman, letter to the author 1997.

[41] I am grateful to Dr Timothy Wilson for his comments on the flags depicted.

[42] Dr Ian Friel discussion with the author, 22 Apr. 1997.

Drake of her navy's victory.[43] Natalie Mears has recently been researching a number of provincially commissioned and executed applied examples of Armada imagery – including wall-paintings and tomb carvings – and has found them to be associated with Puritan patrons.[44] A painting on panel of about 1610 by the otherwise unknown Robert Stephenson shows the Spanish fleet as a dragon encircling the tiny but ultimately triumphant English. It was displayed in a Lincolnshire church to remind parishioners of God's favour to England, as its inscription makes plain.[45]

The association is made even more clearly in another picture showing Elizabeth I with the Spanish Armada, a well-known painted panel in Gaywood church, near King's Lynn in Norfolk, which is actually part of a diptych – the other panel shows the trial of the conspirators of the Gunpowder Plot. An early seventeenth-century incumbent, Thomas Hales (rector 1598–1635) is said to have presented the pair.[46] These seem to be regional works, of little aesthetic sophistication, unlike the Apothecaries' picture. The text inscribed at the foot of the Gaywood picture is similar to that published in a sermon by William Leigh in 1612 as the Tilbury speech.[47] Queen Elizabeth is seen twice – once, as in the Apothecaries' painting, on the shore, and again, at the top, presiding over the entire course of events, with a cartoon-like bubble coming from her mouth with the words 'Blessed be the great God of my Salvation'. Mears has found that Hales had matriculated from the Puritan Trinity College, Cambridge, in 1588.

A further major outburst of anti-Catholic rhetoric took place around the time of the proposed marriage between the future king Charles I and a Spanish princess in 1623. This may well be the context for an image embroidered in silk on linen canvas depicting 'The Defeat of the Armada and the Gunpowder Plot', closely based on an engraving entitled *The Double Deliverance*, devised by a Puritan preacher, Samuel Ward of Ipswich, and published in Amsterdam in 1621. Within a single rectangle are shown, to the left, the Armada in the familiar crescent formation, at the centre back 'Tilbry Campe', with Philip III of Spain setting up the Gunpowder Plot at the front and to the right Guy Fawkes sneaking into

[43] Michael Dobson and Nicola J. Watson, *England's Elizabeth* (Oxford, 2002), 58–9.

[44] Natalie Mears's paper 'Wall-Paintings of the Spanish Armada and the Popularity of James VI and I in England' was delivered at the conference, *James VI and I* (Reading University, 9–11 July 2003).

[45] See *Armada NMM*, 281, no. 16.30, from the church of St Peter and St Paul, Bratoft.

[46] Francis W. Steer, 'Painting in a Norfolk Church of Queen Elizabeth at Tilbury', *Essex Review*, 53 (1944), 1–4; see also the note by Arthur Chilton in following issue (210, Apr. 1944), 68. However, Dr John Alban, Norfolk County Archivist, in a letter to the author of 25 Mar. 1997 confirms that this gift is not mentioned in Thomas Hares's will, proved 1634/5 by the Consistory Court of Norwich (181 Playford). The Armada painting is reproduced in *Armada NMM*, 282–3, no. 16.31.

[47] Quoted Frye, 'The Myth of Elizabeth I at Tilbury', 101–2.

Westminster Hall.[48] I would suggest that the details outlined above add up to an indication that the Apothecaries' picture is from slightly earlier in the seventeenth century. A Protestant individual of high status and some sophistication probably commissioned it from a currently unidentified Flemish-trained painter. Indeed, more than one painter may have been involved in making a work of this size and complexity. There seems to have been no tradition of producing paintings on canvas of this type in Britain – so, while it may have been painted here, it could also have been made in the Netherlands, where such images had first arisen, though by someone who was well briefed as to details of the events.

The subsequent popular view of the Armada was shaped by centuries of interpretation and propaganda.[49] Some of the legend evolved soon after the events in question, but much of it emanates from the nineteenth century when the continuing notion of the successful defence of the British islands by an effective navy echoed the preoccupations and aspirations of Victorian empire-makers. A clear expression of this was T. B. Macauley's patriotic poem *The Armada* of 1832, and it continued, for instance, with Charles Kingsley's historical novel *Westward Ho* of 1855. It was against this background that Mr Nussey made what, seen in this light, becomes a surprisingly resonant gift.

John Nussey (Figure 2) was born in Yorkshire in 1794, the eldest of thirteen children – the youngest of whom, Ellen, was to become known to posterity as the lifelong friend of the novelist Charlotte Bronte.[50] In 1809 he was apprenticed to his kinsman Richard Walker, the prince of Wales's Apothecary, who practised at 17 St James's Street in London. Nussey was admitted Freeman of the Society of Apothecaries in May 1816. When the prince became George IV in 1820, Nussey became Apothecary to the King's Household. Upon his marriage in 1825 to Walker's daughter Mary, Nussey moved to No. 4 Cleveland Row, opposite St James's Palace, which remained the address of his practice until his retirement in 1860. Nussey attended George IV on his deathbed, carried out the autopsy and even embalmed the body. He later told a contemporary that 'the King [had] confided to him all his secrets, and that the knowledge, if written down would set all England in a blaze'. This writer added that 'Nussey was a man deservedly esteemed; he had that gracious manner which

---

[48] See Xanthe Brooke, *The Lady Lever Art Gallery: Catalogue of Embroideries* (Stroud, 1992), 18–20, no. LL5292, where both the canvas and Ward's print are reproduced. Natalie Mears has been investigating other appropriations of this image in embroidery and in other media.

[49] A theme explored by a number of writers, most recently Michael Dobson and Nicola Watson (see n. 43 above).

[50] John T. M. Nussey, 'Walker and Nussey – Royal Apothecaries 1784–1860', *Medical History*, 14 (1970), 81–9; Helen G. Nussey, *The Nussey Family* (privately printed, 1957), and letter to author from Natalie Nussey Prior, 3 July 1997. See also Barbara Whitehead, *Charlotte Bronte and her 'Dearest Nell'* (Otley, 1993).

Figure 2 Portrait of John Nussey, by an unidentified artist (location of original unknown, here reproduced from glass negative in possession of the Worshipful Society of Apothecaries of London).

comes often from enjoying the confidence of the great.' He also attended William IV, and in 1833–4 served as Master of the Apothecaries' Society.

Upon the accession of the young Queen Victoria in 1837 he became Apothecary to her Person, a post he held until he retired. He prepared the anointing oil for her coronation and officiated at the births of several of her children, including the future Edward VII. He represented the Apothecaries' on the General Medical Council in 1858 and died at his country home in Chislehurst in 1862. It has not proved possible to locate any relevant personal documents of Nussey's, but he was clearly a keen collector of paintings. In 1861, the year before he died, Nussey sold part of his collection – more than seventy-five paintings – through Christie's auction-house.[51] From the catalogue, we can see that they were mainly Dutch, English and Flemish, with a few Italian examples. It is interesting to get an idea of his personal taste. Few of the pictures are portraits – the majority are landscapes, with seven seascapes and no fewer than fifteen river views. But none were anything like as early in date as the present picture.

It is at least possible to suggest where he first encountered the Armada painting. The Getty Trust's database of auction records reveals that a picture entitled 'Queen Elizabeth reviewing the Fleet after the defeat of the Spanish Armada' and said to be by Nicholas Hilliard was entered in a sale at Christie's on 20 November 1824 by an individual named Holmes.[52] 'Holmes' is also recorded as the name of the buyer, which presumably means that the painting failed to sell at that time, and was 'bought in'. Perhaps this was the work now owned by the Apothecaries? Christie's were – as they still are – based in King Street, St James's – just round the corner from John Nussey's practice.

When John Nussey presented this picture to the Society in 1846, his most celebrated client, Queen Victoria, had been on the throne a mere eight years. A female monarch seemed an extraordinary and alarming phenomenon to contemporaries – the previous one, Queen Anne, had died in 1714, more than 120 years earlier. Nussey's gift, however, referred back explicitly to Elizabeth I – England's greatest queen, who had presided over what posterity now viewed as a golden age. This picture, moreover, depicted her taking, as it were, an active role in the preservation of her country. Its presentation could be viewed as a vote of confidence in the new queen and as a delicate public compliment to her. But above all, it surely also emphasised to his peers Nussey's own professional association with the young queen. There may even have been an additional personal significance for, according to his granddaughter, it was a Nussey family tradition that they were descended from an illegitimate son of William (the Silent) of Nassau – one George Nusse – said to have fled to England from the duke of Alba's persecutions in the late 1560s.[53]

---

[51] Christie's, London, 17 June 1861, *Catalogue of the Small Collection of Capital Pictures by Italian, Flemish, Dutch and English Masters of John Nussey Esq Who, in Consequence of Ill-health, Is Retiring into the Country.* It consisted of eighty-one items, seventy-five of which were paintings, and was to 'be viewed at Mr Nussey's Residence, 4 Cleveland Row'.

[52] Getty Provenance Index Databases: Sale Catalogue Br-12442, lot 143, described as 'Queen Elizabeth reviewing the fleet, after the defeat of the Spanish Armada by N. Hilliard.'

[53] See Nussey, *The Nussey Family*; in fact, 'George Nusse' never existed. There was also a connection between the site of Apothecaries Hall in Black Friars Lane and Howard of Effingham, of which Mr Nussey could have been aware. In 1546 the guesthouse of the former

In 1846, no one could know that Victoria herself would preside over the vast consolidation of the British Empire, or by how many years she would outlive her celebrated predecessor, Elizabeth. This painting must originally have been commissioned as a significant political visual statement. When it re-emerged, more than two hundred years later, it was appropriated for a rather differently nuanced form of public display. It reminds us how complicated it can be to investigate the context of an image – and how diverse can be the successive purposes for which it can be used.

Dominican priory of Black Friars was acquired by George Brooke, 9th Lord Cobham, and ten years later it was noted that he had a substantial dwelling and gardens on the site, Cobham House. Subsequently, the 11th Lord Cobham married Effingham's daughter who in 1609 gave Cobham House to her brother William Howard and his wife, Lady Anne. The Apothecaries purchased the property from Lady Anne's executors in October 1632 for £1,800 (information kindly supplied by Dee Cook).

Transactions of the RHS 14 (2004), pp. 141–51 © 2004 Royal Historical Society
DOI: 10.1017/S0080440104000210   Printed in the United Kingdom

A CENTURY ON: PEPYS AND THE
ELIZABETHAN NAVY*

By C. S. Knighton

ABSTRACT. The year 2003 was also a commemoration of Pepys, whose lifespan corresponds exactly with that of Elizabeth a century before. The Navy was Pepys's professional concern, and in his Diary and other writings he frequently, and with increasing shrewdness, compared Elizabethan glories with the poorer record of his own day. Pepys also collected and bequeathed important sources for the history of the Elizabethan Navy. This paper uses these materials to consider the perceived failure of Restoration seamen to match the achievements of their grandfathers.

On 13 June 1666 in St Mary's, Whitechapel, the funeral took place of Vice-Admiral Sir Christopher Myngs, a casualty of the massive engagement known laconically as the Four Days' Fight. Myngs was a controversial figure, and not many top men were present to pay their respects. But among them were two Navy commissioners, Sir William Coventry and Samuel Pepys; and after the service they were approached by a group of Myngs's men, who asked to be appointed to crew a fireship, to avenge their commander's death. It was, Pepys recalled, one of the 'most Romantique' things he had ever heard – and by 'romantic' he meant not sentimental, but heroic.[1] Myngs had died courageously, but this alone cannot have prompted his men to volunteer for what might amount to a suicide mission. Myngs had that special charisma which attracts a following,[2] which Drake and the great Elizabethans had, and which in time would pass to Beatty and Mountbatten. Myngs's most famous exploit was a raid on the Spanish Main when twenty-two chests full of treasure were seized, which then mysteriously disappeared. It was widely and no doubt rightly believed that Myngs had simply shared the loot with his crew, in cheerful disregard of the laws of prize, which had frustrated him on a

---

* I am grateful to Professor David Loades for reading a draft of this paper.
[1] *The Diary of Samuel Pepys*, ed. R. C. Latham and W. Matthews (11 vols., 1970–83) [hereafter Pepys, *Diary*], VII, 165.
[2] Cf. N. A. M. Rodger, *The Wooden World: An Anatomy of the Georgian Navy* (1986; repr. 1988), 119–24; *Samuel Pepys and the Second Dutch War: Pepys's Navy White Book and Brooke House Papers*, ed. R. C. Latham (Navy Records Society [hereafter NRS], CXXXIII, 1995) [hereafter Pepys, *White Book*], 209, 216, 227, 231.

previous mission. He was too much of a hero, and too well connected, to be in trouble for long.[3] Of all the flag officers of the Restoration, he was the one most obviously cast in the Elizabethan mould – yet he is now a quite unfamiliar figure. Perhaps Myngs and his fellows had little chance of joining the Elizabethan sea-dogs in the memory of later generations. The Stuarts and their servants have no place in the Protestant creation epic. Since it has proved impossible to dislike the Dutch for long, the three wars fought against them in the seventeenth century seem particularly futile. Even the English naval successes of 1665 and 1666 are inevitably overshadowed by the disasters which followed in 1667 and 1688. The overall view of the Dutch wars, that the Navy failed its first great test after the Armada, is in itself an important rider to the Elizabethan naval myth.

It seems appropriate to consider how the Elizabethan Navy was viewed a century on, and to take that view through the eyes of Pepys, for whom 2003 is also a commemorative year. Pepys is an unrivalled commentator on his own times; and was the lynchpin of the Navy's administration for almost the whole of the Restoration era. What he says, and what he assumes, about the Elizabethan achievement in naval and maritime affairs is therefore relevant to the theme of these papers. Pepys has also transmitted to us a substantial body of the materials, printed and manuscript, on which the history of the Elizabethan Navy has been, and is yet to be, written.

Pepys imbibed the Elizabethan myth with his mother's milk; or, as he less fancifully put it, he 'sucked in so much of the sad story of Queen Elizabeth' from his cradle that he was 'ready to weep';[4] he was alluding to the troubles of the queen's early life, but he would have sucked up the good parts as well. As an intelligent and impressionable boy in the 1630s and 1640s he would have met the Elizabethan legend in all the potency of its first flowering. There is no reason to suppose he had any special interest in its naval aspects, or in maritime affairs at all, until he was brought into the Navy Board in 1660, by the patronage of his cousin, Lord Sandwich. Pepys was made clerk of the acts – an office which could be traced back to that of the medieval clerk of the king's ships, but, as that of secretary to the Navy Board, it was of Henry VIII's creation. Pepys had yet to learn this. The board had been replaced by other agencies during the Commonwealth, and so did not exist when Pepys entered government service in the late 1650s. Its re-establishment in 1660 was a part of the larger restoration of traditional structures. In time Pepys would find reasons to defend that system of naval administration

³ F. E. Dyer, 'Captain Christopher Myngs in the West Indies', *Mariner's Mirror* [hereafter *MM*], 18 (1932), 168–87. For Myngs, see also C. H. Firth, 'The capture of Santiago, in Cuba, by Captain Myngs, 1662', *English Historical Review*, 14 (1899), 536–40, and *Oxford DNB*.
⁴ Pepys, *Diary*, VIII, 388 (17 Aug. 1667).

inherited from the Tudors – with which his own job security was of course now linked. At first he was more interested to discover that one of his predecessors, Peter Buck, the last of the Elizabethan clerks of the acts, had been knighted.[5] This proved to be a false trail, since no other clerk received that honour. Pepys might have been better encouraged had he known that John Hawkins had a reversion to the clerkship, though he never took it up.

Pepys may have retained some blind spots about the origins of his own office, but he set himself to learn all he could of the general history of the Navy; this frequently prompted comparison between present practice and that of the Elizabethans. His conversation with colleagues at the Navy Board or Trinity House often turned that way – more so, perhaps, than to recollection of more recent naval adventures.[6] Pepys's original colleagues at the Navy Board all had extensive and distinguished careers afloat; the oldest of them, Sir John Mennes, had served in the Jacobean Navy; Sir George Carteret had been second-in-command of a hostage rescue mission which was Charles I's greatest naval success, and had later sheltered Charles II on Jersey; Sir William Penn had been naval commander of the expedition which took Jamaica; Sir William Batten had the distinction of being a flag officer on both sides in the Civil War. Yet Pepys passes to us disappointingly little of their stories. But then, theirs were awkward memories for recent antagonists now serving together – the Restoration Navy simply could not refer to its immediate past with any collective esprit de corps. This was another reason why the Elizabethan Navy remained everyone's model.

Its old-fashioned ships Pepys regarded with an amused condescension. A few Elizabethan warships were still afloat in his youth, and one survived as a hulk until 1683,[7] but little was remembered of them. Did they really fire 18-inch diameter stone shot? So it appeared, from a warship, presumed Elizabethan, found when Deptford dock was excavated in 1662.[8] How could Drake and company have sailed round the world in the tiny ships they did? (One reason, Pepys was told, was that they carried a lot of corn, which took up less space than the meat with which modern ships were overloaded).[9] Mostly Pepys's information came not from archaeology or oral tradition, but from books. As owner of two-thirds of the Anthony Roll, Pepys had a unique view of the Tudor

---

[5] *Ibid.*, I, 318 (14 Dec. 1660).

[6] E.g. *ibid.*, III, 187 (4 Sept. 1662), VIII, 293 (25 June 1667).

[7] N. A. M. Rodger, *The Safeguard of the Sea: A Naval History of Britain*, I: *660–1649* (1997), 480.

[8] Pepys, *Diary*, VIII, 188 (28 Apr. 1667).

[9] *The Tangier Papers of Samuel Pepys*, ed. E. Chappell (NRS, LXXIII, 1935) [hereafter Pepys, *Tangier Papers*], 232.

Navy.[10] An earlier acquisition was the treatise on shipbuilding begun by Elizabeth's master shipwright Matthew Baker, to which Pepys gave the name 'Fragments of Ancient English Shipwrightry' – fragmentary indeed, but nevertheless the first of its kind in English. Only when the Navy Record Society's projected edition is published will we fully appreciate our debt to Pepys for preserving this manuscript; we can, I think, already forgive him for liberating it from a weak-minded subordinate.[11]

Pepys wanted the Baker volume as a curiosity, and for its artistry. The mathematics, even if he could have deciphered it, would certainly have been beyond his grasp. Administrative records were a different matter. He acquired from John Evelyn one of the account books of Benjamin Gonson – who been Navy treasurer from 1549 to 1577, and who was the ancestor of Evelyn's wife. Evelyn was eventually prevailed upon to part with eight of Gonson's books; two remain among the Rawlinson collection in the Bodleian, with other Elizabethan accounts. By related descents came journals and accounts of Captain Edward Fenton, and some original letters of Hawkins to the earl of Leicester. Pepys was initially put off by the horridness of sixteenth-century script ('Lord, how poorly methinks they wrote in those days, and on what plain uncut paper').[12] Overcoming his aversion to secretary hand, he put his researches to practical use. After the Second Dutch War a commission asked searching questions about the Navy's finances; one issue was the Navy treasurer's rake of 3d in the pound for sums he received at the Exchequer. The

[10] Magdalene College, Cambridge, Pepys Library [hereafter PL] 2991. *The Anthony Roll of Henry VIII's Navy*, ed. C. S. Knighton and D. M. Loades (NRS Occasional Publication 2, 2000), which accepts Pepys's claim that the 1st and 3rd rolls were given to him by Charles II in 1680. But the 3rd roll appears to have been among maps which Pepys was supposed to pass from James II to Lord Dartmouth in October 1688: Bodleian Library, Oxford, Rawlinson MS [hereafter Bodl. Rawl. MS] A. 171, fo. 17 (I owe this reference to Mr Peter Barber).

[11] PL 2820. Cf. Pepys, *Diary*, V, 108 (1 Apr. 1664); M. Blatcher, 'Chatham dockyard and a little-known shipwright, Matthew Baker (1530–1613)', *Archaeologia Cantiana*, 107 (1989), 155–72; R. A. Barker, 'Fragments from the Pepysian Library', *Revista da Universidade de Coimbra*, 32 (1986), 161–78; S. A. Johnston, 'Making Mathematical Practice: Gentlemen, Practitioners and Artisans in Elizabethan England' (Ph.D. thesis, Cambridge University, 1994), 107–65.

[12] Pepys, *Diary*, VI, 307–8 and n. 1 (24 Nov. 1665); Bodl. Rawl. MS A. 200–6 (A. 200 and A. 202 contain Gonson's accounts for 1562–4); cf. Pepys, *Tangier Papers*, 219; PL 513 (Fenton accounts), 2133 (Fenton journals and related matter, printed *The Troublesome Voyage of Captain Edward Fenton, 1582–1583*, ed. E. G. R. Taylor (Hakluyt Soc., second series, CXIII, 1959 for 1957), 49, 83–149, and *The Third Voyage of Martin Frobisher to Baffin Island, 1578*, ed. J. McDermott (Hakluyt Soc., third series, VI (2001)), 64–5, 66–9, 136–76; PL 2502, p. 427, 2503, p. 371 (Hawkins letters, printed in Historical Manuscripts Commission, *Report on the Pepys Manuscripts Preserved at Magdalene College, Cambridge*, ed. E. K. Purnell (1911) [hereafter HMC, *Pepys MSS*], 65–6, 173–4). Mary Evelyn's grandmother was Gonson's daughter Thomasine, wife of (1) Fenton, and (2) Christopher, son Sir Richard Browne (head of Leicester's household). Cf. Simon Adams, 'The Papers of Robert Dudley, Earl of Leicester. I. The Browne-Evelyn collection', *Archives*, 20 (1992), 63–85.

commission could find no precedent from Elizabeth's day, but Pepys was able to cite a ledger of his own, presumably one of the Gonson accounts, tracing this practice back to 1566.[13] Both sides felt their case was adequately proved by appeal to Elizabethan custom.

More generally Pepys convinced himself that the naval management restored in 1660, the Navy Board of professional commissioners, was innately superior to the controlling committees of the Commonwealth, which were packed in the mercantile and shipowning interests. After the Second Dutch War the duke of York asked for a thorough review of current practice, and Pepys duly reported in favour of the traditional system.[14] That remained his view even when, paradoxically, he persuaded James II to suspend the Navy Board in 1686 and replace it with a temporary Special Commission, stuffed with his own cronies. This was, as he pointed out, well justified by Jacobean precedent.

Even so, the more Pepys informed himself of the past, the more he became aware that things had not always been wonderful, and he was proud to distinguish improvements in his own time, particularly those in which he had some part. Two things especially concerned him: training for sea service, and caring for those whose service was over. In both cases he saw much that was defective in Elizabethan practice. It appalled him to learn that men discharged from the victorious ships in 1588 were reduced to beggary. He thought it disgraceful that, in the absence of adequate public relief, seamen had clubbed together to establish the Chatham Chest. He wanted to know what was discussed in parliament, and to what extent the statutes which did eventually provide relief were concerned with sailors as well as soldiers. On the same tack he noted sourly that Elizabeth's collegiate foundation at Westminster gave places for old soldiers, but not old sailors (though in this he was mistaken).[15] Pepys worked closely with the Sick and Wounded Commissioners and with the governors of the Chest to achieve a better level of health care and charity than the Elizabethans had managed;[16] though it must be said that it was not until five years after Pepys left the Admiralty, in 1694, that improvements of the most substantial kind came into being.

Pepys ran a long campaign to improve education for seamen, and particularly for naval officers. He was puzzled by the negligence of previous generations; especially when, as he allowed, navigation and sea discoveries were 'in a great degree' new in Queen Elizabeth's time, and

---

[13] Pepys, *White Book*, 378–9, 387, 400; PL 2874, p. 367.

[14] *Further Correspondence of Samuel Pepys, 1662–1679*, ed. J. R. Tanner (1929), 230–5; Pepys, *Diary*, IX, 525 and n. 1 (18 Apr. 1669).

[15] *Samuel Pepys's Naval Minutes*, ed. J. R. Tanner (NRS, LX, 1926) [hereafter Pepys, *Naval Minutes*], 74, 85, 171, 232 and n. 2, 254–5, 262, 391; Pepys, *Tangier Papers*, 105–6.

[16] J. J. S. Shaw, 'The Commission of Sick and Wounded and Prisoners, 1664–1667', *MM*, 25 (1939), 306–19.

so the better recorded and valued.[17] He himself acquired a number of early printed navigational books, which he formed into one of the sub-collections in his library, now at Magdalene; the earliest of these 'Sea Tracts' as he called them is the work of Antonio de Guevera's in the translation by Edward Hellowes of 1578. He had three copies of Cortés's *Arte of Navigation* in Richard Eden's translation, the first from 1572. Bourne's *Regiment for the Sea*, an edition of 1592, and the works of Borough, Hood and Norman were on his shelves.[18] In this there was more than bibliographical interest. Pepys endorsed Borough's argument, in the preface to his *Discourse on the Variation of the Cumpas*, that the publication of these navigational aids in English, and the use of the instruments which they taught, meant English seamen would be less dependent on maps produced by the Spanish and Portuguese.[19] It was, Pepys felt, bad enough that England's first discoveries were owed to a foreigner.[20] He realised that exploration (except, he supposed, in the remotest parts) must ultimately belong to all nations, and he was critical of Drake for abandoning a pilot to the alligators in the interests of navigational security.[21] He could not, however, imagine why the Elizabethan government published charts of the English coasts just months after the Armada had passed, and when fresh attempts were expected. This was the atlas of Lucas Janszoon Waghenaer, from whose name all such works are called 'waggoners', translated as *The Mariners Mirrour* by Anthony Ashley, with a dedication to Lord Chancellor Hatton. Who was this Ashley, Pepys wondered, sitting in St James's Palace correcting his proofs when the queen's ships were at sea, and when disaster was averted in part because the Spanish did not know the coasts well enough? It is not difficult to see why this touched Pepys so sharply. During the Popish Plot he had himself been accused of passing maps and charts of the English coast to the French. The chief promoter of these and other fabrications was Anthony Ashley's descendant and namesake, the first earl of Shaftesbury.[22]

---

[17] Pepys, *Naval Minutes*, 133.

[18] A. de Guevera, *A Booke of the Inuention of the Art of Nauigation* (1578: STC 12425); M. Cortés, *The Arte of Nauigation* (1584: STC 5801); W. Bourne, *A Regiment for the Sea* (1592: STC 3427); T. Hood, *The Marriners Guide* (1592: STC 13696); R. Norman, *The New Attractiue* (1585: STC 18648); W. B[orough], *A Discovrse of the Variation of the Cumpas* (1585: STC 3390). These form PL 1077(1–6); other edns of Cortés at PL 1078(1) [1596], 1478(1) [1572].

[19] Pepys, *Naval Minutes*, 229 and n. 7, alluding to Borough ('Burrows'), Preface, sig. A. iii.

[20] Sebastian Cabot ('Gobot'): Pepys, *Naval Minutes*, 229.

[21] *Ibid.*, 4 and n. 2; the story is from Sir W. Raleigh, *Judicious and Select Essayes and Observations upon the First Invention of Shipping* (1650: Wing R170), 19 [PL 294].

[22] Pepys, *Naval Minutes*, 347–50. *The Mariners Mirrour . . . for the Use of Englishmen by Anthony Ashley* (1588: STC 24931). Pepys bought his copy in 1663 (*Diary*, IV, 240 and n. 1), and later acquired the Dutch original, *Teerste deel vande Spieghel der Zeevaerdt* (Leiden, 1584), and the Latin version *Speculum Nauticum* (Amsterdam, 1591–2); they stand together at PL 2798–800: Pepys, *Catalogue of the Pepys Library at Magdalene College, Cambridge* [hereafter Pepys, *Catalogue*],

Pepys naturally had his Hakluyt and Purchas, and read them avidly.[23] It nevertheless struck him as shameful that 'no admiral or secretary of the Admiralty ever wrote a history of the Navy', and that the best to hand was the work of a 'poor private minister'; he means Hakluyt, who was a canon of Westminster. He suspected, correctly, that Purchas was no better.[24] What most upset Pepys was Hakluyt's failure to establish a navigation lecture in London, such as had been founded in Seville by Charles V. Drake had offered £20 a year, and £20 more for instruments, but nobody would bring the salary up to £40, for which the chosen candidate held out.[25] Here Pepys could and did do something, by promoting the foundation of the Royal Mathematical School at Christ's Hospital in 1673, and using his contacts in the Royal Society to support that foundation through some early difficulties.[26]

Technical training for sea officers was part of the wider profession-alisation of the naval service, with which Pepys was much associated. The Restoration Navy has been conventionally described as a contest between the gentlemen and the tarpaulins, the hereditary military caste and the professional sea captains. That polarisation has been exaggerated; as warships and naval fighting became more sophisticated, there was less relevance to the old distinction between the master directing the ship and the captain directing the fight. Charles II and his brother recognised this, and worked to create an officer corps on which they could rely for political loyalty and professional competence.[27] Pepys nevertheless has done much to persuade later generations that there was a contest, and on the whole he sided with the tarpaulins. He was, after all, a meritocrat like them. Naturally he looked back to the Elizabethan Navy to support his argument, and it pleased him to find that in 1588, 'though there was a nobleman Admiral, they were fain to make two plain tarpaulins, Drake and Hawkins, their Vice- and Rear Admirals'. He was scornful of the crowd of noblemen and gentlemen who flocked to the ships in

---

IV, *Maps*, comp. S. Tyacke (Cambridge, 1989), 40 (nos. 189–90), 49–50 (no. 230). Pepys took every opportunity to denigrate Ashley's 'pretended improvement': *Naval Minutes*, 19, 42, 58, 305, 391–2.

[23] R. Hakluyt, *The Principal Navigations, Voyages, Traffiques and Discoveries of the English Nation* (1599–1600: STC 12626, 12626a) [PL 2111–12]; S. Purchas, *Purchas his Pilgrimes* (1625: STC 20509), and *Purchas his Pilgrimage* (1626: STC 20508.5) [PL 2511–15]. Cf. the many entries indexed in Pepys, *Naval Minutes* and *Tangier Papers*.

[24] Pepys, *Tangier Papers*, 148 and n. 1.

[25] Pepys, *Naval Minutes*, 229–30, 378, 415; R. Hakluyt, *Diuers Voyages Touching the Discouerie of America* (1582: STC 12624), Epistle Dedicatorie, sig. ¶3r–v [PL 1077(8)].

[26] N. M. Plumley, 'The Royal Mathematical School, Christ's Hospital', *History Today*, 23 (1973), 581–7.

[27] J. D. Davies, *Gentlemen and Tarpaulins: The Officers and Men of the Restoration Navy* (Oxford, 1991).

1588, when plunder was in prospect, but who disappeared after the first excitement was over. At the same time Pepys respected the social order and was keen to trace the landed connections of Drake and the other great seamen. It impressed him that so many of Elizabeth's ministers and favourites 'understood the sea.' He even detected 'a spirit extraordinary stirring among our nobility and gentry in Queen Elizabeth's time towards the sea, beyond what appears to have been ever before or since; imputable, I think, to their then fervour for religion and against Spain, joined with the general better morals of that age'.[28]

Much of the politics of the Restoration was transacted, quite literally, against the backdrop of Elizabethan naval success, the Armada tapestries on the walls of the House of Lords.[29] Pepys saw in them evidence of that respect for maritime service which his own age had lost, though he could not resist sneering that they were designed by a Dutchman.[30] He had his own copy of the original Ryther engravings of 1589, which he bound up with a manuscript version of the accompanying text by Ubaldini – regrettably another foreigner.[31] After the Second Dutch War Pepys sourly suggested that the House should be redecorated with images of 1667 rather than 1588.[32] Some months earlier, in the immediate aftermath of the Chatham disaster, he saw a revival, in the presence of the king and his brother, of '*Queen Elizabeths Troubles, and the History of Eighty-Eight*' (Thomas Heywood's *If You Know Not Me*). Pepys spent the previous evening swotting up the history; he does not tell us whether the performance restored or further weakened public confidence in the regime.[33]

---

[28] Pepys, *Naval Minutes*, 10, 46, 119, 171, 215, 376.

[29] See K. Hearn, '*Elizabeth I and the Spanish Armada*: A Painting and its Afterlife' in this volume.

[30] Pepys, *Naval Minutes*, 94, 380, 392.

[31] P. Ubaldini, *Expeditionis Hispanorum in Angliam vera Descriptio* (1589: STC 24481a), with MS text [PL 2806]; Pepys, *Catalogue*, IV; *Maps*, 40 (no. 188). Pepys also had two copies of the printed English text, *A Discovrse concerning the Spanishe Fleete Inuadinge Englande* (1590: STC 24481) [PL 1077(11), 1431(23)]. *Naval Minutes*, 392 and nn. 2, 3. Cf. *State Papers relating to the Defeat of the Spanish Armada*, ed. J. K. Laughton (NRS I–II, 1894), I, 1–18, II, 388–90. G. P. B. Naish, 'The Spanish Armada', in *The Naval Miscellany, Volume IV*, ed. C. Lloyd (NRS, XCII, 1952), 30–82. The other item is a much smaller list of personnel and munitions, passed to Pepys by Evelyn: PL 2503, p. 445 (HMC, *Pepys MSS*, 181). *Particular Friends: The Correspondence of Samuel Pepys and John Evelyn*, ed. G. de la Bédoyère (Woodbridge, 1997) [hereafter de la Bédoyère, *Particular Friends*, 125 (Evelyn to Pepys, 6 Dec. 1681).

[32] De la Bédoyère, *Particular Friends*, 67 (Pepys to Evelyn, 8 Feb. 1668).

[33] Pepys, *Diary*, VIII, 387, 388 (16 and 17 Aug. 1667). Cf. T. Grant, 'Drama Queen: Staging Elizabeth in *If You Know Not Me You Know Nobody*', in *The Myth of Elizabeth*, ed. S. Doran and T. S. Freeman (Basingstoke, 2003), 120–1, 135–6, 141–2 (n. 50), noting that W. C. Hazlitt had supposed a connection between the play's revival and the Chatham raid: *A Manual for the Collector and Amateur of Old Plays* (1892), 113. Cf. M. Dobson and N. J. Watson, *England's Elizabeth: An Afterlife in Fame and Fantasy* (Oxford, 2002), 67–9, 84.

Awkward comparisons between Chatham and the Armada could at least be qualified by detecting blemishes in the Elizabethan record. Pepys was perhaps thinking of the laying up of the fleet in 1667 when he criticised orders sent to bring in four of the great ships just as the Armada came into view. Operations then as in his own day, he realised, could be jeopardised by bad intelligence. From the Spanish angle he saw that the enterprise was compromised not by inferior seamanship or for want of pilots, but by 'imprudent orders', and that lack of adequate charts which *The Mariners Mirrour* would have given them.[34] Pepys obtained a couple of authentic Armada souvenirs: one being the 500-page victualling manifest which may have been recovered by that same Anthony Ashley from the *Nuestra Señora del Rosario*.[35] Pepys found little at fault with the operational command on the English side, and thought it remiss that Lord Admiral Howard received no parliamentary thanks.[36] Maybe he was recalling the shower of honours after the victory of Lowestoft in 1665, or the lionising of Rupert and Albemarle by parliament in the following year.

Pepys and his contemporaries thought much on the Armada. What worked then ought to work again. Fireships had been famously successful against the Spanish, when they were set adrift towards ships at anchor. They were deployed urgently, but to little effect, against the Dutch in the Medway. And in the general actions they were notoriously two-edged weapons. The Dutch used them more intelligently, against ships they had already disabled with chain-shot. Pepys tells us that before the Second War, the Dutch proposed mutual renunciation, but this was refused on Sandwich's advice.[37] Sandwich would die as the result.

In retirement Pepys devoted his time to completing the library he would leave to his old College, and to a projected history of the Navy. This was never written, but in the process he gathered a great body of record material, much of it relating to the Elizabethan Navy. In many cases the originals are now lost or, as with the Cotton MSS, so damaged that the Pepys copies are now a primary source.[38] Enquiries he addressed to Evelyn and others show that his grasp of Elizabethan history remained shaky,[39] and his research was never pure. He was still keen to prove that

---

[34] Pepys, *Naval Minutes*, 49, 74, 231, 342.

[35] PL 2269 (*Libro de Cargos*): Pepys, *Catalogue*, V, *Manuscripts*, II, *Modern*, comp. C. S. Knighton (Cambridge, 1981), 55–7. Cf. P. Martin, *Spanish Armada Prisoners: The Story of the* Nuestra Señora del Rosario *and her Crew, and of Other Prisoners in England, 1587–97* (Exeter Maritime Studies, I, Exeter, 1988), 33–4.

[36] Pepys, *Naval Minutes*, 95, 262.

[37] *Ibid.*, 360; Pepys thought piloted fireships were an improvement on those merely set adrift (as at Gravelines).

[38] See particularly Simon Adams, 'The Armada Correspondence in Cotton MSS Otho E VII and E IX', in *The Naval Miscellany, Volume VI*, ed. M. Duffy (NRS, CXLVI, 2003), 37–92, where *lacunae* in Cotton originals are supplied from PL copies.

[39] De la Bédoyère, *Particular Friends*, 100–1 and *passim*.

the Elizabethan commanders were more honourable than those he had known. The Elizabethan gentlemen captains, whom he once criticised for serving for plunder only, were commended because they never asked or received a shilling more than the common wages of the Navy – in contrast to those of the Restoration era who demanded pensions or half-pay. Some of the noblemen, he acknowledged, had served against the Armada entirely at their own charges. The tarpaulins went 'chearfully' back to the merchant service, without having their morals corrupted by public service.[40] Pepys's enduring veneration for Drake is evident from this the smallest of his books, a nautical almanac printed in Brittany in 1546; on the first leaf is written 'F. Drak.'. It is nothing whatsoever like the great man's usual flourished signature, but that is beside the point: Pepys believed it was genuine, and he preserved this copy in his library rather than another he owned, which had belonged to Henry VIII. The reject passed to his family, and was bought by the National Maritime Museum in 1931.[41]

While Pepys was planning his history, there was a naval victory – La Hogue – which some thought the equal of the Armada. Pepys himself was sceptical of the comparisons, especially as delivered from the pulpit. Both actions were, he concluded, 'the results purely of accident, in exclusion of all extraordinariness either of conduct or courage'.[42] But he has also left us, in his Ballad Collection, the tabloid verdict:[43]

> The Downfall of Lewis le Grand is reckon'd
> So far above that of Philip the Second...
> 'Twas in Eighty Eight Queen Bess swept the Main
> In Ninety Two Queen Mary the same...
> Now... chant forth the praise of those Protestant Queens,
> Now all English lads not enter'd their Teens,
> Shall chant forth the Praise of those Protestant Queens,

[40] *Private Correspondence and Miscellaneous Papers of Samuel Pepys, 1679–1703*, ed. J. R. Tanner (2 vols., 1926), II, 244–7.

[41] Tidetables (untitled), comp. G. Brouscon (Conquet, 1546). Cf. L. Dujardin-Troadec, *Les cartographes bretons du conquet* (Brest, 1966), 48. 'Drake' copy: PL 1; facsimile with notes by D. Howse (1980). 'Henry VIII' copy: NMM, MS NVT 40; see *Magdalene College Magazine*, 5, no. 4 (issue no. 36, Mar. 1921), 127.

[42] Pepys, *Naval Minutes*, 298. Pepys thought Archbishop Tillotson had compared the victories of 1588 and 1692 at the thanksgiving service for the latter, but this sermon contains only a general allusion to the operation of divine providence in warfare: J. Tillotson, *A Sermon Preached before the King and Queen at White-Hall, the 27th of October ... for the Signal Victory at Sea* (1692: Wing T1246), 10 [PL 1432(14)]. Pepys collected printed eulogies for Mary II; only one suggests a comparison with Elizabeth, then retracts it lest it 'offend as fulsome': D. Pead, *A Practical Discourse upon the Death of our Late Gracious Queen* (1695: Wing P962), 23 [PL 1528(13)].

[43] *A Merry New Ballad, on the Great Victory over the French Fleet, May the 19th. 1692* (1692: Wing M1870B) [PL 2510, pp. 382–3; reproduced in Pepys, *Catalogue*, facsimile volumes, *The Pepys Ballads*, ed. W. G. Day (5 vols., Cambridge, 1987), V, 382–3].

Protestant Queens! Protestant Queens!
Shall chant out the Praise of those Protestant Queens.

So Gloriana was at last reincarnated in the person of Mary II. This trivial piece suggests one further reason why the heroes of the Restoration Navy were forgotten by posterity: the monarchs they served not only favoured the wrong religion, and picked the wrong fight: they belonged to the wrong sex.

Transactions of the RHS 14 (2004), pp. 153–74 © 2004 Royal Historical Society
DOI: 10.1017/S0080440104000180   Printed in the United Kingdom

QUEEN ELIZABETH AND THE MYTH OF SEA-POWER IN ENGLISH HISTORY

By N. A. M. Rodger

ABSTRACT. This paper identifies an English 'national myth' of sea-power, based on the folk-memory of the Elizabethan naval war, which powerfully shaped public attitudes and political choices throughout the seventeenth and eighteenth centuries. This myth associated true, patriotic and ever-victorious English sea-power with political liberty, financial profit and, above all, Protestantism. The public judged successive governments on their willingness and ability to realise this programme. Most of them failed on one or both counts, until the elder Pitt made the myth work, and the French revolutionaries changed the rules.

This is a study of things that never happened, or never in the way they were understood and remembered. It is a history of ideas, but not an intellectual history, for it deals with the thoughts of men who were not accustomed to thinking in any profound and analytical fashion. It is a study of the memory of the Elizabethan age as it was shaped into an English national myth[1] about sea-power, the distorting lens through which generations of public men perceived and understood real naval activity. In this subject historians have sometimes been too apt to believe that political debate had to do with reality, that the issues discussed in parliament and print were real issues. This is curious, for it is a matter of common experience that even in our own day, when information circulates more freely than it ever did in the past, public policy is often formed and discussed in terms dictated more by politicians' preconceptions than by a dispassionate regard for facts. We ought to expect the same thing in a greater degree in the past, and so indeed we find it. For centuries sea-power and naval affairs mattered a great deal in English political life, but the shipping which men discussed in parliament was not exactly the same as the shipping which actually put to sea.

The English naval myth was built on the events of Queen Elizabeth's reign, but its precise origin does not seem ever to have been located. This may possibly be because it is to be found somewhere where British naval

[1] I use the word 'English' deliberately, even for the period after the union of the crowns, because the tradition I want to outline is essentially English. Scotland has, or had, its own ideas about the sea, but they were not the same.

historians have not traditionally looked for patriotic inspiration; namely France, and specifically in English cooperation with the Huguenots of La Rochelle and the Norman ports during the wars of religion. Until the 1560s English seamen were skilled in the coastal pilotage of northern European waters, but lacked any knowledge of deep-sea navigation. In the West Country especially, they had centuries of expertise in piracy, and the three English experiments with 'reprisals by general proclamation' in 1544, 1557 and 1563 did a good deal to revive the pirate culture in England, but it remained a matter of local rather than national importance, and it was only beginning to acquire any religious overtones. All this was changed by English support for the French Huguenots, and in particular by covert government assistance in the years 1568 to 1572. This support came via a group of West Country seamen led by Sir Arthur Champernowne, the vice-admiral of Devon, and his old business associates the Hawkins brothers of Plymouth, veterans of many joint ventures with Huguenot interests. Together they organised a joint Anglo-Huguenot fleet, sailing under letters of reprisal issued by the Huguenot leaders Henry of Navarre (as admiral of Guyenne, 1563–89) and Gaspard de Coligny (as admiral of France, 1552–72) out of Plymouth and La Rochelle as opportunity offered, against the shipping of all nations, but especially of Spain. By March 1569 there were as many as forty Huguenot cruisers in the Channel. At the same time Queen Elizabeth's own ships and seamen were supplying the French rebels. When Sir William Winter escorted the annual wine convoy to Bordeaux in December 1568, he sent ammunition into La Rochelle in passing, while next year John Hawkins with another squadron relieved the city, returning with cargoes of wine, prize goods and church bells.[2] The bells are an apt symbol of the wars of religion by land and sea; the fruit of the destruction of French country churches, carried to England to the profit of English ship-owners to be melted down and recast into guns with which to continue the war of religion.

The tie that bound the Huguenots to their English associates was religion, for Calvinism and piracy were intimately connected. The connection was not of course a theological one; the reformers did not encourage armed robbery in principle. In practice, however, in France, the Netherlands, Scotland and elsewhere, even the most scrupulous of

---

[2] Charles de La Roncière, *Histoire de la marine française* (6 vols., Paris, 1899–1932), IV, 102–18; B. Dietz, 'The Huguenot and English Corsairs during the Third Civil War in France, 1568 to 1570', *Proceedings of the Huguenot Society*, 19 (1952–8), 278–94 [hereafter *Proc. Hug. Soc.*]; James A. Williamson, *Hawkins of Plymouth*, 2nd edn (1969), 165–70; Patrick Villiers, *Les corsaires du Littoral: Dunkerque, Calais, Boulogne, de Philippe II à Louis XIV (1568–1713)* (Villeneuve d'Ascq, 2000), 26–7; D. J. B. Trim, 'The "Secret War" of Elizabeth I: England and the Huguenots during the Early Wars of Religion, 1562–77', *Proc. Hug. Soc.*, 27 (1999), 189–99 (I am indebted to Dr Trim for copies of this and his other paper cited below).

Protestant dissidents found themselves fighting to preserve their liberty of conscience, and obliged to find the sinews of war by whatever means the Lord might put into their hands. One of the best means was reprisals at sea,[3] and their best allies were the English. Thus the English, and at the same time the Dutch, rebels joined the Huguenots and their long-standing Scottish associates in what we may call the Calvinist International. Religion now sanctioned a private war against the shipping of the Catholic powers, which, providentially, formed much the largest and richest part of the sea-borne trade of Europe.[4] Most English seamen were now conscientiously convinced 'that we cold not do God better service than to spoyl the Spaniard both of lyfe and goodes, but indeed under color of religion al ther shot is at mens mony'.[5]

Though the immediate crisis passed in 1572, the links that the West Countrymen had established remained active. With French advice and encouragement, the English began to move out into the Atlantic and even, in small numbers, across to the West Indies.[6] Huguenot navigators like Guillaume Le Testu now took English seamen by the hand and

[3] For the legal doctrine of reprisals see: D. A. Gardiner, 'The History of Belligerent Rights on the High Seas in the Fourteenth Century', *Law Quarterly Review*, 48 (1932), 521–46; René de Mas Latrie, 'Du droit de marque ou droit de représailles au moyen âge', *Bibliothèque de l'Ecole des Chartes*, 27 (1866), 529–77, 29 (1868), 294–347, 612–35; Marie-Claire Chavarot, 'La pratique des lettres de marque d'après les arrêts du parlement (XIIIe-debut XVe siècle)', *Bibliothèque de l'Ecole des Chartes*, 149 (1981), 51–89; Pierre Chaplais, 'Règlement des conflits internationaux franco-anglais au XIVe siècle (1293–1377)', *Le Moyen Age*, 57 (1951), 259–302; Florence E. Dyer, 'Reprisals in the Sixteenth Century', *Mariner's Mirror*, 21 (1935), 187–97 [hereafter *MM*]; *Documents relating to Law and Custom of the Sea*, ed. R. G. Marsden (Navy Records Society vols. 49–50, 1915–16), I, 119–24 [hereafter NRS].

[4] Mickaël Augeron, 'Coligny et les Espagnols à travers la course (c. 1560–1572): une politique maritime au service de la cause protestante', in *Coligny, les protestants et la mer*, ed. Martine Acerra and Guy Martinière (Paris, 1997), 155–76; Ralph Davis, *The Rise of the Atlantic Economies* (1973), 77–80; David Loades, *England's Maritime Empire: Seapower, Commerce and Policy, 1490–1690* (2000), 85–114; Timothy George, 'War and Peace in the Puritan Tradition', *Church History*, 52 (1984), 492–503; D. J. B. Trim, 'Protestant refugees in Elizabethan England and confessional conflict in France and the Netherlands, c. 1562–c. 1610', in *From Strangers to Citizens: The Integration of Immigrant Communities in Britain, Ireland and Colonial America, 1550–1750*, ed. Randolph Vigne and Charles Littleton (Brighton, 2001), 68–79; Alan James, 'Between "Huguenot" and "Royal": Naval Affairs during the Wars of Religion', in *The Adventure of Religious Pluralism in Early Modern France*, ed. Keith Cameron, Mark Greengrass and Penny Roberts (Oxford and New York, 2000), pp. 101–12.

[5] *An Elizabethan in 1582: The Diary of Richard Madox, Fellow of All Souls*, ed. Elizabeth S. Donno (Hakluyt Society, second series, CXLVI, 1976), 144. Few English sea chaplains were as sceptical as Madox, who made himself very unpopular by preaching that armed robbery was not invariably warranted by Scripture.

[6] Kenneth Andrews, *Trade, Plunder and Settlement: Maritime Enterprise and the Genesis of the British Empire, 1480–1630* (Cambridge, 1984), 128–38; *Documents concerning English Voyages to the Spanish Main 1569–1580*, ed. I. A. Wright (Hakluyt Society, second series, LXXI, 1932), xxx–xxxv; G. V. Scammell, 'The English in the Atlantic Islands c.1450–1650', *MM*, 72 (1986), 295–317, at 302–3.

showed them how to raid the Spanish empire. The young Francis Drake and his contemporaries who began to range the Caribbean in search of 'some little comfortable dew from heaven'[7] were strongly motivated by religion as well as money. More eminent figures like Sir Richard Grenville, who owned men-of-war but did not go to sea himself until much later, belonged to the same current of opinion. His powerful galleon the *Castle of Comfort* was often encountered in the 1570s, and never in honest trade. She sailed with French letters of reprisal against the enemies of reformed religion, while at home in Cornwall, Grenville enthusiastically persecuted his Catholic neighbours and their priests, whom most of the Cornish gentlemen would have been quite happy to ignore. He was responsible for the execution of Cuthbert Mayne, the first of the seminary priests, at Lostwithiel in 1577.[8]

Religious war at sea, 'to God's glory and our comfort',[9] was linked with religious persecution at home. At first it was only in the West Country, but Pius V's bull *Regnans in excelsis* of 1570, which excommunicated Queen Elizabeth, made Protestantism patriotic and Catholicism matter of treason, while the outbreak of the Spanish War in 1585 allowed the West Country seamen to teach the nation the skills they had learnt from the Huguenots. Without this connection, founded on a common religion and a common sense of a mortal threat from resurgent Catholicism, it is far from certain that English piracy would have spread beyond the coasts of the Channel and the Bay of Biscay. Though the period of active cooperation in open war lasted less than four years, it gave a powerful impetus to the future development of English sea-power, and English ideas about sea-power. The intimate connection between Protestantism, patriotism and plunder that the English learnt at La Rochelle was to become a distinctive and formative part of the English national myth. In France, ironically, it was the ideology of the losers, destined to be rubbed out and overwritten by the very different ethos of royal absolutism.[10]

The Spanish War of 1585 to 1603 fixed the essential elements of the English idea of sea-power in the national consciousness. This was a war fought only partly by the queen's ships. Their strategic role was largely defensive, their operations for the most part confined to nearby waters. Only once, in 1588, did the Royal Navy take the lead in a campaign

[7] *The Expedition of Sir John Norris and Sir Francis Drake to Spain and Portugal, 1589*, ed. R. B. Wernham (NRS, CXXVII, 1988), 179, quoting Drake to Sir Francis Walsingham, 2 June 1589.

[8] A. L. Rowse, *Sir Richard Grenville of the Revenge: An Elizabethan Hero* (1937), 117–21, 132–44.

[9] *English Privateering Voyages to the West Indies 1588–1595*, ed. K. R. Andrews (Hakluyt Society, second series, CXI, 1959), 339 n. 4, quoting the account book of the London privateer owner Thomas Middleton for the voyage of the *Vineyard* in 1603.

[10] Jean Meyer, 'La course: romantisme, exutoire sociale, réalité économique', *Annales de Bretagne*, 78 (1971), 307–44, at 311. The recent collection, *Coligny, les Protestants et la mer*, ed. Acerra and Martinière, marks a stirring of French interest in this long-neglected subject.

that caught the national imagination. The offensive part of the naval war was largely in private hands, the work of a coalition of seamen (notably but no longer solely from the West Country), gentlemen and London capitalists making war on the common enemy for profit. The intellectual and political leadership of this coalition came from the radical Protestant group at court. The queen was unable and unwilling to take their wilder projects seriously; it was not in her interest to overthrow Spanish power, and it was not remotely within her capabilities, but many of them truly believed, in Sir Walter Raleigh's words, that 'if the late Queen would have believed her men of war as she did her scribes, we had in her time beaten that great empire in pieces and made their kings kings of figs and oranges as in old times'.[11]

By the end of the war the essential elements of the English naval myth were securely in place. The war had been fought for England's freedom, against the mortal threat of Catholic tyranny. It had been a naval triumph, and would have been more so but for the queen's hesitancy and parsimony. It had been fought at little public expense, and yielded enormous private profit. It had endowed English history with an ample stock of Protestant heroes. Above all, that part of the naval war which had seized the national imagination had been fought by private interests rather than by the crown, so that the prestige did not go to strengthen an image of royal power, but one of national liberty. It made English sea-power the ideal expression of the nation in arms. Reality, of course, did not altogether correspond with the myth, but it is too dismissive to follow a recent historian's judgement: 'the idea that the privateers were Protestant crusaders is nonsense. Like the lord admiral and his chief judge, they were primarily cheerful thieves.'[12] In fact the idea is not complete nonsense; there was some truth in it, and in each of the elements of the new naval myth, for cheerful theft and Protestant crusading were entirely compatible.[13]

At the core of the English political idea of sea-power as it was now established lay a trinity of associations: religion, freedom and money. True, natural and national English sea-power was securely attached to these three, and the three belonged together as inseparable parts of a single system. First, English sea-power was essentially Protestant, exercised for the defence of true religion and the destruction of Catholicism. English

[11] R. B. Wernham, 'Elizabethan War Aims and Strategy', in *Elizabethan Government and Society: Essays Presented to Sir John Neale*, ed. S. T. Bindoff, J. Hurstfield and C. H. Williams (1961), 340–68, quoted at 340.

[12] Bruce Lenman, *England's Colonial Wars 1550–1688: Conflicts, Empire and National Identity* (Harlow, 2001), 85.

[13] Kenneth R. Andrews, *Elizabethan Privateering: English Privateering during the Spanish War 1585–1603* (Cambridge, 1964), 6, 9, 16, 232–5; Andrews, *Trade, Plunder and Settlement*, 17–36, 248; Loades, *England's Maritime Empire*, 111–25; Geoffrey Scammell, *The World Encompassed: The First European Maritime Empires, c. 800–1650* (1981), 498.

sea-power fought for religious freedom, therefore; meaning the religious freedom of the people who mattered, English Protestants, and it was naturally associated with that most English of religious freedoms, the freedom to persecute Catholics. It was equally integral to its character to be on the side of political freedom, not simply by defending the country against foreign invasion, but by associating with those domestic policies which defended the liberties of Englishmen, and in particular the liberties of parliament. Finally, true English sea-power was profitable; it was the means by which the English nation in general, English seamen and merchants in particular, made their fortunes. Initially these fortunes came mainly from plunder; later foreign trade came to play the dominant part, but the underlying idea remained the same.

Throughout the seventeenth and eighteenth centuries the national use of the sea was commonly understood as a unity, in which merchant shipping and trade formed a common system with the Royal Navy and private men-of-war. In the words of a 1615 pamphlet,

> As concerning ships, it is that which every one knoweth and can say, they are our weapons, they are our ornaments, they are our strength, they are our pleasures, they are our defence, they are our profit; the subject by them is made rich, the Kingdom through them strong, the Prince in them mighty.[14]

Various terms were used to refer to this 'maritime-imperial system';[15] I have chosen to use the word 'sea-power', but I do not mean to limit it to the Royal Navy as an organisation. Public debate very often centred on the Navy, if only because it cost so much money and public money was the proper business of the House of Commons, but the subject as a whole is broader.

The modern observer naturally thinks of sea-power in the context of foreign policy, economics and war. For public men in seventeenth- and eighteenth-century England, however, its leading associations were more domestic than foreign. The political liberty which belonged to true English sea-power was English liberty, at home in England, a permanent and prominent element of English political life, not just the occasional military requirement for defence against foreign invasion. Likewise the religious liberty native to English sea-power was chiefly invoked in the domestic context; it was both a privilege and an obligation flowing from the status of the English as God's new elect, his chosen instruments to

---

[14] Norman Clayton, 'Naval Administration, 1603–1628' (Ph.D. thesis, University of Leeds, 1935), 281, quoting Robert Kayll, *The Trade's Increase* (1809). Cf. Brian Dietz, 'The Royal Bounty and English Merchant Shipping in the Sixteenth and Seventeenth Centuries', *MM*, 77 (1991), 5–20, at 5.

[15] The phrase used by Daniel A. Baugh in 'Maritime Strength and Atlantic Commerce: The Uses of "A Grand Marine Empire"', in *An Imperial State at War: Britain from 1689 to 1815*, ed. Lawrence Stone (1994), 185–223.

defeat the hellish designs of the Antichrist. It certainly involved defence against Catholic powers overseas, but even more it called for the proper enforcement of the penal laws against Catholics at home, for Rome was the centre of a single, worldwide conspiracy whose agents were at work everywhere, and had to be fought everywhere.[16] Foreign policy and war were remote and difficult subjects belonging to the prerogative of the crown. Domestic policy was within the competence and the understanding of members of parliament, and it was mainly in their sphere of home affairs that their ideas of sea-power were deployed.

Naval policies which conformed to the true and proper character of English sea-power could be confident of public support. War which promised to put money in the pockets of Englishmen (if not always of their government), war which strengthened the authority of parliament rather than the crown, above all war against Catholic rather than Protestant enemies, was warmly received by the political nation. But naval policies which appeared to serve the interests of the crown rather than the private citizen; policies tainted with arbitrary government, or its natural associate, religious toleration; above all policies of alliance with Catholic powers, were liable to be rejected as a false, unnatural and unpatriotic perversion of true English sea-power.

For the early Stuarts, the English naval myth was a minefield lying in the path of every attempt to use English sea-power. English parliamentarians of the day were not trying to assume the crown's prerogative powers to handle foreign policy and war. Their business was to represent their localities, and to avoid taking responsibility for these complex and expensive national burdens. Fortunately, there was no need for them to do so, since the secret of making war at sea without taxes was already discovered. In so far as taxes might be needed, they should be granted as a reward for virtue, that is to say after an aggressively Protestant foreign policy had proved its inevitable success. There was no point of contact here with the reality of James I's situation. To guard English independence from resurgent Habsburg power, to achieve his main foreign-policy objective of restoring his nephew to the Palatinate, called for alliance with France, which could only be bought by some relaxation of the penal laws against Catholics. For the House of Commons, this was popery and tyranny, the negation of a true English naval policy. What was worse, it was promoted by the duke of Buckingham, a kinsman of Catholics, a commander of armies and consequently an enemy of true freedom. So the naval expeditions of the 1620s were wrecked, and

---

[16] David Cressy, *Bonfires and Bells: National Memory and the Protestant Calendar in Elizabethan and Stuart England* (1989), 110–23; Carol Z. Wiener, 'The Beleaguered Isle: A Study of Elizabethan and Jacobean Anti-Catholicism', *Past and Present*, 51 (1971), 27–62 [hereafter *P&P*]; John Miller, *Popery and Politics in England 1660–1688* (Cambridge, 1973), 67–90.

Charles I inherited a situation in which his naval ambitions and those of his subjects were incompatible. For them the first essential of naval policy was to enforce the penal laws against Catholics; to invoke the blessing of God, and to bring in the rich prizes that were the inevitable fruit of a good and godly use of sea-power. 'We may enjoy peace and prosperity', as Isaac Pennington proclaimed; 'I mean peace with all the world, but war with Spain.' Sir John Eliot agreed: 'War only will secure and repair us' – meaning war with Spain, to be paid for by recusant fines.[17] Meanwhile the earl of Warwick and his associates of the Providence Island Company showed what a truly English naval policy should be, mounting a private naval war in the Caribbean against Spain, and in other seas against all comers. Warwick's piratical activities split the Virginia Company and nearly destroyed the East India Company, but in the eyes of public opinion they were a standing example, and reproach, to Charles I. It was no accident that it was John Hampden who was put up to oppose the legality of Ship Money, for as a director of the Providence Island Company he was a representative of true, patriotic English naval warfare.[18] Charles I's great fleet was a symbol of all his opponents regarded as wrong in his policy. It was maintained by extra-parliamentary taxation levied by prerogative power. It was associated with Laudian policies at home, and *de facto* Catholic alliance abroad. Without going to war it deterred foreign powers and supported the authority of the crown; instead of fighting to protect English trade and bring home lucrative prizes, as it should have done. When the civil war broke out and parliament gained control of the fleet, Warwick, the man who had shown Charles I how it ought to be done, was parliament's inevitable choice as its naval commander-in-chief.[19]

Under the Commonwealth and Protectorate the realities of power exposed some of the contradictions inherent in the English tradition of

[17] G. M. D. Howat, *Stuart and Cromwellian Foreign Policy* (1974), 52; S. R. Gardiner, *History of England from the Accession of James I to the Outbreak of the Civil War, 1603–1642* (10 vols., 1883–4), V, 191.

[18] Conrad Russell, *Parliaments and English Politics 1621–1629* (Oxford, 1979), 8, 71–83, 284–5, 290; Thomas Cogswell, 'Foreign Policy and Parliament: The Case of La Rochelle', *English Historical Review*, 99 (1984), 241–67 [hereafter *EHR*]; Roger Lockyer, *Buckingham: The Life and Political Career of George Villiers, First Duke of Buckingham, 1592–1628* (1981), 190, 244, 266, 467–74; S. L. Adams, 'Foreign Policy and the Parliaments of 1621 and 1624', in *Factions and Parliament: Essays on Early Stuart History*, ed. Kevin Sharpe (Oxford, 1978), 139–71; Simon Adams, 'Spain or the Netherlands? The Dilemmas of Early Stuart Foreign Policy', in *Before the English Civil War: Essays on Early Stuart Politics and Government*, ed. Howard Tomlinson (1983), 79–101; W. Frank Craven, 'The Earl of Warwick, a Speculator in Piracy', *Hispanic American Historical Review*, 10 (1930), 457–79; 'The Earl of Warwick's Voyage of 1627', ed. Nelson P. Bard, in *The Naval Miscellany V*, ed. N. A. M. Rodger (NRS, CXXV, 1984), 15–93; Nelson P. Bard, 'The Ship Money Case and William Fiennes, Viscount Saye and Sele', *Bulletin of the Institute of Historical Research*, 50 (1977), 177–84.

[19] Miller, *Popery and Politics*, 81–4; N. A. M. Rodger, *The Safeguard of the Sea: A Naval History of Britain*, I: *660–1649* (1997), 379–86, 393–4.

sea-power. For the first time since the tenth century, a fleet was built powerful enough to raise England to the first rank of European powers – a fleet paid for by arbitrary taxation illegally imposed by a military dictatorship which had ruthlessly slaughtered every one of the sacred cows of English liberty for which the civil war had supposedly been fought. This fleet launched into a war of aggression against fellow-Protestants, the Dutch, justified by the tortuous argument that a Presbyterian was next kin to a Jesuit, and that as insufficiently pious Protestants they constituted the first obstacle to the march on Rome. The Spanish War which followed brought disillusionment from another quarter. It was beyond question that such a war must be blessed by God, who had so often blessed the Good Old Cause, all the more so since 'the Spaniards cannot oppose much, being a lazy, sinfull people, feeding like beasts upon their lusts, and upon the fat of the land, and never trained up to warres'.[20] Instead, the war brought heavy expense, heavy loss to trade and no profit whatever. Cromwell's confidence never recovered from the humiliating Hispaniola disaster, the worst defeat the New Model Army ever suffered. In the end the war served not for 'the ruining and the utter fall of Romish Babylon',[21] but only to make England an auxiliary to the aggressive foreign policy of Cardinal Mazarin.[22]

All this might have taught public men a few lessons in the realities of sea-power, but the only one they seem to have learnt, at least in part, was its true financial cost. The Interregnum at least taught the English to pay taxes, and the political debates of Charles II's reign assumed a more realistic, or at least less unrealistic, estimate of the resources needed to make war at sea.[23] In all other respects England's experience of military dictatorship only entrenched the myths of sea-power. The failures of Cromwell's navy were swiftly forgotten, and its successes attributed to

[20] Thomas Gage, in *A Collection of the State Papers of John Thurloe*, ed. T. Birch (7 vols., 1742), III, 60.

[21] Thomas Gage, in *Thurloe State Papers*, ed. Birch, III, 61.

[22] Steven C. A. Pincus, 'Popery, Trade and Universal Monarchy: The Ideological Context of the Outbreak of the Second Anglo-Dutch War', *EHR*, 107 (1992), 1–29; John F. Battick, 'Cromwell's Diplomatic Blunder: The Relationship between the Western Design of 1654–55 and the French Alliance of 1657', *Albion*, 5 (1973), 279–98; Charles P. Korr, *Cromwell and the New Model Foreign Policy: England's Policy towards France, 1649–1658* (Berkeley, CA, 1975); Timothy Venning, *Cromwellian Foreign Policy* (1995); Hans-Christoph Junge, *Flottenpolitik und Revolution: Die Entstehung der englischen Seemacht während der Herrschaft Cromwells* (Stuttgart, 1980); Roger Crabtree, 'The Idea of a Protestant Foreign Policy', in *Cromwell, A Profile*, ed. Ivan Roots (London, 1973), 160–89; Blair Worden, 'Oliver Cromwell and the Sin of Achan', in *History, Society and the Churches: Essays in Honour of Owen Chadwick*, ed. Derek Beales and Geoffrey Best (Cambridge, 1985), 125–45; R. C. Thompson, 'Officers, Merchants and Foreign Policy in the Protectorate of Oliver Cromwell', *Historical Studies Australia and New Zealand*, 12 (1965–7), 149–65.

[23] James Scott Wheeler, *The Making of a World Power: War and the Military Revolution in Seventeenth-Century England* (Stroud, 1999).

virtue and godliness. In a striking witness to the English capacity to build an imaginary world, this military despotism came to be cited as a symbol of political liberty. All this was possible because sea-power, and the Navy in particular, was a subject in which every shade of opinion in Restoration England took pride. Here, and here alone, royalist and republican met on common ground. The Navy was a national concern, one on which every Englishman claimed an opinion. Things could be said about the Navy which could not be said about the state. It was impossible to speak openly in favour of the English Republic in the 1660s – but it was entirely acceptable to argue that the republican Navy had been successful because it had been virtuous and godly, where the Stuart Navy was neither. Right actions at home were the foundation of success abroad. As Charles II fought two wars against the Protestant Dutch, both of them in a context of resurgent royal authority, parliament reacted as it had to his father: when the king asked for money for the Navy, parliament rebuked his false sense of priorities by concentrating on suppressing the Catholics. During 1665 and 1666 it forced through the Irish Cattle Acts, and blamed the papists for the Great Fire. For want of the money the Commons were too busy and too suspicious to vote, the main fleet had to be laid up, opening the way for the Dutch raid on the Medway.[24]

The Third Dutch War, fought in alliance with Louis XIV, on a domestic policy of naked tolerance, initially without parliamentary support, still more strongly aroused all the old English nightmares of popery and tyranny. Parliament's reaction to naval disappointment was to suppress the king's Declaration of Indulgence and impose the Test Act. As always, the essential core of any truly English naval policy was Protestantism, and its most urgent application was in domestic, not foreign policy. Parliament was somewhat reassured by the partial hand-over of the Navy to opposition management in 1673, and by the anti-French alliance of 1678, but all the old paranoia broke out anew with the Popish Plot, and once again the Navy was at the heart of the political crisis because it was seen to embody all that was right or wrong with the nation. The failure to discover the Catholic officers and administrators, alleged to control the Navy, may be said to mark the moment at which the Exclusion Crisis passed its peak, and Charles II's decision to hand over much of the management of the Navy to the opposition in the Commons (and to send into exile his brother the former lord admiral) was perhaps the essential concession which permitted him to weather the storm. In all this the Navy's real connection with the political issues was at best tangential. Even if you believe, as some historians still do,[25] that Charles II genuinely

---

[24] Ronald Hutton, *The Restoration: A Political and Religious History of England and Wales, 1658–1667* (Oxford, 1985), 251–60; Miller, *Popery and Politics*, 103–5.

[25] Lenman, *England's Colonial Wars*, 206.

aimed at imposing a Catholic despotism, there is no doubt that the Navy would have been of little direct help to him, and that he did nothing to make it in the least responsive to such ambitions. But for contemporaries the Navy's connections with liberty and Protestantism were so intimate that any threat to either of them had to be seen as a threat to the Navy's proper identity.[26]

The same arguments presented themselves with redoubled force under James II. Here again most contemporaries believed that toleration and tyranny were inseparably linked, and again some modern historians agree.[27] Once again contemporaries assumed that the perversion of the Navy must be an essential part of the king's wicked plans. In this case their fears were not completely imaginary, in that there were a few real Catholic sea officers, but their obsession with the Mediterranean squadron as a nursery of papists proved to be the exact reverse of the truth.[28] Once again the English view of the foreign world was hopelessly distorted. 'There were two inchanting terms', one of the bishops recalled, 'which at the first pronounciation could, like Circe's intoxicating cups, change men into beasts; namely Popery, and the French interest. Which words, if anyone did but slightly mention in the House of Commons, all serious counsels were immediately turn'd into rage and clamour.'[29] The public mind was obsessed with the risk that James II would crush Protestant liberty with the aid of Louis XIV and Innocent XI, though in reality his Most Christian Majesty was a declared enemy of the pope, and James II was on indifferent terms with both of them. Meanwhile, all unnoticed by the public, a real invasion was preparing in an entirely different quarter.

In many respects the Glorious Revolution sharply increased the gap between myth and reality in English naval power. Charles II and James II had known and cared a great deal about their Navy, so that during their reigns it enjoyed strong and expert leadership. William III had a clear sense of the strategic value of sea-power, but no personal interest in ships. The Revolution settlement indirectly strengthened parliamentary authority in matters financial, and it was natural for him to concede the powers of admiralty to parliament. The Dutch constitution had

---

[26] Steven C. A. Pincus, *Protestantism and Patriotism: Ideologies and the making of English Foreign Policy, 1650–1668* (Cambridge, 1996), 354–70, 410–29; J. D. Davies, 'The Navy, Parliament and Political Crisis in the Reign of Charles II', *Historical Journal*, 36 (1993), 271–88; J. R. Jones, *The Anglo-Dutch Wars of the Seventeenth Century* (1996); Miller, *Popery and Politics*, 125–31.

[27] W. A. Speck, 'Some Consequences of the Glorious Revolution', in *The World of William and Mary: Anglo-Dutch Perspectives on the Revolution of 1688–89*, ed. Dale Hoak and Mordechai Feingold (Stanford, 1996), 29–41, at 31–2.

[28] L. Gooch, 'Catholic Officers in the Navy of James II', *Recusant History*, 14 (1978), 276–80; Peter Le Fevre, 'Tangier, the Navy, and its Connection with the Glorious Revolution of 1688', *MM*, 73 (1987), 187–90.

[29] *Bishop Parker's History of his Own Time*, trans. Thomas Newlin (1727), 379–80; this is Samuel Parker, made bishop of Oxford in 1686.

taught him to regard admiralties as engines of disunity and inefficiency, irretrievably dominated by his republican enemies. His business was to avoid government and control power by acting in secret through a few trusted ministers. He despised the ignorant passions of members of parliament, which he regarded as God's punishment on England, but he permitted them to interfere in the detailed management of the naval war. Terrified by the apparent ease with which the Dutch had invaded in 1688, obsessed by the political treachery which it believed had been responsible, the House of Commons reacted to every naval defeat, and some victories, by impeaching the admirals responsible. It arbitrarily reduced the naval votes to punish want of success, and attempted to manage both operational deployments and warship design by legislation.[30]

The most striking evidence of the extent to which the parliaments of William III and Queen Anne were possessed by naval myth rather than naval reality is the great controversy between 'Gentlemen' and 'Tarpaulins' which was at its height during these years. Ostensibly this pitted the advocates of officers promoted from warrant rank or the merchant service, against those of officers chosen from gentlemen. Historians from Macaulay onwards have believed that this was a real debate about a real naval issue.[31] Once upon a time it had been. Charles II in 1660 had faced a serious political and practical problem, inheriting a Navy commanded entirely by sectaries and republicans, and without any established system for selecting and promoting officers. His success in resolving this issue is one of the great achievements of his reign. Well before his death the sea officers were becoming a united corps. There were still many quarrels amongst them, but they were the professional disputes of rivals for promotion and prize money, having little connection with politics and almost none with social origin.[32] This was still true after the Revolution. There was a new problem with political tensions amongst senior officers, which parliament with its obsessive conspiracy theories did all it could to make worse, but there were no significant social tensions,

[30] J. A. Johnstone, 'Parliament and the Navy, 1688–1714' (Ph.D. thesis, Sheffield University, 1968); T. J. Denman, 'The Political Debate over War Strategy, 1689–1712' (Ph.D. thesis, Cambridge University, 1985); *Archives ou correspondance inédite de la maison d'Orange-Nassau*, fourth series, ed. F. J. L. Krämer (3 vols., Leiden, 1907–9) III, 249–50, 509; John Ehrman, *The Navy in the War of William III, 1689–1697: Its State and Direction* (Cambridge, 1953), 311–20; Brian Lavery, *The Ship of the Line* (2 vols., 1983–4), I, 70–1.

[31] T. B. Macaulay, *The History of England from the Accession of James II* (Everyman edn, 4 vols., 1906), I, 225–8; Norbert Elias, 'Studies in the Genesis of the Naval Profession', *British Journal of Sociology*, 1 (1950), 291–309.

[32] J. D. Davies, *Gentlemen and Tarpaulins: The Officers and Men of the Restoration Navy* (Oxford, 1991); Bernard Capp, *Cromwell's Navy: The Fleet and the English Revolution, 1648–1660* (Oxford, 1989), 387–96.

and the rapidly expanding Navy of the 1690s provided good promotion prospects for all comers.[33]

The 'Gentlemen versus Tarpaulins' controversy was conducted by politicians, few of whom knew anything about the real Navy. The Navy mattered very much to them, and it was perhaps the only major national institution that everyone supported. The Church, the monarchy, parliament, the army – all these were intensely divisive in the 1690s. Only the Navy united the political world, and provided a common language of political rhetoric. It was a screen on which every party could project its own ideology – a blank screen, thanks to their ignorance of what it was really like. Those who supported the 'Tarpaulins' praised not only their superior skill, but even more their superior virtue; they were more English, more manly, more Protestant and more courageous than Frenchified courtiers, cruel, effeminate and cowardly. The advocates of gentlemen likewise invoked the virtues which only breeding conferred, and which contrasted with the brutish ignorance of the common men. In between there were other positions, notably Lord Halifax's famous *Rough Draught of a New Modell at Sea* of 1694, arguing for a combination of both characters.[34]

In all this the Navy provided the language of political debate, not the subject. To speak for the superior virtue of Tarpaulin officers was to praise the Cromwellian Navy, and by implication the republican cause. Thus the author of *An Enquiry into the Causes of our Naval Miscarriages*, a pamphlet of 1707, quoted 'an old Cromwellian captain' on the moral collapse allegedly brought about by the Restoration:

> Instead of the good Morals, and harmless Conversation of our Seamen in the Parliament-time, there was nothing but Cursing, Swearing, Damning, Sinking, and obscene nasty Discourse, to be heard on board our Fleet; so that it look'd more like the Suburbs of Hell, than a Christian Navy.

He did not literally mean that the recent successes of Forbin and Duguay-Trouin against Channel convoys had been made possible by an outbreak of bad language in the English Navy almost half a century before; he meant that naval, and therefore national, success sprang from the virtue which a godly, republican system generated.[35]

There was a tendency for parliamentarians to become somewhat less ignorant about the Navy during the course of the wars of King William

---

[33] David Davies, 'The English Navy on the Eve of War, 1689', in *Guerres Maritimes (1688–1713)* (Vincennes, 1996), 1–14; N. A. M. Rodger, 'Commissioned Officers' Careers in the Royal Navy, 1690–1815', *Journal for Maritime Research* [www.jmr.nmm.ac.uk] (July 2001), graphs 1.1, 2.1, 3.1, 6.1, 6.2.

[34] *The Works of George Savile, Marquis of Halifax*, ed. Mark N. Brown (3 vols., Oxford, 1989), I, 296–314; Robert E. Glass, 'The Image of the Sea Officer in English Literature, 1660–1710', *Albion*, 26 (1994), 583–99.

[35] Glass, 'The Image of the Sea Officer', 587–9.

and Queen Anne. The lapse of the Licensing Act in 1695 promoted the circulation of information and argument, some of it sound, and Queen Anne's desire to resign to parliament many decisions that William III had kept to himself encouraged a less irresponsible attitude.[36] Nevertheless the parliamentarians of the eighteenth century still thought naturally in terms of agreeable stereotypes, and many if not most would probably have agreed with Henry Pelham: 'My observation as to foreign affairs is, that the less one knows of them the better.'[37] Ignorant and credulous public men, informed or misinformed by ignorant and credulous journalists, were easily roused to xenophobia, and still obsessed by fears of popery and arbitrary government.[38]

An obvious example of this is the popular hysteria which forced Walpole's government into war with Spain in 1739. The public remained almost as convinced as Cromwell's government had been over eighty years before that Spain was wealthy, effete and vulnerable, though ministers were much better informed. A 'mad and vain nation... warmed and hardened by pride and prejudice',[39] identified with the traditional, patriotic myths of national naval superiority which dictated that a war against Spain must necessarily be easy, glorious and profitable. Pious, virtuous and blessed by God, English sea-power could not but be prosperous. It might cost money, but that money was in the nature of an investment which would yield a sure return. 'What we give towards the support of a War seems to be but a kind of Venture to the Sea, which may return again with great Profit which makes us Contribute with Alacrity towards the Charges of such a War.'[40] In the words of the title of a pamphlet of 1727, *Great Britain's Speediest Sinking Fund is a Powerful Maritime War, Rightly Manag'd, and Especially in the West Indies.*[41]

---

[36] Johnstone, 'Parliament and the Navy', 57–8 and 493–5; Denman, 'The Political Debate over War Strategy', 18–19; John B. Hattendorf, 'The Machinery for the Planning and Execution of English Grand Strategy in the War of the Spanish Succession, 1702–1713', in *Changing Interpretations and New Sources in Naval History: Papers from the Third United States Naval Academy History Symposium*, ed. R. W. Love, jr (New York, 1980), 80–95.

[37] To Lord Essex, 21 July 1735: Jeremy Black, 'British Neutrality in the War of the Polish Succession, 1733–1735', *International History Review*, 8 (1986), 345–66, at 358.

[38] J. C. D. Clark, *The Dynamics of Change: The Crisis of the 1750s and English Party Systems* (Cambridge, 1982), 11–12; Paul Langford, 'William Pitt and Public Opinion, 1757', EHR, 88 (1973), 54–80, at 58–9; J. R. Jones, *Britain and the World 1649–1815* (Brighton, 1980), 12–13; James T. Boulton, 'Arbitrary Power: An Eighteenth-Century Obsession', *Studies in Burke and his Times*, 9 (1968), 905–26; David Armitage, *The Ideological Origins of the British Empire* (Cambridge, 2000), 143–4, 173.

[39] Philip Woodfine, 'The Anglo-Spanish War of 1739', in *The Origins of War in Early Modern Europe*, ed. Jeremy Black (Edinburgh, 1987), 185–209, quoting at 185–6 the ministerial writer Henry Etough.

[40] Ruth Bourne, *Queen Anne's Navy in the West Indies* (New Haven, 1939), 20, quoting Dr James Drake, *An Essay concerning the Necessity of Equal Taxes* (1702).

[41] Daniel A. Baugh, *British Naval Administration in the Age of Walpole* (Princeton, 1965), 15.

The Cromwellian regime was now less fashionable, and the naval virtues were once again evoked by references to the glories of Queen Elizabeth's reign. Thomson and Arne united to remind the Opposition of Britannia's glories, and to conjure up a future golden age in which 'Don Roberto' would be ejected from power, British sea-power restored and Britons nevermore be slaves. The Navy, 'as essential to our Safety & Wealth as Parliament or Magna Charta', was the guarantor of freedom, virtue and conquest.[42] Those like Admiral Vernon whose victories gave substance to these myths were immediately elevated to the status of Protestant heroes.[43] Those who failed to do their duty by the myths of sea-power, like Mathews, Lestock or Byng, were condemned to public execration, if not execution.[44] Popular religious sentiment remained strong, and anti-Catholicism was sharply revived by the 1745 Jacobite rebellion, so that Protestantism, prosperity and naval mastery remained closely connected.[45] From the 1750s, public attention tended to turn to France rather than Spain, but sea-power was as ever the guarantor of all that really mattered.

> All true Englishmen, since the decay of the Spanish monarchy, have ever taken it for granted, that the security of their religion, liberty and property; that their honour, their wealth, and their trade depend chiefly upon the proper measures to be taken from time to time against the growing power of France.[46]

The proper measures were of course naval, and by the end of the Seven Years War sea-power was still more deeply entrenched as the supreme

---

[42] Philip Woodfine, *Britannia's Glories: The Walpole Ministry and the 1739 War with Spain* (Woodbridge, 1998), quoting (at 235) the diplomat Sir Everard Fawkener; *idem*, 'Ideas of Naval Power and the Conflict with Spain, 1737–1742', in *The British Navy and the Use of Naval Power in the Eighteenth Century*, ed. Jeremy Black and Philip Woodfine (Leicester, 1988), 71–90; Richard Harding, *Amphibious Warfare in the Eighteeth Century: The British Expedition to the West Indies 1740–1742* (Woodbridge, 1991), 22–6.

[43] Gerald Jordan and Nicholas Rogers, 'Admirals as Heroes: Patriotism and Liberty in Hanoverian England', *Journal of British Studies*, 28 (1989), 201–24; Kathleen Wilson, 'Empire, Trade and Popular Politics in Mid-Hanoverian Britain: The Case of Admiral Vernon', *P&P*, 121 (1988), 74–109.

[44] Bob Harris, '"American Idols": War and the Middling Ranks in Mid-Eighteenth Century Britain', *P&P*, 150 (1996), 111–41, at 119–21; Nicholas Rogers, *Crowds, Culture and Politics in Georgian Britain* (Oxford, 1998), 61–3.

[45] Jeremy Black, *Natural and Necessary Enemies: Anglo-French Relations in the Eighteenth Century* (1986), 161; Colin Haydon, '"I Love my King and my Country, but a Roman Catholic I Hate": Anti-Catholicism, Xenophobia and National Identity in Eighteenth-Century England', in *Protestantism and National Identity: Britain and Ireland, c. 1650–c. 1850*, ed. Tony Claydon and Ian McBride (Cambridge, 1998), 33–52; Armitage, *Ideological Origins*, 7–8.

[46] *The Fourth Earl of Sandwich: Diplomatic Correspondence 1763–1765*, ed. Frank Spencer (Manchester, 1961), 7, quoting Israel Maudit, *Considerations on the Present German War*, 4th edn (1761), 10.

symbol of the national character and virtue.[47] A generation later Admiral Keppel briefly attained the status of Protestant hero, not for having won a victory, but for having diverted the Navy from oppressing the Americans back to its proper role of fighting Catholics and defending English liberties. It was even insinuated that his enemy Admiral Palliser was a secret Catholic in league with the administration to subvert English freedom.[48]

Since liberty was a defining characteristic both of sea-power and of Britain, the methods used to man the Navy presented certain intellectual and moral inconsistencies which neatly illustrate the gap between myth and reality. For those professionally concerned with the efficiency of the Navy, the manning problem was a permanent nightmare. Seven times between 1696 and 1758 government bills were introduced into parliament which offered to move at least some way away towards methods more equitable and less arbitrary than the press. Only the first was enacted, and its failure reinforced prejudice against all plans of registration, however limited and voluntary. Liberty and the Navy were intimately associated, and the symbiosis of trade and sea-power provided the Navy's manpower by an automatic mechanism which required no government intervention. Consequently, there could be no manning problem; or if there appeared to be, it was only because of Walpole's malice and tyranny.[49] His 1740 scheme proposed, the Opposition claimed, 'not only to enslave, for the best part of their lives, upwards of 150,000 free born subjects, and to invest the crown with an absolute power over them; but also, thereby to give the crown a farther power of influencing of the

[47] Stephen Conway, 'War and National Identity in the Mid-Eighteenth-Century British Isles', *EHR*, 116 (2001), 863–93, at 884–6; Peter Krahé, *Literarische Seestücke: Darstellungen von Meer und Seefahrt in der englischen Literatur des 18. bis 20. Jahrhunderts* (Hamburg, 1992), 29–43; Juan A. Ortega y Medina, *El conflicto anglo-español por el dominio oceanico (siglos XVI y XVIII)* (Mexico City 1981); Geoff Quilley, '"All Ocean Is her Own": The Image of the Sea and the Identity of the Maritime Nation in Eighteenth-Century British Art', in *Imagining Nations*, ed. Geoffrey Cubitt (Manchester, 1998), 132–52.

[48] Rogers, *Crowds, Culture and Politics*, 122–51; Kathleen Wilson, *The Sense of the People: Politics, Culture and Imperialism in England, 1715–1785* (Cambridge, 1995), 256–8; *The Private Papers of John, Earl of Sandwich, First Lord of the Admiralty 1771–1782*, ed. G. R. Barnes and J. H. Owen (NRS, LXIX, LXXI, LXXV, LXXVIII, 1932–8), II, 191; A. M. W. Stirling, *Pages & Portraits from the Past, Being the Private Papers of Admiral Sir William Hotham, G.C.B. Admiral of the Red* (2 vols., 1919), II, 311; Stephen Conway, *The British Isles and the War of American Independence* (Oxford, 2000), 255–6.

[49] J. S. Bromley, 'Away from Impressment: The Idea of a Royal Naval Reserve, 1696–1859', in *Britain and the Netherlands*, VI: *War and Society*, ed. A. C. Duke and C. A. Tamse (The Hague, 1977), 168–88; Gillian Hughes, 'The Act for the Increase and Encouragement of Seamen, 1696–1710. Could it Have Solved the Royal Navy's Manning Problem?', in *Guerres Maritimes*, 25–34; Christopher Lloyd, *The British Seaman 1200–1860: A Social Survey* (1968), 173–93; Baugh, *British Naval Administration*, 234–40; Stephen Gradish, *The Manning of the British Navy during the Seven Years' War* (1980), 107–10.

elections throughout England'.[50] Genghis Khan, James II and the Spanish Inquisition were invoked to illustrate its horrors. The modest 1749 plan to establish a voluntary reserve of 3,000 men was denounced as intending 'to circumscribe public liberty, and augment the number of those, whom ministers desired to reduce to a state of slavery'.[51] Those who opposed reserve or registration schemes as a threat to the liberty of the subject were implicitly declaring that impressment was a lesser threat, or none at all, but perhaps understandably, they tended not to push their case to its logical conclusion. For the Wilkite and pro-American radicals later in the century who directly attacked impressment as an infringement of English liberties this graceful elision was not so easy. Taking impressment in isolation, their case almost made itself, but it presented difficulties when they fully subscribed to the traditional idea of British sea-power as a temple of Protestant liberty, and demanded that the Navy be mobilised at the same time as denying it an essential source of manpower. A figure like Granville Sharp neatly illustrates the contradictions. A leader of the City of London opposition to impressment during the American War, Sharp was also founding chairman both of the Anti-Slavery Society and later of the Protestant Union. There was nothing in the least contradictory, of course, in campaigning simultaneously for the emancipation of slaves and against that of Catholics. The suppression of Catholicism had always been regarded as an essential element of English liberty, and remained so for the popular radicals of the period. The difficulty for Sharp, and those who campaigned with him against impressment, was that the Navy also was so inseparably connected with English liberty that it was difficult to campaign against the tyranny of the press without appearing to be a friend of tyranny.[52]

Their solution lay not in explicit arguments, which might have been somewhat vulnerable, but in skilful insinuations that impressment,

---

[50] Lord Gage, in *The Parliamentary History of England*, ed. William Cobbett (36 vols., 1806–20), XI, 422.

[51] William Coxe, *Memoirs of the Administration of the Right Honourable Henry Pelham* (2 vols., 1829), II, 67, quoting Lord Egmont.

[52] John A. Wood, 'The City of London and Impressment 1776–1777', *Proceedings of the Leeds Philosophical and Literary Society*, 8 (1956–9), 111–27; Nicholas Rogers, 'Liberty Road: Opposition to Impressment in Britain during the American War of Independence', in *Jack Tar in History: Essays in the History of Maritime Life and Labour*, ed. Colin Howell and Richard J. Twomey (Fredericton, NB, 1991), 53–75; Bromley, 'Away from Impressment', 170–1; Prince Hoare, *Memoirs of Granville Sharp*, 2nd edn (2 vols., 1828); John Sainsbury, *Disaffected Patriots: London Supporters of Revolutionary America 1769–1782* (Gloucester, 1987), 134–9; Linda Colley, 'Radical Patriotism in Eighteenth-Century England', in *Patriotism: The Making and Unmaking of British National Identity*, ed. Raphael Samuel (3 vols., 1989), I, 169–87; Stephen Conway, 'The Politics of British Military and Naval Mobilization, 1775–83', *EHR*, 112 (1997), 1179–201; Conway, *British Isles*, 153, 255–6; Margarette Lincoln, *Representing the Royal Navy: British Sea Power, 1750–1815* (Aldershot, 2002), 66.

however the crown might try to justify it, was not really a method of manning the Navy at all.[53] The prints and engravings of the anti-impressment movement are a rich source of these ideas. In Gillray's celebrated 'The Liberty of the Subject' of 1779, for example, a press gang is discovered at work in a London square. To judge by the architecture and the clothes of the bystanders, the scene is somewhere in Mayfair, and we are meant to understand that the press gang is a threat, not to the poor and propertyless, but to people who matter, the sort who could afford to buy a one-shilling coloured print like this. The gang is in the process of seizing a tailor. Tailors were notoriously impotent, in every sense, and clearly outside the press-warrant's definition of 'Seamen, Seafaring Men and Persons whose Occupations or Callings are to work in Vessels and Boats upon Rivers.' To take a tailor, therefore, was both illegal and pointless: an arbitrary exercise of power which was of no service to the Navy, and which the patriot could oppose with a clear conscience. The print, in short, depicts an imaginary world which it was convenient for opposition radicals to believe in. Real impressment took place largely at sea. Press-gangs on shore did exist, but they were not promenading in Berkeley Square at noon, they were raiding the waterside pubs of Wapping and Shadwell at midnight. Nor were they illegally taking landsmen; they were selectively looking for the one category of manpower of which the Navy was critically in need: seamen, and above all topmen.[54]

Another imaginary world in which not only metropolitan radicals but all sorts of MPs devoutly wished to believe was that in which the Navy acted as an instrument to purify as well as to defend society, freeing it of 'idle and reprobate Vermin by converting them into a Body of the most industrious People, and even, becoming the very nerves of our State'.[55] Hence the regularity with which every naval bill, regardless of its other provisions, enacted means by which magistrates might despatch paupers and petty criminals into the Navy. This was more than a cynical exercise in reducing the poor rates, it represented a deep-seated feeling about the purifying and cleansing effect of righteous war which can be traced back to Protestant writers of the sixteenth century.[56] This was what ought to have been a function of a truly national force acting in a just cause, and

---

[53] The idea survives among American Marxists, for example, Jesse Lemisch's assertion that 'the navy pressed because to be in the navy was in some sense to be a slave'. J. Lemisch, 'Jack Tar in the Streets: Merchant Seamen in the Politics of Revolutionary America', *William and Mary Quarterly*, third series, 35 (1968), 371–407, at 383.

[54] N. A. M. Rodger, *The Wooden World: An Anatomy of the Georgian Navy* (1986), 164–82.

[55] Rogers, *Crowds, Culture and Politics*, 88, quoting a pamphlet of 1751 by 'Philonauta' (usually identified as Admiral Sir Charles Knowles).

[56] George, 'War and Peace in the Puritan Tradition', 499; J. R. Hale, 'Incitement to Violence? English Divines on the Theme of War, 1578 to 1631', in *Renaissance War Studies* (1983), 487–517, at 494, 498.

therefore, in the minds of public men, it was. In reality, though magistrates occasionally tried to exercise these powers, there was no provision to force the Navy to accept their offerings, and it was usually reluctant to do so.[57]

By the late eighteenth century, sea-power had been an essential part of the patriotic English self-image for over two centuries, and patriotism had always been the first resort of the opposition. Governments might be obliged to take some account of inconvenient facts, but oppositions could always triumph in the virtual reality of the English political imagination, in which sea-power was ever-victorious, in the right kind of war, against the right kind of enemy. A government which declined to fight such a war, like Walpole's in the 1730s, stood self-condemned as unpatriotic, cowardly and tyrannical. A government which accepted the challenge was doomed either to fail, demonstrating incompetence if not treachery, or to succeed, as Walpole's administration did in sending Vernon to attack Porto Bello in 1740, in which case the victory was immediately transformed in Opposition eyes into 'our honest admiral's triumph over Sir Robert and Spain'.[58] Governments, in short, could not win. As late as 1790, the Nootka Sound crisis aroused all the old anti-Spanish certainies so powerfully that the younger Pitt's government was driven by public opinion into claiming a right (to trade anywhere in Spanish territory regardless of Spanish law or policy) which it knew was indefensible, and which it expected would lead to war.[59]

The Navy was still, in the words of the *Gentleman's Magazine* in 1798, 'the sacred palladium of our laws, our religion, and our liberties, not to perish or be overthrown but with the downfal [*sic*] of Great Britain itself'.[60] Already, however, the moral and political value of sea-power was changing. In the Seven Years War the elder Pitt (with a little help from Frederick the Great) made the national myth work for the government. In the American War, the spectacle of Whig peers openly rejoicing at British naval defeats, and Whig admirals refusing to fight the French,

---

[57] Baugh, *British Naval Administration*, 160–1; D. Hay, 'War, Dearth and Theft in the Eighteenth Century: The Record of the English Courts', *P&P*, 95 (1982), 117–60, at 157; Gillian Russell, *The Theatres of War: Performance, Politics and Society, 1793–1815* (Oxford, 1995), 8; Clive Emsley, 'The Recruitment of Petty Offenders during the French Wars 1793–1815', *MM*, 66 (1980), 199–208; Rogers, 'Liberty Road', 70–1; Conway, *British Isles*, 37; Philip Woodfine, '"Proper Objects of the Press": Naval Impressment and Habeas Corpus in the French Revolutionary Wars', in *The Representation and Reality of War: The British Experience: Essays in Honour of David Wright*, ed. Keith Dockray and Keith Laybourn (Stroud, 1999), 39–60; Lincoln, *Representing the Royal Navy*, 79, 91; Bob Harris, 'Patriotic Commerce and National Revival: The Free British Fishery Society and British Politics, c. 1749–58', *EHR*, 114 (1999), 285–313, at 207, 302–3.

[58] Stanley Ayling, *The Elder Pitt, Earl of Chatham* (1976), 66.

[59] John M. Norris, 'The Policy of the British Cabinet in the Nootka Crisis', *EHR*, 70 (1955), 562–80.

[60] Quoted by Lincoln, *Representing the Royal Navy*, 99.

did a good deal to disgust public opinion and uncouple sea-power from the Opposition.[61] After the war, still aided by the folly of its opponents, and later by the violence of the French revolutionaries, the younger Pitt's government began to appropriate naval patriotism for itself. Anti-Catholicism, for so long an essential part of the English definition of liberty, began to wilt in the 1790s in the face of aggressive atheism. The Navy now became the 'characteristic and constitutional defence' of the country, as Wellington called it,[62] and its adoption as part of the political constitution of the state (as opposed to the moral constitution of the nation) marks a significant development. The nationalisation of patriotism changed the symbolic value of the Navy. Where formerly an abstract sea-power had embodied the national virtues, now sea officers and seamen in person were elevated from honest but somewhat comic figures of the stage, to the status of symbolic national heroes. Their plain, manly sincerity exemplified all that was truest in the English character, and contrasted with the disloyal, Frenchified effeminacy of the Whig aristocracy, and the atheistic republicanism of the radicals.[63] To the consternation of the old-fashioned, real seamen were allowed to walk in the 1797 procession organised by the government to give thanks for recent naval victories. Naval temples in which to celebrate the new national cult were proposed, and in some cases built. Naval monuments to the fallen heroes were erected at public expense.[64] Poets good and bad turned to the Navy – 'the scene of our Triumphs, the source of our Wealth, and the safeguard of our Empire', in the words of the Poet Laureate Henry Pye – for inspiration.[65] William Pitt had caught the Whigs bathing and stolen their clothes.[66]

Radical critics could no longer appeal to the easy certainties of the English naval myth, for Queen Elizabeth now belonged to the government. Naval warfare still came naturally to them as the language

[61] M. D. George, *English Political Caricature to 1792: A Study of Opinion and Propaganda* (Oxford, 1959), 163–6.

[62] John Ehrman, *The Younger Pitt: The Years of Acclaim* (1969), 313.

[63] Lincoln, *Representing the Royal Navy*, 2–6, 29–32; Gerald Newman, *The Rise of English Nationalism: A Cultural History, 1740–1830* (1987), 80–2, 92, 129–33, 194, 213–21; Paul Langford, *Public Life and the Propertied Englishman 1689–1798* (1991), 536–41; Emma Vincent Macleod, *A War of Ideas: British Attitudes to the Wars against Revolutionary France 1792–1802* (Aldershot, 1998), 185.

[64] Alison Yarrington, *The Commemoration of the Hero, 1800–1864: Monuments to the British Victors of the Napoleonic Wars* (1988), 7. The as-yet unpublished work of Dr Holger Hoock will also explore this theme.

[65] Lynda Pratt, 'Naval Contemplation: Poetry, Patriotism and the Navy 1797–99', *Journal for Maritime Research* [www.jmr.nmm.ac.uk] (Dec. 2000), 4.

[66] Linda Colley, 'The Apotheosis of George III: Loyalty, Royalty and the British Nation 1760–1820', *P&P*, 102 (1984), 94–129, at 128; Newman, *English Nationalism*, 36–82, 129–33, 230–1; Jordan and Rogers, 'Admirals as Heroes', 214–22; Russell, *Theatres of War*, 88; J. E. Cookson, *The British Armed Nation, 1793–1815* (Oxford, 1997), 215–17; Langford, *Public Life*, 536–41.

of political rhetoric, but they had to invent new myths of sea-power of their own. Thus, in the unpublished early version of his epic poem *Madoc*, finished in the same year as the naval procession of 1797, the young Robert Southey enriched English literature with a lengthy description of the (otherwise unrecorded) naval battles between Prince Madoc of Gwynedd and the Aztecs, in which the brutally efficient Welsh stand as figures for the Royal Navy; while the freedom-loving Aztecs, their piety and domestic virtues marred only by the occasional human sacrifice, represent the French republicans.[67]

Here we have come full circle, back to the original (and only genuine) British empire of Humphrey Llwyd and John Dee, in which Prince Madoc's most eminent descendant Elizabeth Tudor was to rule over the Welsh-speaking Indians of North America.[68] On this fantastic scene, we may draw this brief survey to a close. The English naval myth was by no means dead, but in its new guise as the property of the state it no longer represented a radical critique of reality. Much about it was still fictional, but henceforward the fictions were different, and in different service. Queen Elizabeth still had a long afterlife ahead of her, but for the historians of the nineteenth century she and the English seamen of her age were the private property of the Royal Navy.[69]

Much of the afterlife of Elizabethan sea-power in the seventeenth and eighteenth centuries can only be understood by carefully distinguishing the history of the real sea, and the sea as viewed from Westminster. There were connections between the two, of course. There was a good deal of correct information in the public domain, competing with much inaccuracy and fantasy.[70] There were men in public life with first-hand knowledge of the realities of sea-power, though their expertise often aroused as much suspicion as respect. In practice the degree of divergence between the reality of naval power, and the image of it as perceived by the political nation, varied at different periods, and on different issues. It did not vary in a random fashion, for the discrepancy was not simply caused by ignorance. Most public men were ignorant of the remote and highly technical world of the seamen, but the problem was not so much that they knew too little, but that they knew too much, or thought they did. 'The men of both these parties are alike in being open to conviction; but so many convictions have already got inside, that it is very difficult to find the openings.'[71] For centuries a set of simple, powerful and tenacious

[67] Pratt, 'Naval Contemplation'.

[68] Gwyn A. Williams, *Madoc: The Making of a Myth* (1979), 31–67.

[69] Cynthia Fansler Behrman, *Victorian Myths of the Sea* (Athens, OH, 1977).

[70] Clark, *The Dynamics of Change*, 10–13.

[71] F. M. Cornford, *Microcosmographia Academica, Being a Guide for the Young Academic Politician* (Cambridge, 1908), 4.

concepts occupied that part of the minds of English public men which was devoted to the sea, and left little room for inconvenient facts which could not be accommodated to the established image. English, later British, sea-power benefited essentially from a breadth and depth of public support which had no equivalent in any other naval power. Without that support it seems very unlikely that Britain would ever have risen to be a dominant trading and later industrial power – but it was not based on the rational analysis of accurate information. In many areas of history, the scholar needs to master the complex and technical world of real seafaring, but to understand policy and high politics we must put aside the inconvenient complications of the facts, to enter into the alternative reality of English sea-power as English politicians imagined it: a myth strong and simple, like all the best myths, with just enough truth to sustain credibility, and not too much to muddle or perplex the public mind.

Transactions of the RHS 14 (2004), pp. 175–84 © 2004 Royal Historical Society
DOI: 10.1017/S0080440104000192   Printed in the United Kingdom

MATHEMATICS AND THE ART OF NAVIGATION: THE ADVANCE OF SCIENTIFIC SEAMANSHIP IN ELIZABETHAN ENGLAND

By Susan Rose

ABSTRACT. This paper examines the extent to which English seamen in the later sixteenth century began to employ astronomical observations and mathematical calculations in navigation instead of relying largely on practical experience. It discusses the manuals of seamanship that were published in increasing numbers at this period and also looks at the availability of instruction in the necessary mathematics. The popularity of some texts including Waghenaer's the *Mariner's Mirrour*, a book combining charts and sailing directions with the tables needed to use astronomical observations, are, it is suggested, an indication of the progress made in this respect by the early seventeenth century.

In 1561 Richard Eden, introducing his translation of Martin Cortes's *Arte of Navigation* (or *Arte de navegar*) piously remarked, 'What can be a better or more charitable dede than to bring them into the way that wander; what can be more difficult than to gyde a shippe engouffed where only water and heaven can be seene?'[1] Eden had undertaken this translation from Spanish at the urging of Stephen Borough who had close connections with John Dee and had also been involved with his brother William in the preparations for the voyage of Willoughby and Chancellor in 1553 in search of a North-East passage to the Orient. Borough, alone among English sixteenth-century mariners, had visited the Spanish pilots' school in Seville and greatly admired the training provided there. Even if his scheme to introduce something similar in England got nowhere, the publication of Eden's book seems to mark a decisive point in English attitudes to navigation. This was to be based in the future not on experience and intuition alone but also on astronomical and mathematical principles.

Both Eva Taylor and David Waters, to whose invaluable work in this field I am greatly indebted,[2] have pointed out how slow the English were

---

[1] Richard Eden, *The Arte of Navigation Translated out of Spanyshe into Englyshe* (1561). This quotation is from D. Waters, *The Art of Navigation in Elizabethan and Early Stuart Times* (1958), 1.

[2] E. G. R. Taylor, *The Haven-finding Art* (1956); Waters, *Art of Navigation*.

to develop an appreciation of scientific navigational skills compared with the Portuguese, the Spanish and the French. The old attitudes associated with Chaucer's Shipman, one of the best known of all the Canterbury pilgrims, persisted into the sixteenth century. The Shipman could:

> reckon well his tides,
> His streams and his dangers him besides,
> His harbour and his moon, his lodemanage.

He had expert knowledge of havens:

> From Gotland to the Cape of Finisterre,
> And every creek in Brittany and Spain.[3]

The understanding of astronomy and mathematics that allowed Portuguese and Spanish mariners from the mid-fifteenth century onwards to make use of navigational instruments and tables to fix their position at sea and to set courses based on the knowledge of the latitude of a location was not commonly found in England before the middle of the next century. William Bourne, one of the foremost of the Tudor exponents of mathematical navigation, remarked in 1571,

> I have known within this 20 years that them that were auncient masters of shippes hathe derided and mocked them that have occupied their cardes and plattes and also the observation of the Altitude of the Pole saying; that they care not for their sheepskinne for he could keepe a beter account upon a boord.[4] And also when they dyd take the altitude they would call them starre shooters and would aske if they had stricken it.[5]

Yet as Waters states, the English 'mastered the art of oceanic navigation so rapidly and effectively that within thirty years they had defeated half the leading maritime states in battle at sea'.[6]

This paper examines the nature of this change in navigational techniques, linking it not only to the historical context but also to the realities of conditions at sea. It will consider whether the change was as dramatic as has been suggested and to what extent the so-called 'new' methods penetrated the world of the mariner.

It is certainly the case that the would-be navigator of the later part of the sixteenth century and the early seventeenth century had no shortage of printed books to instruct him in this new science and the necessary ancillary mathematics. Many were also reprinted at regular intervals which indicates the extent of the demand for this kind of 'how to' book.

---

[3] Geoffrey Chaucer, *The General Prologue to the Canterbury Tales*, ll. 401–4, 408–9. http://www.courses.fas.harvard.edu/~chaucer/ includes the full text with an interlinear version in modern English.

[4] Bourne's 'old salt' is talking about a traverse board, a wooden board with a compass rose drawn on it linked by pegs and cords to a series of pegholes beneath it. It allowed a helmsman to keep a rough check of the time sailed on each rhumb of the wind.

[5] Quoted in E. G. R. Taylor, *Tudor Geography 1485–1583* (1930), 160.

[6] Waters, *Art of Navigation*, 80.

Eden's translation mentioned above was reprinted four times before a completely new edition appeared in 1596.[7] This was in print until 1630. William Bourne's *Regiment for the Sea: Containing Very Necessarie Matters for All Sorts of Sea-men and Trauailers, as Masters of Ships, Pilots Mariners and Marchants*, described by Taylor as being 'the English sailor's *vade mecum* for a generation and more',[8] first appeared in 1574 as an extension and more homely version of his *Almanack and Prognostication for iii Yeares with Sexten Rules of Navigation*, first published in 1567.[9] The *Regiment* needed ten reprints between 1574 and 1631 not including three editions of the version translated into Dutch. By the end of Elizabeth's reign books like Blundeville's *Exercises*[10] said (on the title page) to be 'very necessarie for all young gentlemen that have not been exercised in such disciplines and yet are desirous to have knowledge as well in cosmography astronomie and geography as also in the arte of navigation in which it is impossible to profite withoute the help of these or such like instruction'; Edmund Wright's *Certain Errors in Navigation*,[11] which strongly advocated the use of charts based on Mercator's projection and John Davis's *Seaman's Secrets*,[12] which contains the first clear description of how to set out the tabular log book of a voyage, were also in print. In his *Accidence for Young Sea-men: Or Pathway to Experience* published in 1626, John Smith, 'sometime Governour of Virginia and Admirall of New-England', as he described himself, listed the works a young seaman should study and the instruments he should possess. His list included Wright's *Certain Errors*, both *A Regiment for the Sea* and the *Seaman's Secrets* and also 'waggoner', the most used pilot book, and Robert Hues's book on the use of the globes published in 1592. As well as these books a young navigator also needed 'the sea-mans glasse for the skale, the new attractor for variation',[13] good sea cards or charts, two pairs of compasses, an astrolabe, a quadrant, a cross staff, a back staff and a nocturnal (a device for estimating time at night by the stars). A full idea of the extent of the publications on navigation available to the studious inquirer later in the seventeenth century is clear from the catalogue of a Newcastle bookseller dated 1656. This includes thirteen titles, said to be the most 'vendible' books on navigation. Some later

---

[7] The annotated bibliography of E. G. R. Taylor, *The Mathematical Practitioners of Tudor and Stuart England* (Cambridge, 1954), lists all works on navigation as well as mathematics printed before 1715.

[8] Taylor, *Haven-finding Art*, 201.

[9] Bourne's works have been edited by E. G. R. Taylor, *A Regiment for the Sea and Other Writing on Navigation* (Hakluyt Society, second series, CXXI, 1963).

[10] First published in 1594.

[11] First published in 1599.

[12] This is included in *The Voyages and Works of John Davis the Navigator*, ed. A. H. Markham (Hakluyt Society, LIX, 1880).

[13] An azimuth compass is meant here.

titles are included, like Manwaring's *Seaman's Dictionary* of 1644 and John Smith's *Seaman's Grammar* of 1653 (an expanded version of his *Accidence for Young Sea-men* mentioned above), but Davis's *Secrets* is still listed along with Richard Polter's *A Pathway to Perfect Safety*, published in 1605.[14]

How closely were these books and others like them informed by practical experience of seafaring? Some authors, like Davis, the intrepid searcher for the North-West passage, were, of course, among the most prominent seamen of the age. Davis was also close to that group of interrelated Devon gentlemen, the Gilberts and the Raleighs, who so greatly extended England's reputation as a seafaring nation. Others like Bourne had a humbler background, but still one moulded by experience of the maritime world. He was described by a contemporary as 'an expert artisan', a 'cunning and subtle empirique even if 'unlectured in schooles and unlettered in books'.[15] He was brought up in the world of those whose livelihood depended on the difficult waters of the Thames estuary. His family came from Gravesend and were deeply involved in the business of running the so-called tide barges on the Thames, taking freight from Gravesend to Billingsgate Stairs, going up river on the flood tide and coming down on the ebb. Despite Gabriel Harvey's somewhat patronising comments on his lack of formal education quoted above, Bourne had studied the works of Tudor mathematicians like Digges and himself taught navigation on mathematical principles, a stimulus for the writing of his invaluable book.[16] An account of its contents can in fact serve well as an introduction to the best current navigational practice of his day, though it also includes certain innovations which will be discussed below.

Bourne first of all describes the desired characteristics of a navigator. He should be knowledgeable about tides, soundings, the nature of the ground and both leading marks and landmarks. All this may sound a little familiar; it is very similar to the skills of our friend Chaucer's Shipman. The book, however, includes after this introduction a table of declinations to be used when finding latitudes from sun or star sights. Similarly the chapters on how to ascertain the phases of the moon and to use them to establish the direction of tidal streams are followed by detailed directions in the use of the cross staff and mariner's astrolabe. These instruments had long been used for taking sights from fixed stars, principally the pole star and the sun. In the fifteenth century, the Portuguese pioneers of this method of using the height of a heavenly body above the horizon to determine latitude had probably had to go on shore at first to use their astrolabes, but the Elizabethan versions were certainly intended

[14] E. G. R. Taylor, *Late Tudor and Early Stuart Geography 1583–1650* (1934), 79.
[15] Taylor, *Tudor Geography*, 161.
[16] *A Regiment for the Sea*, ed. Taylor, xvi–xxiv.

for use at sea. Bourne's practicality and empiricism are clearly displayed here in his attempt to deal with the problem of parallax caused by the eye of the observer not being on the centre line of the instrument. His suggestion 'you must pare away a little of the end of the staff' would not improve accuracy greatly but at least he was aware of the probability of error. Illustrations in Bourne's and other manuals perhaps served only to compound this difficulty and that caused by the height of the observer himself above the horizon line. One woodcut intended to explain the use of the cross staff has an apparently disembodied head floating in the sea with the eye at water level. No horizon at all is indicated in the rather more sophisticated engravings of Christ's Hospital boys using the cross staff and back staff from Jonas Morre's *A New Systeme of the Mathematicks*, published as late as 1681.

Bourne goes on to deal with the use of the astrolabe or mariner's ring, the problems caused by compass variation and the way to use almanacs and tables of declinations in varying circumstances. Chapter 14, which is mainly concerned with the need for a navigator to make rough sketches of coastal views, contains a clear description of the use of the log and line with a time glass to estimate a vessel's speed through the water. This is the sole English contemporary invention in the field of navigational instruments but, despite its utility, was not widely adopted by other seafaring nations at the time. The final chapters deal with the finding of longitudes by dead reckoning and the need for careful soundings when entering channels.

The book, in fact, takes navigational practices that had been part and parcel of English seamanship for generations and links them to newer ideas. It would always have been hard for any seafarer in the waters of North-West Europe to ignore tides and there is plenty of evidence that the effect of the waxing and waning of the moon on the direction, strength and timing of tidal streams was well understood before the sixteenth century. This information was probably originally held in a mariner's memory or recorded in treasured handwritten notes. There are only a few rare printed survivors of the many tidetables and the like that probably once existed but were used until they fell apart. Particularly good examples still exist from Brittany, which link an outline of the coast taken from a chart to a compass rose. This, however, is needed to show not wind direction but the timing of the new moon at high water, at a particular port, each compass point being taken to represent forty-five minutes. This was how the so-called establishment of a port was described: e.g. moon north-east-south-west, full sea meant high tide was at 3 pm. Further tables allow differences to be calculated according to the age of the moon, while a calendar was also included. It is interesting that no contemporary material seems to take much notice of the issue of the speed of tidal streams, something which can be of great concern when trying to round a headland or in areas like the waters off the north of Scotland.

Here experience and local knowledge would have been all-important. Similarly, the use of soundings combined with knowledge of the nature of the seabed as a location aid had a long history. This kind of information is an important feature of the rutters or pilot books of which English versions can be found in rare manuscripts from the fifteenth century.[17] The use of the compass, and the need to take bearings, were also part of normal maritime practice well before the sixteenth century. What is relatively new in Bourne's book, in this respect, is the inclusion of information on the need to allow for the variation between magnetic and true North.

This feature, along with the directions on the use of the cross staff and astrolabe for the taking of the altitude of either the pole star or the sun according to the circumstances and the position of a vessel, introduce the need for a navigator to have knowledge of and skill in mathematics. The theoretical and astronomical basis of the calculations needed was well established. The Portuguese *Regimento do Astrolabio e do Quadrante*, which gives directions for observing the pole star, the Rule for raising the Pole, the Rule of the Sun and a list of altitudes from the equator northwards together with a calendar and table of declinations dates from the last decades of the fifteenth century (the earliest surviving printed edition is from 1509). John Dee had close contacts with both Frisius and Mercator and had instructed Stephen Borough in spherical geometry and trigonometry. Leonard Digges published a work called *Prognostication* in 1553. This was a calendar and tide table with additional information regarding the graduation of dials on navigational and surveying instruments. He also designed for his own private pupils what he called 'an instrument for navigation most commodious' which was intended to simplify the finding of tangents and cotangents of angles. Little if any of the work of these scholars was, however, easily accessible to the ordinary seaman, something Bourne was well aware of from his own experience as a teacher.

Mathematics was not taught in schools in Tudor England and those who needed to keep reckonings of various kinds probably picked up the most basic kind of arithmetic 'on the job'. This is clear by implication from the layout of mathematical textbooks in English, which began to appear at much the same time as the earliest of the navigational manuals mentioned previously. Blundeville begins his *Exercises* (which appeared as late as 1594)

---

[17] An example is British Library, Lansdowne MS 285. The sailing directions of Pierre Garcie, dating from *c.* 1483–4 and first printed in 1502–10, have been edited by D. W. Waters, *The Rutter of the Sea: The Sailing Directions of Pierre Garcie* (New Haven and London, 1967). Another example dating from *c.* 1460–80 can be found in the Hastings manuscript at the Society of Antiquaries. This concludes with a picture of a ship entering the Channel taking soundings; the text states that if the vessel is in 80 fathoms, 'yf it be stremy grounde it is between huschant and cille in the entre of the chanel of fflaundres and soo goo yowre cours til ye have sixti fadum deep than goo est northe est a longs the see'.

with 'a very easie arithmetic so plainle written that any man of a mean capacitie can easily learn the same without help of any teacher'. This section begins with an explanation of adding, subtracting, multiplication and division, but even so his assertion is somewhat optimistic when he begins discussing more complex matters. Robert Recorde wrote a series of mathematical and cosmographical textbooks in English in the middle of the century including one called *The Pathway to Knowledge Containing the First Principles of Geometry* (1551). He begins this text with basic definitions of a straight line and a crooked line, pointing out that there is only one kind of straight line but 'innumerable diversities' of crooked ones. He also includes a rousing poem setting out the intrinsic usefulness of geometry in virtually every area of contemporary life but then admits in the preface some doubts as to the best way to teach the subject. He felt men would not understand the mathematical process unless he discussed effects before causes even if 'the cause do go before the effect in order of nature'.[18] As well as the general lack of formal teaching in numeracy (to use the modern term) Recorde faced another problem. Even in the mid-sixteenth century the use of Arabic numerals had not fully replaced Roman numerals. One of the examples from an accounting manual, James Peele's *The Manner and Fourme how to Kepe a Reconyng*, published in 1553, makes this clear. In this example of 'the inventorie or state of soche goodes as unto me Fraunces Bonde of London Grocer dooeth perteine', sums of money, which had to be reckoned up, are in Arabic numerals, but everything else (including final totals, the rates of exchange in various currencies and the values of jewellery) is still written in Roman figures. A teacher had to introduce and explain the use of Arabic figures before moving on to more advanced matters.

All this gives one considerable admiration for the navigators of Elizabeth's reign, taking into account the amount of new material and new techniques they had to master. First of all they had to make observations with cumbersome instruments. Trying to get a passably accurate reading from an astrolabe on deck in any kind of a seaway must have been extremely difficult; the bland illustrations in the various manuals give no hint of this whatsoever. The cross staff also had disadvantages, not the least being the need to look directly at the sun (if using it to take the altitude of that body), something which the use of smoked glass vanes did little to ameliorate. One modern seafarer who used a cross staff on the *Golden Hind* replica voyage of 1976 found that the experience gave him greatly increased respect for the navigators who had been forced to rely on it.[19] The back staff, designed by John Davis, someone with immense

---

[18] This book is not paginated.
[19] A. N. Stimson and C. St J. H. Daniel, *The Cross Staff: Historical Development and Modern Use* (1977), 13.

practical experience of both cross staff and astrolabe, particularly in high latitudes, got away from the danger to one's eyes inherent in the cross staff (since the operator stood with his back to the sun whose rays were reflected in a mirror), but it did not entirely replace the earlier instrument.

Once the observations had been made, however dubious their accuracy, the navigator then had to calculate his position. Here his mathematical skills became all important. A publication from 1749, *The Mariner's Compass Rectified*, had fairly clear worked examples but the same cannot be said of most sixteenth-century navigational guides. The different calculations necessary according to whether the mariner's vessel was in the northern or southern hemisphere and according to whether the sun's meridian was north or south of the equator at the relevant date were not easy to explain in simple terms. In fact W. E. May, in his *History of Marine Navigation*, was of the opinion that by the beginning of the seventeenth century there was a conflict between the rule of thumb navigation understood by most mariners and the rules propounded by theoretical mathematicians. In his view 'works on navigation were clogged with much mathematical material of no real value to the seaman and by frightening him with a mass of unnecessary rules must actually have delayed his progress'.[20] This observation related, of course, to the difficulties of mariners attempting not only the calculation of latitudes but also the laying of courses including such matters as allowing for compass variation and using the rules for great circle sailing. Solving problems in spherical geometry on board ship, perhaps in very bad weather and until 1614 without the benefit of Napier's logarithms, would probably make modern navigators, who rely on electronic aids linked to satellites to fix their position and to lay a course, quail and admit the ease with which problems can now be solved. Davis would probably have agreed heartily with May since, having briefly mentioned some of the more complex uses of trigonometry in navigation he concludes, 'because seamen are not acquainted with such calculations I therefore omit to speake further thereof, sith this plaine way before taught is sufficient for their purpose'.[21]

Despite these problems, it is not the case that Tudor seamen themselves completely retreated from a more scientific approach to navigation, or that the maritime community was divided between those who were experienced in oceanic navigation and those who were more adept at coastal pilotage. Davis's *Seaman's Secrets*, the fruit of a lifetime at sea, is divided into two books. The first teaches (in his words)

> three kinds of sailing, Horizontal, Paradoxall and sayling upon a great circle; also a horizontal tide table for the easie finding of the ebbing and flowing of the tides with a

---

[20] W. E. May, *A History of Marine Navigation* (Henley, 1973), 17.
[21] *Voyages and Works of John Davis*, ed. Markham, 267.

regiment newly calculated for the finding of the declination of the sun and many other most necessary rules and instruments not heretofore set for them by any.[22]

This first part includes most of the material already discussed together with details of the azimuth compass for finding the variation of the sea compass. Davis also discusses the problem of charts and the projection on which they are based: as he points out 'in the sea chart all these courses are described as parallels without any diversity, alteration or distinction to the contrary whereby the instrument is apparently faulty'.[23] On short voyages this is of no account (in his view) but on longer voyages in high latitudes true rather than plane charts are a necessity. His most useful addition is the description of a 'Table showing the order how the seaman may keep his accounts' or log book. Every twenty-four hours the latitude with course, distance, wind direction and altitude should be set down with an extra column for 'any breefe discourse for your memory'.[24] Sailors had often made such notes (a so-called traverse book kept by Davis himself on his Arctic voyage of 1587 exists), but setting it out in a tabular format made for more systematic and uniform recording and a formula which could be taught. The second part of the book, which is concerned with the use of the globe, was probably of less concern to many, but the two together demonstrate a further development of the kind of amalgam of 'old' and 'new' practices we have already seen in Bourne's work some thirty years earlier.

A similar approach is visible in the 'Exhortation to the Apprentices of the Art of Navigation' written by Lucas Janszoon Waghenaer as a preface to his *Spieghel der Zeevaerdt* or *Mariner's Mirror* as it became in the English translation by Anthony Ashley first published in 1588. This was a publication that combined many of the features of a rutter, or book of sailing directions, with charts, adorned with coastal views, tide tables, tables of the phases of the moon, the declination of the sun and fixed stars (including those in the southern hemisphere) and instructions in the use of the cross staff and astrolabe. Earlier rutters and even some published in Elizabeth's reign contained information on soundings, directions for entering harbours and tides, but none of this invaluable extra material. In the Exhortation the user is directed to be highly observant of landmarks when approaching the coast, drawing sketches and taking bearings. In Waghenaer's view experience is all important 'for that which any man either old or young exerciseth, searcheth out and observeth himself sticketh faster in memory that that which he learneth of others'. Nevertheless he must also learn all he can from the ship's

[22] *The Seaman's Secrets*, title page.
[23] *Ibid.*, 271.
[24] *Ibid.*, 281.

master and practise with the cross staff and astrolabe 'the two principall instruments next the compasse that belong to safe and skilfull seafaring'.[25]

It is no wonder that the book itself remained in print for much of the succeeding century, and in fact books of this type were soon known familiarly as waggoners in England. Its collection of charts, sailing directions and soundings together with instruction in basic navigational practice was hugely useful to the generality of mariners. This was despite the fact that, as Taylor points out, the charts took no account of the problems of projection. Moreover, the charts themselves, though of high quality for the Dutch coast, including indications of anchorages and the presence of seamarks, are very sketchy when it comes to some regions of England. It was the combination of elements that aided the mariner; the sailing directions for entering the Solent at the West End of Wight (for example) were accurate even if the chart itself was not based on a good survey. The sailor was instructed:

> to go in at the West End of Wight you muste looke well to the tide for the flood sets very sore upon the Needles and the ebb likewise westward upon the Shingles and chalke rocks which lie westward of the Needles and it is very narrow between the Needles and the Shingles. Wherefore sail directly with Wight very neare them and keep the inner point of the isle right without the Needles and when you are so come within the Needles beare somewhat off the Island between the Chesell and the Isle's point because of the rocks called the Wardens which lie on Wight-side neare the shore.[26]

He was finally advised to anchor over against Calshott in 7 or 8 fathoms.

Thus the English mariner, who had had little published material to help him acquire the skills necessary to bring a ship in safety to its destination until the middle of the sixteenth century, could rely on a plethora of publications by its end. These varied from the highly theoretical to those which were clearly of enormous value to the whole seagoing community, both those voyaging in home waters and those setting out to cross unknown seas. Knowledge of the use of the instruments necessary to calculate latitudes and to employ difference in latitudes to lay off courses was by the end of the century, I would suggest, expected of the great majority of master mariners. Equally the kind of instinctive appreciation of the way of a ship needed for successful dead reckoning was well appreciated. Some of the more arcane skills of greatest use in the longest passages were rarer, but by the seventeenth century navigation as practised in England could be described as both an art and a science, and as an essential skill for a seafarer.

---

[25] Exhortation to the Apprentices of the Art of Navigation, *The Mariners Mirrour*, trans. A. Ashley (1588), fA2h. Published in facsimile by Theatrum Orbis Terrarum , Amsterdam, 1966.

[26] *The Mariners Mirrour*, facsimile edn, 22.

Transactions of the RHS 14 (2004), pp. 185–98 © 2004 Royal Historical Society
DOI: 10.1017/S0080440104000131   Printed in the United Kingdom

WAS ELIZABETH I INTERESTED IN MAPS – AND DID IT MATTER?

By Peter Barber

ABSTRACT. It tends to be assumed that Queen Elizabeth was interested in maps and globes, not least because she was frequently depicted in their vicinity. Investigation strongly suggests that this was not the case. It is argued that this did matter. By depriving her of an independent source of spatial information, it made her more dependent on her ministers and, in particular, it meant that the royal estates were not mapped before 1600, with long-term financial and possibly constitutional consequences for the crown.

There is probably no English or British monarch who was portrayed more meaningfully in the vicinity of maps and globes than Elizabeth I. This should cause little surprise for in the course of her lifetime the use of maps and globes moved from the fringes into the centre of English life.[1] In the process, as their practical potential as well as their frequent aesthetic appeal were realised, they aroused an enthusiasm among Elizabeth's contemporaries that was comparable to that which accompanied the appearance of the internet over the past decade.

Many of the most important people in Elizabeth's life are known to have been map enthusiasts. The most prominent and active as a patron from the early 1530s was Henry VIII himself but, within their more limited spheres, Thomas Cromwell and Thomas Cranmer were not far behind. Those who were young or were growing up in the 1520s and 1530s were particularly likely to be excited by maps. Elizabeth's tutor, Roger Ascham, almost certainly used Ptolemy's maps to instruct his young charge in history as recommended by Sir Thomas Elyot in his influential treatise, *The Boke Named the Governour* of 1531. Thomas Seymour and his brother Edward, duke of Somerset and Lord Protector to Edward VI,

---

[1] Peter Barber, 'England I: Pageantry, Defense and Government: Maps at Court to 1550', and 'England II: Monarchs, Ministers and Maps 1550–1625', in *Monarchs, Ministers and Maps. The Emergence of Cartography as a Tool of Government in Early Modern Europe*, ed. David Buisseret (Chicago, 1992), 26–98. More generally, see David Buisseret, *The Mapmakers' Quest – Depicting New Worlds in Renaissance Europe* (Oxford, 2003).

were adept at using maps for their own purposes.[2] The inventories of Leicester House and Kenilworth reveal that Elizabeth's great love, Robert Dudley, had an extensive collection of maps for information as well as display.[3] William Cecil first entered Elizabeth's life as surveyor of her lands from 1550.[4] His enthusiasm for maps of all kinds of has been extensively documented.[5] Other courtiers and ministers were similarly fascinated. Sir Francis Walsingham regularly used them and had his galleries on the Strand adorned with wall maps.[6] In 1587–8, Elizabeth's 'Dancing Chancellor', Sir Christopher Hatton, paid Anthony Ashley to translate into English Waghenaer's *Spieghel der Zeevaerdt* (1584), the first purpose-made printed atlas of sea charts of the coasts of Europe with sailing directions.[7] Walter Raleigh commissioned Thomas Harriot and the artist John White to map the Virginia colony in America from 1584 and his Irish estates a decade later.[8]

Elizabeth's wider circle also included numerous map enthusiasts. The polymath, mapmaker and visionary, John Dee, student of Gemma Frisius, and friend of Gerard Mercator, was one of her principal advisers on colonial and navigational matters. Sir Henry Sidney, her long-serving, capable and pragmatic lord deputy in Ireland and the Welsh Marches, the father of Sir Philip Sidney (whose cartographical interests are also recorded), was the patron of Jenkinson's map of Muscovy (1562), the earliest known regional map by an Englishman to be printed in England, and between 1569 and 1572, of Robert Lythe's epoch-making relatively detailed though unpublished mapping of the whole of Ireland.[9]

With this background it would be natural to assume that Elizabeth took more than a passing interest in maps. The visual evidence strongly suggests this.[10] The best known of the 'Sieve portraits' (that by Quentin Matsys the younger, *c.* 1580, now in Siena), shows her next to a large

[2] *Calendar of State Papers Domestic, 1547–1553* (repr. 1992), 87, no. 188. Barber, 'England I', 40–2.

[3] Cited in Simon Adams, 'The Papers of Robert Dudley, Earl of Leicester III: The Countess of Leicester's Collection', *Archives*, 22 (1996), 1–27.

[4] Susan Doran, *Queen Elizabeth I* (2003), 29. In this case taking its traditional meaning of supervisor and overseer.

[5] See particularly R. A. Skelton and John Summerson, *A Description of Maps and Architectural Drawings in the Collection Made by William Cecil, First Baron Burghley. Now at Hatfield House* (Oxford, 1970).

[6] Barber, 'England II', 68–9.

[7] *Ibid.*, 65.

[8] *Ibid.*, 62–3.

[9] *Ibid.*, 67.

[10] For the subsequent paragraph: Roy Strong, *Gloriana: The Portraits of Queen Elizabeth I* (1987), and Susan Doran, 'Virginity, Divinity and Power: The Portraits of Elizabeth I', in *The Myth of Elizabeth*, ed. Susan Doran and Thomas S. Freeman (Basingstoke and New York, 2003), 171–99.

globe with the sun shining on England and ships sailing westwards while the rest of the world is thrown into darkness. The Armada portraits show her with her hand resting over the Americas on a smaller globe. In the Ditchley portrait of about 1592 she is depicted, armillary spheres hanging from her ears, actually standing on a globe, with her feet on an oversized map of England, protecting it from the storms raging to her right over the war-torn European mainland. It was followed in 1596 by Crispin van der Passe's engraving commemorating the sacking of Cadiz. It shows Elizabeth in front of part of a globe representing Spain, with smoke rising from what would seem to be Cadiz and another port.[11] Perhaps the most intriguing cartographic depiction of the queen, however, is to be found as the preface to John Case's *Sphaera Civitatis* of 1588. Elizabeth is shown embracing a version of the Ptolemaic universe containing allegories of her ministers as fixed stars in a genuine court of the Star Chamber, the spheres representing the virtues of her rule, such as prudence, steadfastness, religion, clemency and unbending justice with the queen as the unmoving earthly centre. Older viewers would have recognised that the image was copied from a type of medieval mappamundi showing God as the prime mover embracing the world or universe.[12]

During the course of her reign, Elizabeth was the dedicatee of at least three highly significant cartographic works. The earliest was Christopher Saxton's atlas of the counties of England and Wales of 1579 with an allegorical frontispiece attributed to Remigius Hogenberg depicting Elizabeth enthroned. It has been argued that Elizabeth was personally involved in its composition even to the extent of insisting on the re-engraving of her robes so that in the second state they appeared to fall more naturally over her knees.[13] In 1591–2 she was the recipient of Emery Molyneux's first terrestrial and celestial globes.[14] Engraved by the Flemish émigré mapmaker Jodocus Hondius and with diameters of 62 inches, they were then among the largest printed globes ever to have been produced. Undoubtedly the most outstanding cartographic dedication, however, was of the *Atlas* of Gerard Mercator, probably the best-known cartographer of all time, on the appearance of its final part in 1595. The term Atlas was henceforth to be associated with all such books of maps. The dedication, in 1570, to Philip II of the first true modern atlas, the *Theatrum Orbis Terrarum* by its editor and publisher, Mercator's friend and

[11] Doran, 'Virginity, Divinity and Power', 179–80.

[12] Cf. British Library, Additional Manuscripts [hereafter BL, Add. MS] 28681, fo. 9v.

[13] Ifor M. Evans and Heather Lawrence, *Christopher Saxton: Elizabethan Map-Maker* (Wakefield, 1979), 20.

[14] Anna Maria Crino and Helen Wallis, 'New Researches on the Molyneux Globes', *Der Globusfreund*, 35–7 (1987), 14–15.

rival, Abraham Ortelius, must have made the Mercator dedication all the sweeter.

At court Elizabeth encountered maps at almost every turn. The Privy Gallery in Whitehall continued to be adorned with the maps that had been there in her father's day, including one presented to Henry in 1524 by Girolamo da Verrazzano.[15] To them had been added, since 1549, a printed world map by Sebastian Cabot,[16] and by the 1590s the manuscript world map showing the route of Drake's circumnavigation, which Drake had personally presented to Elizabeth on his return.[17] The queen's portrait is found on a small map of England of 1590 by Jodocus Hondius[18] and her arms appear on all of Saxton's county maps, associating her and her government with every part of her mainland dominions. Behind the grand galleries maps were brought into use to assist in running the court. A rudimentary but perfectly usable routes plan, for instance, almost certainly derived from Saxton's recently published county maps was drawn up when Elizabeth's progress into Suffolk and Norfolk in 1578 was being planned.[19]

Elizabeth's official writings often convey the impression of a genuine interest in maps and an understanding of their potential for government and administration, particularly in the case of Ireland. Throughout her reign, the governance of Ireland abounded in the mixture of distant military, colonial and administrative problems which maps are particularly good at elucidating. A manuscript map of Ireland, probably resembling the 'Goghe' map drawn in that year,[20] was evidently being consulted during the composition of a letter of 11 June 1567 in which the queen, condoling Lord Deputy Sidney, on 'your paynfull long journey from the end of January until the middest of April', proceeded to recite his route through most of central and southern Ireland in considerable detail. Later in the same letter the queen turned to the planting of Protestant English families in Ulster which, following the defeat of Shane O'Neill, was enjoying a brief period of stability. She asked Sidney to inform her 'what contreys there are to be taken and kept by the English people and

[15] Laurence C. Wroth, *The Voyages of Giovanni da Verrazano 1524–1528* (New Haven, 1970), 167.

[16] Barber, 'England I', 44.

[17] Helen Wallis, 'The Cartography of Drake's Voyage', in *Sir Francis Drake and the Famous Voyage, 1577–1580: Essays Commemorating the Quadricentennial of Drake's Circumnavigation of the Earth*, ed. Norman Thrower (Berkeley, CA, 1984), 121–63.

[18] Günter Schilder, 'Jodocus Hondius: Creator of the Decorative Map Border', *The Map Collector*, 32 (1985), 40–3.

[19] The National Archives (Public Record Office), State Papers [hereafter TNA (PRO), SP] 12/25 fo. 98, reproduced in Catherine Delano-Smith and Roger J. P. Kain, *English Maps. A History* (1999), 144.

[20] TNA (PRO), MPF 68. There was no sufficiently detailed printed map available at that time. See Andrew Bonar Law, *The Printed Maps of Ireland 1612–1850* (Dublin, 1997).

what be the names of the contreys, the ports, the castells and such lyke', and added as an afterthought:

> And if you can speedely cause the situation of contrees to be described in platte, and sent by some hable to infourme us therof, you shall therby much satisfy us, for in planting and stablishing of our people in contrees to have perpetuitee we cannot sodenly nor without good information resolve... Sense our determination of writing thus farre, thinking more of the maner of the planting of the people in that contrey of Ulster, we ar very desirous to be infourmid from you what parts in that contrey do properly belong unto us, as our demeane of our Earldome of Ulster, or any other title which we have by inheritance therto. And what be the other parcels that have been the possessions of other Irish and Englishe and yet holden by them of us by any kynde of service and rent... And for the better understanding therof, if you can fynde some skilfull person there that can make a more particular description, then already we have by any card, it wolde helpe us to the under-standing of that which you shall write.[21]

Yet, persuasive though this evidence for a genuine interest in and understanding of the potential of maps appears to be at first glance, the reality was rather different. Elizabeth did not commission the Molyneux globes and the grand paintings and the engravings showing her in the vicinity of maps and globes. Far from being an expression of her own inclinations, they were probably intended as a means of flattering a reluctant queen into supporting the policies implicit in the images. The patrons, who to greater or lesser extents selected the imagery and allegories,[22] were almost all strongly Protestant, anti-Spanish and imperial-minded individuals who conspicuously commissioned and used maps.[23] Francis Drake is traditionally said to have commissioned the prototype of the Armada portraits (and had himself portrayed, appropriately, with a globe).[24] Hatton, the patron of the Siena Sieve portrait, was the dedicatee of Case's tract and employer of the surveyor Ralph Treswell.[25] William Sanderson, the wealthy merchant who paid £1,000 for the creation of the Molyneux globes was closely linked to

[21] *Sidney State Papers 1565–70*, ed.Tomás O'Laichlin (Dublin, 1962), 61, 69 no. 41. For similar sentiments see also 71–2 (no. 42), 111 (no. 65) (Elizabeth I to Sidney, 6 July 1567, 6 June 1569).

[22] Doran, 'Virginity, Divinity and Power', 187, 190.

[23] J. H. Andrews, *Shapes of Ireland. Maps and their Makers 1564–1839* (Dublin, 1997), 57, 58, 80, 83; Sir Henry Lee, ostensibly a 'hermit' from court by 1592, was an exception but he had close links across the political spectrum with known map enthusiasts and with the Board of Ordnance. See E. K. Chambers, *Sir Henry Lee* (Oxford, 1936).

[24] *Elizabeth: The Exhibition at the National Maritime Museum*, ed. Susan Doran (2003), 231–2, no. 238; Strong, *Gloriana*, 131–3; Karen Hearn, *Dynasties. Paintings in Tudor and Jacobean England 1530–1630* (1995), 88, no. 43. Karen Hearn has, however, informed me (private communication) that recent research suggests that the Tyrwhitt-Drake family only purchased its version of the Armada painting, said to have been commissioned by Francis Drake, in the mid-nineteenth century.

[25] Barber, 'England II', 79, 82; Hearn, *Dynasties*, 85–6, no. 40.

Drake, the Hakluyts and Dee, and was married to Raleigh's niece, while Molyneux himself had served under Drake.[26]

On closer inspection, there is no evidence that the queen took any particular interest in the maps, globes and the atlas dedicated to her. There is no sign of personal involvement in the course of Saxton's surveying activities, unlike Burghley who was presented with proofs of the county maps as they came off the press. Indeed the incorporation into the royal library presumably after 1598 of the atlas that Burghley constructed around these maps suggests that until then the library had lacked such a comprehensive cartographic survey.[27] The dedication of the maps to Elizabeth I, then, seems to have been a formality.

The dedications on the Molyneux globe and in the preface to Mercator's *Atlas* also give no hint of the queen's personal interest. They are instead implicit petitions for support from her. The dedication on the Molyneux terrestrial globe, significantly placed over North America, pleads for her to support naval expansion by lauding the extent of the globe controlled by her naval forces.[28] The dedication fronting Mercator's *Atlas* was addressed to her as the patron of English overseas discovery in the hope that, at a time of increasing wartime censorship and security precautions, she would allow her subjects to communicate information about their discoveries to Mercator's heirs, living though they were as ostensible Catholics in Catholic Europe.[29] But perhaps the most significant indicator of Elizabeth's lack of cartographic interest is to be seen in her failure to respond in any way to John Norden's direct address to her for patronage of his *Speculum Britanniae* series of guidebooks to the English counties illustrated by maps which provided far more administrative and economic information (such as the location of ironworks) than had Saxton's of two decades earlier.[30]

The contrast with Elizabeth's predecessors and fellow monarchs is striking. Her father's hunger for maps can be read not only in the

[26] Crino and Wallis, 'New Researches', 13.

[27] Now BL, Royal MS 18.D.III. Skelton and Summerson, *Hatfield House*, 20; Evans and Lawrence, *Saxton*, 9–19, 143–7. The only Old Royal Library copy of Saxton's atlas, bound with Robert Adams's charts of the defeat of the Armada (now BL, Maps C.7.c.1), seems only to have entered the Royal Library under James I (R. A. Skelton, *County Atlases of the British Isles 1579–1850. A Bibliography*, I: *1579–1703* (Folkestone, 1970), 9, 209).

[28] Crino and Wallis, 'New Researches', 14.

[29] Most recently, Nicholas Crane, *Mercator. The Man who Mapped the Planet* (2002), 286–7.

[30] Frank Kitchen, 'John Norden (c. 1547–1625): estate surveyor, topographer, county mapmaker and devotional writer', *Imago Mundi*, 49 (1997), 46, 48. The omnibus manuscript volume that he presented to the queen is now BL, Add. MS 31853. I am grateful to Catherine Delano Smith for this observation. Kitchen excuses Elizabeth on the grounds of the other pressures on her ('Ireland . . . rising prices . . . rumours of another armada'), but a real enthusiast would have found the money, as did William Sanderson who paid for the publication of Norden's maps of Hampshire and Sussex in 1595–6.

directives that he sent to the gentry resident on the coasts of England between 1538 and 1540 but also in his dynamic communications with his representatives in France in the mid-1540s, not the least of whom was the military engineer and cartographer John Rogers. Geoffrey Parker and Barbara Mundy have described the energy with which Philip II personally commissioned medium- and large-scale surveys of his American and European dominions because – in words that could have been written by Burghley – 'things crop up every day which can only be clearly and properly understood by knowing the distances, the rivers and the borders', even though these ambitious enterprises remained incomplete and in manuscript.[31]

Detailed investigation of the drafts of Elizabeth's instructions to Sir Henry Sidney in the National Archives again shows that things were not as they seemed. The basic text is always in a scribal hand and was almost certainly dictated by Burghley. The language and mindset are very similar to those to be found in Burghley's letters to Sir John Norris during the Rouen campaign in 1591.[32] Before the final version was prepared Burghley went through the drafts and the particularly cartographic references to surveys, to routes, to plats and to the purposes that they were intended to serve are in his hand. It was only then that the drafts were shown to the queen for approval, usually being returned without further amendments.

This impression of the queen's reliance on Burghley in cartographic matters can be read into John Dee's account of his presentation to Elizabeth of the 'two rolls' containing his arguments for her rights to sovereignty over most of North America. These rolls no longer seem to survive, but a map in the British Library[33] is probably derived from them, the endorsements being a summary of the arguments contained in one of the rolls and the autograph manuscript map of the northern hemisphere on the recto, illustrating them, being a copy of the second roll.[34] Dee recorded how he had given the rolls to the queen personally while they were in the garden at Richmond Palace in the morning of 3 October 1580. The queen arranged to discuss them with him that afternoon in her privy chamber 'where the L. Treasurer also was, who . . . did seem to doubt much that I had or could make the argument for her Highness' title so as I pretended'. A week later the queen visited

---

[31] Geoffrey Parker, 'Philip II, Maps and Power', in Geoffrey Parker, *Empire, War and Faith in Early Modern Europe* (2002), particularly 107 (Philip II to the viceroy of Naples, 1566); Barbara E. Mundy, *The Mapping of New Spain: Indigenous Cartography and the Maps of the Relaciones Geográficas* (Chicago, 1996).

[32] See, for example, *List and Analysis of State Papers Foreign Series Elizabeth I: III (September 1591–April 1592)*, ed. R. B. Wernham (1980), 269, no. 418 (Burghley to Norris, 27 July 1591).

[33] BL, Cotton MS Augustus I.i.1.

[34] William H. Sherman, *John Dee: The Politics of Reading and Writing in the English Renaissance* (Amherst, 1995), 183–7.

Dee at his home in Mortlake, and 'told me that the Lord Treasurer had greatly commended my doings for her title, which he had to examine'.[35] A monarch with a known enthusiasm for maps, like her father or Philip II, would probably have found time to look at the maps himself and not have relied purely on his minister's judgement.[36]

In fact, Elizabeth seems to have lacked the graphic, visual dimension that characterised her father, her favourites and her most trusted minister. In December 1545 Elizabeth presented her stepmother, Katherine Parr, with an English translation of Calvin's *Institutions*. Despite their hostility to the worship of images, Protestant theologians, notably Calvin, were not unconditionally opposed to the arts, and least of all to picture/map making as evidenced by the cartographic illustrations in their Bibles. So Elizabeth would have been under no theological pressure to express her preferences in any particular way. Though doubtless influenced by her tutors, it seems quite likely that she was expressing her own views when in the accompanying letter, she wrote that despite their laudable efforts, painters and sculptors 'could and cannot yet represent or reveal by their works the mind, or wit, the speech or understanding of any person'. By contrast writing and letters 'seems to me the most clever, excellent and ingenious' of the arts 'For through their ordering not only can the aforesaid bodily features be declared, but also (which is more) the image of the mind, wiles and understanding, together with the speech and intention of the man, can be perfectly known.'[37] The care she took with her own elaborate signature would further support the importance that she attached to the written word.

If one looks at other indices the impression of a lack of interest in maps grows stronger. Marcus, Mueller and Rose's authoritative edition of Elizabeth's authenticated personal writings contains not a mention of maps in contrast to the later letters of Henry VIII and the letters and annotations on documents of Philip II, Henri IV, Burghley and Sully who regularly mentioned them. Again had Elizabeth been really excited by maps, one might expect someone of her literary ability to utilise Shakespearean-style cartographic allegories in her poems, speeches and prayers.[38] Again, there is no sign. One might also expect observers to comment on her excitement about maps, in the way that Laurence

---

[35] *The Diaries of John Dee*, ed. Edward Fenton (Charlbury, 1998), 11.

[36] For examples of Philip II studying maps intensively and critically see Parker, 'Philip II, Maps and Power', 97–8, 111–12.

[37] *Elizabeth I: Collected Works*, ed. Leah S. Marcus, Janet Mueller and Mary Beth Rose, (London and Chicago, 2000), 11.

[38] For which see Nigel Morgan, 'The Literary Image of Globes and Maps in Early Modern England', in *English Map Making 1500–1650*, ed. Sarah Tyacke (1983), 46–56.

Nowell, in 1563, commented on the 'especial pleasure' that Cecil was known to take in maps.[39] But no such reference is known.

Someone interested in maps might be expected to commission them for their private use and to treasure them – and even perhaps to draw them. Henri IV of France sketched the plan of a proposed fort, asked for (and was sent) a chart 'diapré et doré' of Drake's circumnavigation in 1585 and had the *Galerie des Cerfs* at Fontainebleau decorated with detailed semi-pictorial plans of his palaces and their surrounding parks.[40] Lord Burghley also drew several sketch maps in order to clarify issues for himself.[41]

Elizabeth's role, however, was entirely negative as demonstrated by an unfinished manuscript hydrographic atlas commissioned by Mary I for her husband Philip from the Portuguese chart maker Diogo Homem.[42] According to an unverifiable tradition, rather than having the atlas completed, as someone with an interest in maps may have done, she gouged Philip's arms out from the royal arms over England. The gesture, if understandable, further suggests a lack of aesthetic sensibility. There is no mention of her having attempted to draw a map. She seems never to have commissioned a map in a private capacity. Elizabeth does not seem even to have looked after the numerous maps that she inherited from her father, many of which disappeared into the private archives of her ministers and notably Lord Burghley.[43] Again this contrasts with Philip II who knew perfectly well what maps he owned and attached great importance to them, though he could not always succeed in laying his hands on the particular ones that he wanted.[44]

One can only conclude that Elizabeth was not excited by maps, though she was well aware that others were and that maps could play a valuable propaganda role. She was evidently familiar with them and was prepared to request them on her ministers' behalf: local corporations and justices of the peace were forced into commissioning and utilising them during her reign because of her privy council's insistence on receiving maps to illustrate any issues that had a spatial element.[45] It is quite possible though

---

[39] BL, Lansdowne MS 6, fo. 135, as translated in R. A. Skelton, *Saxton's Survey of England and Wales with a facsimile of the Wall-Map of 1583* (Amsterdam, 1974), 15–16.

[40] Buisseret, *Maps and Monarchs*, 107; Wallis, 'Cartography of Drake's Voyage', 123; Peter Barber, 'Maps and Monarchs in Europe 1550–1800', in *Royal and Republican Sovereignty in Early Modern Europe*, ed. Robert Oresko, G. C. Gibbs and H. M. Scott, (Cambridge, 1997), 111–13.

[41] Barber, 'England II', 70, 72–3.

[42] BL, Add. MS 5414A, illustrated in *Lie of the Land: The Secret Life of Maps*, ed. April Carlucci and Peter Barber (2001), 54–5.

[43] Barber, 'England II', 71–2.

[44] Philip II to Francisco de Erasso, 5 July 1568, quoted in Parker, 'Philip II, Maps and Power', 97–8.

[45] Peter Barber, *History of Cartography III* (Chicago, forthcoming).

that Elizabeth herself never voluntarily took a close, analytical look at a map.

Did this really matter? Some of Elizabeth's contemporaries certainly thought it did, because of the value they attached to maps as instruments of government. In June 1571 Sir Henry Sidney's secretary, Edmund Tremayne, wrote that Lythe's manuscript map of Ireland would enable Sidney

> to describe every part of [Ireland] with their frontiers, and with all the borders, havens, creeks and rivers with other notable commodities. By the same Your Lordship is able to describe every man his country, of what power he is, and what he hath been, and how it is neighboured, what quarrels he hath, and how [in] every war each of them is affected. [Also] how straight you found the English Pale, and how it is now enlarged. The places that be fortified already will appear. And so may you with good commodity thereupon express what your opinion is for fortifications in any other place that your lordship shall think good. And so of the bridge that your lordship hath builded [at Athlone] and any other that you think meet to be builded or repaired. And finally by these means you shall describe what commodity hath grown of such things as are done and what her highness shall embrace by proceeding onward, ever abating cost behind as she shall bestow forward.[46]

It might be argued that Tremayne was somewhat overstating the case and that Elizabeth's lack of cartographic interest did not matter since in all important matters she could rely on the cartographic enthusiasm and analytical skills of her ministers and courtiers. Yet had she been interested – though, admittedly she would have had to have been a different person – she would have had an independent means of evaluating the advice of her ministers as a basis for reaching decisions herself, particularly in wartime when, as Paul Hammer has pointed out, as a woman her freedom of action was severely limited.[47] In these situations, Henry communicated directly with his mapmakers, ordering them to produce maps from which he could evaluate – apparently objectively – the proper site and design of a defensive fort, the line of a border or the strategy to be adopted in a siege.[48] Elizabeth's lack of interest in maps deprived her of these advantages. It increased her dependence on her ministers in the detailed formulation and execution of policy. At the same time it reinforced the negative nature of her role in government: delaying decisions and vetoing certain courses of action without being able to suggest positive alternatives (though she clearly personally preferred to be in a position where she could disown or repudiate rather than take responsibility for actions).

Nor could she always rely on the loyalty of her ministers to bring her the benefits of cartographic sophistication. The administration of the crown

---

[46] Quoted from TNA (PRO), SP 63/52/66, by Andrews, *Shapes of Ireland*, 67.

[47] Paul Hammer, *Elizabeth's Wars: War, Government and Society in Tudor England 1544–1604* (Basingstoke and New York, 2003), 6, 59.

[48] *The History of the King's Works*, ed. H. M. Colvin *et al.*, IV (1982), 391–2.

lands was a case in point. Elizabeth derived between 30 and 34 per cent, or about £86,000 to £111,000 annually of her income from them.[49] While a princess in the 1550s she had demonstrated a gritty determination to protect and shepherd her private estates in Bedfordshire.[50] When at the start of the 1560s she was forced to sell sizeable amounts of crown lands in order to finance the war in France, she learnt a lesson in economy that she did not forget[51] and it was only during the still more expensive wars of the 1590s that she was reluctantly forced into further mass sales.

It would have been in her interest to have had the crown lands surveyed, particularly after the mid-1570s when estate plans drawn to a consistent scale put in their first appearance.[52] These complemented the traditional written surveys in two important ways. First they enabled boundaries and abutments to be depicted with great clarity and with a permanence that could not be matched by the written word. One practical consequence was that encroachments could easily and rapidly be identified. Estate maps would have enabled the crown to dispense with most of the self-interested bounty hunters who secured very favourable leases on the concealed or 'drowned' crown lands which they discovered. Elizabeth could have increased her income and avoided the social conflicts and the unpopularity that attached to the crown as a result of the bounty hunters' activities.[53] Secondly estate plans enormously facilitated long-term estate strategy by showing at a glance the most profitable potential land exchanges, purchases or enclosures.

Yet hardly any surveys of the crown lands – let alone mapped surveys – were carried out under Elizabeth. She obtained some maps, such as the plan of the early 1560s showing manors in North Dorset, from the archives of episcopal lands that were acquired by the crown.[54] Burghley saw to it that the lands of minors, which were being administered by the crown, were sometimes mapped.[55] Similarly confiscated lands and those that fell to the crown when a see was empty were sometimes mapped, though

[49] David Thomas, 'The Elizabethan Crown Lands: Their Purpose and Problems', in *The Estates of the English Crown, 1558–1640*, ed. R. W. Hoyle (Cambridge, 1992), 58–9.

[50] Doran, *Queen Elizabeth I*, 29; Elizabeth to the privy council, 31 May 1553, in *Collected Works*, ed. Marcus, Mueller and Rose, 39–40.

[51] Hammer, *Elizabeth's Wars*, 67, 69.

[52] P. D. A. Harvey, 'Estate Surveyors and the Spread of the Scale-Map in England 1550–1580', *Landscape History*, 15 (1993), 40.

[53] David Thomas, 'Leases of Crown Lands in the Reign of Elizabeth I', in *Estates of the English Crown*, ed. Hoyle, 180–2; R. W. Hoyle, '"Shearing the Hog's Back": The Reform of the Estates 1598–1640', in *ibid.*, 211–12.

[54] BL, Add. MS 52522; P. D. A. Harvey, 'An Elizabethan Map of Manors in North Dorset', *British Museum Quarterly*, 29 (1965), 82–4 n. 5. See also H. M. T. Cobbe, 'Four Manuscript Maps Recently Acquired by the British Museum', *Journal of the Society of Archivists*, 4 (1973), 646–52.

[55] Skelton and Summerson, *Hatfield House*, 54–5, no. 60.

not necessarily to scale.[56] But apart from a few written surveys of lands in Wales and Cornwall and a plan of Tottenham Court in Middlesex of 1591 by one William Necton, no detailed surveys, written or mapped, of the older Elizabethan crown lands are known.[57]

This worried some contemporaries. In 1602, Sir Robert Johnson, a skilled estate surveyor and mapmaker[58] as well as a loyal servant of the crown, wrote to Robert Cecil that 'whenever I have heard of the sale of Her Majesty's lands, I have observed that the value was seldom known . . . The chief foundation of mischief has been the want of authentic surveys . . . of every ten manors, there is not one perfect survey.'[59] In 1606, Henry Woodhouse estimated that the crown had lost £100,000 since 1583 because it had, through ignorance, sold its estates at valuations far below the ancient rent.[60]

Yet it has been argued that the estates did not primarily exist to generate revenue.[61] Some, notably hunting parks, were not intended to be profitable.[62] All were the major source for royal patronage, and as Elizabeth ruefully commented to William Maitland of Lethington as early as 1561, 'no princes revenues be so great that they are able to satisfy the insatiable cupidity of men'.[63] Some were granted away, knowing they would immediately be resold, without entry fines being charged.[64] Even the administration of the royal estates was a form of patronage and the crown had no alternative but to tolerate the corruption, the gross waste and the failure to collect the monies that were due.[65] Indeed any attempt to maximise the return from the estates was likely to provoke social dislocation and resentment from lessees and officeholders (often noblemen and justices of the peace on whom the national administration

[56] BL, Royal MS 18. D. III, fos. 91v–92; BL, Add. MS 71126 (map of the Seven Marshland Lordships, c. 1582).

[57] Heather Lawrence, 'John Norden and his Colleagues: Surveyors of Crown Lands', Cartographic Journal, 22 (1985), 54; Skelton and Summerson, Hatfield House, 50 no. 48 (CPM II. 19); Thomas 'Crown Lands', 66, 76.

[58] See for example his superb estate atlas of the Welsh lands of the earl of Worcester of 1587 now in the National Library of Wales (Badminton 3).

[59] Quoted by Heather Lawrence, 'John Norden', 54.

[60] Thomas, 'Crown Lands', 67. See also Hoyle, '"Shearing"', 205.

[61] Thomas, 'Leases', 173.

[62] Thomas, 'Crown Lands', 81–2.

[63] Collected Works, ed. Marcus, Mueller and Rose, 66. In the 1580s and 1590s Burghley's efforts to cut back on patronage won Elizabeth a reputation for 'princely parsimony', but royal revenues from the crown lands nevertheless continued to decline. John Cramsie, Kingship and Crown Finance under James I (Woodbridge, 2002), 29.

[64] Joyce Youings, Sixteenth-Century England (Harmondsworth, 1984), 162–3. Despite inflation, average entry fines and rents did not rise after 1560 until the late 1590s. Ibid., 161–2, 174; Thomas 'Crown Lands', 76.

[65] Thomas, 'Crown Lands', 71–2, 74–5.

depended) and their tenants at times when the crown could least afford it.

It has also been pointed out that for much of her reign, Elizabeth did not desperately need the additional sums involved. Until 1576 she had a surplus on her ordinary income and in the 1580s she earned enormous profits from her investment in privateering ventures.[66] The situation only became critical as the strains of war grew in the course of the 1590s – and by the end of the decade the need for money was so pressing that there simply was not the time to survey the crown estates before selling them off – often at prices that were known to be unrealistically low.[67] Nevertheless, Elizabeth would undoubtedly have welcomed more income. She managed to keep her accounts in balance for as long as she did only because of the windfall of great confiscated estates that fell to the crown between 1569 and 1572 and through the practice of extreme economy and political passivity, which frustrated numerous of her courtiers and ministers if not herself. However, even with regard to the crown estates, she was in the hands of her ministers.

The lord treasurer and the chancellor of the exchequer were responsible for their day-to-day administration and it would seem that the queen trusted them to get on with the work without interference from her.[68] Of the holders of these posts in the relevant decades, Burghley was outstandingly cartographically sophisticated. Indeed in 1587 Burghley criticised the master of All Souls College in Oxford for not having commissioned a mapped survey of a piece of land to ascertain a proper valuation for the entry fine before leasing it out.[69] Yet he never seems to have recommended a similar course of action to his mistress. But then, as beneficiaries of the prevailing lax regime, as lessees of crown lands, as stewards of crown lands in Lincolnshire and rangers of Enfield Chase,[70] he and his family had good reasons for inaction.

Elizabeth was no different from most other landowners of her time in showing a lack of interest in estate mapping.[71] Some surveyors, such as John Norden, themselves claimed that it could prove to be an expensive luxury, which achieved no more than far less costly written surveys.[72] Nevertheless such considerations would not have deterred a real map

[66] *Ibid.*, 78–9; Hammer, *Elizabeth's Wars*, 80–1.

[67] Youings, *Sixteenth-Century England*, 161–2; Thomas, 'Crown Lands', 85–7.

[68] Thomas, 'Crown Lands', 73.

[69] Peter Eden, 'Three Elizabethan Estate Surveyors: Peter Kempe, Thomas Clerke and Thomas Langdon', in *English Map Making*, ed. Tyacke, 71.

[70] Thomas, 'Crown Lands', 63, 71; Hoyle, '"Shearing"', 207–8, 213.

[71] Sarah Bendall, 'Estate Maps of an English County: Cambridgeshire, 1600–1836', in *Estate Maps in the Old and New Worlds*, ed. David Buisseret (Chicago, 1996), 70. In court circles, however, the balance was probably different.

[72] Lawrence, 'Norden', 54–5.

enthusiast. By the 1580s, however, Elizabeth's essential lack of interest in graphic means of representation was reinforced by her growing conservatism and hostility to such 'newfangleness'[73] as the mapping of estates to a uniform scale.

It cost her dear. The essential reason why virtually no action was taken to increase the revenues from the crown estates before 1600 was because, in this rare case and primarily for reasons of self-interest, Elizabeth I's cartographically minded ministers were not prepared to serve their mistress's long-term interests. On her part the queen was not sufficiently cartographically knowledgeable or motivated to take matters into her own hands and to insist on a general survey at a time – the later 1570s and 1580s – when England was (relatively) at peace, the technical expertise was available and the imposition of raised rents and dues could have been justified on patriotic grounds.

It was only after Burghley's death in 1598, and at the instigation of his successors as lord treasurer, Lord Buckhurst, and from 1608, Salisbury, that the royal estates began to be actively managed.[74] Enthusiastically supported by James I, the new approach culminated in the survey of the royal woods, commissioned in 1607, the surveys of the lands of the duchy of Cornwall and of the honour of Windsor, both commissioned from John Norden, and the 'Great Survey' of the crown lands undertaken from 1608. Though mainly written, there was a sizeable cartographic element.[75] However, the survey came too late. The additional revenues, limited by custom and by the absence of any overriding patriotic justification, were insufficient to meet the crown's needs. The freshly surveyed lands had to be sold and the king still remained dependent on parliamentary subsidies.

Had the general survey taken place earlier, the increased income generated would have made the prosecution of war in the 1590s easier and less politically damaging to the queen. It might also have spared at least some of the more precious crown lands from the extensive sales at bargain prices in the 1590s and again after 1610 that were cumulatively to weaken the monarchy's power base under her successors. In the final analysis, it did matter that Elizabeth was not interested in maps.

[73] Speech at the closing of parliament, 29 Mar. 1585, in *Collected Works*, ed. Marcus, Mueller and Rose, 183.

[74] Hoyle, '"Shearing"', 204, 211–12, 224.

[75] *Ibid.*, plate 9.1, for the costs of the maps, and p. 211, for the atlases of estate and woodland maps that were created, though many maps have not survived.

Transactions of the RHS 14 (2004), pp. 199–207 © 2004 Royal Historical Society
DOI: 10.1017/S0080440104000209   Printed in the United Kingdom

BRINGING THE WORLD TO ENGLAND:
THE POLITICS OF TRANSLATION IN
THE AGE OF HAKLUYT

By William H. Sherman

ABSTRACT. Elizabethan travel books – and particularly the epoch-making antho-
logies of Richard Hakluyt – have been seen (and celebrated) as evidence of England's
first great age of maritime expansion. This paper suggests, in terms first suggested
by F. O. Matthiessen, that the work of the translator was closely connected with that
of the voyager and the merchant. The role played by the translation of Classical
and Continental materials is crucial to understanding the intellectual and practical
outlook of those involved in overseas ventures and, in particular, to contextualising
Hakluyt's patriotic claims and strategies in his *Principle Navigations* (1598–1600).

> A study of Elizabethan translations is a study of the means by which the Renaissance
> came to England. The nation had grown conscious of its cultural inferiority to the
> Continent, and suddenly burned with the desire to excel its rivals in letters, as well as
> in ships and gold. The translator's work was an act of patriotism. He, too, as well as
> the voyager and merchant, could do some good for his country: he believed that foreign
> books were just as important for England's destiny as the discoveries of her seamen, and
> he brought them into his native speech with all the enthusiasm of a conquest.[1]

These are the opening words from a little-known book by a well-known
author. Before he produced his path-breaking account of the *American
Renaissance*[2] – which did more than any other text to make the American
literary tradition a legitimate subject in its own right – F. O. Matthiessen
turned his attention to the English Renaissance and wrote the first major
study of translation in the Elizabethan Age. In *Translation: An Elizabethan
Art*, Matthiessen concerned himself only with the importation of literary
and historical works, and he was here borrowing the terms of maritime
expansion to describe the translations of Hoby (Castiglione's *Courtier*),
North (*Plutarch*), Holland (*Livy* and *Suetonius*) and Florio (Montaigne's
Essays). But in the formative years of the British Empire, the roles of the
translator, the voyager and the merchant were closer than Matthiessen's
analogy suggests: his description of the use of books to translate the wider

---

[1] F. O. Matthiessen, *Translation: An Elizabethan Art* (Cambridge, MA, 1931), 3.
[2] F. O. Matthiessen, *American Renaissance: Art and Expression in the Age of Emerson and Whitman*
(Oxford, 1941).

world to an England that felt it was at once inferior to its Continental rivals and destined to outpace them applies most directly to the work of writers, editors and translators of travel texts. His image of the textual expert as *conquistador*, in particular, provides a resonant frame for the figure of Richard Hakluyt – not least because Hakluyt's career as the pioneering collector of English travel narratives began and ended with translations of foreign works.[3]

No conference on the legacy of Elizabethan expansion can afford to ignore travel writing, either the record it preserves or the issues it raises. Participants in the conference that generated these essays were asked to assess the reality behind Hakluyt's claim, in the first edition of his *Principal Navigations . . . of the English Nation* (1589), that, during the reign of Queen Elizabeth I, 'her subjects . . . in searching the most opposite corners and quarters of the world . . . have excelled all the nations and peoples of the earth'.[4] For Victorian scholars celebrating the 300th anniversary of Elizabeth's death, Hakluyt's tribute testified to her founding role in the great age of maritime expansion. One hundred years later, the British Empire and Elizabeth's role in creating it look very different: revisionist scholarship has tended to replace celebration with scepticism, and Hakluyt's words (and the worldview they represent) are now seen as at best wishful and at worst reprehensible. If we turn to the literature of travel and trade produced by Hakluyt and his contemporaries, however, we find that its creators were already acutely aware of the debate over what would later be called the Elizabethan outreach. Indeed, as we shall see, Hakluyt himself was capable of considerable scepticism, and attending to the fuller context for his 1589 claim will give us some purchase on the rhetoric and the reality of Elizabethan expansion.

Hakluyt's claim that, with the queen's 'peerless' support, the Elizabethan explorers 'have excelled all the nations and peoples of the earth' would certainly have struck the nations and peoples of the earth in 1589 as perverse; and even the queen's own subjects and ministers would have raised their eyebrows in surprise rather than thumped their tables in agreement.[5] At the end of Elizabeth's reign, the English reputation abroad was more for insularity and piracy than for global mastery. In 1599, just as Hakluyt was unveiling his three-volume monument to

---

[3] F. M. Rogers, 'Hakluyt as translator', in *The Hakluyt Handbook*, ed. D. B. Quinn (2 vols., Hakluyt Society, 1974), I, 37–47.
[4] Richard Hakluyt, dedicatory epistle to Sir Francis Walsingham, *The Principal Navigations, Voyages, Traffiques and Discoveries of the English Nation* (1589), *2v.
[5] The State Papers are full of complaints about her reluctance to sponsor overseas ventures and her willingness to let her favourites stifle the spirit of enterprise with their dormant monopolies on potential markets and trade routes.

English travel, the massively expanded edition of the *Principal Navigations*, the Swiss physician Thomas Platter visited London on the kind of Grand Tour that was not yet popular among the English. After attending two plays and a bear-baiting he recorded in his journal, 'With these and many more amusements the English pass their time, learning at the play what is happening abroad... since the English for the most part do not travel much, but prefer to learn foreign matters and take their pleasures at home.'[6] From the outset, in fact, the rapidly growing English enthusiasm for the literature of voyages and ventures was accompanied by a steady undertow of scepticism about the benefits of travel: in his mock-utopia, *Mundus Alter et Idem*, and his satirical essay *Quo Vadis?*, Bishop Joseph Hall argued that travel was dangerous (since the only things travellers picked up abroad were foreign fashions, vices and diseases) and ultimately unnecessary (since everything essential could be learned from books and maps in the comfort of one's own study). And while Ben Jonson seems to have celebrated England's nascent colonialism and London's incipient consumer culture in some of his masques (particularly in the recently discovered 'Entertainment at Britain's Burse', written in 1609 for the opening of the New Exchange), he is better known for his satirical attacks on materialism and upward mobility and for his parodies of travellers who all but lose themselves in their pursuit of foreign novelties.[7]

Hakluyt's words from 1589 may be giving voice to some post-Armada bravado, but more sober accounts – by Englishmen as well as their enemies – would make more of the fact that the Elizabethans were latecomers to the European project of exploring and mapping the wider world. At the beginning of Queen Elizabeth's reign they had barely begun to travel to, write about and take possession of other parts of the globe. By the end of her reign they finally had their Magellan in Drake and their Ramusio in Hakluyt, but there had been very few practical successes in discovering and planting the New World. English soldiers and pirates had made devastating attacks on Spanish outposts in the West Indies; Ralegh's men had established a short-lived laboratory near Roanoke, where John White captured some of the period's most interesting images of native American life; and Drake had nailed an English coin to a tree in what he named 'Nova Albion' before returning to England with unprecedented booty from captured Spanish ships. But a stable colony in Virginia, a navigable Northern Passage to Cathay and a source of endless gold in the

---

[6] Cited in *Three Renaissance Travel Plays*, ed. Anthony Parr (Manchester, 1995), 1.

[7] For a fuller treatment of these sources see William Sherman, 'Stirrings and Searchings (1500–1720)', in *The Cambridge Companion to Travel Writing*, ed. Peter Hulme and Tim Youngs (Cambridge, 2002), 17–36.

Arctic waters of Baffin Bay or the tropical jungles of Guiana all proved painfully elusive.[8]

Hakluyt himself conceded as much in 1601, in his translation of António Galvão's history of global exploration:

> Now if any man shall maruel that in these *Discoueries of the World* for the space almost of fower thousand yeeres here set downe, our nation is scarce fower times mentioned: Hee is to vnderstand, that when this authour ended this discourse, (which was about the yeere of Grace 1555.) there was little extant of our mens trauailes.[9]

Hakluyt's wording here is ambiguous and could be read as suggesting that there were few *texts* of English travel rather than little in the way of English travels for Galvão to draw on; and he is careful, at any rate, to observe that Galvão's account ends before English travellers had hit their stride. He goes on, however, to make a more general and telling acknowledgement:

> [the] trauailes of our men ... be not come to ripenes, and haue been made for the most part to places first discouered by others; when they shall come to more perfection, and become more profitable to the aduenturers, [they] will then be more fit [to figure in such histories of global travel].[10]

This is a surprisingly downbeat assessment for the editor of *The Principal Navigations* to be making in 1601 – exactly one year after he had finished printing accounts of 216 English voyages with 378 supporting documents, stretching back 1,600 years and spread over 1,900 tightly packed folio pages.

This dual sense of belatedness and what Hakluyt called a lack of 'ripeness' haunted the Elizabethans, and it accounts for several features in the pattern of both the texts and the travels of Elizabethan expansionism. The fact that English explorations had largely followed in the footsteps of their Continental rivals and had rarely produced the results that their financial and intellectual backers were hoping for meant, first, that the tone of English accounts could veer between optimism and fatalism. It also meant that they were often marked by an exaggerated rhetoric fuelled by political, religious and commercial competition and mobilized (in Mary Fuller's terms) more often in acts of recuperation than of celebration.[11] In more practical terms, it goes some way toward explaining why piracy and

---

[8] See Michael Foss, *Undreamed Shores: England's Wasted Empire in America* (New York, 1974), and Jeffrey Knapp, *An Empire Nowhere: England, America, and Literature from* Utopia *to* The Tempest (Berkeley, CA, 1992).

[9] Richard Hakluyt, dedicatory epistle to Sir Robert Cecil in his translation of António Galvão's *The Discoveries of the World* (1601), A3v.

[10] Ibid., A4r.

[11] For a sensitive reading of this rhetoric see Mary Fuller, *Voyages in Print: English Travel to America, 1576–1624* (Cambridge, 1995), and her 'Ralegh's Fugitive Gold: Reference and Deferral in *The Discoverie of Guiana*', *Representations*, 33 (1991), 42–64.

privateering occupied such a prominent position in Elizabethan maritime enterprise, and it accounts for the tendency of English explorers to persist in their futile search for a Northern Passage to the riches of the East (in the face of increasingly obvious impediments and a death toll that would reach shocking proportions by the nineteenth century).

This background puts us in a better position to look again at Hakluyt's dedicatory epistle to Sir Francis Walsingham in the 1589 *Principal Navigations*, and to put its rhetoric into a broader context. In the passage leading up to the claim quoted above, Hakluyt sets out to explain why, unlike the collections of his predecessors and his own earlier anthology of voyages to America (the *Divers Voyages* of 1582), the 1589 Principal Navigations would 'meddle ... with the Nauigations onely of our owne nation'. He launches on an autobiographical account, beginning with the now legendary visit (while still a schoolboy) to his cousin and namesake in his chambers at the Middle Temple, where he 'found lying open vpon his boord certeine bookes of Cosmographie, with an vniuersall Mappe' – leading to a geography lesson in which the elder Hakluyt pointed to every region and described its 'speciall commodities, & particular wants, which by the benefit of traffike, & entercourse of merchants, are plentifully supplied'. The lesson left what he described as a 'deepe impression' and, once he had progressed to university, it inspired him to collect 'whatsoeuer printed or written discoueries and voyages I found extant either in the Greeke, Latine, Italian, Spanish, Portugall, French, or English languages', and then to seek out 'the chiefest Captaines at sea, the greatest Merchants, and the best Mariners of our nation'. This led, finally, to a five-year stint as chaplain to Sir Edward Stafford, the English ambassador in Paris where, Hakluyt writes,

> I both heard in speech, and read in books other nations miraculously extolled for their discoueries and notable enterprises by sea, but the English of all others for their sluggish security, and continuall neglect of the like attempts ... either ignominiously reported, or exceedingly condemned ... Thus both hearing, and reading the obloquie of our nation, and finding few or none of our owne men able to replie herein ... [I] determined notwithstanding all difficulties, to vndertake the burden of that worke ... To harpe no longer vpon this string, & to speake a word of that iust commendation which our nation doe indeed deserue: it can not be denied, but as in all former ages, they haue been men full of actiuity, stirrers abroad, and searchers of the remote parts of the world, so in this most famous and peerlesse gouernement of her most excellent Maiesty, her subjects through the speciall assistance, and blessing of God, in searching the most opposite corners and quarters of the world, and to speake plainly, in compassing the vaste globe of the earth more then once, haue excelled all the nations and people of the earth.[12]

If Hakluyt's language was stridently patriotic, its purpose was fundamentally defensive and patently promotional – of his ambitions both for his nation and (as always, in dedicatory epistles) for himself. It responds,

---

[12] Hakluyt, *Principal Navigations*, *2v.

first and foremost, to an expectation among his readers and patrons that a collection of travel accounts would – like *all* earlier models, on the Continent and in England – proceed on geographical rather than national lines.[13]

In the academic, diplomatic and commercial circles that Hakluyt travelled in – the world of what Warren Boutcher has described as a 'vernacular humanism' that was 'closely tied to the active life and practical concerns'[14] – such rhetoric did not cut England off from the wider world but, rather, marked its assumption of a new role in the old history of European political and economic rivalry. And it was indeed on these fronts that Hakluyt had more ammunition against the Platters of the world. Under Elizabeth, English ambassadors had established diplomatic relations with Russian, Ottoman and Indian rulers. And the expansion of England's commercial network was dramatic – even according to Platter. Elsewhere in his travel diary he acknowledged – in almost complete contradiction to his earlier image of an insular nation of armchair travellers – that by 1599 Londoners were deeply involved in global trade, and ideally situated for it: 'most of the inhabitants are employed in commerce: they buy, sell and trade in all the corners of the globe, for which purpose the water serves them well'.[15]

After 1550, new markets for English goods and new products for English and European consumers emerged in Russia, Persia and the Guinea and Barbary coasts, and then in East and Southeast Asia, North America and the Caribbean. The late Tudor and early Stuart periods became the great age of companies chartered for the purpose of overseas commerce and colonisation. Several African ventures pursued a lucrative trade in gold and slaves from the 1530s onward. The Muscovy Company was chartered in 1555 and developed trade with Russia, Persia and Greenland before its decline at the end of the seventeenth century. In 1576–8 the Cathay Company was formed for an exploration and mining venture in the Canadian Arctic. The short-lived Turkey and Venice Companies lost their grants in 1588–9 and were replaced by the Levant Company, which was chartered in January 1592 and flourished until the eighteenth century.

---

[13] See Richard Helgerson, *Forms of Nationhood: The Elizabethan Writing of England* (Chicago, 1992), 152.

[14] Warren Boutcher, 'Vernacular Humanism in the Sixteenth Century', in *The Cambridge Companion to Renaissance Humanism*, ed. Jill Kraye (Cambridge, 1996), 189–202, at 191. Boutcher's comments on English Renaissance library lists are particularly useful for drawing attention to the ways in which figures like Hakluyt would have been trained to move 'between the world of academe and the world of diplomacy and commerce', operating in 'a cultural environment which was not only interdisciplinary but interlinguistic in a particular and highly consistent fashion' (190–1). For Hakluyt's own career in both academic and ambassadorial settings, see ch. 4 in Fuller, *Voyages in Print*, and the 'Hakluyt Chronology' compiled by D. B. and A. M. Quinn for *The Hakluyt Handbook*, ed. Quinn, I, 263–331.

[15] Cited in *Material London, ca. 1600*, ed. Lena Cowen Orlin (Philadelphia, PA, 2000), 93.

The East India Company was chartered in the last year of the sixteenth century and exchanged currency, silks and spices on a truly global scale, despite persistent competition from the Portuguese and the Dutch. The turn of the seventeenth century also saw the emergence of the Virginia Company, the first of a series of new companies for the explicit purpose of 'plantation'.[16]

This is the context in which, at least on paper, the English could begin to hold their own against their Continental rivals; and nobody was in a better position to put that context on to paper than Hakluyt. Hakluyt took advantage of his contacts in the commercial and diplomatic worlds, and exploited both sharpening national identities and a developing book trade to help ripen English travel writing into one of the period's most popular and flexible genres. As travellers made contact with new regions and peoples, authors and editors translated the world for an audience at home that was increasingly eager to hear news of the wider world and to reflect on England's place in it. As Anthony Payne and others have shown, the number of new titles published, and old titles reprinted, during the period suggests that there was a significant market for travel writing and that books such as Hakluyt's quickly took their place – alongside the sugar, tobacco, spices and silk they described – as one of the most reliable new products for English consumers.[17]

In surveying the emergence of this genre between 1500 and 1720 for a recent overview in *The Cambridge Companion to Travel Writing*, I produced a tabular list of sixteenth- and seventeenth-century English travel books by region.[18] However crude such statistics are, they do capture some general patterns that speak to the collective concerns of these essays and the particular emphasis of my own contribution. First, they reveal that by the end of Elizabeth's reign, the only major regions for which readers could not yet turn to English accounts were Australia and Antarctica. And second, they highlight the crucial – and often overlooked – role played by *translation*: in more than half of the regions covered by the period's travellers, works translated into English preceded works written in English. And, not surprisingly, among the regions covered first in English were those closest to home (Western Europe), those in the far north (Northwest Passage/Greenland), and those that did not exist at all (Utopia).

---

[16] See my summary in 'Travel and Trade', in *A Companion to Renaissance Drama*, ed. Arthur F. Kinney (Oxford, 2002), 109–20, and the assessment of David Loades in *England's Maritime Empire: Seapower, Commerce and Policy, 1490–1690* (Harlow, 2000), particularly in Map 2 and ch. 3.

[17] See the contributions to *Journeys through the Market: Travel, Travellers, and the Book Trade*, ed. Robin Myers and Michael Harris (Folkestone, 1999).

[18] Sherman, 'Stirrings and Searchings', Table 1.

G. B. Parks reminded us several decades ago that in the 1580s, when Hakluyt began his publishing career, English bookshops were still dominated by accounts of foreign travels.[19] What it is still easy to forget, however, is that the books that informed the voyages of the great Elizabethan explorers tended to be in Latin, Italian, Spanish and French rather than in English. We have only begun to assess the presence and use of books by (among others) Ramusio, Thevet and de Bry in England – despite the fact that they clearly outnumber English publications in most of the major Elizabethan libraries we have catalogues for. Almost without exception, in those library catalogues where geography and travel are listed as a separate category, the English books form a small list at the end of much longer lists of titles in Classical and Continental languages. Thanks to the research of Pamela Neville-Sington and Anthony Payne, we have a good sense of the circulation of Hakluyt's work and a detailed census of surviving copies of his major collections.[20] What we know almost nothing about is the circulation and assimilation of the Continental materials collected by everyone with a serious interest in geography, travel and empire – and, indeed, used by virtually all of the scholars and seamen involved in Elizabethan expansionism.

It is important to recall that Hakluyt himself began, once he had gone to university and picked up the requisite language skills, by reading 'whatsoeuer printed or written discoueries and voyages I found extant either in the Greeke, Latine, Italian, Spanish, Portugall, French, or English languages'. Giovanni Battista Ramusio's three-volume collection of *Navigationi et Viaggi* (published in Venice between 150 and 1559) would have been near the top of his reading list: it has been called 'the first great collection of travel literature' and it created an editorial template for those who followed in his footsteps.[21] When Hakluyt drew up the list of important geographical writers at the beginning of his first collection of (mostly European) travels, the *Divers Voyages* of 1582, he included the understated acknowledgement, 'John Baptista Ramusius, hee gathered many notable things.'

While Ramusio set out to document the entire history of world travel, Hakluyt decisively chose to limit his collection to the activities and

[19] George B. Parks, 'Tudor travel literature: a brief history', in *The Hakluyt Handbook*, ed. Quinn, I, 97–132; cf. David B. Quinn, 'The Literature of Travel and Discovery, 1560–1600', in his *European Approaches to North America, 1450–1640* (Aldershot, 1998), 119–44.

[20] Anthony Payne, 'Richard Hakluyt and his Books', and P. A. Neville-Sington and Anthony Payne, 'An Interim Census of Surviving Copies of Hakluyt's *Divers Voyages and Principal Navigations*', The Hakluyt Society Annual Talk 1996 (London: The Hakluyt Society, 1997).

[21] See Gian Battista Ramusio, *Navigationi et Viaggi*, facsimile edition with an introduction by R. A. Skelton and an analysis of the contents by George B. Parks (3 vols., Amsterdam, 1970), III, v.

achievements of the English (and to issue his translations, for the most part, in discreet volumes). It is worth trying to imagine how English travel writing and the history of the British Empire would look now had Hakluyt simply translated Ramusio's collection and added the English materials as a sort of supplement (like the two English compilers of travel narratives before him, Richard Eden and Richard Willes). Granted, this is not on the same level, as Elizabethan counterfactuals go, with 'What if Elizabeth had married one of her suitors and produced a legitimate heir?' or 'What if the Spanish Armada had made it to the coast of England?' But it does help to highlight the long-term success of Hakluyt's patriotic project: had he followed in the footsteps of Eden and Willes, he certainly would not have been credited by the Victorians with compiling the 'great prose epic of the English nation', and the premier society for the history of English travel writing would probably not have named itself after him. What may be more productive to ponder is the long-term influence of Hakluyt's rhetorical and editorial strategies on setting the agenda for research on English travel and its texts. As with recent arguments about the need to attend to the pervasive influence of Latin texts and Catholic books in Tudor and Stuart England, a strong case could be made for paying more attention to the pre-existing voyages and texts that brought the world to Elizabethan England.

If Elizabethan translation, as Matthiessen suggested in the passage that opened this paper, was the means by which the world of the Renaissance came to England, then Elizabethan travel writing was (along with new consumer goods, captured natives, pirates' booty and adopted words) the means by which the wider world – and the dream of mastery over it – were imported for English readers. All Elizabethan travel writing, and not just those texts based explicitly or implicitly on foreign texts, participated in this project of translation in which the 'strange' (both civil and savage) was at once co-opted and occluded.[22]

---

[22] Eric Cheyfitz, *The Poetics of Imperialism: Translation and Colonization from* The Tempest *to* Tarzan (expanded edition, Philadelphia, PA, 1997).

Transactions of the RHS 14 (2004), pp. 209–22 © 2004 Royal Historical Society
DOI: 10.1017/S0080440104000234   Printed in the United Kingdom

GLORIANA RULES THE WAVES: OR, THE ADVANTAGE OF BEING EXCOMMUNICATED (AND A WOMAN)*

By Lisa Jardine

ABSTRACT. In the last quarter of the sixteenth century England embarked on a strategic rapprochement with the Ottoman Empire. Elizabeth I's excommunication by Pope Pius V in 1570 removed the papal levies for trading with the 'infidel', opening up commercial opportunities. England also explored the possibility of calling upon Ottoman military might to support her against the Catholic powers of mainland Europe. One product of this East–West engagement is a remarkable correspondence and exchange of gifts between Elizabeth and the sultana, Walide Safiye. Although the Anglo-Ottoman political accord failed, the exchanges between Elizabeth and the sultana set the tone for England's subsequent trading position in the East.

Talking to the infidel

On 7 March 1579, the Ottoman sultan Murad III wrote from Constantinople to Queen Elizabeth I, promising security by land and sea to all English merchants trading in the Ottoman territories, and requesting her friendship in return. The letter was a work of art in itself: the calligraphy of the Turkish original was elaborate, the text of the letter composed in the stylised and effusive terms of traditional Ottoman Turkish rhetoric, the whole thing crowned with the sultan's official signature and lavishly sealed. It was passed to the official interpreter Mustapha for translation into Latin. Then the letter was placed in a satin bag and fastened with a silver capsule, and original and translation were dispatched together to England.

---

* This paper is dedicated to Dr Susan Skilliter, who was a senior scholar at Newnham College where I was an undergraduate and graduate student, and a neighbour when I returned to Cambridge to live in 1976. Dr Skilliter's work on Elizabeth I and the Ottomans was so far ahead of its time that its ground-breaking originality has only recently come to be fully appreciated outside the expert circles of Ottomanists. I have drawn here extensively on her published work: her book on William Harborne and an important early article: S. A. Skilliter, *William Harborne and the Trade with Turkey 1578–1582: A Documentary Study of the First Anglo-Ottoman Relations* (Oxford, 1977); 'Three Letters from the Ottoman "Sultana" Safiye to Queen Elizabeth I', in *Documents from Islamic Chanceries*, ed. S. M. Stern, first series (= *Oriental Studies* 3) (Oxford, 1965), 119–57.

According to modern Ottomanists, such an unsolicited letter from a ruling sultan represented an unheard-of honour for the recipient. It was customary for Murad to respond only to carefully framed and formally constructed epistolary approaches made by petitioners in their own name, even if those petitioners were of royal status equal to his own.

On 25 October 1579, Queen Elizabeth I replied from Greenwich, in terms as fulsome and flattering as those of the original letter, and which acknowledged the magnitude of the honour which had been bestowed on her – she had evidently been well briefed:

> Elizabeth by the grace of the most mightie God, . . . the most invincible and most mightie defender of the Christian faith against all kinde of idolatries, of all that live among the Christians, and falselie professe the name of Christ, unto the most Imperiall and most invincible prince, Zuldan Murad Chan . . .
>
> Most Imperiall and invincible Emperor, we have received the letters of your mightie highness written to us from Constantinople the fifteenth day of March this present yeere, whereby we understand how gratiously, and how favorably the humble petitions of one William Harebrowne [Harborne] a subject of ours, resident in the Imperiall citie of your highnesse presented unto your Maiestie for the obteining of accesse . . . to come with merchandizes both by sea & land, to the countries and territories subiect to your governement, and from thence againe to returne home with good leave and libertie, were accepted of your most invincible Imperiall highnesse.[1]

So in fact Murad's letter had indeed come as a response to an English approach, carried to Constantinople by an English merchant, Willliam Harborne, under orders from the queen herself. As a result of his efforts, England and the Ottoman Empire signed a trade agreement in 1581, granting English merchants preferential trading rights superior to any currently in existence with other European trading nations (chief amongst them France and Venice).[2]

The story of how this Anglo-Ottoman accord came about is a fascinating one, and is an important reminder, in these disturbingly islamophobic days, that Elizabeth I's strategies for outflanking her European economic and commercial competitors reached a long way to the East, far beyond the familiar boundaries of the Mediterranean region – beyond Christendom itself. Remarkably, English foreign policy between the 1570s and the late 1590s shows a marked inclination to foster good relations with the Ottomans, for both trade and power-political reasons. In the period 1570 to 1590, there were good reasons, as we shall

---

[1] R. Hakluyt, *The Principall Navigations, Voyages, Traffiques & Discoveries of the English Nation*, 2nd edn (3 vols., 1598–1600; repr., 12 vols., Glasgow, 1903–5), V, 165–6. Taken from Skilliter, *William Harborne*, 69–70.

[2] 'On 11 September 1581 the Turkey company which later . . . united with [the] Venice [Company] to become the Levant Company was founded by royal charter. The Ottoman government lowered the customs rate for the English to 3 per cent, the French and other foreigners paying 5 per cent until 1673.' H. Inalcik, *The Ottoman Empire: The Classical Age 1300–1600* (1994), 138.

see, for Elizabeth to believe that she had more in common with the
Ottoman Turk than with the Spanish Catholics.

Heretics trading with infidels

The trigger for Elizabethan initiatives to the East was Pope Pius V's
decision, issued in a Papal Bull in February 1570, finally to excommunicate
Elizabeth 'pretended Queen of England, and her followers' – and to
pronounce the entire nation 'heretics'. The papal intention was further
to isolate England from the rest of Catholic Europe – although in fact its
immediate effect was to generate an upsurge of English patriotism and
loyalty. An unlooked-for consequence of the Bull, however, was that it
freed English merchants from the Catholic Church's embargo on (and
punitive fines for) trading in the infidel oriental marketplace. Heavily
embroiled in hostilities in the Mediterranean and having embarked on a
crippling war with Persia, the Ottoman Turks were more eager than ever
in the later 1570s to import munitions.

> The English were now free and eager to export cloth for soldiers' uniforms and metal
> for arms, especially the precious tin. Flaunting their liberty, English ships would carry to
> the infidel the scrap-metal resulting from the upheavals of the Reformation – lead from
> the roofs of ecclesiastical buildings, old bells, and broken metal statuary . . . It cannot be
> a coincidence that the new contraband trade with Turkey followed almost immediately
> after the Queen's excommunication.[3]

An unlooked-for outcome of formal exclusion from the 'club' of
Catholic trading nations, then, was a clear rapprochement between
England and the Ottomans, bringing with it significant commercial
benefits. In November 1579 the Spanish ambassador Bernardino de
Mendoza reported anxiously to the Habsburg emperor the increasingly
cordial Anglo-Turkish trade alliance, based on England's exemption from
papal sanctions:

> The Turks are also desirous of friendship with the English on account of the tin which
> has been sent thither for the last few years, and which is of the greatest value to them, as
> they cannot cast their guns without it, whilst the English make a tremendous profit on
> the article, by means of which alone they maintain the trade with the Levant. Five ships
> are ready to sail thither now, and I am told that, in one of them, they are sending nearly
> twenty thousand crowns worth of bar tin, without counting what the rest of them take.[4]

Elizabeth's flouting of the papal embargo was, moreover, more than a
piece of commercial wheeler-dealing – it was also potentially a political
challenge by the Protestant sovereign to the power of Catholic Spanish.
'This sending tin to the infidel is against the apostolic communion, and
your Majesty has ordered that no such voyage shall be allowed to pass

---

[3] Skilliter, *William Harborne*, 23.
[4] Cit. *ibid.*, 24.

the Messina light, to the prejudice of God and Christianity', observed Mendoza.

Nor was Mendoza wrong to be alarmed at the advantage England was gaining in international trade terms. A second letter from Elizabeth accompanied the one just cited. It was addressed to Mustafa Beg, who answered to both the sultan and Elizabeth's English agents, and was in charge of translation and transmission of official documents between the two, and it specified even more clearly the extent of the commercial rights being extended to the English, above those held by France and Venice (the traditional European commercial interests in the region).

The English rapidly consolidated the advantage excommunication had given them in the Turkey trade. By the mid- to late 1570s English ships were operating commercially, freely and with confidence, in the Levant. An 'estimate for a voyage to the Levant', drafted by John Hawkins in June 1577, survives, headed 'The determynacion of a voiage, to be made by the swallow of 300 tonne & the pellycan of 120 tonne to alexandria tripoly constantynople &c.' This records a cargo which includes:

    40 tonne of brasyll [hardwood] caled farnandoboucke
    20 hundredweight of tynne
    90 fodder [a fodder = 19.5 cwt] of ledd
    2000 ordynary blew Hamshere Karsyes [Hampshire Kerseys]
    100 clothes [cloths] of all sorts chose for that country of mete collers
    [colours].[5]

This combination of prohibited military materials (hardwood, tin and lead) and sought-after English cloth products was to become the standard lading for the Levant trade. En route, Hawkins intended to take on board currants and sweet malmsey and muscadel wines at Crete and Zante. If attempts were made by hostile powers to intercept his ships, they would sail direct to Alexandria, and collect the currants and wine on the return journey. At Alexandria the English cargo would be sold and '50 or 60 tonne of the best and clenest spice' purchased. Thus the merchants would arrive home with a major cargo of spices, currants, malmsey and muscadel for the English market at competitive European prices.[6]

Initiatives like Hawkins's drew the attention of Sir Francis Walsingham and the earl of Leicester to trading initiatives and opportunities in the Levant.[7] Encouraged by the lucrative prospects and military advantages such enterprises brought with them Walsingham drafted a position paper

---

[5] *Ibid.*, 20. Skilliter suggests that the *Pelican* did not in fact go East, but became the lead ship for Sir Francis Drake's circumnavigation of the world. See also K. R. Andrews, *Trade, Plunder and Settlement: Maritime Enterprise and the Genesis of the British Empire 1480–1630* (Cambridge, 1984).

[6] Skilliter, *William Harborne*, 20–1.

[7] Walsingham was interested in Levant trade as early as 1577 (Conyers Read, *Mr Secretary Walsingham and the Policy of Queen Elizabeth* (3 vols., Oxford, 1925), III, 372). The earl of Leicester

in 1578, in which he outlined the reasons for encouraging English trade with Turkey.[8] Trade into Turkey, he advised, would mean employing England's 'greatest ships' in profit-making enterprises, thereby increasing and strengthening naval resources for the national defence. By selling English products direct, rather than through foreign middlemen, and, similarly, purchasing Turkish commodities at source, greater profits could be made, 'which before did fall into strangers hands'. If English merchants themselves imported and distributed Turkish goods throughout Europe, Walsingham counselled, English profits would be all the greater: 'You shall furnishe not onlie this Realme, but also the most parte of the hyther parte of Ewrope with suche Commodyties as are transported out of the said Turkes dominions, to the great enrichinge of this realme.'[9]

Against this had to be set the fact that English trade with Turkey would create hostility amongst the French and Venetian merchants who had previously held the monopoly of such trade, and anger the king of Spain. Both would try to impede England's access to Constantinople – diplomatically and physically. To counter this, Walsingham proposed secretly sending an emissary to the sultan:

> To meete with these inconveniencies, and to provide som probable waie of suertie, the fyrst thinge that is to be done to withstande theyr fines is to make choice of some apte man to be sent with her Majestes letters unto the Turke to procure an ample safe conducte, who is allwaies to remaine there at the charge of the merchantes, as Agent to impeache the indirect practises of the [French and Venetian] Ambassadours.[10]

It was Walsingham's initiative which led to the secret dispatch of William Harborne (who had previously acted as factor for the merchant Edward Osborne, already trading in the East) to Constantinople in 1578. Hakluyt describes the beginning of that adventure:

> The sayd M. Harborne the first of July 1578 departed from London by the sea to Hamburgh, and thence accompanied with Joseph Clements his guide and a servant, he travailed to Leopolis in Poland, and then apparelling himselfe, his guide, and his servant after the Turkish fashion . . . by good means he obteined favour of one Acmet Chaus

---

was involved in trade with Morocco as early as 1572. See T. S. Willan, *Studies in Elizabethan Foreign Trade* (Manchester, 1959), 'The Leicester Partnership', 118; also 240–65.

[8] For full discussion of Walsingham's 'A Consideration of the Trade into Turkey' see Read, *Mr Secretary Walsingham*, III, 229–30; Skilliter, *William Harborne*, 27–33. Skilliter redates the 'Consideration' from 1580 to 1578, and all scholars since have accepted her revised dating.

[9] Skilliter, *William Harborne*, 28.

[10] *Ibid.*, 29. Walsingham continues, with positively Alistair Campbell-like awareness of 'spin': 'whose repaire thither is to be handled with grett secrecie, and his voyage to be perfourmed rather by lande than by sea, for that otherwise the Italians that are here will seeke under hande that he may be disgraced at his repayre thither, and therefore it shalbe verey well done to geve owt that in respect of the daunger of the trafficque her majestie cannot be induced that hir subiects shall trade thither'.

the Turks ambassadour then in Poland, and readie to returne to Constantinople, to bee received into his companie and carovan.[11]

The story of Harborne's successful negotiation of preferential trading rights for the English, and his personal success in building cordial relations with key members of the sultan's entourage has been told before.[12] His is a remarkable tale of East–West, Christian–Islamic bridge-building. Of particular interest here are some of the political consequences of the Anglo-Ottoman accord so carefully brokered by Harborne on behalf of England's mercantile interests.

United against the idolators

By 1582 it was clear that merchants in Constantinople required an official English government presence to guarantee their rights and safety. Accordingly, after assiduous lobbying by Edward Osborne and Richard Staper of the Turkey Company, and building on the careful groundwork laid during Harborne's first period at the Ottoman court, William Harborne was eventually sent as England's first ambassador to the Ottoman Turks.[13] As if to confirm that the ambassador's function was seen as first and foremost one concerning English trade and commercial interests, his salary and all his expenses were to be paid by the Turkey Company.

Harborne took up his residency in 1583.[14] Throughout his time as English ambassador to the Ottoman Turks (he returned to England finally in 1588), Harborne (who had, we recall, begun his Turkish career as a secret emissary) continued to be briefed and directed by Walsingham in his capacity as head of Elizabeth's intelligence operations.[15] It is as a result of the survival of Walsingham's briefing letters to Harborne that we can see how closely England's Turkish trading ventures were tied up with European power politics during the same period.

[11] Hakluyt, *The Principall Navigations*, V, 168–9.
[12] For the full story see Skilliter, *William Harborne*.
[13] 'Anglo-Ottoman diplomatic relations were first established in 1583 when William Harborne arrived in Constantinople as Queen Elizabeth's ambassador, carrying her letters and delivering the royal present, due at the installation of every ambassador, to the Sultan – in this case to Murad III (1574–95). Harborne returned to England in August 1588, leaving behind as agent his secretary, the then twenty-five years old Edward Barton.' Skilliter, 'Three Letters', 143.
[14] The queen's commission was delivered to Harborne (who had returned to London) on 20 November 1582. It began: 'Know ye, that wee thinking well, and having good confidence in the singular trustinesse, obedience, wisedome, and disposition of our welbeloved servaunt William Hareborne [Harborne], one of the Esquiers of our body, towards us, and our service, doe by these presents, make, ordaine and constitute him our true and undoubted Orator, Messenger, Deputie, and Agent.' Skilliter, *William Harborne*, 199–200.
[15] See, in addition to Skilliter, Read, *Mr Secretary Walsingham*, III, 225–8 and 326–32.

In the spring of 1585 Harborne received verbal instructions, via a messenger dispatched by Walsingham, to incite the Ottomans to attack Spain, 'thereby to divert the dangerous attempt and designs of the said King [of Spain] from these parts of Christendom'. Walsingham elaborated on these instructions in a cyphered letter dispatched on 8 October 1585.[16] Elizabeth having finally resolved to go to war with Spain (following the assassination of the prince of Orange), Walsingham instructed Harborne to press for an Ottoman offensive against Spain:

> Her Majesty being, upon the success of the said King of Spain's affairs in the Low Countries, now fully resolved to oppose herself against his proceedings in defence of that distressed nation, whereof it is not otherwise likely but hot wars between him and us, wills me again to require you effectually to use all your endeavour and industry in that behalf.[17]

The sultan might, Walsingham suggested, be encouraged to keep the Spanish forces 'thoroughly occupied' by 'some incursions from the coast of Africa', or by attacking his Italian territories from the sea. Failing this, Harborne was to try to persuade the sultan at least to pretend aggression:

> If you shall see that the Sultan cannot be brought altogether to give ear to this advice you shall, after you have done your best to gain this first point, procure at least that, by making show of arming to the sea for the King of Spain's dominions, hold the King of Spain in suspense, by means whereof he shall be the less bold to send forth his best forces into these parts, which may serve to good purpose if you fail of the first.[18]

Walsingham wrote similarly to Harborne in 1587 – a year before the Armada – once again urging the ambassador to encourage the Ottoman sultan to 'attempt somewhat presently for the impeachment of the said Spaniard's greatness, by setting such princes as are in Barbary at his devotion upon the King of Spain, which with small cost shall give him great annoyance'.[19] It is clear, then, that the English government was able

---

[16] Read, *Mr Secretary Walsingham*, III, 226: 'As by instructions given to Jacobo Manuci for to impart to you about VI months since, I did advise you of a course to be taken there for procuring the Grand Seigneur, if it were possible, to convert some part of his forces bent, as it should seem by your advertisements, from time to time wholly against the Persians, rather against Spain, thereby to divert the dangerous attempt and designs of the said King from these parts of Christendom.'

[17] *Ibid.*

[18] *Ibid.*, 226–8. By contrast with the official correspondence, Walsingham represents this as setting one bunch of heretics against another: 'It would be no small advantage to her Majesty presently, but to all Christendom hereafter; the limbs of the devil being thus set one against another, by means thereof the true Church and doctrine of the gospel may, during their contention, have leisure to grow to such strength as shall be requisite for the suppression of them both.' As a result of such 'mixed messages' to Harborne, modern historians have great difficulty deciding whether Elizabeth and her ministers really wanted an alliance with the Turks against the Spanish, or merely gesture politics in that direction.

[19] Read, *Mr Secretary Walsingham*, III, 330 (complete letter transcribed 329–32). Edward Barton, Harborne's successor as Ottoman ambassador, was dismayed when he received

to exploit the strong commercial base established by English merchants (under the agency of Harborne) in Constantinople to significant effect, in relation to the European political arena.

The axis around which the Anglo-Ottoman political negotiations were conducted was the supposedly shared values and beliefs of Lutheran Protestantism and Islam. Returning to that exchange of letters between Queen Elizabeth and Sultan Murad with which this paper began, what is perhaps as remarkable as the personal contact between Elizabeth I and Murad III itself is the appeal clearly made to shared beliefs and principles of Protestantism and Islam, in order to cement good relations between the two realms. Skilliter is at pains to point this out:

> In both her letters . . . the Queen insists on her title 'Defensatrix Fidei', her worship of the one, true God, and her abhorrence of idolatry which brings her to overthrow images. She is appealing unmistakably to the basic religious tenets of her Islamic correspondents and separating herself from her Catholic neighbours.[20]

This appeal to shared tenets of religious observance matches those made explicit in other communications with Protestants on the part of the Ottoman sultan in the period, for instance, this one from Murad III to 'members of the Lutheran sect in Flanders and Spain' in 1574: 'As you, for your part, do not worship idols, you have banished the idols and portraits and bells from churches, and declared your faith by stating that God Almighty is One and Holy Jesus is His Prophet and Servant.'[21]

Beyond these careful formal expressions of shared beliefs, European Protestants apparently recognised themselves as occupying a similar place to Muslims in the arena of European power politics. In the face of their common plight, threatened because of their beliefs by Spanish Imperial might, European Protestants, dubbed infidels and heretics alongside Turk and Jew, readily interpreted turbaned figures in contemporary art as

---

forceful instructions from Walsingham to try to get Mehmed III to make peace with Rudolph, emperor of Hungary. See I. I. Podea, 'A Contribution to the Study of Queen Elizabeth's Eastern Policy', *Mélanges d'Histoire Générale*, 2 (Cluj, 1938), 423–76: 'Until the middle of July 1593, and before receiving the Queen's instructions, Barton continued to encourage the warlike disposition of the [sultan] . . . War [with the emperor Rudolph] became inevitable after the great defeat sustained by the Turks near Sissek, where Hassan died in the river Kulpa together with two other Pashas. On July 20 . . . Barton received the instructions from the Queen and the Lord High Treasurer: "We have great desire to try all meanes in our parte possible to stay the intended warre, and though our advises maie comme somewhat late yet if it might be, as in like former times hath been used, a surseau or truce might be made on both parts for some time" [PRO SP 97/2 fos. 194–5].' Podea, 'A Contribution to the Study of Queen Elizabeth's Eastern Policy', 469–70.

[20] Skilliter, *William Harborne*, 74–5. The fact that this emphasis is clearer in the letter to Mustafa (which Skilliter transcribes from the official Latin copy in the PRO, rather than taking from Hakluyt) suggests that Hakluyt may have modified his original to avoid offending his Christian readers.

[21] *Ibid.*, 37.

themselves, and identified with the figure of the Turk in paintings and tapestries.[22]

Thus the Protestant viewers saw themselves in the conventional rendering of the vanquished infidel trampled under the hooves of the Imperial warrior in a painting like Titian's *Charles V at the Battle of Mühlberg*: 'Under the heel of the Hapsburg master lie crushed, together, the hopes and aspirations of Protestant Europe and the Muslim East. Eastwards and westwards, circulated to Muslim, Jew and Lutheran alike in the early modern global community, this image and its threat were provocative and unmistakable.'[23]

In the political iconography of Anglo-Spanish and Protestant–Catholic hostilities, there is, in other words, a tendency towards identification of Protestant with Turk – both dubbed 'infidel' by the pope and the Holy Roman emperor, both practising the 'true' Religion of the Book, free from alienating rituals, superstition and idolatry. In many ways it suited the English to let it be known that they flirted seriously (certainly not a tautology in terms of Elizabethan diplomacy), throughout the 1580s and 1590s, with Anglo-Turkish political accord.

Entering the harem

That flirtation was aided by one further significant feature of Elizabethan rule. The sovereign ruler of England, Defender of the Faith, was a woman. Her sex meant that friendship (even epistolary) with the sultan with whom she sought to establish cordial relations – and who evidently reciprocated her enthusiasm – was limited by the bounds of protocol. Yet the absolute curiosity of her status in relation to Islam and the Ottoman state gave her a notable advantage over male European rulers: she could entertain direct personal relations with the sultana – something no male representative of a European power was allowed to do.[24]

Murad III's and Mehmet III's reigns were famously considered to be periods in Ottoman history when the state was ruled from the harem.

---

[22] For an account of the complexity of English Protestants' cultural relationship with Islam and the Ottoman Turks see M. Dimmock, *New Turks: Dramatizing Islam and the Ottomans in Early Modern England* (Aldershot, 2005).

[23] L. Jardine and J. Brotton, *Global Interests: Renaissance Art between East and West* (2000), 181.

[24] 'During the sultanate of Murad, the grandfather of the present Padishah [Ahmed I, 1603–17], the ruler of the Lutheran kingdom among the Franks took of old the road of submission to the Padishah of the House of Osman and at that time was, it is said, a woman, Queen of a sizeable kingdom. This person, in order to approach the Abod of Majesty and the shadow of its protection, sent as a gift a masterpiece of craftsmanship, a clock[work organ] . . . The aforementioned Queen expended boundless wealth and unlimited treasure, while the experts who build the clock[work organ] laboured for many years, toiling and preserving, to complete and perfect it.' Cit. G. M. MacLean, *The Rise of Oriental Travel: English Visitors to the Ottoman Empire, 1580–1720* (Basingstoke, 2004), xi.

When Edward Barton (who had been Harborne's secretary) replaced William Harborne as English ambassador in 1588, he advised the queen that for sound political reasons, in addition to sending the compulsory gifts to the sultan to accompany his letter of commission, she should also write to the Walide Safiye, and should send gifts to her too.[25]

The first letter which survives from the correspondence between Elizabeth and the Albanian-born Walide Safiye (the sultana, Murad III's wife and Mehmed III's mother) was written in November 1593, and is her formal response to the letter and gifts sent – rather tardily – at Barton's request. Skilliter describes this richly beautiful missive as follows:

> The document is a single sheet of Oriental paper, which at first sight resembles parchment and is thick, yellowish and inclined to break at the folds... The script is a beautiful calligraphic *naskh*, partially vocalised... In every line except the last the scribe changes the ink at least three times, using altogether five colours, black, blue, crimson, gold, and scarlet. In these changes of colour purely aesthetic considerations seem to have prevailed; thus the last line is written entirely in black, suggesting an intention to stress the closing.[26]

The letter's seal – its crowning glory – is lost, but is described in the inventory which accompanied the letter and gifts: 'one shell of gould which couered the seale of her lettere to her Magestie uppon which was sett ii smale sparkes of Dyamondes and ii small sparkes of rubies mighte bee worth £20.00.00'.[27]

Safiye's letter acknowledged the one she had received from Elizabeth, together with the accompanying lavish gifts, all of which were presented

[25] 'In order to achieve full ambassadorial status Barton needed to procure a new present and it was only after a long and hard struggle on his part that in 1593 the Queen's second gift left England, so that in the October of that year he was at last able to deliver the royal letters and present to the Sultan. At the same time a special letter and gifts also arrived for the Sultana, sent on the advice of Barton who wished to encourage his good relations with the harem.' Skilliter, 'Three Letters', 143–4.

[26] *Ibid.*, 120–1. 'A letter in Turkish from the Sultana Safiye to Queen Elizabeth, written 25 November – 4 December 1593. British Museum Cotton MS Nero B. viii, ff. 61–2.' See also L. Pierce, *The Imperial Harem: Women and Sovereignty in the Ottoman Empire* (New York, 1993).

[27] Skilliter, 'Three Letters', 148. Skilliter describes the text as equivalently lavish: 'Just as the letter is beautiful from the point of view of decoration and calligraphy, so it is elaborate in its style, being composed in a very involved and flowery rhyming prose with many poetical comparisons. In this showpiece of rhetoric, the actual communication which the Sultana has to make occupies less than half of the twenty-four lines.' *Ibid.*, 122–3. See e.g.: 'towards the support of Christian womanhood, [the elected of the triumphant] who follow the Messiah, bearer of the marks of pomp and majesty, trailing the skirts of glory and power, she who is obeyed of princes, cradle of chastity and continence, ruler of the realm of England, crowned lady and woman of Mary's way – may her last moments be concluded with good and may she obtain what she desires! – with the intention of her following the guidance in the right path, let there be made a salutation so gracious that (all) the rose-garden's roses are but one petal from it and a speech so sincere that the (whole) repertoire of the garden's nightingales is but one stanza of it, a prayer which bestows a fortunate end, a praise which brings felicity in this world and the next!' *Ibid.*, 131–2.

by the ambassador Edward Barton to the 'Agha or keeper of the Gate [to the seraglio]', who in turn gave them to Walide Safiye.[28]

We have a first-hand account of the presents Elizabeth sent Safiye, from Richard Wrag, who travelled from England to Constantinople in 1593, aboard the same ship which carried them:

> The Present sent her in her majesties name was a jewel of her majesties picture, set with some rubies and diamants, 3 great pieces of gilt plate, 10 garments of cloth of gold, a very fine case of glasse bottles silver & gilt, with 2 pieces of fine Holland.[29]

In return, Mehmed's mother – on the advice of Barton that 'a sute of princely attire being after the Turkish fashion would for the rarenesse thereof be acceptable in England' – sent 'an upper gowne of cloth of gold very rich, an under gowne of cloth of silver, and a girdle of Turkie worke, rich and faire'.

In the letter of thanks, almost buried under the weight of the flowery compliments, the sultan's mother, the power behind the throne of Mehmed III, promised to do all she could to promote Elizabeth's interests:

> While striving for that illustrious princess's and honoured lady's salvation and Her success in Her desires, I can repeatedly mention Her Highness's gentility and praise at the footdust of His Majesty, the fortunate and felicitous Padishah, the Lord of the fortunate conjunction and the sovereign who has Alexander's place, and I shall endeavour for Her aims.[30]

Here, then, is a pledge of friendship between the queen mother in Constantinople and the sovereign queen of England, which is explicitly aimed at promoting her interests – commercial and political. True to her promise, Safiye shortly afterwards attempted to influence her son on Elizabeth's behalf in the political decision of the moment: in 1592 Mehmed was set on all-out war with Hungary, while Elizabeth had instructed her ambassador Edward Barton to try to influence the sultan to seek a truce with the emperor Rudolph instead. Safiye intervened – unsuccessfully – to try to persuade the sultan to allow Barton to act as mediator between the sultan and the emperor. The Venetian ambassador Zane reported on 4 December 1593: 'I hear that the Sultana has tried

---

[28] 'After her Felicitous Majesty's presents and gifts had been accounted for, . . . by the hand of Her ambassador [Edward Barton] . . . a special letter, full of marvels, whose paper was more fragrant than pure camphor and ambergris and its ink than finest musk, notifying indescribable and immeasurable consideration towards (me) Her well-wisher, reached (me) by the good offices of the Agha of the Door of chastity and modesty.' *Ibid.*, 132.

[29] Hakluyt, *The Principall Navigations*, VI, 94–118. The ship left London in March 1593 and reached Constantinople in September. The gifts were presented by Barton to the sultan on 17 October.

[30] Skilliter, 'Three Letters', 132–3.

to persuade the Sultan to allow the English Ambassador to mediate for peace, but that his Majesty would lend no ear to her.'[31]

Two-way traffic in exotic goods

Queen Elizabeth wrote to the sultana again in 1599. Following Barton's death in January 1598, when his secretary Henry Lello had been introduced as ambassador, an official letter and appropriate gifts for the sultan were expected. These were finally dispatched from London in March 1599 aboard the ship *Hector*.[32] This was the occasion on which the queen sent the sultan the famous organ, much talked of in contemporary travel literature.[33] Less well known is the fact that the ship also carried a beautiful coach for the Walide Safiye. On board to supervise these state-of-the art pieces of English technology and ensure they were delivered in perfect working order were the coachman Edward Hale and the organ-maker Thomas Dallam of Lancashire.[34]

[31] *Ibid.*, 149. Barton found himself in an extremely awkward position, since he had, on Walsingham's instructions, been lobbying equally forcefully in favour of war with Hungary only months earlier. 'Barton met the Grand Vizier near Constantinople. He found such "could entertainment touching Her Majesty's desire" that he was forced to change his arguments and explain that the Queen was anxious to have peace in Hungary, not because of any friendship with the Emperor, but because she considered that the war would prevent the Sultan from attacking the king of Spain, as he had formerly promised the Queen to do. Barton's letters came so unexpectedly that the Vizier suspected they had been forged, especially as they were produced precisely on the day of his departure to the camp. In his report the ambassador excused the failure of his intervention by showing that matters had advanced too far to be arrested; however, he was ready to accompany Sinan to the war in order to intervene whenever the moment should prove more favourable for the conclusion of a truce . . . In September the ambassador wrote that his attempts to realize the Queen's desire "hath greatly impaired Her Majesty's creditt and my reputation with these ayders and fautors unto the Emperor". To save his position at the Porte he tried to explain that the Queen only wished to give the Sultan the possibility of attacking the king of Spain.' Podea, 'A Contribution to the Study of Queen Elizabeth's Eastern Policy', 471–3.

[32] Letters and presents were also due to congratulate the sultan upon his accession in January 1595. Barton wrote anxiously in September 1595: 'Hitherto Mr Barton hath excused the sending of her Maties present; but . . . he hath now no further excuse for delay; it is needful therefore, it be presently provided & sent; for the longer it is delayed, the lesse affection it will represent.' Cit. MacLean, *Rise of Oriental Travel*, 34. The long time delays successive English resident ambassadors in Constantinople experienced in getting formal letters, gifts and policy instructions from London is a reminder of the immense distances involved, and the difficulties of travel across the intervening regions.

[33] For a full account of the remarkable fortunes of Dallam and his clockwork organ at the court of the sultan see MacLean, *Rise of Oriental Travel*, 1–47. As MacLean points out, although Dallam's organ has become a standard anecdote in accounts of Anglo-Ottoman relations, many of the previous stories told about it have been fanciful, misinformed and misleading. MacLean also has a clear account of the destruction of the organ by Mehmed III's son Ahmed.

[34] This account of the delivery of the coach (which MacLean mentions only in passing) is closely based on Skilliter, 'Three Letters', 149–51.

The *Hector* reached Constantinople at the end of August. The organ had been damaged during the long voyage (all the gluing had failed, and some of the pipes were broken), and it was at first suggested that the coach might be substituted as the sultan's gift. This idea had to be abandoned, however. As Lello reported to Sir Robert Cecil:

> The coach must of necessity be givne to the old Sultana because itt hath byn brutted here longe agone by some out of Ingland thatt hir highnes had ordayned the same, for hir, who longe seince have taken notice ther of and nowe sheweth hir selfe to be glade, havinge alredie sente to me thatt I wold sende for two horses, out of hir owne stable, to drawe the same.

Excitement and curiosity began to mount. 'So excited was she by news of the carriage she was about to receive, that Safiye peremptorily send "two horses out of her own stable, to drawe the same".'[35] On 12 September Safiye went by water to view the English ship, following the sultan in his golden caique. By 21 September Dallam had repaired the organ and had begun to set it up in the sultan's private quarters. He noted in his diary: 'The same Daye, our Imbassader sente Mr. Paule Pinder, who was then his secritarie, with a presente to the Sultana, she being at hir garthen. The presente was a Coatche of six hundrethe poundes vallue.' Ambassador Lello reported the enthusiastic reception of the gift by Walide Safiye with delight:

> The Sultana sente me worde, thatt I should sende hir the Queen's lettere and the Coatche, which she harde was destined for hir to the courte wher shee was with hir sonne, which accordingly I sente together with a fanne by my Secrettarie accompanyed with Ientlemen and Merchanttes of the which she made a great demonstration of Ioy by hir Agent or Aga, and tooke itt very gratfully sendinge to them three vestes of cloath of silver, 300 chequins of gold and 40. chequins to the Coatchman the like have never byn seen or herde here thatt any of these have given any like rewardes, also proferinge hir selfe readye to doe all the service she could for the Queen and our nation, and thatt I should bouldlye come to hir agent or Aga for any busines whatsoever, and should fine hir my frinde. The Sultan and she have often tymes byn abroade in the Coache, and seince she have sente to me to sende hir the Queen's picture to behold, which I have her given order to make by one thatt came with the shipp.[36]

In line with the evident success of the gift, Walide Safiye responded with a letter written by one of the harem scribes – a personal letter, then, distinguished by its poor command of the scribal formalities of Ottoman diplomatic correspondence, and its primitive calligraphy. Once again Safiye promises friendship, and a commitment to continuing to protect

---

[35] MacLean, *Rise of Oriental Travel*, 34. Lello, whose difficult relations with Dallam MacLean vividly conveys, complained 'at having to stable and feed them while the carriage was being repaired and repainted'. Lello to Cecil, 8 Sept. 1599, PRO SP 97/4, fo. 45.

[36] Lello to Cecil, 22 Sept./2 Oct. 1599, PRO SP 97/4, fos. 49b, 50a. Cit. Skilliter, 'Three Letters', 150–1.

the queen of England's interests:

> Your letter has arrived and reached (us); whatsoever you said became known to us.
> God willing, action will be taken according to what you said. Be of good heart in this respect! We will not cease from admonishing our son, His Majesty the Padishah [Mehmed III], and from telling him: 'Do act according to the treaty!' [the first English capitulation of 1580] God willing, may you not suffer grief in this respect!
> May you, too, always be firm in friendship! God willing, it will never fail. And you sent us a coach; it has arrived and has been delivered. It had our gracious acceptance.
> We, too, have sent you a robe, a girdle, a sleeve, two gold-embroidered handkerchiefs, three towels, one crown studded with pearls and rubies.

These final gifts, transported at enormous effort and expense from London to Constantinople, somehow symbolise the escalating scale of the English adventure in the East. Organ and coach were absurdly complicated items to attempt to transport across the enormous distances involved, and both required constant attention to keep them in good running order. Both objects incorporated the most elaborate of Western technology, and were effectively extravagant boasts, announcing England's international power and prestige to the Eastern world.

By 1599, with an ageing queen on the throne who had no intention of involving herself in European mainland wars, England's power in the Levant was commercial, not political. The organ and the coach – baroque occasions for largely pointless extravagance – surely say that, loud and clear.[37] So too does a letter which accompanied Walide Safiye's thank-you letter, written by her Jewish agent (or Kira), Esperanza Malchi, suggesting that the queen might help in the acquisition of cosmetics and other 'female' luxury items.[38]

England might have been, in the end, largely bluffing politically in the Ottoman arena, but her merchants were entirely in earnest. And whereas the supposed close analogies between Protestant and Muslim situations and beliefs were in the end merely gestural, there really was a good match between the fundamentally mercantile ethos of Islam and English entrepreneurial spirit (Mohammed was, as Muslims will be keen to tell you, a merchant). Elizabeth's pursuit of a close relationship with the Ottoman sultan was ultimately unsuccessful as a political strategy. It contributed significantly, nevertheless, to England's establishing herself in the next generation as the foremost European trading nation in the East.

---

[37] The gifts sent to Murad III when Harborne was first installed as English resident ambassador in 1582 included an elaborate mechanical clock: 'One clock valued at 500 pounds sterling; over it (above it) was a forest of trees of silver, among which were deer chased with dogs, and men on horseback following, men drawing water, others carrying mine ore in barrows: on top of the clock stood a castle and on the castle a mill. All these were of silver. And the clock was round beset with jewels.'

[38] 'A letter in Italian from Esperanza Malchi, the Sultana's Jewish agent, to Queen Elizabeth; dated 16/26 November 1599.' Skilliter, 'Three Letters', 142–3. This letter reminds us that there is also an Anglo-Jewish dimension to Elizabeth's gift and other commercial transactions with the Ottoman court.

Transactions of the RHS 14 (2004), pp. 223–42 © 2004 Royal Historical Society
DOI: 10.1017/S0080440104000143   Printed in the United Kingdom

FRANCE AND ELIZABETHAN ENGLAND*

By Charles Giry-Deloison

ABSTRACT. Descriptions of Tudor England by French visitors are scarce, but in the 1560s and 1570s a renewed interest in 'all things English' is perceptible amongst the French elite. The new religion, parliament, the eventuality of a royal marriage and genuine curiosity in such a strange country contributed to distract the attention of a few Frenchmen from Italy and Spain. In the 1580s, a major change was to occur: more books on England were being published in French, but their sole purpose was religious propaganda and many were translations of English pro- or anti-Catholic pamphlets.

Elizabeth's reign was to witness a major transformation in Anglo-French relations in the sixteenth century, to which only the Perpetual Peace of 1527 might be compared.[1] Seen from a French standpoint, from 1564 onwards (treaty of Troyes, 11 April), England, the old enemy, slowly and more than once with some reluctance (notably after the Massacre of St Bartholomew on 24 August 1572),[2] turned into a critical but staunch ally, with whom a royal wedding was actively sought, and, more dramatically, without whom Henri de Navarre would probably never have become Henri IV, king of France. Henri himself recognised his debt to Elizabeth. Learning of the queen's death, he wrote to Sully: 'Mon ami, j'ai eu avis de la mort de ma bonne sœur la reine d'Angleterre, qui m'aimait si cordialement, à laquelle j'avais tant d'obligations', adding 'elle m'était un second moi-même.'[3] Though one may like to think that this was only a return of the favour that Charles VIII of France had done for Henry Tudor before Bosworth, the words ring true. As Jean-Pierre Babelon has pointed out, one has only to look at the number and the quality of the

---

* I would like to thank Mrs Patricia Burkard for her kind help.

[1] See Charles Giry–Deloison, 'A Diplomatic Revolution? Anglo-French Relations and the Treaties of 1527', in *Henry VIII: A European Court in England*, ed. David Starkey (1991), 77–83, and *idem*, 'Une alliance contre nature? La paix franco-anglaise de 1525–1544', in *François Iᵉʳ et Henri VIII. Deux princes de la Renaissance (1515–1547)*, ed. Charles Giry-Deloison (Lille, 1996), 53–62.

[2] See, for example, Wallace T. MacCaffrey, *Queen Elizabeth and the Making of Policy 1572–1588* (Princeton, 1981), 164–70, and Michel Duchein, *Elisabeth Iʳᵉ d'Angleterre. Le pouvoir et la séduction* (Paris, 1992), 425–9.

[3] Quoted by Duchein, *Elisabeth I ʳᵉ*, 723, following Jean-Pierre Babelon, *Henri IV* (Paris, 1994), 929–30.

ambassadors Henri IV sent to Elizabeth between 1589 and 1603 to realise the importance the king bestowed upon his relationship with the queen[4] even though, in September 1601, he politely declined an invitation to visit her.[5]

Peace brought important changes to Franco-English relations during Elizabeth's reign. The most notable was the political *rapprochement* which allowed the establishment of permanent reciprocal diplomatic representations in the two kingdoms. This, among other things, involved an almost uninterrupted flow of dignitaries crossing back and forth, not only to discuss the queen's marriage to a French prince (which became more and more elusive after the late 1570s), but also to resolve the many deep-rooted misunderstandings, disagreements and fears that still marred relations between the two governments in the early stages (particularly on the English side), as the dramatic events in France blurred the political scene, preventing any plausible forecast, and rendering long-term policy hard to sustain. Nevertheless, the final outcome was the strengthening of the political alignment between the two countries against Spain and its ultra-Catholic allies in France. This resulted in direct English military intervention in Normandy in August 1589 to aid the new king, Henri IV, and which was to last until the peace of Vervins on 22 April/ 2 May 1598.[6] Another major aspect, inseparable from high politics, was the steady arrival of French Protestants seeking safe haven in England. The barbarism of the Massacre of St Bartholomew put a particular strain on Anglo-French relations, but it did contribute greatly to open England to the persecuted Huguenots.[7] Though precise numbers are difficult to ascertain, the French refugee communities in London and the south-east of England grew rapidly during the 1570s and 1580s.[8] Not only did they financially contribute to England's involvement in the Netherlands in 1572,[9] but they also acted as facilitators (particularly through importing and printing of books and pamphlets) in the diffusion of French political thought amongst the English elite.[10] Beyond the pale

---

[4] Babelon, *Henri IV*, 929.

[5] Duchein, *Elisabeth Iʳᵉ*, 715.

[6] See *La paix de Vervins 1598*, ed. Claude Vidal and Frédérique Pilleboue (n.p., 1998).

[7] The foundation of a formal Franco-Dutch Protestant church in London had been achieved at the end of June 1550 (the 'stranger church' as it was known). Though, technically, the French and Dutch congregations were part of one foundation and one church, they used separate buildings: the French rented the Chapel of St Anthony on Threadneedle Street. Andrew Pettegree, *Foreign Protestant Communities in Sixteenth-Century London* (Oxford, 1986), 25, 37.

[8] The only precise figure we have for London is the 1,200 Frenchmen recorded in the Return of Aliens of 1568, Pettegree, *Foreign Protestant Communities*, 255.

[9] *Ibid.*, 255.

[10] Lisa Ferraro Parmelee, *Good Newes from Fraunce. French Anti-League Propaganda in Late Elizabethan England* (Rochester, NY, 1996), ch. 2.

(if not the reach) of governmental policy, and where the interests of merchants were concerned, Anglo-French relations were undoubtedly less easy and commercial rivalry, maritime disputes and piracy, on both sides, remained constant during the whole of the period, probably at the same level as previously.[11]

The lifting, in the 1580s, of the threat of a French invasion or French participation in a Scottish coup or, more worryingly still, in an international Catholic league against England, enabled, to some extent, the expansion of Elizabethan England. According to Jean Bodin, it also curbed the barbarity of the English, who, in consequence, became a more acceptable people: 'Et pour ceste cause les Anglois, qui par ci devant estoyent reputez si mutins et indontables... maintenant depuis qu'ils ont traitté paix et alliance avec la France et l'Escosse, et qu'ils ont esté gouvernez par une Princesse douce et paisible, ils se sont bien fort apprivoisez.'[12]

There remains nevertheless a question that historians have seldom asked: if England was to be their new, and many still said unnatural, ally,[13] how well did the French know their English neighbours? As one would expect with regard to the sixteenth century, English historiography has concentrated on the continental influences in England,[14] while the French have been more interested in the Italian, Spanish and Dutch influences in France. To my knowledge, only one work in French has attempted to cover this aspect of the bilateral relations during those years: Georges Ascoli's *La Grande-Bretagne devant l'opinion française, depuis la guerre de Cent ans jusqu'à la fin du XVIe siècle*, which was published in 1927. Admittedly, before him William Brenchley Rye had written *England as seen by Foreigners in the days of Elizabeth and James the First* (1865),[15] but this book (though still very valuable) only alludes to two sixteenth-century French 'descriptions' of

---

[11] This remains a largely unexplored area of Anglo-French relations since Michel Mollat's thesis, *Le commerce maritime normand à la fin du Moyen Age. Etude d'histoire économique et sociale* (Paris, 1952).

[12] Jean Bodin, *Les Six Livres de la République* (Paris, Jacques Du Puys, 1576), ed. Christiane Frémont, Marie-Dominique Cousinet and Henri Rochais (6 vols., Paris, 1986), V, ch. 1, 51.

[13] As late as 1638 the duke of Sully, who had been an ambassador to England in 1603, noted in his *Mémoires*: 'It is certain that the English hate us, and with a hate so strong and so general, that one would be tempted to list it as one of the natural dispositions of this people', quoted by Robert Gibson, *Best of Enemies. Anglo-French Relations since the Norman Conquest* (1995), 65.

[14] There are several studies of French political and cultural influence on England in the second half of the sixteenth century, see for example: Sidney Lee, *The French Renaissance in England. An Account of the Literary Relations of England and France in the Sixteenth Century* (Oxford, 1910); John H. M. Salmon, *The French Religious Wars in English Political Thought* (Oxford, 1959; repr. Westport, CT, 1981); Parmelee, *Good Newes from France*.

[15] William Brenchley Rye, *England as seen by Foreigners in the days of Elizabeth and James the First* (1865).

England in the introduction.[16] It is mainly concerned with the travels of three German aristocrats between 1602 and 1613.

In sixteenth-century France, the gathering and circulation of information on contemporary England depended upon a certain number of conditions. First, there were several channels through which such material was conveyed to France. The small and disparate English communities abroad were of course important intermediaries: diplomats, soldiers, students, Catholic refugees such as the Jesuit Robert Parsons (or Persons) in 1580–5,[17] and even comedians (there were two visits of English actors to Paris in 1598 and 1603–4).[18] The English government itself sometimes played a key role by allowing, or ordering, pamphlets in defence of the queen to be published in London in French, and then sent abroad. It is difficult to quantify this official propaganda, for most tracts were anonymous and carried no place of publication. For example, it is most likely that the French edition of Cecil's *The Execution of Justice in England for Maintenance of Publique and Christian Peace . . .* , dated 1584, was printed in London as were those in Dutch, Latin and Italian,[19] and as was the 1594 text denouncing the Catholic and Spanish conspiracies against Elizabeth, *Discours veritable de diverses conspirations nagueres descouvertes contre la propre vie de la tres excellente maieste de la roine . . .* [20] Another channel were the nationals of other countries (Scots, Dutch, Italians, Germans) who, having stayed in England and then passing through France, described what they had seen and experienced. But the main conveyors of news were of course the French themselves: those who having sojourned in England brought back information (ambassadors, merchants, students, travellers, Huguenot exiles), and those (no doubt sometimes the same) who translated English books and pamphlets into French. Unfortunately, the majority of the latter remained anonymous, no doubt because most

[16] The *Description des royaulmes d'Angleterre et d'Escosse* by Estienne Perlin and the *Angliae Descriptionis Compendium* by Guillaume Paradin (xlvii and l–li).

[17] He published most of his pamphlets anonymously or under pseudonyms (Doleman, John Philopatris). In 1584 he set up a press in Rouen which printed, among other works, Cardinal William Allen's response to Lord Burghley's *Execution of Justice in England, A True Sincere and Most Modest Defence of English Catholiques that Suffer for their Faith at Home and Abroade: Against a False, Seditious and Slanderous Libel Intituled; The Execution of Justice in England*, etc.

[18] Frances A. Yates, 'English Actors in Paris during the Lifetime of Shakespeare', *Review of English Studies*, 1 (1925), 392–403, reprinted in *idem, Ideas and Ideals in the North European Renaissance. Collected Essays. Volume III* (1984), 83–95.

[19] *L'execution de justice faicte en Angleterre, pour maintenir la paix publique et Chrestienne, contre les autheurs de sedition, adherens aux traistres et ennemis du Royaume . . . traduite en langue Françoise, &c.*, n.p. There were simultaneous editions in Dutch (R. Schilders, Middelburg), Italian (G. Wolfis, London) and Latin (Thomas Vautrollier), all dated 1584.

[20] *Discours veritable de diverses conspirations nagueres descouvertes contre la propre vie de la tres excellente maieste de la roine : par assassinemens autant barbares, comme sa conservation a este miraculeuse de la main du tout puissant, opposee aux desseings pernicieux de ses Anglois rebelles, et aux violences de ses tres puissans ennemis estrangers* (Londres, Charles Yetsweirt, Novembr. 1594).

of their works contained polemical or scandalous material relating to Mary Stuart and the Catholic cause. The two main French translators were François de Belleforest, cosmographer to Henri III, and Jean Benard (or Bernard), 'interprète et historiographe général des langues septentrionales et estrangères'.

Secondly, such information was transmitted and exchanged in speech, writing and print. Conversation was obviously the most common means of communication but, unfortunately, seldom were spoken words recorded if they were not considered of importance and, consequently, we have little trace of what would have been oral descriptions of England or of its state of affairs. Letters, despatches and reports were rarely meant to be shown outside a small circle of chosen people: royal courtiers, business partners, friends or family. Works in manuscript form were usually reserved for personal use, that of close circles or of a patron, and, though they could be copied at an expense, their circulation was necessarily and purposely limited. For example, the Bibliothèque nationale de France holds three copies of Jean Benard's 'Sommaire discours sur le present estat d'Angleterre', of 1574, two of which are dedicated, one to Catherine of Médicis, the other to Henri III. Similarly, there are at least four copies of his 'Recueil des principaux seigneurs qui passerent la mer avec Guillaume Conquéreur d'Angleterre'. Two are dedicated to Charles IX, but one is dated 1 January 1569 (British Library, MS Egerton 2388) and the other 1 January 1572 (Bibliothéque nationale de France, ms. fr. 19000). It is of course impossible to say who read these manuscripts apart from their recipients.

On the other hand, books and pamphlets were printed to be bought and read by an increasingly wider literate public, and were a means of learning, often weapons of propaganda in the political and religious debates of the day, and merchandise. But as not everything went into print, access to a broader range of information, and probably of better quality, very much depended on belonging to the privileged, educated and well-connected sections of society and also, probably of equal importance, on being part of a network which had links with England. Jean Bodin, who only crossed the English Channel in 1581 (five years after the publication of the *Six Livres de la République*), gained much of his knowledge of English history and institutions, which he used in the *Six Livres*, from conversations with diplomats and from reading their reports. It was owing to the French ambassador's letters that he was made aware of the request that parliament had addressed to the queen in October 1566 to marry and name a successor,[21] and also the particulars of the treaty of the marriage

---

[21] 'Comme j'ay appris par les lettres de l'ambassadeur du roy', Bodin, *Six Livres*, I, ch. 8, 200.

between Mary I and Philip II of Spain.[22] It was from the English envoy, Dr Valentine Dale,[23] that he learnt that a law could only be modified by an act of parliament and the consent of the monarch,[24] and from an anonymous English gentleman that the earl of Worcester, who represented the queen at the baptism of the daughter of Charles IX and Elizabeth of Austria in February 1573, was a descendant of Edward III.[25] According to Georges Ascoli, Pierre de L'Estoile had been able to gain access to the account of the earl of Essex's execution which the French ambassador, Jean de Thumery, sieur de Boissise, had sent to Henri IV on 24 February/5 March 1601. Copies of it apparently circulated in Paris.[26] Another example is the manner in which L'Estoile acquired books from England (in English?) in September 1609. An acquaintance of his in Rouen, M. Justel, wrote to say that he was expecting some books from a friend in England and that he would send him a selection of them as soon as they arrived.[27] The literate public without any such links could only rely on what was in print in France.

Thirdly, we know nothing of the price of these books and pamphlets, nor how many were sold or who read them. We are therefore largely left to guess what success they enjoyed and what impact – if any – they had on the French, though available indications (simultaneous editions in different towns, number of shops in which a book was sold, number and rate of reprints) tend to suggest that several works were widely circulated in France. For example an anonymous political tract entitled *Discours des troubles nouvellement advenus au royaume d'Angleterre, au moys d'Octobre 1569* was published in 1570 by N. Chesneau in Paris and by Michel Jove in Lyons, and reprinted in 1587 in Rouen, by Pierre l'Aignel, and in Paris. Adam Blackwood's *Martyre de la royne d'Escosse*, first published in Paris in 1587, was reprinted in 1588 and again in 1589, each time by the same Parisian

---

[22] 'J'ay appris par les lettres de l'ambassadeur de France, qui lors estoit en Angleterre . . .', *ibid.*, VI, ch. 5, 242.

[23] Dr Valentine Dale (*c.* 1527–89) was ambassador in France from March 1573 to October 1576, Gary M. Bell, *A Handlist of British Diplomatic Representatives 1509–1688* (1990), 93.

[24] 'Les ordonnances faictes par le roy d'Angleterre à la requeste des estats ne peuvent estre cassees sans y appeler les estats. Cela est bien prattiqué, et se fait ordinairement, comme j'ay sceu de M. Dail ambassadeur d'Angleterre, homme d'honneur et de sçavoir: mais il m'a asseuré que le roy reçoit ou refuse la loy si bon luy semble', Bodin, *Six Livres*, I, ch. 8, 201.

[25] 'Comme j'ay appris d'un gentil-homme Anglois', *ibid.*, VI, ch. 5, 240. Elizabeth was godmother to the child who was born on 27 Oct. 1572.

[26] Ascoli, *La Grande-Bretagne devant l'opinion française*, 213.

[27] 'Le dimanche 6 [septembre 1609] j'ay receu, de Rouen, des lettres de M. Justel par lesquelles il me mande ce qui s'ensuit : ". . . Je n'ay encore receu ces livres d'Angleterre, qu'un de mes amis me fait apporter. Vous y aurez vostre part, comme de, etc."', Pierre de L'Estoile, *Mémoires-Journaux. Journal de Henri IV et de Louis XIII: 1574–1611*, X: *1609–1610* (Paris, 1875–99, 1982–9), 7.

printer but under a slightly different title.[28] Nevertheless, of all the printed material in French relating to England, only political and religious tracts and pamphlets were reprinted. As to the cost of such works, Pierre de L'Estoile's *Mémoires-Journaux* give us an insight into the book trade in early seventeenth-century Paris. To take but one example, in September 1609 *L'apologie du roi d'Angleterre*, a pamphlet which had been recently translated from English by his friend Jean de Tourval, sold very well, despite the fact that it was poorly printed, had been banned by the king and was on sale for just a week during which time its price rapidly fell from three-quarters to a quarter of an *écu*. But it must have remained in strong demand (no doubt partly because it had been forbidden) for Pierre de L'Estoile resold one of the two copies he had bought for twice the price ten days later.[29] One can safely assume that prices for similar material in the late sixteenth century were no different.

Allowing for more to be discovered, and excluding diplomatic correspondence (which is of a totally different nature), works relating to Elizabeth's involvement in the Netherlands and the war with Spain, and not taking into account reprints or copies in other languages, there remain in the French and English archives and libraries at least sixty works (fifty-six in French and four in Latin) dealing with England and written in the second half of the sixteenth century. Manuscripts account for 35 per cent (twenty-one) and printed works for 65 per cent (thirty-nine).[30] So information available in France on Elizabethan England was relatively abundant, as it is most likely that there was more in circulation than which is now preserved. For example, one visitor to England, Jacques Esprinchard, warns the readers of his 'Journal' that he will not give any details on England since he has already done so in another manuscript ('je ne diray rien icy, pour en avoir dressé un discours en uns autre

---

[28] *Martyre de la royne d'Escosse, douairiere de France; contenant le vray discours des traïsons à elle faictes à la suscitation d'Elizabet Angloise, par lequel les mensonges, calomnies, et faulses accusations dressées contre ceste tresvertueuse, trescatholique et tresillustre princesse son esclarcies et son innocence averée* (Edinburgh [Paris], J.[Jean] Nafield, 1587). Reprinted in 1588 under the title *Martyre de la royne d'Escosse, douairiere de France . . . Avec son oraison funèbre prononcée en l'église nostre dame de Paris* (Edinburgh [Paris], J.[Jean] Nafield) and in 1589 under the title *Martyre de la royne d'Escosse. Avec deux oraisons funèbres. Et plusieurs poèmes* (Edinburgh [Paris], J.[Jean] Nafield). There is actually only one *oraison funèbre*. These works were also published in Anvers by Gaspard Fleyben.

[29] L'Estoile, *Mémoires-Journaux*, X, 13–14 and 22–3.

[30] I have excluded works in English published in France (i.e. those from Robert Parsons's press in Rouen) as it is doubtful that any Frenchmen could read them, and works concerning Scotland (i.e. Adam Blackwood's denunciation of George Buchanan: *Apologia pro regibus, adversus Georgii Buchanani dialogum de jure regni apud Scotos* (Poitiers, 1581, and Paris, 1589), except those relating to Mary Stuart's death.

papier').³¹ Unfortunately, the document was already lost by the late seventeenth century when Paul Colombiez, a French priest who had settled in London in 1681, was unable to find it.³² Furthermore, it is possible that previous material published in France was still obtainable. For example, Guillaume Paradin, a priest with a keen interest in history, had written two books in Latin in the 1540s and 1550s: a description of the country in 1545 (*Anglicae descriptionis compendium*), and, ten years later, a virulent pamphlet against the religious changes (*Afflictae Britannicae religionis et rursus restitutae exegema*).³³ In 1550 an anonymous tract was published in Paris alerting the population of the religious upheavals in England (*La responce du peuple anglois à leur roy Edouard sur certains articles qui en son nom leurs ont esté envoyez touchant la religiõ chrestienne*).³⁴ In 1557, another pamphlet appeared in France on a related issue (*Epistre envoyée aux Angloys*).³⁵ A few privileged might also have had access to François de Noailles's manuscript 'Journal' of his travel to England in 1554–5.³⁶

Equally, works printed outside France might have been available to the French public. In 1572, the description of England that Humphrey Llwyd had sent in 1568 to his friend Abraham Ortels (Ortelius), who was gathering material for his *Theatrum orbis terrarum*, was published in Cologne: *Commentarioli Britannicae descriptionis fragmentum*.³⁷ A year later, it was translated into English by Thomas Twyne under the title *The Breviary of Britain*.³⁸ Polydore Vergil's *Anglica Historia* enjoyed considerable success on the Continent, the final edition in 1555 being reprinted in Basle in 1556

---

³¹ Esprinchard, 'Journal des voyages de Jacques Esprinchard, 1597–1598', in *Vie de Jacques Esprinchard, Rochelais, et Journal de ses voyages au XVIᵉ siècle*, ed. Léopold Chatenay (Paris, 1957), 85–6.

³² *Ibid.*, 86 n. 7.

³³ *Angliae descriptionis compendium* (Paris, V. Gaultherot, 1545); *Afflictae Britannicae religionis et rursus restitutae exegema* (Lyons, Jean de Tournes, 1555). Guillaume Paradin (*c.* 1510–190) was the author of several works on the history of Burgundy and Savoy and on the wars of 1542–3. His best-known book was *Histoire de notre temps faite en latin par Maistre Guillaume Paradin et par luy mise en françois* (Lyons, 1550). See *Dictionnaire des lettres françaises. Le XVIᵉ siècle*, ed. Michel Simonin (Paris, 1951, 2001), 905. According to Rye (*England as Seen by Foreigners*, xlvii), Paradin never visited England, which, considering what he writes about the country and the English, is most likely.

³⁴ Paris, Robert Massellin.

³⁵ Rouen, Claude Tiphaine (for) Antoine Du Ry.

³⁶ François de Noailles, 'Journal des voyages du protonotaire de Noailles (François de Noailles, plus tard évêque de Dax), en Angleterre, 1554–1555', Bibliothèque nationale de France [hereafter BNF], ms. fr. 20147, fos. 22–142.

³⁷ Cologne, J. Birckmannum, 1572. Humphrey Llwyd (1527–68) was a physician and antiquary and the author of several books on medicine and history. See his entry in the *Dictionary of National Biography* and Ascoli, *La Grande-Bretagne devant l'opinion française*, 122–3.

³⁸ London, Richard Jones.

and again in 1570.[39] Most – if not all – of those writing on English history or on English institutions openly relied on the *Anglica Historia*, including Guillaume Paradin, Humfrey Lwyd and David Chambers. Though he may not have been his sole source of information, it must nevertheless be a testimony to Vergil's influence that Guillaume Paradin, who never visited England and who was writing in the 1540s, had to interrupt his account of the history of England at the outcome of the War of the Roses because the then available edition of the *Anglica Historia* (the edition printed by John Bebel in Basle in 1534) only covered events up to 1509.[40] The two French leading theorists of sovereignty, the philosopher Jean Bodin and the jurisconsult François Hotman, both explicitly quote Polydore Vergil when describing the origins and the role of parliament: the former in *Les Six Livres de la République* ('nous lisons en Polydore'),[41] the latter in *Franco-Gallia* ('tesmoin Polydore Vergile au livre II de l'histoire des Anglois').[42] Vergil is particularly important to Hotman's demonstration of the primacy of the authority of the 'Concile des Estats' because his narration of the 1328 agreement between Edward III and Philip de Valois for the succession to the throne of France is in accord with those of French historians, affirming that the two kings agreed to comply to the 'concile's' decision. Corroborated by acknowledged authorities on both sides, Hotman's interpretation of this key event in Anglo-French relations becomes therefore indisputable:

> l'autorité du Concile des Estats, est plus grande que celle du Roy, puisque ces deux Roys [Edward III and Philippe VI de Valois] s'assujettirent au jugement d'iceluy : ce qui est asseuré, non seulement par nos historiens mais aussi par Polydore Vergile historien Anglois au 9. Li. de son Histoire.[43]

In fact, Polydore Vergil was already a well-known author in France. His *De Inventoribus Rerum* (Venice, 1499) had been published in Paris in 1528 by Robert Estienne following the enlarged Basle edition of 1521.[44] In 1544 it was translated into French (possibly by Jacques Regnault or Jean Ruelle) and in 1576 François de Belleforest produced another translation, which

---

[39] There was also a composite reprint at Ghent in 1556–7, see Polydore Vergil, *The Anglica Historia of Polydore Vergil A.D. 1485–1537*, ed. Denys Hay (Camden Society, third series, LXXIV, 1950), xvii.

[40] *Ibid.*, xiii.

[41] Bodin, *Six Livres*, I, ch. 8, 201.

[42] François Hotman, *Franco-Gallia* (Geneva, Jacob Stoer, 1573). The work was translated into French in 1574, possibly by Simon Goulart: *La Gaule françoise de François Hotoman jurisconsulte nouvellement traduite de Latin en François* (Cologne, Hierome Bertulphe, 1574; ed. Christiane Fremont, Paris, 1991), 98.

[43] *Ibid.*, 146.

[44] *Polydori Vergilii de inventoribus rerum prior editio, . . . cui e editioni adglutinavit Institua omnia nostre Christianae religionis aliamrumve gentiu[m] ac eorum primordia undique diligenter quasiter, etc.* (Paris, R. Stephanus, 1528). On the influence of the *De Inventoribus Rerum*, see Hay, *Polydore Vergil. Renaissance Historian and Man of Letters* (Oxford, 1952), in particular ch. 3.

was reprinted in Paris in 1582 under a slightly different title.[45] André Thevet, the first 'cosmographe du roi', drew heavily on the *De Inventoribus Rerum* (or its French translation) whilst preparing *Les singularitez de la France antarctique* which went to print in 1557[46] and was to bring him both fame and criticisms.[47]

Finally, the French could turn to an increasingly popular and abundant geographical literature, which, in most instances, contained some information on England. For example, the two French cosmographies published in 1575, *La cosmographie universelle* by André Thevet[48] and *La cosmograhie universelle de tout le monde* by François de Belleforest,[49] had entries on European countries, as did Gabriel Chappuys's *L'estat, description et gouvernement des royaumes et républiques du monde tant anciennes que modernes*, which was published in Paris in 1585.[50] A map of the British Isles, with an accompanying commentary drawn from Humfrey Llwyd's manuscript (as we have seen) but also from other authors, notably Nicholas Chalcondyle, was to be found in Abaham Ortels's famous *Theatrum orbis terrarum*, which was translated into French in 1581 (*Théâtre de l'univers*).[51]

The sixty books, pamphlets and manuscripts which were written in French or in Latin during Elizabeth's reign fall into four categories: descriptions of England (eight), road-books and journals (four), histories of England (seven) and accounts of current events in England (forty-one). These accounts represent 68 per cent of the total available material and 87 per cent of the printed output. In other words, the information on Elizabethan England that circulated in France was predominantly about the political and religious situation of the country. This is confirmed

---

[45] *Pollidore Vergile, hystoriographe nouvellement traduict de latin en francoys, declairant les inventeurs des choses on estre* (Paris, Jean Longis et Vincent Sertenas, 1544). François de Belleforest, *Les memoires et histoire de l'origine, invention et autheur des choses. Faicte en Latin, et divisee en huic livres, par Polydore Vergile natif d'Urbin: et traduicte par François de Belle-forest Comingeois* (Paris, Robert Le Mangnier, 1576; 2nd edn, 1582).

[46] André Thevet, *Les singularitez de la France antarctique, autrement nommée Amerique: et de plusieurs Terres et Isles decouvertes de nostre temps* (Paris, les héritiers de Maurice de la Porte, 1557 and 1558; ed. Frank Lestringant, Paris, 1997).

[47] See Lestringant, *L'atelier du cosmographe ou l'image du monde à la Renaissance* (Paris, 1991), 91–101.

[48] Thevet, *La cosmographie universelle d'André Thevet cosmographe du Roy. Illustree de diverses figures des choses plus remarquables veües par l'Auteur, et incogneuës de noz Anciens et Modernes* (4 tomes in 2 vols., Paris, Pierre L'Huillier et Guillaume Chaudière, 1575).

[49] Belleforest, *La cosmographie de tout le monde, en laquelle . . . sont au vray descriptes toutes les parties habitables et non habitables de la terre et de la mer, . . . auteur en partie Munster, mais beaucoup plus augmentée, ornée et enrichie par François de Belle-Forest* (2 tomes in 4 vols., Paris, M. Sonnius, 1575).

[50] Gabriel Chappuys, *L'Estat, description et gouvernement des royaumes et républiques du monde tant anciennes que modernes* (Paris, Pierre Cavellat, 1585).

[51] Abraham Ortels (Ortelius), *Théâtre de l'univers, contenant les cartes de tout le monde, avec une brieve declaration d'icelles, par Abraham Ortelius. Le tout reveu, amendé, & augmente de plusieurs cartes & declarations par le mesme autheur* (Anvers, C[hristophe] Plantin, 1581).

by the fact that seven of the eight descriptions of England, four of the seven histories and three of the four road-books and journals remained in manuscript form. Nevertheless, as impressive as these percentages may be, they should not come as a surprise. The ideological confusion, the break-down of the social fabric and the barbarity of the civil wars provoked by the Reformation (particularly in France) created throughout Europe a dramatic climate of fear of the present and uncertainty for the future, destroying most people's social and intellectual bearings. Confronted with the extreme difficulty of interpreting the events they were witnessing or partaking in, many looked to other countries to find similarities or differences which could help them to make sense of their own experiences. News from abroad was therefore important. It also built on the new interest for history and foreign worlds (and England was undoubtedly a strange world for the French), the Renaissance having stimulated a desire for learning among the educated classes. Gervais Mallot, who printed Jean Benard's *Discours des plus mémorables faicts des roys & gra[n]ds seigneurs d'Angleterre depuis cinq cens ans* in 1579, remarked on the importance of knowing the history, laws and customs of neighbouring countries and the growing number of such books: 'combien il est necessaire de cognoistre ce que font noz voisins: & au contraire, quelle messeance c'est d'ignorer leurs gestes, loix & coustumes'. [52]

One must not forget either the more mundane concern of printers and booksellers. Their main preoccupation was trade. In such a troubled era, political pamphlets sold well and there was a growing market for them, particularly in Paris: twenty of the twenty-six printers whose names we know were Parisians. The jurist and memorialist Pierre de L'Estoile noted that many people in Paris bought satirical tracts just for the pleasure of a laugh at the expense of well-known figures.[53] The description of the tragic fate of Mary, queen of Scots, held all the ingredients for a commercial success in France (a Catholic, a queen of Scotland, a dowager queen of France, executed by order of her Protestant cousin); but, curiously, though at least eight books in French were published between her execution (8 February 1587) and 1589, only three carry the name of a printer (Guillaume Bichon, Jean Nafield and J. Poitevin). No bookseller or printer specialised in polemical literature, but some do appear to have been supporters of the Catholic cause: Guillaume Bichon, Thomas Brumen and Jean Nafield (a pseudonym for an unidentified printer) in Paris, Michel Jove and Jean Pillehotte and probably Jean Didier in Lyons. Likewise, in La Rochelle, Adam de Monte, the pseudonym for another unidentified printer who published the puritan divine Walter Travers's

---

[52] Mallot, *Discours des plus memorables faicts, Epistre*, ii. The manuscript is dated 1 Jan. 1571, Arsenal, ms. 3729, fos. 1–64 and 89–92.

[53] L'Estoile, *Mémoires-Journaux*, X, 1.

work on ecclesiastical discipline and the decline of the Church of England (*Ecclesiasticae disciplinae*...),[54] was no doubt a Protestant sympathiser. It is interesting to note the role played by provincial presses: La Rochelle was a Protestant stronghold while Lyons, under the control of the governor of Lyonnais, Charles-Emmanuel de Savoie, duc de Nemours, and the archbishop of Lyons, Pierre d'Espinac (or Épinac), adhered to the Catholic *Ligue*.

Another particularity of the printed material is that only twelve of the thirty-nine texts can be ascribed with certainty to French writers, while ten others are the works of known British authors and one of the bishop of Silves, Osorius. Though the French were quite logically more numerous (they were nine: François de Belleforest, Pomponne de Bellièvre, Jean Benard, Dominique Bourgoing, Louis Dorleans, Joachim Du Bellay, Jean Du Tillet, Jacques La Guesle, Etienne Perlin), they produced proportionally less than their five British counterparts (the Englishmen Lord Burghley, Robert Parsons and Walter Travers, the Scots Adam Blackwood and David Chambers, Lord Ormont). Similarly, among the sixteen anonymous texts, seven are of unknown origin, three were probably French, five are translations (three from English, one from Scottish and one from Italian) and one was directly printed in French in London. This imbalance is also noticeable in the coverage of current events: nine texts had British authors, eight French ones.

These figures and the numerical importance of the accounts of current events tend to indicate that the motives for writing about England were mainly political and polemical. This is confirmed by the contents of the printed works, the date of publication of most and the known religious and political affiliations of their authors. The literature on current events covers eight main topics: the capture of Calais (one); the war against France in 1562 (one); the Northern Rising of 1569 (five); the execution of the duke of Norfolk in 1572 (five); the fate of Mary Stuart (eight); the conspiracies against Elizabeth in 1584 and 1594–5 (three); religion (fourteen); miscellaneous (four). Calais was the subject of a poem by Joachim Du Bellay, *Hymne au roy sur la prinse de Calais*, but does not appear to have generated further writings. The war of 1562 led to the translation into French of a pamphlet masterminded by the English government in defence of Elizabeth's policy: *Protestation faicte par la royne d'Angleterre*. For Condé, who was actively publishing tracts in justification of his rebellion, it appeared at the right moment. Condé's *Mémoires* acknowledge the apparent support Elizabeth was giving to his cause:

> la tres illustre Roine d'Angleterre...sans pretendre en cecy aucun proffit particulier, seulement pour la conservation de la Religion & de la Justice a faict une si louable &

---

[54] *Ecclesiasticae disciplinae et Anglicanae ecclesiae ab illa aberrationis plena è verbo dei & dilucida explicatio* (La Rochelle, A.[Adam] de Monte, 1574).

opportune entreprise, moyennant laquelle nous devons attendre en bref, avec l'aide de Dieu, ou une paix saincte . . . ou bien une heureuse et prompte victoire. [55]

All the other books and pamphlets dealing with current events have in common the question of religion. The Catholic camp and the Stuart devotees were particularly virulent in the aftermath of the abortive Northern Rising, in 1587 when Mary Stuart was executed and in the 1580s and 1590s when the English Catholics and the Jesuits set up seminaries on the Continent, and Robert Parsons and others had found refuge in France. Except for four texts,[56] all the literature on these events comes from those factions. French readers were kept well informed of the Northern Rising, no doubt because at a time when Protestantism was gaining ground in France, it showed the strength of the Catholic opposition in England and the martyrdom that a true Christian (the earl of Northumberland) would inevitably suffer at the hands of a heretic monarch. A first anonymous book was published in 1570 with details of the Rising in November 1569. It was soon followed by a second one, which brought readers to the end of the rebellion in December and the murder of the regent of Scotland, James Stewart, earl of Moray, on 23 January 1570. These were most likely the work of Jean Benard, who had prepared a manuscript text, which is very similar to the books.[57] In 1572 two texts were published, one describing the dignified death of Thomas Percy, earl of Northumberland (misleadingly stiled 'duke' in the pamphlet), who was executed on 22 August 1572 (after the Scots sold him to Elizabeth for £2,000),[58] the other attempting to exculpate Mary Stuart from any participation in the Rising. The latter was written by François de Belleforest, the newly appointed (1568) historiographer of France.[59] Finally, the French could read about three other events that had occurred in England; none was to the advantage of the English. Two anonymous pamphlets demonstrated how the country was being punished by God: *Histoire merveilleuse advenues par feu du ciel en trois villes d'Angleterre* (1577?) and *Histoire*

[55] Condé, *Mémoires de Condé, ou recueil pour servir à l'histoire de France, contenant ce qui s'est passé de plus mémorable dans ce rouyaume sous les règnes de François II et Charles IX* (6 vols., Claude du Bosse, 1740), IV, 15–16. At least one of Condé tracts was translated into English: *Declaration faicte par monsieur le prince de Condé, pour monstrer les raisons qui l'ont contrainct d'entreprendre la defense de l'authorité du roy, du gouvernement de la royne, & du repos de ce royaume. Avec la protestation su ce requise* ([Paris?], 1562), trans. R. Hall for E. Sutton, 1562).

[56] Bellièvre, *La harangue faicte à la royne d'Angleterre pour la desmouvoir de n'enteprendre aucune iurisdiction sur la royne d'Ecosse* (n.p., 1588); Travers, *Ecclesiasticae disciplinae* (La Rochelle, A. [Adam] de Monte, 1574); *Apologie ou defense de l'honorable sentence & execution de Marie Steuard* (n.p., 1588); [Whitaker, William], *Confutatio respontionis Gul. Whitaleri ad rationes decem quibus fretus Edmundus Campianus jesuita certamen anglicanae ecclesiae ministris obtulit in causa fidei* (Paris, 1582).

[57] BNF, ms. fr. 1905, fos. 1–14.

[58] John Guy, *Tudor England* (Oxford, 1990), 275.

[59] *L'innocence de la très illustre, très chaste et débonnaire princesse Madame Marie, royne d'Escosse.*

advenue en Angleterre vers l'an 1586 contenant le discours d'une étrange maladie et mortalité subite advenue en la ville d'Oxford, en l'instant d'une sentence donnée contre Roland Jenker... traduite d'anglois en françois (1589). In 1589, another anonymous document described the capture, by the *ligueur* Claude de Lorraine (the chevalier d'Aumale) of two vessels that Elizabeth had sent to Henri de Navarre.[60]

If controversy and the danger of supporting a rebellion had led authors to remain cautiously anonymous in 1570–2, the death of the Scottish queen and the acrimonious debates about religion were seized upon by well-known French and English Catholics to publish extremely virulent anti-Protestant pamphlets. The Stuart adherent and Parisian Adam Blackwood, the Jesuit Robert Parsons and the *ligueur* Louis Dorleans were responsible for most of the output (eight). Nevertheless, though published in France, these texts were not all pursuing the same goal. Those written by Blackwood and Parsons, and the anonymous tracts translated from English, were primarily directed against the queen and her councillors, while the works by Dorleans and the anonymous French writers were addressed to French Catholics, warning them of the dangers they would encounter should Henri de Navarre become king of France. In fact, England was no more than a pretext in the French Catholics' internal wars. For example, in 1586 Louis Dorleans wrote the *Advertissement, des catholiques anglois aux françois catholiques, du danger où ils sont de perdre leur religiõ [n]*, in which he drew a parallel between the fate of the English Catholics and their French co-religionists in the event of France falling in the hands of the then Protestant Henri de Navarre. The work, which was reprinted in 1587, was answered, also in 1587, by moderate French Catholics in two pamphlets entitled *Response d'un gentil-homme françois à l'advertissement des catholicques anglois* and *Response à un ligueur masqué du nom de catholique anglois*. Their purpose was not to discuss the affairs of England or English Catholics, but to defend the inheritance of the crown of France by Henri III's legitimate heir, Henri de Navarre.

At the other end of the political and religious spectrum, a similar divide between English and French documents is visible. Five pamphlets were produced for the French market by the privy council, or under its patronage. Their sole purpose was to justify the government's actions in the Throckmorton Plot of 1584 (*L'execution de justice faicte en Angleterre, pour maintenir la paix publique et chrestienne*), the execution of Mary (*Apologie ou defense de l'honorable sentence & execution de Marie Steuard*), the manner in which the 1594–5 subversive threats were dealt with (*Discours veritable de diverses conspirations nagueres descouvertes contre la propre vie de la tres excellente Maieste de la Roine* and *Discours veritable des deux dernieres compensations & attentats sur la*

---

[60] *Discours de la prinse de deux grands navires.*

personne de la royne d'Angleterre) and the Cadiz voyage of 1596.[61] Two books were printed in French in London and three translated, two of which were published, in Paris, jointly with the text in English. As Blackwood and Parsons had reminded the French of the plight of English Catholics, so the English government strove to convince the same French public of the merits of its policy and win them to its cause. Clearly, all this information was biased, but in this war of words, the Stuart and Catholic camp was certainly more productive and probably more effective judging by the number of editions of most of their tracts. On the French side, the only official text which went into print was the speech delivered by Henri III's envoy, Pomponne de Bellièvre, before Elizabeth in November 1586 in an attempt to deter her from executing Mary Stuart (see n. 56). Bellièvre had been received coldly in London and his mission much criticised in France by the ultra-Catholic *ligueurs*, who accused Henri III of secretly supporting Mary's execution. Like the publications of the English government, the harangue was primarily an exercise in communication; in this instance, to help the king regain some control over French public opinion at a time when his kingdom was increasingly becoming the prey of seditious factions.

Relations between France and England and the political situation of the Tudor kingdom also dominated most of the other works included in our thirty-nine printed texts. The aftermath of Mary Stuart's involvement in the Northern Rising and the execution of the earl of Northumberland were the occasion for the Scottish historian and judge David Chambers (another ardent partisan of Mary in exile in France), to present Charles IX with an *Histoire abrégée de tous les rois de France, Angleterre et Ecosse* in 1572. It was enlarged in 1579 with a *History of Scotland* and a dissertation on the succession of women to the crown. The renewed Anjou marriage negotiations in 1579 prompted the posthumous publication of two works by Jean Benard, under the name of Bernard: *La Guide des chemins d'Angleterre* and the *Discours des plus mémorables faicts des roys & gra[n]ds seigneurs d'Angleterre depuis cinq cens ans.*[62] The Parisian printer and bookseller Gervais Mallot explained why he had decided to publish them. The main reason for the *Discours* was the difficulty of finding a history of England in French, although there were an increasing number on other foreign countries. For Mallot this was a regrettable *lacuna* resulting from the fact that the English were islanders who shared little with foreigners and who only wrote in their native tongue. The *Guide des chemins* was for those who travelled to England or passed through the kingdom on their way to

---

[61] *Declaration des iustes causes qui ont meu la royne d'Angleterre de mettre sus une armee navalle pour envoyer vers l'Espagne. Jouxte la copie imprimée à Londres par les deputez de Christophle Barker* (Paris, J.[Jean] Le Blanc, 1597). It is a reprinting of the French text of 1596.

[62] Paris, Gervais Mallot, 1579.

Scotland. In other words, both books would be most useful at a time when more Frenchmen than usual were likely to be crossing the Channel. In 1588 the heirs of the lawyer and historian Jean Du Tillet added to the second edition of his *Recueil des rois de France* (first published in 1580)[63] a whole volume entitled *Les guerres et traictez de paix, trefves et allianses d'entre les roys de France et d'Angleterre*. Du Tillet had presented Charles IX with a manuscript of the *Recueil* in 1566. It covered events up to the reign of Henri II (1547–59) but had remained in manuscript form until Du Tillet's death in October 1570. In 1578, his family obtained a twelve-year *privilège* to have it printed. Though his heirs gave no reason for its publication in 1588, it did coincide with a renewed interest in England due to the war with Spain and the English involvement on the Continent.

Finally, there is only one book that appears to have been published outside any political or religious context. In 1558 a French student at the Sorbonne, Estienne Perlin, presented the king's sister, Marguerite de France, duchess of Berry, with a 'Description des royaulmes d'Angleterre et d'Escosse' which was subsequently published in Paris by François Trepeau. His declared purpose was to please the duchess, an 'amatrice des lettres & des hommes doctes'. Perlin had already written a book on medicine the same year, apparently well received by the king, and maybe the author was in search of further patronage.

So, despite an important number of printed works written in French, information on Elizabethan England available to the French literate public was limited in scope and, most often, biased by political considerations. First, the four published descriptions and histories of England were all written between 1558 and 1572: the *Description des royaulmes d'Angleterre et d'Escosse* by Estienne Perlin ends with the death of Mary I; *Les guerres et traictez de paix, trefves et allianses d'entre les roys de France et d'Angleterre* by Jean Du Tillet, with the accession of Henri II of France in 1559; David Chambers's *Histoire abrégée de tous les rois de France, Angleterre et Ecosse* in the late 1560s; and Jean Benard's *Discours des plus mémorables faicts des roys & gra[n]ds seigneurs d'Angleterre depuis cinq cens ans* with the beheading of the earl of Northumberland in 1572. To discover and understand what may have occurred after 1572, the French had to turn to political tracts issued by the English government and the pro- and anti-Catholic factions in England and abroad. The fact that none of these works was ever reprinted in the last decades of the sixteenth century confirms this lack of real interest in English history and in England among the French population.

Even the *Guide des chemins* was a translation of William Harrison's 'Of our Innes and Thorowfaires', which was published in 1577 in his *Description*

---

[63] Jean Du Tillet, *Recueil des rois de France, leurs couronne et maison; ensemble les 'Rangs des grands de France'*, par Jean Du Tillet, sieur de La Bussière … plus une chronique abrégée, contenant tout ce qui est advenu … entre les rois et princes (Paris, J.[Jacques] Du Puys, 1580).

of England and Holinshed's *Chronicles of England*. As Herbert Fordham has shown, the nine principal lines of communication described by Benard, with interspersed historical and descriptive paragraphs relating to the more important places, are all to be found in Harrison, though sometimes with a slightly different mileage. They correspond to the main trunk roads of the country and the pilgrimage route from London to the shrine of Our Lady of Walsingham. The mileage given appears to be the reputed distance in the sixteenth century. In fact, Jean Benard was following in the footsteps of the very popular, though anonymous, *La Guide des chemins de France*, which the printer Charles Estienne published in 1552, to the extent of adopting the style, details and dimension of the book.[64] But Benard's *Guide* never enjoyed the success of Etienne's, which was reprinted and enlarged thrice in the space of a few years.

Secondly, contrary to the treatment of Italian or even Spanish books, there was no lasting attempt to translate, into French, English works that did not relate to a specific political context. Only a few Frenchmen (Belleforest, Benard) acted as facilitators between the two countries and most of Benard's translations were never printed. In fact, only two of the fourteen known manuscripts he wrote on England were published, and furthermore only posthumously. The ignorance of the French regarding the English language, as Gervais Mallot remarked, rendered the importation of English books impossible:

> mais bien peu de noz voisins les Anglois & Escossois: pource qu'il semble que ces insulaires ayent seulement voulu communiquer leurs faicts, & esté nez pour eux-mesmes, sans que les autres peuples ayent recueilly le fruict de plusieurs belles choses, qui s'y sont passees : tant leurs escrivains ont prins plaisir de les rediger en leurs langues maternelles, comme la Britannique, Saxonique, Angloise.[65]

This lack of interest was certainly not helped by the absence of any Franco-English grammar or dictionary ('dialogues' as they were known) published in France in the sixteenth century. To learn even a few words of English, if ever such a strange idea occurred to them, French travellers could only rely on foreign publications or, in London, on books published by Huguenot refugees. It is difficult to say if such works were ever introduced in France.

Thirdly, if one looks at any foreign events that the French could read about, and in which England was involved, none appear very favourable

---

[64] Herbert G. Fordham, *An Itinerary of the 16th Century. 'La Guide des Chemins d'Angleterre', Jean Bernard, Paris, 1579* (Cambridge, 1910), 4 and 8.

[65] In Benard, *Discours des plus mémorables*, epistre, A ii. The situation was not to improve for over a century: in 1665, the *Journal des Savants* informed its readers that 'la Société Royale de Londres produit tous les jours une infinité de bons ouvrages, mais parce qu'ils sont pour la plupart écrits en langue anglaise, on n'a pu jusqu'à présent en rendre compte dans ce journal', quoted by André Morize, 'Samuel Sorbière (1610–1670) et son "Voyage en Angleterre" (1664)', *Revue d'histoire littéraire de la France*, 14 (1907), 235.

to the English. For example, the *Copie de la requeste presentée au Turc par l'agent de la royne d'Angleterre, le 9 de novem. 1587*,[66] curiously translated from German, no doubt left the French under the impression that Protestants, contrary to good Catholics, were natural allies of the other heretics, the Turks. It may have reminded some Frenchmen of a political pamphlet published in 1576 entitled *La France-Turquie, c'est-à-dire conseils et moyens tenus par les ennemis de la Couronne de France, pour réduire le royaume en tel estat que la tyrannie turquesque.*[67] Ironically, in 1591, Henri IV was to solicit the Turkish sultan Murâd III in his struggle against Philip II of Spain.[68] Even during the Armada campaign, the French were not spared from the propaganda circulated in the summer of 1588 by a Spanish agent in Rouen. One of his tracts explained how Sir Francis Drake and the English navy had been defeated off the Orkney Islands by the marquis of Santa Cruz, Don Alvaro de Bazán.[69] Unfortunately, Santa Cruz had died in February 1588! In other words, even for English matters that did not directly concern them, French *libraires-imprimeurs* were not very punctilious when it came to the accuracy of what they handled.

One is left with mixed impressions. There was undoubtedly a surge of interest in England in the 1560s and 1570s when a matrimonial union seemed possible, and when, in the midst of the religious wars, some French political theorists (Jean Bodin, François Hotman) turned to England and its parliament to find inspiration for possible constitutional reforms. In the late 1580s, triggered by the acrimonious debate between moderates and ultra-Catholics, the French looked again to England. But it was no longer England as such that interested the French, but specific events (the fate of Mary, queen of Scots, the English Catholics and their plots) and information which circulated in France was, by then, biased. Furthermore, the lack of new descriptions and of histories of England after 1572, the lack of re-editions of previous books, the absence of any translations of English works and of any Anglo-French dictionary published in France tend to demonstrate that there was no real and lasting interest, in France in England and the English.

On the other hand, those who belonged to the inner circle of power, or who had the right connections, were no doubt able to read

---

[66] *Copie de la requeste presentée au Turc par l'agent de la royne d'Angleterre, le 9 de novem. 1587, traduicte sur la coppie imprimée en Allema[n]de ... Certaines lettres du sultan à la roynez d'Angleterre* ([Paris], 1589).

[67] Orléans, Thibaud des Murs.

[68] Babelon, *Henri IV*, 507.

[69] See also *Copie d'une lettre envoyée de Dieppe* ([Rouen?], le Goux, 1588); *Discours véritable de ce qui s'est passé entre les deux armées ... depuis 29 juillet 1588 jusques à 11 Aoust* ([Paris?], 1588). For the propaganda around the Armada see Garrett Mattingly, *The Defeat of the Spanish Armada* (1959), ch. 30, and Bertrand T. Whitehead, *Brags and Boasts. Propaganda in the Year of the Armada* (Stroud, 1994).

at least some, if not all, of the unpublished works on England. Not only do manuscripts account for over a third of our corpus but they also cover topics that, apparently, were not deemed of interest to the general public, or commercially viable: the state of English affairs and diaries of travels through England. Jean Benard, in his capacity of 'historiographe... interprète pour la langue angloise', gathered much political information for Charles IX and Henri III directly from English sources: on the parliament of 1564, on the state of England in 1569, 1572 and 1574, on the execution of the duke of Norfolk (which, rather unexpectedly, was never printed). In 1578, 1584 and 1586 several reports were made on the state of England (1578), of its finances (1586) and on the succession to the crown (1584). In 1596, on his return from having accompanied the French diplomat Nicolas Harlay de Sancy on his embassy to Elizabeth, Guillaume Du Vair wrote his 'Advis sur la Constitution de l'Estat d'Angleterre & accidens desquelz il semble estre menacé', though it is unclear if it was meant for publication or just to be an *aide-mémoire*. As with the printed material, most of these documents were drawn up when a closer union was being discussed or when the death of Elizabeth became a matter of discussion in international politics.

Similarly, the three surviving *journals* kept by Frenchmen who crossed the Channel remained in manuscript form and, therefore, were only circulated in a very small circle: Jacques Esprinchard's *Journal* of his trip to England in 1593, the duke of Rohan's *Voyage* in 1600 and Jean de Tourval's *Direction pour le voiageur d'Angleterre* of 1603. The duke of Rohan was the most explicit in explaining the reasons for keeping an accurate account of a journey. It was first to supply the deficiency of his memory: 'ayant veu plus de choses remarquables que ma memoire ne sçauroit retenir, je l'en veux soulager par ce petit abbregé de ma peregrination'. Secondly it was to give him a better understanding of the diversity of the world:

> afin d'en tirer s'il m'est possible de l'utilité pour moy... L'utilité que je pense en devoir prendre, c'est ceste diversité que je vois aux hommes aussy souvent comme ils changent de Climat: d'ou provient la diversité de leurs loys & gouvernements, la situation des villes ou j'ay passé, leurs origines, leurs accroissements, & leurs maintiens.

Thirdly it was to entertain his friends with a light account of his travels and to allow them to follow in his footsteps without leaving the comfort of their homes: 'du contentement pour mes amys; ayant moyen avec ce rafraichissement de les en entretenir quand ils le desireront... Le contentement de mes amis sera de leur pouvoir raconter... ce qu'ils pourront desirer de ce que j'auray veu.'[70] The relation of his peregrinations must have enjoyed some success among

---

[70] Rohan, *Voyage du duc de Rohan*, 1–2.

these armchair-travellers since it was published after his death in 1646. Jean de Tourval's *Direction pour le voiageur d'Angleterre*, written while he was in England with Sully, was probably intended for those wishing to visit London and the south of England, since he describes the road from Dover to London, then to Oxford and Cambridge. His friend Pierre de L'Estoile, on hearing of this manuscript in September 1609, requested his son to produce a copy.[71] The fact that none was published during Elizabeth's reign would confirm the idea that no market existed for them, contrary, for example, to the very popular literature on the discovery of the New World. Whatever may be, the quality and depth of information, in particular political, contained in all these unpublished works was far greater than what could be found in most of the available books and printed pamphlets.

In 1664, Samuel Sorbière wrote confidently in his *Relation d'un voyage en Angleterre*: 'L'Angleterre est le pays du monde le mieux connu; parce que Cambdenus par ordre du Roy Jacques en fit une description, à laquelle il employa plusieurs années de voyages faits tout exprés.'[72] If a hundred years before this was certainly not the case, it remains nevertheless that Elizabeth's England did attract some interest in France and that, consequently, at the end of her reign, England was probably a lesser unknown quantity for the French than previously.

---

[71] 'Le samedi 12 [septembre 1609], Tourval m'a donné . . . avec une direction faite par ledit Tourval pour ceux qui veulent voir l'Angleterre, laquelle j'ay baillé à François Delestoille pour me la copier', L'Estoile, *Mémoires-Journaux*, X, 13. Jean Loiseau de Tourval, *Direction pour le voiageur d'Angleterre, du sieur De Tourval*, (*c. 1603*), Bibliothéque municipale Rouen, collection Coquebert de Montbret, ms. 96, fos. 300r–306r. It has been edited by Alison Clarke, 'Jean Loiseau de Tourval: A Huguenot translator in England, 1603–31', *Proceedings of the Huguenot Society of London*, 20 (1960), 36–59, appendix 54–9.

[72] Samuel Sorbière, *Relation d'un voyage en Angleterre, où sont touchées plusieurs choses, qui regardent l'estat des sciences, & de la religion, & autres matieres curieuses* (Cologne, Pierre Michel, 1666), ed. Louis Roux (Saint-Etienne, 1980), 18.

Transactions of the RHS 14 (2004), pp. 243–60 © 2004 Royal Historical Society
DOI: 10.1017/S0080440104000167   Printed in the United Kingdom

THE KING (THE QUEEN) AND THE JESUIT: JAMES STUART'S *TRUE LAW OF FREE MONARCHIES* IN CONTEXT/S

By Peter Lake

ABSTRACT. The paper argues that Robert Parsons's tract *The Conference* about the next succession provides the immediate polemical and political context in which James VI wrote his *True Law of Free Monarchies*. The argument is not that that tract is a simple reply to Parsons but rather a response to the position occupied both by Parsons and Buchanan, which in fact were very similar. James's pamphlet was occasioned, however, by Parsons's book and the concerns raised therein about the succession to the English throne and forms part of a concerted campaign to defend James's rights in that regard and to assert his view of kingship against the monarchomach theories of both Protestants and Catholics.

Recent writing on the reign of Elizabeth I, most notably a series of brilliant articles by Patrick Collinson, has presented the politics of the period as dominated by a conjuncture of dynastic and confessional issues that Collinson has dubbed 'the Elizabethan exclusion crisis'. The essence of that crisis lay in a series of threatening counterfactuals centred on the unsettled nature of the succession and the prospect, should Elizabeth die childless and/or without nominating a successor, of the accession of the Catholic Mary Stuart. It was a 'crisis', or at least a conjuncture, that lasted more or less from the moment the queen came to the throne until Mary Stuart's death in 1587.[1] Now the destruction of the Catholic reversionary interest centred upon Mary, the focus of Catholic hopes and plots for over twenty years, might be thought to have brought this particular 'crisis' to an end. However, the demise of Mary Stuart did not destroy the basic dynastic structures that had underpinned the exclusion crisis for the previous two and a half decades. Indeed, it might plausibly be argued that Mary's death merely removed one set of problems, centred on the

---

[1] Patrick Collinson, 'The Monarchical Republic of Queen Elizabeth I', an article first published in the *Bulletin of the John Rylands Library* in 1987 and subsequently reprinted in Collinson's *Elizabethan Essays* (1994), 31–57. For a further development of the same case see Collinson's Raleigh lecture, 'The Elizabethan Exclusion Crisis and the Elizabethan Polity', *Proceedings of the British Academy*, 84 (1995), 51–92. For the subsequent application and development of Collinson's insights see S. Alford, *The Early Elizabethan Polity: William Cecil and the British Succession Crisis, 1558–1569* (Cambridge, 1998), and John Guy, *My Heart Is My Own: The Life of Mary Queen of Scots* (2004).

need to exclude one claimant in particular from the field of possibilities, only to replace it with another, centred on the multiplicity of possible candidates left by the still unsettled succession to fight it out after the old queen's death.

And this second problematic promised to be at least as threatening as the first. After all, the threat of a Catholic reversionary interest centred on Mary had, for the most part, acted on the regime as a centripetal force, pulling all the major figures in the Protestant establishment (not to mention their clients and dependants in the provinces) together in common cause against an outcome likely to prove disastrous both for themselves and for the Protestant state over which they presided. However, the increasingly pressing questions of just who was going to succeed Elizabeth and who (in England, but, of course, not only in England) was going to manage and therefore profit from that process were likely to operate in an altogether different, centrifugal, manner, opening and exacerbating divisions within the inner circle, as different groups and individuals positioned themselves, in a spirit of rivalry and mutual suspicion, before the inevitable prospect of regime change.[2] We have here, *in potentia* at least – and the *potentia* in question was at least as serious, severe and threatening as that underlying Collinson's exclusion crisis – a situation with all the makings of the sort of confessional and dynastic, ideological, political and indeed geo-political, meltdown that was currently tearing apart the French monarchy, which, of course, at this very moment, was in the throes of a succession crisis and religious civil war caused by the prospect of the accession to the French throne of the heretic Henry IV.

I

If we want to register just how seriously that prospect was taken in England, where, of course, any overt discussion of the succession and related issues was strictly prohibited, we need only to remind ourselves of the appetite, displayed in the popular and not so popular press, for news of events in France and of the vogue, on the popular stage from the late 1580s on, for history plays obsessed with dynastic civil wars, rebellion, usurpation and the nature of legitimacy, with narratives often organised around competing claims to both the English and French thrones, noble faction and feud and campaigns in and against France.[3] On this basis, we might conclude that as they contemplated, with some trepidation,

    [2] Helen Stafford, *James VI of Scotland and the Crown of England* (New York, 1940).
    [3] Lisa Parmalee, *Good News from France: French Anti-League Propaganda in Late Elizabethan England* (Rochester, 1996); Paul J. Voss, *Elizabethan News Pamphlets: Shakespeare, Spenser, Marlowe and the Birth of Journalism* (Pittsburgh, 2001); Richard Hillman, *Shakespeare, Marlowe and the Politics of France* (Basingstoke, 2002).

the decidedly uncertain prospect before them, English people had two
main models with which to shape and control their fears, fantasies and
political calculations – in the present, the nature and course of the exactly
contemporaneous French succession crisis and religious civil war and, in
the relatively recent past, the nature and course of that last great English
dynastic civil war, the wars of the Roses.[4]

In what follows I want to illustrate the dynamics of this situation
through an analysis of one text and (some) of its effects. The text in
question is *A Conference about the Next Succession* by Robert Parsons and
the effects in question are a series of replies which it provoked, the most
significant of which, I will argue, was *The True Law of Free Monarchies*
by none other than James VI himself. The book was dedicated, with
wonderful dead-pan malice, to the earl of Essex, who, as the queen's
favourite, was depicted as the man most likely to have a determinative
influence in matters of succession.[5] Thereafter, Parsons's text sought
systematically both to exacerbate and to exploit the situation and anxieties
sketched above. On the one hand, the book was an extended exercise
in genealogical complication, indeed obfuscation. Parsons produced an
elaborated account of the different claims to an English throne about to be
left vacant by the death of the childless (and heedless) Elizabeth. His aim
was to create a sense of confusion and impending crisis by rendering the
case for the apparently natural successor, James Stuart, less compelling
than it might otherwise have appeared to be and by enhancing the claims
of other less obvious and seemingly less congenial candidates like the
infanta. Having stirred the pot of potential claimants or competitors, and
heightened the aura of anxiety and mutual suspicion surrounding the
succession, Parsons then went on to produce a version of the English polity
(and indeed of all monarchical polities) that left a residual right within
the socio-political whole, the commonwealth, as he called it, to alter or

---

[4] At an elite level we might, of course, add to these the increasing vogue for Tacitean
politick history that was such a feature of precisely this same period and which, by the reign's
end, had started to invade the realm of the popular drama, as well. From a burgeoning
literature see Malcolm Smuts, 'Court Centred Politics and the Uses of Roman Historians,
c. 1590–1630', in *Culture and Politics in Early Stuart England*, ed. K. Sharpe and P. Lake
(Basingstoke, 1994), 21–43.

[5] Robert Parsons, *A Conference about the Next Succession to the Crown of England* (1594). For a
discussion of the question of Parsons's authorship of the tract (which appeared under the
name R. Doleman) see Peter Holmes, 'The Authorship and Early Reception of *A Conference
about the Next Succession to the Crown of England*', *Historical Journal*, 23 (1980), 415–29. The
dedication 'to the right honourable the earl of Essex, of her majesty's privy council' was
justified on the grounds that 'no man is in more high and eminent place or dignity at this
day in our realm then yourself, whether we respect your nobility or calling or favour with
your prince or high liking of the people and consequently no man like to have a greater
part of sway in deciding of this great affair . . . than your honour and those that will assist
you and are likest to follow your fame and fortune'.

divert the succession, when the common good dictated it. This capacity remained in place even when a clear winner in the legitimate hereditary successor stakes could be identified, something which, as we have seen, Parsons denied to be the case in late Elizabethan England. Through an analysis of the current balance of religio-political and dynastic-factional forces operating within and without the kingdom Parsons then proceeded to argue that just such an exercise of the commonwealth's right to settle and, if need be, to divert the succession might well be necessary if England were to avert an otherwise inevitable descent into religiously inflected dynastic strife, on the scale of the wars of the Roses or the French wars of religion.[6]

II

Parsons's tract was, therefore, of pressing interest to James Stuart. When Burghley first acquired a copy he told his son that it should be shown to James immediately to prove to him just what stock the Spanish and the papists set by his claims to the English throne. The book was in James's possession by December 1595.[7] In January one of Burghley's correspondents told him that he had tried to get a sight of the book 'but the king keeps it so charily that it cannot be wanting from its keeper above one night'. Through a friend, he had secured possession of the volume for 'a night and half a day in which time it was sent for thrice by the king'.[8] On this evidence, there can be no doubt that Parsons's book had got James's attention. So much so, that he immediately set about having the book refuted. Letters to England report a preaching campaign against the book throughout January. United in refuting the seditious arguments of a papist troublemaker, so Roger Aston reported, 'the ministers and the king were never so great'.[9] Also in January reports started to flow to England that James was sponsoring written, indeed printed, replies. A 'Mr John Sharpe', an Irish man named Walter Quin and one Dixon 'that taught the art of memory in England' were all mentioned as potential authors of such a work.[10] In February 1597–8 Cecil was told that Robert Waldegrave the exiled puritan and now the king's printer in Scotland was being leant

[6] The first part of the conference was dedicated to questions of political theory and the second to detailed expositions and evaluations of the various available claims to the English throne.

[7] F. Peck, *Desiderata Curiosa* (1779), 169.

[8] *Calendar of Border Papers, 1595–1603* (1896), 102–4, John Carey to Burghley, 1 Feb. 1596.

[9] *Calendar of the State Papers relating to Scotland and Mary Queen of Scots, 1547–1603, XII 1595–7* (1952) [hereafter *Cal. SP Scot.*], 112–15, George Nicholson to Robert Bowes, 7 Jan. 1596; 126, Roger Aston to Robert Bowes, 18 Jan. 1596.

[10] For Sharpe see *ibid.*, 100, George Nicholson to Robert Bowes, 29 Dec. 1596. For Quin see *ibid.*, 119–20, John Colville to Robert Bowes, 12 Jan. 1596. For Dixon see *ibid.*, *XIII 1597–1603*, pt 1 (1969), 167–8, Colville to Robert Cecil, 25 Feb. 1598.

on to print a defence of the king's title to the English throne penned by Quin. Waldegrave wanted nothing to do with this proposal, fearing that if he became involved in so controversial an issue he would have no chance of returning to England, while if he refused to cooperate with James's plans, he would lose the royal patronage that was alone sustaining him in Scotland.[11] By June some of the heat had gone out of the issue, with Nicholson reporting to Cecil that 'the two books by Quin and Mr Dixon are sent out of the country to be printed, for of this long time the printer has not been dealt with for printing them'.[12]

But, of course, the succession issue did not go away and nor did James's itch publicly to assert and defend his rights against Parsons's taunts. In a speech to parliament in 1597, James railed at his treatment at Elizabeth's hands and asked for money to mount a diplomatic campaign across Europe to assert and defend his rights. James, it was reported, had been spooked by rumours coming out of England that the succession was about to be settled by parliament; that the queen was sick and 'a second person' or 'Lord Steward' had been named; that the queen had made provision for the succession and 'cut off the king's title'.[13] Not much came of all this; having secured his money James spent a good deal of it on entertaining Ann of Denmark's brother-in-law.[14] But rumours about Quin and Dixon's books kept circulating through 1598 and the pressure on Waldegrave seems to have been kept up.[15] Certainly, by 1598 Waldegrave had given in, printing two tracts by Peter Wentworth in one volume. The first was Wentworth's *Pithy Exhortation* of 1587 and the second a treatise written in the Tower 'concerning the person of the true and lawful successor to these realms of England and Ireland'. This last took the form of answer to Parsons's *Conference*.

In 1599 Waldegrave produced another pamphlet, this one anonymous, but, since there was now presumably no point in further dissimulation, with Waldegrave's name on the title page. This pamphlet defended James's claim, advocated the wisdom of formally acknowledging him as heir before Elizabeth's death and also refuted central arguments adduced by Parsons in *A Conference*.[16] 1599 witnessed another paroxysm of royal anxiety on the subject of the succession, with James, as ever, desperate

---

[11] *Ibid.*, *XIII 1597–1603*, pt 1, 167–8, George Nicholson to Cecil, 25 Feb. 1598.

[12] *Ibid.*, 216, Nicholson to Cecil, 9 June 1598.

[13] *Ibid.*, 133–4, Nicholson to Cecil, 16 Dec. 1597; 125, Nicholson to Cecil, 21 Nov. 1597; 129, Nicholson to Cecil, 9 Dec. 1597; *ibid.*, 137, Roger Aston to Cecil, 21 Dec. 1597.

[14] *Ibid.*, 217, Aston to Cecil, 12 June 1598.

[15] *Ibid.*, 230, Nicholson to Cecil, 1 July 1598. On Waldegrave's career and predicament see K. S. Van Erde, 'Robert Waldegrave: The Printer as Agent and Link between Sixteenth-Century England and Scotland', *Renaissance Quarterly*, 34 (1981), 40–78.

[16] *A Treatise Declaring and Confirming against All Objections the Just Title and Right of the Most Excellent and Worthy Prince, James the Sixth, King of Scotland, to the Succession of the Crown of England.*

for money telling his parliament that he might have to have recourse to arms to defend his claim. He was reacting, George Nicholson told Cecil in a letter of 24 December, to rumours from Brussels about an intended peace between England and Spain, an intended match between Arbella Stuart and Matthias the emperor's third brother and the arrival at court of Lord Beauchamp, 'which the king accounts to be in his prejudice'.[17]

We can discern here a certain pattern of behaviour, with James's anxieties about the succession peaking at various points, and more than once coinciding with requests for parliamentary supply. On each occasion these outbreaks of activity prompted preparations for the public canvassing of James's claim to the English throne, not merely through royal speeches, the pulpit and diplomacy, but also through the press and in particular in and through replies to and refutations of Parsons's book. Deep background to these developments is provided by James's increasingly close connections with the earl of Essex, connections which gathered strength from the mid-1590s. In a recent brilliant article Nicholas Tyacke has analysed the connections between James and Essex and his circle, connections through which the text of Wentworth's two tracts almost certainly made their way from England (indeed in the case of the second of them, from the Tower) to Scotland, to achieve the apotheosis of print at the hands of the king's printer, Robert Waldegrave. James, it appears, through intermediaries, provided Essex with Scottish intelligence, with Essex, again through intermediaries, reciprocating. Increasingly suspicious of the Cecils, James was looking to build a party in England, while Essex, also suspicious of the Cecils, was looking to crush his rivals at court and to establish himself in the next reign. These connections were to culminate in James's shadowy involvement in the manoeuvres and machinations behind what became Essex's rebellion; a project to establish James's status as successor once and for all, prompted by suspicion that Cecil and his allies were caballing with Spain, looking to conclude a peace and intrude the infanta as the next successor as part of the deal.[18] What we have here is James inhabiting precisely the same perfervid world of uncertainty, prognostication, mutual suspicion and anxiety, making the same sorts of political calculation and pre-emptive

---

For an account of which see James Lyell, 'A Tract on James VI's Succession to the English Throne', *English Historical Review*, 51 (1936), 300–1.

[17] *Cal. SP Scot., XIII 1597–1603*, pt 1, 587, Nicholson to Cecil, 24 Dec. 1599, a letter which also mentions James's desire to clear himself 'of the printing of the book written in Mr Wentworth's name'.

[18] Nicholas Tyacke, 'Puritan Politicians and James VI and I, 1587–1604', in *Politics, Religion and Popularity*, ed. T. Cogswell, R. Cust and P. Lake (Cambridge, 2002), 21–44; Stafford, *James VI*, esp. ch. VII; Paul E. J. Hammer, *The Polarisation of Elizabethan Politic: The Political Career of Robert Devereux, 2nd Earl of Essex, 1585–1597* (Cambridge, 1999), 164–72.

manoeuvre as those described and conjured in Parsons's book. To that extent the world of *A Conference* was also the real world and Parsons's tract not only a marker of that fact but also a remarkably effective move to render it more and more the case.

Waldegrave also printed another tract in 1598 – James's *True Law of Free Monarchies* – which, as will be seen, was also a response to Parsons's tract. Not, of course, that *The True Law* so much as mentioned the issue of the succession. Entirely innocent of the sort of detailed genealogical and historical materials and argument deployed throughout *A Conference*, *The True Law* was a work of political theory, concerned, as its title suggests, with the nature and defining characteristics of free, hereditary monarchy. But then, of course, in addition to its genealogical excavations and political provocations, Parsons's book was also a work of political theory. Part one provided an account of the origins and nature of political power, designed to underpin the claim, central to the Jesuit's immediate argumentative purposes, that all monarchies, no matter how apparently or formally committed they were to the hereditary principle, were also, in effect or at bottom, elective.

On Parsons's account man was a social and political animal. For the peace and welfare of the social whole, that whole, what Parsons termed 'the commonweal', needed the coercive power and authority of the civil magistrate. Accordingly, the commonwealth set up the office of magistrate or prince for the purpose of defending its own integrity or interests.[19] But because the very sin that rendered such a move necessary also meant that any such power left in human hands would inevitably be subject to abuse, the magistrate or prince thus created had to be subject to the constraint of law; constraint through which the magistrate could be made to serve and protect rather than to harm, undermine or even destroy the interests and integrity of the commonwealth. Indeed, on Parsons's account, in all monarchies the prince's hold on power was rendered conditional on his accepting such formal legal restraints on its exercise.[20] This happened most visibly in the coronation oath which functioned as a formal contract or bargain struck between ruler and ruled, between the commonwealth and the prince, whereby if the ruler broke the law, thus threatening the safety or even the survival of the social whole, he became subject to resistance, chastisement or even finally deposition at the hands of the commonwealth or its representatives.[21]

On one level, then, Parsons's political theory was a theory of political resistance, but this was not the central point which his formal analysis of political power or authority was intended to establish. Rather, his

[19] Parsons, *A Conference*, part 1, 5–7, 17.
[20] *Ibid.*, 72–3.
[21] *Ibid.*, 76–8, 81.

main aim was to establish the basic point that all monarchies, however committed to the hereditary principle they may in practice have been, remained, at bottom, elective and that therefore there inhered in the entity he called the commonwealth a basic right to alter or divert the succession if the interests of the common good seemed to dictate that such a change was necessary. It was at this point that the theoretical arguments adduced in the first part of Parsons's tract came together with the genealogical and dynastic, the confessional and politique, arguments contained in the second.

It is, of course, not hard, on this basis, to see *The True Law* as some sort of reply to Parsons. It was of the essence of James's argument there to deny that all monarchies were in effect elective, founded on a reversible transfer of power from the commonwealth to the prince or magistrate. There were such things as free hereditary monarchies and both Scotland and England were prime examples of that type of polity, founded on the free exercise of royal will and/or on the right of conquest. Within such free hereditary monarchies there could be no legitimate right to resist the monarch nor any residual right to alter or divert the succession inhering in the commonweal or social whole. Here the operative principle was the king is dead, long live the king. In such polities coronations recognised something that had already happened rather than constituting some sort of conditional transfer of power from the commonwealth to the prince. The coronation oath was not a form of contract, breech of which could leave the prince subject to the legitimate resistance of his subjects. True enough, the oath represented a promise to the people, but it was a promise of which God was the only judge and guarantor. All these central contentions in *The True Law*[22] represented direct contradictions of propositions central to the argument of Parsons's tract. On this basis, we can see *The True Law* as part of a 'one two' punch, one side of a royally sponsored reply to both parts of the Conference, with Wentworth's tracts covering the genealogical and political arguments of part two and James (anonymously) dealing with the political theory contained in part one.

III

But there remains a major fly in the ointment here. The conventional view of *The True Law* is not that it was written in response to Parsons but rather to George Buchanan's tract *De Iure Regni apud Scotos* and the fact is that Buchanan's account of the central issues canvassed in

[22] I cite from the text of the *True Law* contained in *King James VI and I, the Political Writings*, ed. Johann Sommerville (Cambridge, 1994) [hereafter *True Law*]. Not all monarchies elective, 72–3, 76; on the coronation oath and the role of God as the only judge of whether the monarch has kept it, 80–1; only God has the power either to make or unmake the king, 68; king chosen by both God and the people in an irreversible transfer of power, 69.

these tracts was strikingly similar to that of Parsons.[23] Both men argued that given the ends and jural or moral structure of political society, reconstructed from the basic data of human nature and natural law, and illustrated from a comparative analysis of a wide range of historical data, all monarchies were in some sense elective and legally limited, with the law proceeding from some sort of mixed constitution, comprising prince, council and people. Just as the power of the magistrate or prince had, in the first instance, been conferred on him by, in Buchanan's terms, 'the people' or, in Parsons's, by 'the commonwealth', so, in monarchies at least, the essentially contractual relationship between ruler and ruled was instantiated or enshrined in the exchange of vows and obligations between prince and people transacted during the coronation, when, as at the first, the ruler was once more elected by his people. If the ruler thereafter failed to observe his side of the bargain to govern according to law and in the interests of the social whole or commonwealth, the compact between prince and people was deemed to have been broken and the prince became subject to legitimate resistance, regulation and indeed deprivation by the people or commonwealth. Buchanan's vagueness on just who the people were and on the nature of the institutional and legal mechanisms through which they might best seek to remove or discipline the prince was paralleled by Parsons's equal lack of clarity in describing just who, at any given moment, might be taken to represent or personify the commonwealth in its dealings with a peccant ruler and just how (precisely) they might best control or depose him. Such vagueness was a necessary part of making, in Parsons's case, a wide variety of different political societies and periods of human history both fit within and confirm his underlying theory of political power; and, in Buchanan's case, of making the often erratically violent course of medieval (and more recent) Scottish history do the same. In both, the resulting lack of precision about legal, institutional and constitutional mechanisms served a political as well as an intellectual and rhetorical end; allowing the authors to posit a range of different types of resistance, originating in a variety of different social and institutional locales, as essentially legitimate expressions of 'the commonwealth' or 'the people' defending its or their interests and asserting its or their rights in the face of tyranny.

In making this case, both authors produced what we might term a-confessional, even 'secular' theories. Parsons, for one, largely eschewed

---

[23] See, for instance, Roger Mason, *Kingship and the Commonweal: Political Thought in Renaissance and Reformation Scotland* (East Linton, 1998), chs. 7 and 8; J. H. Burns, *The True Law of Kingship: Concepts of Monarchy in Early Modern Scotland* (Oxford, 1996), esp. chs. 6 and 7, both of which contain excellent expositions of Buchanan's thought. In what follows I cite from the admittedly somewhat problematic translation of Buchanan's *De Iure Regni apud Scotos* by Charles Arrowood, *The Powers of the Crown of Scotland* (Austin, 1949).

distinctively 'Catholic arguments' for resistance, i.e. arguments centred on the papal primacy or deposing power. On the very rare occasions when the papacy was mentioned in Parsons's multifarious accounts of successful and legitimate exercises of resistance or the alteration of strict lineal succession, the pope figured only as confirming the original exercise of powers resting firmly within the commonwealth or political society in question. The foundations of the Jesuit's argument were based on natural law, the dictates of which he extracted from such classical authorities as Aristotle and Cicero. He then ran those same principles through a comparative analysis of myriad historical examples taken from the classical, the medieval and the more recent past, as well, of course, as from what Peter Holmes has calculated was his most frequently cited source, the Old Testament. While the Old Testament functioned in his argument very often as just another source of historical example, that role was, of course, over-determined by the status of the Old Testament as the history of what Parsons termed 'God's own peculiar people', 'his commonwealth'.[24] Thus were the conclusions that Parsons had extracted from natural law (and a variety of classical, pagan texts) confirmed in ways that showed that, on the issue of legitimately resisting princes and diverting successions, God too was on side.[25]

Buchanan's procedures were very similar. He, too, based his account on natural law, a natural law extracted from the same range of classical authorities. Aristotle and Cicero again bulked large. His historical examples tended to be far more narrowly Scottish and he made far less use of scripture than did Parsons. Indeed when he did discuss the authority of scripture he tended to do so only to remove it from the case in hand. Thus the passage in the book of Samuel cited by his opponents to show that resistance was never legitimate was explained away as an exception.[26] Again, the passages in the New Testament about obeying the powers that be as of God were similarly contextualised away. Buchanan placed them in an immediate contemporary debate about the legitimacy of any form of political authority to be exercised over Christians.[27] Paul's injunctions were thus denuded of any direct relevance to the question of resistance to a tyrant ruling within a Christian polity. Buchanan did mention the pope and the papacy; once as a prime example of the abuses of power

---

[24] Parsons, *A Conference*, part 1, 12.

[25] See the account of Parsons's political philosophy in Peter Holmes, *Resistance and Compromise: The Political Thought of the Elizabethan Catholics* (Cambridge, 1982), 149–57; on Parsons's authorities see *ibid.*, 151. While the papal deposing power scarcely figured in the English version of *A Conference*, when Parsons produced a Latin version for circulation in Rome he added a chapter on that subject thus moving it far closer to the centre of his argument. See *ibid.*, 152–7, and Holmes, 'The Authorship and Early Reception', 423.

[26] Buchanan, *The Powers of the Crown of Scotland*, 70

[27] *Ibid.*, 112–16.

that inevitably followed when a prince was allowed to interpret the laws set in place to limit his own actions and authority, and then to illustrate the role of the distinction between the person of the office holder and the nature of the office (what has become known as the doctrine of 'the king's two bodies') in legitimating resistance to monarchical power.[28] These instances, and the language in which they were couched, were enough to show that this was a tract written by an opponent of popery but they certainly did not render Buchanan's theory distinctively or exclusively Protestant.[29]

IV

On the interpretation being advanced here it was James's extended engagement with Parsons's book and the need publicly to vindicate his claim to the English throne that provided the immediate trigger for his writing the *The True Law*. This certainly explains the timing of the book, which has always provided something of a conundrum for those who wanted to see it as a response to Buchanan. As Craigie has observed, 'nineteen years seems a long time to wait before seeking to controvert another man's arguments, especially when that other book had been written when its nominal addressee was only four years old'.[30] And yet such was the similarity between the structure of the argument in Buchanan's and Parsons's tracts that even as James read and responded to Parsons's book he could not help but recall his old tutor Buchanan's arguments. As even the most persuasive makers of the case for *The True Law*'s status as a reply to the *De Iure* have been forced to conclude, Buchanan remains 'something of an elusive quarry' in the pages of James's pamphlet.[31] But then the same applies to Parsons. It is necessary, therefore, to see James's book as in some sense a response to both.[32] In *The True Law* he can be seen using images, apothegms and arguments drawn from

---

[28] *Ibid.*, 75–7, 118–19.

[29] In the words of Robert M. Kingdom, 'there is little within the *De iure regni apud Scotos* that is explicitly protestant much less Calvinist'. Robert M. Kingdom, 'Calvinism and Resistance Theory, 1550–1580', in *The Cambridge History of Political Thought, 1450–1700*, ed. J. H. Burns and Mark Goldie (Cambridge, 1991), 193–218, quotation at 218.

[30] *Minor Prose Works of James VI and I*, ed. James Craigie (Scottish Texts Society, 1982), 193–4.

[31] Mason, *Kingship and the Commonweal*, 233.

[32] In short, I want to endorse, appropriate and modify J. H. Burns's exemplarily cautious formulation that 'there cannot be much real doubt that Buchanan's *De iure regni apud Scotos* was in James's mind as he wrote *The True Lawe*' (Burns, *True Law of Kingship*, 234) by adding that there also cannot be much real doubt that Parsons's *A Conference* was also in his mind, and provided the immediate occasion for James's taking up his pen to write against both men, in this way and at this time.

one text against the other, positioning himself within and between the arguments and structures of both Buchanan's and Parsons's books.

Certainly such a view helps explain many of the otherwise, if not odd, then at least distinctive, features of James's screed. As we have seen, both Parsons and Buchanan based their argument on natural law. James responded with scripture and in particular the text from the book Samuel with an exposition of which *The True Law* so famously opens. This was a passage which Parsons and Buchanan had both treated in precisely the same way. The sort of monarchy that the Israelites were asking for in that passage, they explained, was the same sort as that enjoyed by the neighbouring peoples of the contemporary near east, that is to say it was a form of Asiatic tyranny, entirely unlike the legally limited monarchies of the Christian west.[33] As such, the political structures being discussed in that passage could have no direct application to or relevance for contemporary political experience. As a number of commentators have pointed out, other opponents of monarchomach theory, like the Scottish émigré Adam Blackwood, took a very different tack. For Blackwood, Samuel's description of the powers to be enjoyed by Saul and his successors as kings of Israel was a simple description (and, of course, a divine endorsement) of the powers enjoyed by any and every monarch.[34] Throughout *A Conference* Parsons had constructed his own case against what he presented as just such a tyranny-legitimating 'absolutist' other, in his case taken not from the works of Blackwood but from another French Catholic politique defender of Henry of Navarre, Pierre du Belloy.[35]

James was well aware of the danger of being painted into such a polemically unappealing corner, of being portrayed not merely as an opponent of the right to resist and defender of hereditary succession, but also as a charter member of the party of Saul and Nero, a veritable spokesman for tyranny. To avoid this fate James used his own reading of the crucial passage from Samuel to triangulate between the positions adopted by Blackwood and du Belloy, on the one hand, and Buchanan and Parsons, on the other. He used Samuel's speech to the Israelites to make two points: first, that kings were of God and could be removed by and were accountable to no one but him and, second, that even when they were initially elected (as Saul was) by the people, the transfer of power thus effected was neither conditional nor reversible. Rather, it constituted a once and for all grant or transfer of power.[36] Having used

---

[33] Buchanan, *The Powers of the Crown of Scotland*, 70, 117; Parsons, *A Conference*, 111.

[34] Mason, *Kingship and the Commonweal*, 222.

[35] For Parsons's use of du Belloy in this role see, for instance, *A Conference*, part 1, 64, 67–9, 121, 123, 124–5.

[36] *True Law*, 66–70.

the passage to make these two basic minimum points, James then made it clear that Samuel's terrifying account of how the powers of the king might well be used represented an account of tyrannical abuse rather than a simple value-free exposition of the ways in which any and every free hereditary monarch could legitimately behave, if the mood took him. James was here endorsing and employing Parsons's estimation of the Old Testament as the record of God's own commonwealth against Buchanan's marginalisation of the testimony of scripture for the discussion of pressing issues of contemporary political theory. Thereafter, he changed tack, pursuing Parsons into the other scriptural passages used by the Jesuit to legitimate rebellion, either, as with the later history of the relations between David and Saul, to argue that they proved the opposite of what Parsons claimed, or else, with Buchanan, to claim that they were exceptional, reporting 'extraordinary' actions and examples undertaken directly by God himself or by his divinely inspired agents and thus of no relevance to contemporary political conduct.[37]

Having thus trumped, with the direct testimony and authority of scripture, the resort of both the Jesuit and the Presbyterian to natural law arguments, James turned next to history and in particular to the history and laws of Scotland. Both Buchanan and Parsons had admitted that there was a range of different sorts of legitimate polity in the world. But by its very nature their analysis of the origins and nature of political authority had tended to push all such polities towards an ideal of elective, legally limited, mixed polities or monarchies.[38] James, on the other hand, chose to emphasise difference. There were in the world a number of different types of polity with different origins and histories. Amongst these, and greatly superior to the rest, were free hereditary monarchies; polities that owed their origins to the exercise of royal power or will or to conquest. According to James both Scotland and England were polities of this sort; the powers of the English monarchy based on the military triumphs of William the Conqueror and those of the Scottish crown on the untrammelled exercise of the regal status of King Fergus.[39] Famously James pictured Fergus's creating a kingdom in Scotland almost *ex nihilo*, forging, 'by his own friendship and force', a monarchical polity out of the scattered, entirely pre-political, human materials that he found there. This account represented, as it were, not merely a local refutation of Buchanan's version of an ancient Scottish constitution, but also a more general refutation of both Parsons's and Buchanan's account of the

---

[37] *Ibid.*, 70–1. For Parsons's deployment of these and other such examples for precisely contrary purposes see *A Conference*, part 1, 68–72.

[38] See, for instance, Buchanan, *The Powers of the King of Scotland*, 57, 108, 129–30.

[39] *True Law*, 73–4. For the legitimacy of other sorts of elective monarchies or aristocratic and limited polities see 76.

origins of political power. For, as we have seen, both writers had located the origins of magisterial or princely power in a transfer of the same from a pre-existing social whole, variously termed 'the people' by Buchanan or 'the commonwealth' by Parsons, to the magistrate or monarch. But, on James's account, in Scotland at least no such social whole had existed before Fergus had called it into being through the exercise of a royal authority he brought with him to Scotland from Ireland.

Only after he had adduced arguments from scripture and history did James turn at last to what he termed natural law. Here he did not proceed so much by citing the sort of maxims or aphorisms, the general moral principles, drawn from classical antiquity or scripture of the sort deployed by Buchanan and Parsons, as through a series of what he termed 'similitudes',[40] presented as obvious or transparently apposite parallels between the natural and the political orders. These similitudes served both to naturalise and to patriarchalise James's version of political society and monarchical authority. Parsons had used the image of the king as head of the body politic, arguing that the body had the right to remove or replace its own head if such radical surgery were necessary for the preservation of the whole. This, of course, conjured up the rather incongruous image of a body tearing off its own head for medicinal purposes, an image Parsons tried to remove from the reader's mind by distinguishing between the civil and the natural body and claiming that, unlike the natural body, the civil body could have more than one head. Omitting Parsons's distinction between the civil and natural bodies, James appropriated the image, to argue for the unnaturalness, indeed the impossibility, both moral and physical, of the people removing the prince, their head, from the bleeding trunk of the body politic.[41] Buchanan had used the image of the king as father of his people to illustrate the sorts of moral and legal considerations and constraints that naturally defined and limited the nature and use of royal power; a power he presented as an instrument designed solely in the interests, and for the protection, of the child/subject, rather than for the gratification or glory of the parent/ruler. James used precisely the same image to show once again how much against nature was the very idea of resistance by the children/people to the authority of the father/king.[42]

---

[40] *Ibid.*, 76.

[41] *Ibid.*, 76–8; for the same image see Parsons, *A Conference*, 38–9.

[42] *True Law*, 76–7. For Buchanan's use of the same analogy, see *The Powers of the Crown of Scotland*, 83. This appropriation of basic principles and apothegms from Buchanan for purposes opposite to those for which his former tutor had used them is typical of James's procedure in *The True Law*. See, for instance, his deployment of the image of the king as a speaking law and the law as a dumb king and the tag *summum ius, summum inuria* to defend an account of the royal prerogative that Buchanan had used the very same authorities to denounce as a tyrants' charter, *True Law*, 75. For Buchanan, see *The Powers of the King of Scotland*, 58, citing Cicero *De Legibus*, III, 2. On the perils of such a view of the prerogative,

But these images served another, secondary but still crucial, purpose for James. Even as he used the passage from Samuel as the basis for his defence of 'true monarchy', James had sedulously avoided a reading of that text that might seem to make it a blueprint for tyranny. On James's account Samuel was not there outlining the powers of kings, merely showing the Israelites how badly bad kings could and did act. While his basic point remained that even a Saul or a Nero could never be subject to the just resistance of his subjects, he also wanted to make it plain that good kings (like himself) did not behave like Saul or Nero. His deployment of those two images of the king as head of the body and father of his people served to emphasise that the interests of the ruler were naturally coterminous with those of the ruled. As such both those images were designed to show that Nero-style tyranny was not only evil but also unnatural, and therefore unlikely. On this view, therefore, Constantines and Solomons were not only a more congenial but a more 'natural' (and thus a far more likely) outcome of free hereditary monarchy than were Sauls or Neros. In agreeing with James you were thus far more likely to end up with Solomon than with Saul, with Constantine rather than with Nero, and, it might be added, given James's calming assurances that, all things being equal, good kings (like him) governed according to law, in deciding for him as your king you were indeed getting a Solomon and not a Saul, a godly Christian prince and not a tyrant.[43]

V

The suspicion that *The True Law* had something to do with Parsons's tract is anything but a new idea; D. H. Wilson, Maurice Lee and Peter Holmes have all suggested as much.[44] But surprisingly little has been made of the resulting juxtaposition. On the contrary, of late James's tract has tended to be read in an exclusively Scottish context.[45] The result has been to insulate his reign in England from the absolutism expounded in *The True*

---

see 74–5. Given the commonplace nature of the tags and images in question such echoes and parallels cannot constitute anything like conclusive proof that the one text was answering or echoing the other. They merely add to the different types of admittedly circumstantial evidence being adduced here to make that case.

[43] James might be thought to have brought this argument full circle in his *Basilicon Doron* (which was, of course, written at about precisely this time) where he presented himself as the very epitome of a godly prince, a Solomon or a Constantine indeed.

[44] C. H. Wilson, *King James VI and I* (1956), 149; Maurice Lee, *Great Britain's Solomon* (Urbana, 1990), 82–3; Holmes, 'Authorship and Early Reception', 426–8.

[45] Jenny Wormald, 'James VI and I, *Basilicon Doron* and *The Trew Law of Free Monarchies*: The Scottish Context and the English Translation', in *The Mental World of the Jacobean Court*, ed. L. L. Peck (Cambridge, 1991), 36–54; Mason, *Kingship and the Commonweal*, chs. 7 and 8; Burns, *The True Law of Kingship*, ch. 7. The argument presented here is intended to modify and develop, rather than to contradict, those advanced by Mason and Burns.

Law and to privilege the conceptual primacy of the 'new British history' in interpreting his reign. But, if the book is to be restored to the immediate polemical and political contexts that produced it, it will be seen that none of this will quite do.

It is necessary to pause for a moment to consider the nature of the text to which James was, in all probability, most immediately replying. It was a book about the English succession, produced by an English Jesuit exile, published in Flanders to agitate English opinion but also intended (in its Spanish and Latin translations and recensions) as a position paper for both the king of Spain and the pope.[46] It was written out of the ideological context of the French wars of religion, mobilising arguments about the nature of political and monarchical power, about the right to resist and about hereditary succession and legitimacy that were grounded in the confrontations in France between the Catholic League and its enemies, between Henry of Navarre and his both Catholic and Protestant supporters and various forms of monarchomach assertion. Parsons's use of the Gallican politique de Belloy as his absolutist whipping boy points us to a wider context for and influence upon James's own political development in French politique thought, as J. H. Burns, John Salmon and others have long argued.[47] *A Conference* then sought to apply such arguments and associations to an incipient English, indeed incipiently British, succession crisis, pictured as a cross between the wars of the Roses and the French wars of religion, a crisis, or rather a prospect, that (as the Essex rebellion was to show) was currently helping to destabilise the politics of both England and Scotland. Parsons's book, in short, places James and his little pamphlet at the centre of the ideological, political, dynastic, confessional and geo-political maelstrom that was western Europe in the period after the Reformation.

The other text to which James was replying (Buchanan's *De Iure*) had been written in the late 1560s as a theoretical counterpart to the rather more *ad feminam* justifications produced by Buchanan for the revolutionary ructions (both aristocratic and popular) that forced Mary Stuart from her throne in Scotland and into the 'protective' custody of the Elizabethan regime. It was published in 1579 during the height of the fuss over the Anjou match.[48] As such it represented the most radical face of the 'monarchical republicanism' in two kingdoms that (as Steven Alford

---

[46] Holmes, 'Authorship and Early Reception', 423.

[47] Burns, *True Law of Kingship*, passim, but esp. chs. 6 and 7; J. M. H. Salmon, 'Catholic Resistance Theory, Ultramontanism, and the Royalist Response, 1580–1620', in *Cambridge History of Political Thought, 1450–1700*, ed. Burns and Goldie, 219–53. For the insistence that the course of English Catholic political thought and polemic must be set within the wider context of developments in France see Holmes, *Resistance and Compromise*, passim.

[48] See Collinson, 'Elizabethan Exclusion Crisis', 86. More generally on the radical ideological resonances of the Anjou affair, see Blair Worden, *The Sound of Virtue* (1996).

and John Guy have argued) represented the central organising (both ideological and practical) project of the *regnum Cecilianum* for over two decades.[49] If they are to be understood aright, it is in these overlapping and mutually reinforcing transnational ('European') contexts that this text and the events that produced it need to be set, not in an exclusively 'British' history, either old or 'new'.

In reacting against these texts James was in effect reacting against the sediment, to mix the metaphor, hacking away at the scar tissue, accumulated by thirty years of confessional and dynastic politicking and polemicising throughout western Europe. In so doing he was participating in a wider 'absolutist' reaction against the more radical 'republican', populist and resistance-centred currents that had swept through the second half of the sixteenth century. In more narrowly English terms, his little book thus provides a crucial transition point between 'the monarchical republicanism of the reign of Elizabeth I' and the 'divine right absolutism' of the early Stuarts.[50] Small wonder, then, that we can discern in this text and its contexts the emergence of several habits of thought and action that were to remain central elements of James's style of rule, his mode of kingcraft. Of these the first and most obvious (and yet still the most 'controversial') was, of course, the rhetorically cushioned, but nevertheless explicit absolutism of *The True Law*, which, as Sommerville, amongst others, has argued, stayed with James for the rest of his life.[51] The second was the propensity to see Jesuits and radical puritans as identical and equivalent threats to his authority as a king. This, too, was to remain a central theme in James's political credo and style of rule and manoeuvre. And finally, we have what Lori-Anne Ferrell has termed, James's 'government by pen or polemic', his tendency to use the press and other forms of public and polemical statement to insert his own authority as king and author into the centre of public discourse. In this mode, James was seeking not to close down or simply control by royal fiat, but rather to exploit, indeed in some ways further to open, a realm of public political positioning and case-making in order to set the terms of debate and manipulate opinion in his own favour. This became a rooted propensity, a mode of behaviour to which James was to return again and

---

[49] Alford, *The Early Elizabethan Polity*; Guy, *My Heart Is My Own*.

[50] For the English, largely anti-puritan, aspects of this reaction see P. Lake, *Anglicans and Puritans? Presbyterianism and English Conformist Thought from Whitgift to Hooker* (1988), and *The Reign of Elizabeth I: Court and Culture in the Last Decade*, ed. John Guy (Cambridge, 1995), introduction and ch. 6.

[51] See, for instance, Johan Sommerville, 'James and the Divine Right of Kings: English Politics and Continental Theory', in *The Mental World of the Jacobean Court*, ed. Peck, 55–70. This subject remains 'controversial' largely due to the pertinacity of Professor Glenn Burgess. See, for instance, his *Absolute Monarchy and the Stuart Constitution* (1996).

again – particularly at moments of crisis – throughout his English reign.[52] That tendency surely had its origins in his experiences as king of Scotland and candidate for the throne of England, in his confrontations with Parsons and with Buchanan.

Certainly, at least in retrospect, James regarded this little set-to as a success. Not only, along with the massive production of *Basilicon Doron*, discovered by Peter Blayney, were there at least four reprints of *The True Law* in London in 1603, it was also included in the king's works. On this basis, it is difficult to agree with Jenny Wormald's estimation of the book as an academic treatise, written largely for James's own edification.[53] Rather, it was a book produced to meet the greatest single challenge to his right to succeed to the English throne, as well as a long-postponed reply to, indeed ideological revenge upon, his tutor and nemesis, George Buchanan. As its subsequent publication history also shows, this was not a book that James took lightly, and neither should we.

[52] Lori-Anne Ferrell, *Government by Polemic* (Stanford, 1998); Kenneth Fincham and Peter Lake, 'The Ecclesiastical Policy of King James I', *Journal of British Studies*, 24 (1985), 173–92.
[53] Blayney's findings are noted in Wormald, 'James VI and I, *Basilicon Doron* and *The Trew Law of Free Monarchies*', 51.

Transactions of the RHS 14 (2004), pp. 261–68 © 2004 Royal Historical Society
DOI: 10.1017/S0080440104000155   Printed in the United Kingdom

ELIZABETH I: A SENSE OF PLACE IN STONE, PRINT AND PAINT

By Maurice Howard

ABSTRACT. The image of Elizabeth I has its own significant historiography, with each decade over the past half-century appropriating the legacy of paintings and prints to discuss current issues of historical and social enquiry. Most recently, the representation of Elizabeth after her death, from her monument in the Abbey to the latest film, has been the subject of several monographs. This paper looks again at the diverse original contexts of these images, both in terms of physical space and of ideological intention, and places sculptural depiction more centrally than is often credited.

Much of the recent scholarship about the imagery of Elizabeth I has made exciting and thought-provoking observations on the longer history of this phenomenon; indeed two of the most recent publications deal not with Elizabeth in her own time at all but with the legacy of the making of images of her down to modern times in places far from the original localities in which she was portrayed and in forms of media unknown to Tudor England.[1] My title, however, is a retooling of a phrase first used by the chief of all scholars of the imagery of Elizabeth I, Roy Strong. It introduces my attempt to retrieve something of the original contexts in which her portraits were viewed. More than a generation ago Strong first taught us to think of the queen's portraiture as the rich container of material references taken from other visual and textual sources.[2] These images were variously made sometimes in anticipation of public occasions or subsequently to record them, at others they might be made to forward marriage negotiations, at yet others to express (and here we get closest to the queen's own preferences) the crucial differences between her public and private lives. Two particular ways of understanding the imagery of Elizabeth emerged from Strong's work. First, and crucially (and to a greater or lesser extent almost all subsequent scholarship has

---

[1] Michael Dobson and Nicola J. Watson, *England's Elizabeth. An Afterlife in Fame and Fantasy* (Oxford, 2002); Julia M. Walker, *The Elizabeth Icon 1603–2003* (Basingstoke and New York, 2003).

[2] Roy Strong, *Portraits of Elizabeth I* (Oxford, 1963); idem, *The English Icon: Elizabethan and Jacobean Portraiture* (1969); idem, *The Cult of Elizabeth: Elizabethan Portraiture and Pageantry* (1977).

stepped back from Strong's achievement to look for more insular, more nationalistic concerns), both Strong and his mentor at the Warburg Institute, Frances Yates, stressed the European context for Elizabeth's sovereignty as displayed in these works.[3] It was important that she was viewed by contemporaries as the equal to, and sharing the regal and quasi-imperial attributes of, her European rivals. Secondly, by Strong's inclusion, just as one example of his view of things, of his analysis of the *Henry Unton Memorial Portrait* in *The Cult of Elizabeth* (1977) he stressed that Elizabeth was not only present in her own image but by its reflection in the self-imaging of those around her. These contexts give us a particular sense of place for Elizabeth's portraits, suggesting a map of inter-related connections across Europe and a world of special locations, notably the houses and funerary chapels of her courtiers. Since a sense of place and locality is important for the view taken on these images in this paper, in many ways it joins the long line of Strong's followers who have tried to leap over the years between and get back to a genuine sense of acknowledging and applying Strong's high standard of scholarship and close attention to the nuances of making portraits for their first audiences.

Much of the foundations of Strong's work belongs to the 1960s, though *The Cult of Elizabeth*, a re-casting of and re-thinking of earlier articles, and his book *Gloriana: The Portraits of Elizabeth I* came later. It was followed, through the 1970s and beyond, by lively, provocative and often hard-hitting work that began with feminist analysis which drew less on visual traditions than the enormous support structure of contemporary conduct books, sermons on patriarchy and what was often perceived to be a decline in the post-Reformation state of an earlier promising encouragement of education for upper-class women in early Tudor England.[4] The issue of Elizabeth's virginity, its symbolic value to her and its perceived disempowerment of her in the eyes of others also led in many directions, not least towards the further investigation of Elizabeth as a recast Virgin Mary.[5] For other scholars, Elizabeth's iconography increasingly came to be seen as part of a larger pattern of the Tudor monarchy's appropriating imagery to serve the propagandistic needs of the dynasty, a kind of constant reminder of where power lay to disguise the fact that its authority was always dubious and at best rested on an assumed consensus.[6] So strong was this assertion that propaganda was the key to the original production of portraiture that some questioned the

[3] Frances Yates, *Astraea. The Imperial Theme in the Sixteenth Century* (1975).

[4] A. Heisch, 'Queen Elizabeth and the Persistence of Patriarchy', *Feminist Review*, 4 (1980), 45–56.

[5] Helen Hackett, *Virgin Mother, Maiden Queen: Elizabeth I and the Cult of the Virgin Mary* (1995).

[6] Christopher Lloyd and Simon Thurley, *Henry VIII. Images of a Tudor King* (1990); Maurice Howard, *The Tudor Image* (1995); David Howarth, *Images of Rule* (Basingstoke, 1997).

notion, arguing that images of sovereigns were not ever as widely known as often claimed or as talismanic.[7] The power and terror of the image was, in this debate, at the very heart of discussion about the efficacy of imagery more generally: in what sense were the depictions of Protestant (or at least non-Catholic) sovereigns replacing the supremacy of the image of the godhead? Historians such as John King explored the search for new (in the sense of newly explored), safe and uncontentious heroes and heroines from the Bible and classical history and myth that could serve as prototypes: so, in Elizabeth's case she became Judith, Deborah, Esther as protector and champion of her people.[8] King explored this 'permitted sphere' of new iconography mainly through the print medium, but others have recently begun to stress the equal significance of the domestic realm with the appearance of these figures in tapestry, on overmantels in wood or stone, in chairbacks and bench-ends. Here too a sense of particular place begins to emerge.[9]

All scholars have stressed the multivalence of Elizabeth's imagery, the different layers of meaning that could be applied, suggesting a variety of audiences and avenues of interpretation. Much of the imagery on which the portraits of Elizabeth draw is double-edged, like the pelican, which can be read as the gift of blood to the young but equally as the brood callously accepting the parental bounty, the tension between parental self-sacrifice and a filial struggle to be independent of deference that is the key to Shakespeare's *King Lear*.[10] The realisation that images of the queen could be misinterpreted and thus misused emerges from the frequent proclamations seeking to control how Elizabeth was shown, most notably that of 1563.[11] It is generally agreed that governmental control was fitful and sporadic since a great range of people, individuals and corporate bodies claimed a part of her and constructed images to meet their needs and their own personal sense of loyalty to queen and state.

It could be thought that the potentially most dangerous images of Elizabeth would be those in sculpture, first because so many of these would be seen in public situations and secondly because three-dimensional representation might be viewed as idolatrous. Unquestionably the most celebrated and influential of the public images would have been that which formed part of the series of sovereigns on the upper floor of the great court of the Royal Exchange, probably set up in the early 1570s

---

[7] Sydney Anglo, *Images of Tudor Kingship* (1992).

[8] John N. King, *Tudor Royal Iconography* (Princeton, 1989).

[9] Tara J. Hamling, 'Narrative and Figurative Imagery in the English Domestic Interior 1560–1640' (Ph.D. thesis, University of Sussex, 2002).

[10] Stephen Orgel, 'Gendering the Crown', in *Subject and Object in Renaissance Culture*, ed. Margarita de Grazia, Maureen Quilligan and Peter Stallybrass (Cambridge, 1996), 133–65.

[11] Strong, *Portraits*, 5–12.

and shown in the Frans Hogenberg engraving made shortly thereafter.[12] However, it has recently been contended that there were only a very few sculpted images of the queen produced in her lifetime and this may be true in the sense that the majority of the surviving three-dimensional images of her are part of a cult of commemoration that developed in the century and more beyond her death.[13] Even the famous statue that once adorned the Ludgate and now placed above an archway to the east of the church of St Dunstan in the West has recently been convincingly attributed not to an earlier accepted date of 1586 but to a re-making in the 1670s after the Great Fire.[14] Other images, such as that in the courtyard at Cadhay in Devon, also part of a small set of four, date from after her death, in this case from 1617. The wooden image in St Mary Redcliffe, Bristol, is of uncertain date but if from the sixteenth century it would be a rare piece commemorating an occasion, the equal of the great 'Ditchley' painted portrait for Sir Henry Lee, since it could record the queen's visit to the city in 1574. The original placing of these images is all-important to understanding their impact and their ability to construct the royal image in unconventional ways. The sculpture at Cadhay is in a courtyard, not accessible to many and therefore bridging the experience of sculpture between the world of the public at the Exchange and the more private circumstances within the palace or the country house under which Elizabeth was viewed.

Elizabeth as a sculpted image appears again in the famous Lumley busts, recorded in the inventory of 1590.[15] Crucial here is the sense that Elizabeth is seen with due reverence but very much in relation to making a point about someone else, for she serves, along with her father, brother and sister, also represented, as testament to the service John, Lord Lumley, has rendered to a run of Tudor sovereigns. Even more particular and private, though remaining in the public space for which it was made, is the representation of the queen on the tomb of Blanche Parry at Bacton in Herefordshire.[16] Blanche Parry died at the age of eighty-two in 1590 after long service to Elizabeth as her chief gentlewoman and keeper of her jewels. The monument shows Blanche kneeling sideways on to us before the queen, who is facing outwards in full majesty, bearing her orb and sceptre. The scale of the two figures is different, underlining the commemorative and symbolic quality of the tableau before us rather than any pretence of realism. Blanche presents

[12] *Elizabeth. The Exhibition at the National Maritime Museum*, ed. Susan Doran (2003), no. 46.
[13] *Ibid.*, no. 199.
[14] Nicola Smith, 'The Ludgate Statues', *Sculpture Journal*, 3 (1999), 14–25.
[15] *Dynasties. Painting in Tudor and Jacobean England 1530–1630*, ed. Karen Hearn (1995), nos. 36–9.
[16] Nigel Llewellyn, *Funeral Monuments in Post-Reformation England* (Cambridge, 2000), 277.

the queen with a case, which doubtless refers to the best diamond she possessed, left to Elizabeth. The tomb was erected in 1595–6 by her kinsman Thomas Powell, in accordance with her will. The intention here is a highly personal rendition of Blanche Parry's service, expressed in the twenty-eight lines of verse which she doubtless composed, ending with an unembarrassed, celebratory equation of her virgin state with that of the queen:

> So that my tyme I thus dyd passe awaye
> A mayde in courte and never no mans wyffe
> Sworne of Quene Elisbeths bedd chamber alwaye
> Wythe maeden quene a maede dyd ende my lyffe

But this is not the only funerary monument to Blanche Parry, for she is also commemorated in St Margaret's Westminster. Here she kneels alone, beneath an arch and turns to face the body of the church. The inscription, rather than emphasising the link between queen and subject in so personal a way as at Bacton, records her origins and her life of service in more conventional terms, imitating the style of documenting service to state and sovereign much in the same manner as the grander monuments going up in Westminster Abbey nearby at this very period. So here the context of the depiction of Elizabeth and the accompanying verse is highly significant: what is acceptable and tolerated in a remote Herefordshire church would have been inappropriate, even indecorous, in a church in the shadow of the Abbey in London.

It is perhaps more with this forging of new conventions of appropriateness that we can see the persistence of pre-Reformation notions of how and when spectators were exposed to images. Just as Catholic images were veiled for exposure only at certain times of year, so the court of Elizabeth invented rituals of public and private viewing of the portrait. This has been most thoroughly examined in connection with the miniature, the most private of all realisations of individual sitters.[17] The famous and often retold story of the Scottish ambassador Sir James Melville's attending on Elizabeth and her playful exposing and withholding of Leicester's miniature portrait is testament to the sense that contemporaries were developing towards the power of images when revealed for effect, in this case for the granting of what has to be read as a very special privilege. By contrast to that private, domestic setting, just as the altarpiece in the churches of pre-Reformation England reminded the worshipper of repeated rituals and the constant presence of spiritual support, so the presence of the royal arms in the body of the church reminded faithful subjects of the royal governance of their spiritual lives.

---

[17] Patricia Fumerton, '"Secret Arts": Elizabethan Miniatures and Sonnets', *Representations*, 15 (1986), 57–97.

Other public spaces also carried images of the queen and stressed her supervision of her subjects' conduct. The portrait of Elizabeth purchased by the corporation of Dover in 1598 and remaining in Dover Town Hall to this day, shows the queen flanked by the three theological and the four cardinal virtues. The format of three-quarter length with the figure close to the picture plane allows the impression that the queen is seated and as if in perpetual presence at the deliberations of local government. Contexts here thus can explain a great deal about both the pose of the sitter and the meaning of these works.[18]

In great country houses, the context for Elizabeth's portraits gives us two significant clues as to the construction of her identity and the loyalty of the house owner in relation to this. The first clue is about the presence of portraits amongst other objects. At Hardwick Hall the 1601 inventory lists four portable images of her, in the High Great Chamber, the Low Great Chamber and two in the Gallery, one noted as smaller than the other.[19] At Hardwick only a handful of the rooms are listed with any pictures at all, so the presence of Elizabeth's image in so relatively many of them is significant. However, as has often been noted, the imagery of Elizabeth in a wider sense is everywhere in this house, especially as its owner, the countess of Shrewsbury, was herself a woman of remarkable longevity of years and sought to share the royal virtues by similar association with the heroines of biblical and classical texts. Whilst the countess's own arms stand atop the fireplace in the Hall, in the similar place in the High Great Chamber are the royal arms and above, in the frieze, the image of Diana as huntress, usually interpreted as a direct reference to Elizabeth. Thus the context for the specific image of the royal features is one of repeated acknowledgement of the queen in other ways at every turn in the progression through this great house.

The second context provided in the world of the country house is that European (and indeed wider) sense of the queen that was mentioned earlier through the presence of the queen's portrait as part of a set of images of rulers. The gathering of these collections of images has been found to be largely cumulative; the images, for example, now in the Brown Gallery at Knole and all homogenised as a 'set' in eighteenth-century frames were in fact collected by the Sackville family over a number of generations and date from various periods.[20] But the origins of these portable sets of historical kings and queens undeniably lie in the heady world of the invented genealogy of the sixteenth century and nothing could better have served the purpose of the Tudor dynasty in bedding itself into tradition and continuity. Here, the religious differences of the

---

[18] *Elizabeth Exhibition*, no. 200.

[19] *Furniture History Society*, 7 (1971).

[20] R. Sackville-West, *Knole* (National Trust, 1998), 16.

century between Tudor sovereigns and across national boundaries could be subsumed both in a common allegiance to blood ties and in the right to rule. In a celebrated seventeenth-century set of fixed painted panels in the hall at Astley Hall, Lancashire, Elizabeth takes her place alongside leading Catholics (Philip II) and Protestants (Leicester, Henri IV, William the Silent), together with discoverers and military heroes from all over Europe.

Within the realm of England, the queen's subjects were always aware of the queen's presence alongside the replication of her, or at least the potential of it. Within the area of the south-east, the midlands, East Anglia and the south-west as far as Bristol, a great many people saw the queen herself at some point. It is important therefore to consider how her imagery worked in the context beyond England and in particular to ask how far, in lands over which England essentially held military or trading dominion, images of the queen were used quite specifically to instill loyalty, whether freely given or not. Images were dispersed among loyal Irish chieftains and many were doubtless dutifully displayed. Ireland has the most accomplished contemporary rendition of Elizabeth in the medium of plaster in the overmantel of the gallery at Ormond Castle.[21] This was carried out for Thomas Butler, tenth earl of Ormond, cousin of the queen through the Boleyn family, sometime between 1565 and 1575 at a period when he returned to Ireland to urge his rebellious brothers to sue for the queen's mercy. It opened a sustained period of the Butler family's loyalty to the crown. In 1581 Geoffrey Fenton, the Irish Council's principal secretary, asked Walsingham 'To send her majesty's picture. It would be to good purpose to hang by the cloth of estate, especially for the great assembly of the county to the parliament.'[22] However, dissent was equally forceful. In 1596 William Lyon, bishop of Cork and Ross, told Lord Hunsdon that in an inspection of school books, the queen's style and title were observed to be torn from many books of grammar. Without over-emphasising one incident, the famous report by John Jewel in 1600 of an instance where he found Philip II's image at the head of an Irish table whilst the queen's was placed ignominiously behind the door (and thus a potentially treasonous act) is too good a story not to consider here because it gives a rare glimpse of the sense that the very placing of the object was significant and that domestic spaces could have a basic sense of the hierarchy of signification within the room that echoed somewhat the hierarchy of display in the pre-Reformation church. The abuse of the queen's image was actually part of the indictment for high treason of Sir Brian na Murtha O'Rourke in 1591. Accused of keeping the Feast

---

[21] Jane Fenlon, 'The Decorative Plasterwork at Ormond Castle – A Unique Survival', *Architectural History*, 41 (1998), 67–81.

[22] *Calendar of State Papers Ireland, 1574–85*, 297.

of the Nativity five years earlier, in 1586, 'according to the Romishe and Popish computation' he also caused 'a woman's pycture' to be dragged through the streets declaring to all that this was 'her highnes pycture, and that he caused the same to be so used in despighte and contempt of her Majesty, tearmynge her highnes the mother and nurse of all herisies and heretiques'.[23] More than one historian has suggested that if there is any evidence that some perceived the distributing of the royal portrait as encouraging a cult which replaced the image of the Virgin Mary by that of Elizabeth, then it is found here and mocked by someone loyal to Catholicism.[24]

This paper has been about contexts temporal and physical. Without challenging the immense and fruitful effort that has gone into so much of the exploration of Elizabeth's imagery, the wealth of discussion now in print sometimes neglects the material nature of the objects it discusses. It is undeniable, however, that the inevitable reconstruction of her by each generation to explore its own preoccupations began with Elizabeth herself who used imagery to particular and often conflicting purposes. The evidence is stronger in the power of the words she used than the little we know of her views on the making of her visual likeness. In speeches she could certainly summon up a powerful metaphor for herself that had visual punch to it, whether in the Tilbury speech (though doubts have been cast upon the detail of that)[25] or the 1566 confrontation with parliament on the question of her marriage where, it has been argued, she evokes the story from the Decameron of Gualtieri and Griselda, the wife turned out of doors in her petticoat by her husband, to stress her ability to survive in the face of the tyrannical Commons.[26] But it was less the queen herself who dictated the terms of her imagery than a range of other agents, from courtiers to corporations, who determined where the dialogue began, by placing not just the likeness of the queen herself but a myriad of allusions to her power and beneficence into localities public and private throughout Tudor England.[27]

[23] The O'Rourke controversy is discussed by Christopher Higley, 'The Royal Image in Elizabethan Ireland', in *Dissing Elizabeth. Negative Representations of Gloriana*, ed. Julia M. Walker (Durham and London, 1998), 67–70.

[24] On Ireland, see Bruce Lenman, *England's Colonial Wars 1550–1688. Conflicts, Empire and National Identity* (2001), and on the particular incidents of conflict over images, Louis B. Montrose, 'Idols of the Queen: Policy, Gender and the Picturing of Elizabeth I', *Representations*, 68 (1999), 108–48.

[25] Susan Frye, 'The Myth of Elizabeth at Tilbury', *Sixteenth-Century Journal*, 23 (1992), 95–114.

[26] Ann Rosalind Jones and Peter Stallybrass, *Renaissance Clothing and the Materials of Memory* (Cambridge, 2000), 238–9.

[27] Susan Frye, *Elizabeth I: The Competition for Representation* (Oxford, 1993).

Transactions of the RHS 14 (2004), pp. 269–77 © 2004 Royal Historical Society
DOI: 10.1017/S008044010400012X   Printed in the United Kingdom

THE ELIZABETHAN IDEA OF EMPIRE
By David Armitage

ABSTRACT. This paper argues that the English idea of empire in the reign of Elizabeth I was derivative, belated and incoherent. Its sources were classical and continental rather than indigenous. It arose more than a century after the Scottish monarchy had elaborated its own conception of empire. Moreover, it expressed a sense of backwardness, isolation and anxiety that mirrored the English failure to establish any permanent settlements in the Atlantic world. As a result, any balance sheet of empire drawn up on Elizabeth's death in 1603 would have valued prospects in the Mediterranean and the East Indies more highly than possibilities in the Americas.

'Between 1453 and 1558, . . . England, without realizing it at the time, became (if I may be forgiven the expression) an island, in other words an autonomous unit distinct from continental Europe', wrote Fernand Braudel.[1] 1558 was a *terminus ad quem* less for the accession of a Protestant queen to the English throne than for the loss of Calais, the English crown's last territorial toehold on the European Continent. Braudel's remark obviously ignored Scotland, England's insular neighbour to the north. It overlooked Ireland, England's semi-independent dependency to the west. And it also assumed that England's formal geographical displacement from 'Europe' could be taken to imply its geopolitical disengagement as well. However, Braudel's point was not that 'England' became wholly isolated from the rest of the world and sufficient unto itself; rather, its detachment from its traditional trading links with Europe opened it up to a grander destiny as a central player in the emergent Atlantic and global economy. Insularity thereby became the precondition for ever-expanding interchange.

Braudel was not alone among post-war commentators in noting 'English' insularity and its relation to maritime expansion. For example, the German jurist and political philosopher Carl Schmitt remarked in his astonishing opus, *The* Nomos *of the Earth in the International Law of the* Jus Publicum Europaeum (1950), that, after the late fifteenth-century division

---

[1] Fernand Braudel, *Civilization and Capitalism* (1979; 3 vols., trans. Siân Reynolds, New York, 1982–4), III, 353. My thanks to David Harris Sacks for this reference.

of the globe by the Alexandrine Bulls and the treaty of Tordesillas,

> land and sea were divided into *two* separate and distinct global orders within the Eurocentric world order that arose in the sixteenth century...The connecting link between the different orders of land and sea became the island of *England*... The English island remained a part or rather the center of this European planetary order, but simultaneously distanced herself from the European continent and assumed the world-historical intermediary position that for more than three centuries made her 'of Europe, but not in Europe'.[2]

Braudel's and Schmitt's conceptions of English insularity shed new light on the processes classically examined in A. L. Rowse's *The Expansion of Elizabethan England* (1955).[3] How could insular introversion become imperial expansion, and how could navel-gazing turn outward into empire-building? The answer was clear to Schmitt: England was the Hegelian harbinger of a new global order, separate from the Continent, to be sure, but unequalled in its capacity to inaugurate a wholly new 'planetary order'.

Braudel's insular empire and Schmitt's inexorable empire were two sides of the same coin. Both represented different facets of enduring and widespread ideas of England, of empire, and of the reign of Elizabeth I as pivotal for both English and imperial history. Beneath both their conceptions lay the notion of England as an inside-out empire. For both of them, England formed a shrunken insular core, detached both from continental Europe and from the surrounding Atlantic archipelago. This empire was English long before it became a British – or, to be precise, an Anglo-British[4] – empire. In due course, it would be defined as an empire of the seas, distinct from the 'island' of England, cut off by the River Tweed from Scotland, by St George's Channel from Ireland and by the English Channel from the Continent, yet by the end of the Napoleonic Wars it would expand its wooden walls out across the waves to encompass the whole globe. As Schmitt had put it in an earlier work, *Land and Sea* (1942), 'During the forty-five years of [Elizabeth's] reign . . . all the seas of the world converged upon the English Isle.'[5]

Braudel, Schmitt and Rowse, among many others, were the diverse heirs to an enduring idea of the British Empire as characteristically and uniquely Protestant, commercial, maritime and free. On this conception,

---

[2] Carl Schmitt, *The* Nomos *of the Earth in the International Law of the* Jus Publicum Europaeum (1950; trans. G. L. Ulmen, New York, 2003), 173.

[3] A. L. Rowse, *The Expansion of Elizabethan England* (1955; repr. and introd. Michael Portillo, Basingstoke, 2003).

[4] Roger A. Mason, 'The Scottish Reformation and the Origins of Anglo-British Imperialism', in *Scots and Britons: Scottish Political Thought and the Union of 1603*, ed. Roger A. Mason (Cambridge, 1994), 161–86; Colin Kidd, *Subverting Scotland's Past: Scottish Whig Historians and the Creation of an Anglo-British Identity, 1689 – c. 1830* (Cambridge, 1993).

[5] Carl Schmitt, *Land and Sea* (1942; trans. Simona Draghici, Washington, DC, 1997), 23.

island 'England' sat at the centre of an empire of the seas, separated by a *cordon sanitaire* from the imperial diseases that infected all other European empires. The British Empire was the first post-Reformation empire. It was an empire of commerce not conquest, defended by its navy rather than being propagated by an army. It was therefore a benign empire, conducted at healthy distances from the metropolis and posing no threat to domestic liberties while at the same time carrying 'English' liberty abroad along with the common law and a tolerant and non-coercive religion.[6]

This conception of the British Empire had sixteenth- and seventeenth-century roots, though it first flourished in fully recognisable form during the 1730s and 1740s. It reached its apotheosis in the mid-nineteenth century, in the language of J. A. Froude's 'England's Forgotten Worthies' (1852):

> The England of the Catholic Hierarchy and the Norman Baron, was to cast its shell and to become the England of free thought and commerce and manufacture, which was to plough the ocean with its navies, and sow its colonies over the globe; and the first thunder birth of these enormous forces and the flash of the earliest achievements of the new era roll and glitter through the forty years of the reign of Elizabeth with a grandeur which, when once its history is written, will be seen to be among the most sublime phenomena which the earth as yet has witnessed.[7]

Froude provided an enduring vision of the inside-out empire congenial to later ages of imperial introversion and isolationism. It implied that the British Empire was distinct from the English state but still an extension of the English nation; that it was a product of westward 'expansion' in a straight line across the Atlantic, from England via Ireland to the American colonies; and that it was defined against Europe and the other European empires.

If part of an empire's ideology is getting its history wrong, then this idea of empire was exemplary in its errors. The Tudor idea of empire was in fact a product and extension of Tudor state-formation.[8] Its matrix was the triangular set of relationships among England, Scotland and Ireland. It was also what post-colonial theorists would call a 'derivative discourse' that was inconceivable without contemporary European contexts and comparisons.[9] It could hardly have been anything other than derivative. The language of empire was common to all claims to authority, sovereignty and territory in early modern Europe and all

---

[6] David Armitage, *The Ideological Origins of the British Empire* (Cambridge, 2000).

[7] [J. A. Froude], 'England's Forgotten Worthies', *Westminster Review*, new series, 2, 1 (1852), 22.

[8] Michael J. Braddick, *State Formation in Early Modern England, c. 1550–1700* (Cambridge, 2000).

[9] Partha Chatterjee, *Nationalist Thought and the Colonial World: A Derivative Discourse* (Minneapolis, 1993).

such claims derived ultimately from Roman conceptions of *imperium*.[10] Three such conceptions had been derived from the Roman legacy by the late sixteenth century. In the first, empire meant simply authority or sovereignty. In the second, it meant the territory over which such authority or sovereignty was claimed. In the third, it meant rule over many dominions, either descriptively, as a term denoting 'multiple' or 'composite' monarchy, or evaluatively, as a shorthand for domineering 'universal' monarchy.[11] Each of these three conceptions had its own peculiar afterlife in Elizabethan England.

The idea of empire as sovereignty was the very foundation of the Tudor state's claim to independent authority. It derived from the famous claim, made in the preamble to the 1533 Act in Restraint of Appeals, that 'this realm of England is an empire'. The claim to recognise no superior authority necessarily possessed a territorial dimension. The Henrician acts of 1536 and 1543 incorporating Wales into the Tudor state and the Irish parliament's declaration of Henry VIII's kingship (rather than simply lordship) over Ireland in 1541 confirmed this. Tudor England after the Reformation had become, in short order, a composite monarchy (by incorporating Wales) and a multiple kingdom (by the addition of the crown of Ireland to Henry's regal appurtenances). In retrospect, it can be seen that these developments made possible the first claims to an 'empire of Great Britain' which were made by propagandists for English dominion over Scotland in the 1540s on behalf of Henry VIII and then on behalf of his son, Edward VI. Indeed, the language both of 'British' empire and of 'colonies' as the cultural expression of that empire both arose first in the context of Anglo-Scottish relations and hence on the island of Great Britain, not in Ireland, the Caribbean or North America.[12] Elizabeth would not follow her father or her brother's regents in making such aggressive claims to suzerainty over Scotland though there were those, like John Dee and Edmund Spenser, who would make such claims on her behalf from the 1570s to the 1590s. The expansion of Elizabethan England to incorporate Scotland would only be achieved after her death and by a Scottish king, James VI, when he acquired the crowns of England and Ireland by his accession to the English throne as James I in 1603.

That it should have been a Scottish king who created the kingdom of Great Britain was less ironic than inevitable. After all, it had been the fifteenth-century Stewart monarchy in Scotland rather than the

---

[10] J. S. Richardson, '*Imperium Romanum:* Empire and the Languages of Power', *Journal of Roman Studies*, 81 (1991), 1–9.

[11] Anthony Pagden, *Lords of All the World: Ideologies of Empire in Spain, Britain and France c. 1500 – c. 1800* (New Haven, 1995), 12–17.

[12] David Armitage, 'Making the Empire British: Scotland in the Atlantic World, 1542–1707', *Past and Present*, 155 (1997), 39–41.

sixteenth-century Tudor monarchy in England that had first pioneered the language of empire in Britain.[13] Henry VIII's assertion that his realm was an empire looks distinctly belated when compared to the claim made on behalf of James III of Scotland, more than half a century earlier in 1469, that he possessed 'ful Jurisdictioune and fre Impire' within his realm.[14] As later in England, so in Scotland did an abstract assertion of jurisdictional independence rapidly become the basis of a set of territorial claims, in James III's case to the Orkneys and the Shetlands, to land in France and, later, to the Western Isles of Scotland. These Scottish appeals to the language of empire revealed, perhaps even more clearly than later English usage, that this was a pan-European discourse rather than an autochthonous product of Britain. Their origins lay in a French legal discourse of sovereignty which, in turn, derived from the Europe-wide revival of Roman civil law since the twelfth century.[15] There was nothing peculiarly Scottish about the particular language in which this particular Scottish declaration of independence was couched. This was, of course, even more strikingly true of the later English language of empire deployed in defence of the Tudor church and state.

The Elizabethan idea of empire was belated and unelaborated, even in comparison with the Scottish idea of empire, which had found expression in law and statute, coinage and architecture, decades before any similar manifestations in England.[16] The backwardness and derivativeness of the Elizabethan imperial idea appear even more starkly when it is compared with continental European conceptions. The classic treatment of those conceptions and their relationship with Elizabethan imperial imagery and ideology remains Frances Yates's *Astraea: The Imperial Theme in the Sixteenth Century* (1975). Despite all her extraordinary efforts to show how various and fertile that relationship was, Yates offered little evidence that the traffic from England to the Continent was in any way comparable to that travelling from the Continent to England. Indeed, she acknowledged that, though the 'imperial theme' in Elizabethan England was an index of nascent nationalism, it was nonetheless forged almost entirely from alien ancient and modern materials, from Virgil to Giordano Bruno. She took

[13] Roger A. Mason, 'This Realm of Scotland Is an Empire? Imperial Ideas and Iconography in Early Renaissance Scotland', in *Church, Chronicle and Learning in Medieval and Early Renaissance Scotland: Essays Presented to Donald Watt*, ed. Barbara E. Crawford (Edinburgh, 1999), 77–95.

[14] *Acts of the Parliaments of Scotland*, ed. Thomas Thomson and Cosmo Innes (12 vols., Edinburgh, 1814–75), I, 95.

[15] Jacques Krynen, *L'empire du roi: idées et croyances politiques en France, XIIIe–Xve siècle* (Paris, 1993), 388–414.

[16] Roger A. Mason, *'Regnum et Imperium:* Humanism and the Political Culture of Early Renaissance Scotland', in Roger A. Mason, *Kingship and Commonweal: Political Thought in Renaissance and Reformation Scotland* (East Linton, 1998), 126–38.

this fact to be 'a measure of the sense of isolation which had at all costs to find a symbol strong enough to provide a feeling of spiritual security in the face of the break with the rest of Christendom', especially after the papal excommunication of Elizabeth in 1570.[17]

Yates famously found the key to the Elizabethan imperial theme in the reformist apocalypticism of Virgil's Fourth *Eclogue*, with its vision of the Virgin returning to the earth along with the age of gold (*iam redit et Virgo, redeunt Saturnia regna*).[18] Perhaps a better motto, because one more frequently cited by contemporaries, would have been a line from Virgil's First *Eclogue* describing the isolated Britons (*toto divisos orbe Britannos*): as Ben Jonson translated it in 1604, 'this empire is a world divided from the world'.[19] English writers quoted Virgil's words in self-congratulation at their autonomy and indifference to territorial expansion, and at their distance from the bloody struggles for land and dominion being fought in continental Europe. Until the late 1570s and early 1580s, this reinforced an idea of empire that was conservative, backward-looking and fundamentally defensive rather than expansive. This was a conception of a British Empire derived from the legacy of the British king Brutus, dangerous in its effects on Britons (and others) and destined for inglorious collapse: in a nutshell, 'Brutish', nasty and short.

Any reference to a British Empire evoked an anglocentric vision derived from the anti-Celtic ethnography of Geoffrey of Monmouth in the twelfth century. This had provided the historical basis for English claims over Scotland in the 1540s and underpinned the Elizabethan ideas of empire propagated by the Welsh antiquarian Humphrey Llwyd and the Welsh 'wizard' John Dee in the 1570s and 1580s.[20] Dee envisaged 'this incomparable Brytish Empire' as reaching to the north-east coast of America and the coasts of France and Germany and derived these expansive claims from the exploits of King Arthur and the Welsh Prince Madoc, who had allegedly discovered America four centuries before Columbus.[21]

---

[17] Frances Yates, 'Queen Elizabeth I as Astraea', in Frances Yates, *Astraea: The Imperial Theme in the Sixteenth Century* (1975), 59.

[18] Virgil, *Eclogues*, IV. 6; Yates, 'Queen Elizabeth I as Astraea,' 33–8.

[19] Virgil, *Eclogues*, I. 66; Ben Jonson, *Part of the the King's Entertainment in Passing to his Coronation* (1604), in *Ben Jonson*, ed. C. H. Herford, Percy Simpson and Evelyn Simpson (11 vols., Oxford, 1925–52), VII, 84; Graham Parry, *The Golden Age Restor'd: The Culture of the Stuart Court, 1603–42* (Manchester, 1981), 4.

[20] Bruce Ward Henry, 'John Dee, Humphrey Llwyd, and the Name "British Empire"', *Huntington Library Quarterly*, 35 (1972), 189–90.

[21] John Dee, *General and Rare Memorials Pertayning to the Perfect Arte of Navigation* (1577), 8; Dee, 'ΘΑΛΛΑΤΟΚΡΑΤΙΑ ΒΡΕΤΤΑΝΙΚΗ' (8 Sept. 1597), British Library, Harleian MS 249, fos. 95–105; Ken MacMillan, 'Discourses on History, Geography, and Law: John Dee and the Limits of the British Empire, 1576–80,' *Canadian Journal of History*, 36 (2001), 1–25.

Such visions, despite being grounded on a firm conception of first discovery and defended with legal-humanist justifications from history, far outran the ambitions of Elizabeth or most of her councillors. As David Hume would point out in his mid-eighteenth-century *History of England*, Elizabeth herself 'had done little more than give a name to the continent of Virginia'.[22] Elizabethan panegyric, whether in poetry, prose or paint, portrayed the queen as '*Elizabeth*, great Empresse of the world,/ *Britanias Atlas*, Star of *Englands* globe' (in the words of the poet George Peele) or addressed her as 'the most High, Mighty and Magnificent Empress... Elizabeth by the Grace of God, Queen of England, France and Ireland, and of Virginia' (as Edmund Spenser put it in the dedication to his *Faerie Queene* in 1596).[23] However, such panegyrics were expressed upwards, as flattery, rather than downwards, as propaganda.[24]

There is no evidence that the queen possessed any such exalted ideas of her own imperial status. At least one of her subjects, when interrogated by the Inquisition in Lima, argued that it was the queen herself who discouraged English expansion in the Americas: 'Witness understands that if the Queen should die, many will come and pass through the Strait [of Magellan] and found settlements. The Queen is the cause that no one comes.'[25] The contrast here with the comprehensive apocalyptic imperial vision of her adversary Philip II of Spain is especially striking.[26] The few fragments of evidence we do have suggest that Elizabeth's own idea of empire was indeed tinged with the sense of isolation, backwardness and anxiety felt by all but the most fulsomely flattering of her subjects. For example, her reaction upon being presented with the Huguenot cartographer Emery Molyneux's terrestrial globe in 1592 was reported as follows:

> she was pleased to descant, *The whole earth, a present for a Prince; but with the Spanish King's leave*, she said, alluding to his Emblem, a Spanish Genet, in speed upon the Globe of

[22] David Hume, *The History of England* (1762), ed. William B. Todd (6 vols., Indianapolis, 1983), v, 147.

[23] George Peele, *Polyhymnia* (1590), sig. [A2]v; Edmund Spenser, *The Faerie Queene* (1596), sig. [A1]v.

[24] Sydney Anglo, *Images of Tudor Kingship* (1992), 127–8.

[25] 'Thomas Xerores, shipmaster', in 'The Declarations that Were Made by Captain John Oxenham and Other Englishmen... concerning the Exploration of the Strait of Magellan' (20 Feb. 1579/80), in *New Light on Drake: A Collection of Documents relating to his Voyage of Circumnavigation, 1577–1580*, ed. Zelia Nuttall (Hakluyt Society, second series, XXXIV, 1914), 11.

[26] Geoffrey Parker, *The World Is Not Enough: The Imperial Vision of Philip II of Spain, Charles Edmondson Historical Lectures*, 22 (Waco, TX, 2001); Parker, 'The Place of Tudor England in the Messianic Vision of Philip II of Spain', *Transactions of the Royal Historical Society*, sixth series, 12 (2002), 167–221.

the Earth, his fore-feet over-reaching, with this Motto, *Non sufficit orbis* [the world is not enough].[27]

Her reaction indicated as much embattlement as defiance, as well as a reasonable assessment of England's chances of competing for geopolitical dominance with the Spanish Habsburgs. Similarly, her prayer on the sailing of the English expedition to the Azores in July 1597 expressed a more positive conception of England's aims: 'our just cause, not founded on pride's motion nor begun on malice-stock but, as Thou best knowest to whom naught is hid, grounded on just defence from wrongs, hate and bloody desire of conquest'.[28] Such moral self-congratulation was, of course, something of a cheap luxury for a state without the resources to engage in large-scale conquest (as it had discovered repeatedly in Ireland). It was also a sign of a deep-rooted anxiety about the costs of conquest derived from classical sources such as Livy, Tacitus and Sallust, familiar to a well-trained humanist like Elizabeth. Such sources warned against the moral dangers of corruption arising from conquest and expansion, as when Robert Sidney ominously annotated his copy of Tacitus with a comment on 'the servitu[d]e under the Ro[mans]' experienced by the tribes of Britain.[29]

Such anxiety about the costs of empire, when combined with a lack of firm leadership from the top, left the English without any substantial or distinctive conception of empire for most, if not all, of Elizabeth's reign. Richard Hakluyt noted in 1582 that, 'since the first discoverie of America . . . after so great conquests and plantings of the Spaniardes and Portingales there . . . wee of England could never have the grace to set fast footing in such fertill and temperate places, as are left as yet unpossessed by them'.[30] His life's work would be to collect the records of English overseas activity and, just as importantly, to translate the documents of other European enterprises, in order to inspire his countrymen to better efforts at overcoming their reluctance and backwardness. The instruments of that overcoming would mostly be imports from abroad: Huguenot pilots; Spanish navigational aids; Dutch, Flemish and German mapmakers, printers, engravers and painters.[31] As one economic promoter stated of the

---

[27] William Sanderson, *An Answer to a Scurrilous Pamphlet* (1656), sig. [A3]v; Anna Maria Crino and Helen Wallis, 'New Research on the Molyneux Globes', *Der Globusfreund*, 35 (1987), 14.

[28] Elizabeth I, *Collected Works*, ed. Leah S. Marcus, Janel Mueller and Mary Beth Rose (Chicago, 2000), 426.

[29] Andrew Fitzmaurice, *Humanism and America: An Intellectual History of English Colonisation, 1516–1625* (Cambridge, 2003); *C. Cornelii Taciti Opera*, ed. Justus Lipsius (Antwerp, 1585), 234–5, British Library shelfmark C. 142. e. 13 (annotation by Robert Sidney).

[30] Richard Hakluyt, *Divers Voyages Touching the Discoverie of America* (1582), sig. ¶[1]r.

[31] Helen Wallis, 'Émigré Map-Makers in the Late 16th Century and the Protestant New World', *Proceedings of the Huguenot Society of London*, 24 (1985), 210–20; Sarah Tyacke, *Before*

English in 1577, 'We ought to favor the Strangers from whom we learned so grete benefits... because we are not so good devisers as followers of others'.[32] Such a judgement would fit equally well the English overseas project as it would the cloth industry to which he was referring.

Yet even with the forceful manipulation and exploitation of continental European resources, the Elizabethan age ended with an empire nowhere, its monuments the wrecked hopes of lost colonies scattered along the western Atlantic littoral from Kodlunarn Island in the Arctic circle to Ralegh's Guiana in the tropics.[33] The geographer and bishop George Abbot's epitaph for Virginia in 1599 could have been applied just as readily to any of these failed enterprises: 'this voyage beeing enterprised on the charge of private men: and not thorowly beeing followed by the state: the possession of this *Virginia* is nowe discontinued, and the country is at present left to the old inhabitants'.[34] Any risk assessment of English prospects in 1603 would surely have found those prospects most promising in the Mediterranean, Asia and the East Indies, not in the Atlantic, America or the West Indies. Yet, as such an assessment would also have shown, by 1603 it was no longer sufficient to consider the origins of England's empire outside their archipelagic, European and global contexts. In this respect, Braudel and Schmitt were correct: England was never an island, entire of itself.

[32] John Leake, quoted in Anthony Wells-Cole, *Art and Decoration in Elizabeth and Jacobean England: The Influence of Continental Prints, 1558–1625* (New Haven, 1997), 3.

[33] Jeffrey Knapp, *An Empire Nowhere: England, America, and Literature from Utopia to The Tempest* (Berkeley, 1992); Joyce E. Chaplin, *Subject Matter: Technology, the Body, and Science on the Anglo-American Frontier, 1500–1676* (Cambridge, MA, 2001), 46–59; *English and Irish Settlement on the River Amazon, 1550–1640*, ed. Joyce Lorimer (Hakluyt Society, second series, CLXXI, 1989).

[34] George Abbot, *A Briefe Description of the Whole World* (1599), sig. [D8]v.

Transactions of the RHS 14 (2004), pp. 279–93 © 2004 Royal Historical Society
DOI: 10.1017/S0080440104000106   Printed in the United Kingdom

SCOTLAND, ELIZABETHAN ENGLAND
AND THE IDEA OF BRITAIN
By Roger A. Mason

ABSTRACT. This paper explores aspects of Anglo-Scottish relations in Elizabeth's
reign with particular emphasis on the idea of dynastic union and the creation of a
Protestant British kingdom. It begins by examining the legacy of pre-Elizabethan
ideas of Britain and the extent to which Elizabeth and her government sought to
realise the vision of a Protestant and imperial British kingdom first articulated in the
late 1540s. It then focuses on the issues arising from the deposition of Mary Queen
of Scots and her long captivity in England. The dynastic implications of Mary's
execution in 1587 are highlighted and it is argued that Elizabeth's policy towards
James VI and Scotland betrays little or no interest in developing a truly British
agenda.

It is probably not in the best of taste, on an occasion such as this, to
introduce to the proceedings such an unwelcome guest as Mary Queen
of Scots. Yet no commemoration of Elizabeth and Elizabethan England
would be complete without the haunting spectre of the Tudor queen's
cousin, dynastic rival and near-nemesis. Certainly no consideration of
contemporary Anglo-Scottish relations and the idea of a united British
kingdom can afford to ignore her. For nearly three decades, two-thirds of
Elizabeth's forty-five-year reign, Mary Stewart not only cast a threatening
shadow over the Elizabethan regime but also hugely complicated English
attitudes to Scotland and Scottish attitudes to England. Mary's execution
on 8 February 1587, despite the history of indecision that lay behind it,
proved in the end a decisive moment in the dynastic history of both
England and Scotland, opening the way for the succession of James VI
to the English throne and the creation in 1603 of an imperial British
monarchy. What follows is largely concerned with Scottish attitudes to
the Elizabethan regime and Elizabethan attitudes to Mary, James and the
future of Britain. First, however, it is as well to consider some of the
background to the issue of Anglo-Scottish union and the ideological
antecedents of the idea of Britain itself.[1]

---

[1] The paper thus revisits themes first explored in R. A. Mason, 'The Scottish Reformation
and the Origins of Anglo-British Imperialism', in *Scots and Britons: Scottish Political Thought and
the Union of 1603*, ed. R. A. Mason (Cambridge, 1994), 161–86, reprinted in R. A. Mason,

From a Scottish and, signally, a British perspective, 1603 is a date whose resonances are profound and far-reaching. So profound and far-reaching, indeed, that it seems astonishing that, in 2003, we should be memorialising Elizabethan England rather than celebrating Jacobean Britain. To be sure, the emphasis of this conference is on Elizabeth and the wider world, or at any rate the expansion of England, and there is clearly a sense in which 1603 was – and perhaps still is – viewed simply as the absorption of Scotland into an expanding English imperial system.[2] But there are obvious problems with such a view. After all, leaving the shambles of Ireland aside, Elizabethan expansionism amounted to little more than a failed North American colony and some (admittedly spectacular) piracy and free enterprise overseas trade and exploration. In fact, Elizabeth's greatest contribution to the expansion of England was to die, unmarried and childless. It was the Stewart succession that led to a substantial extension of the English (or, as James insisted, British) crown's dominions, and it was in the reigns of James VI and I and his successors that the real foundations of overseas empire were laid.[3] In so far as England expanded at all in Elizabeth's reign, it was not territorially, but in terms of self-knowledge and awareness. The last decades of the sixteenth century witnessed a remarkable cultural renaissance that, *inter alia*, saw the creation and enrichment of multiple, over-lapping and often contradictory English religious, political and legal identities.[4] There is no little irony in the fact that the final realisation of England's long-looked-for hegemony over mainland Britain was brought about by the accession of a Scottish king whose fanciful notions of a new British monarchy threatened actually to unEnglish the English. It is perhaps not surprising that the myth of an Elizabethan golden age – a quintessentially *English* golden age – developed so quickly and proved so resilient.[5] In 1603, English self-perceptions were rudely challenged, first, by the accession of a Scot to the throne of England, and, second, by the deliberate promotion of ideas

---

Kingship and the Commonweal: Political Thought in Renaissance and Reformation Scotland (East Linton, 1998), 242–69.

[2] A. L. Rowse's *The Expansion of Elizabethan England* (1955), from which this conference derived its title, is as much concerned with the expansion of Elizabethan civilisation into England's Celtic fringes – 'in various stages of deliquescence, decay and regeneration' (p. 3) – as it is with overseas expansion. In Rowse's view, however, the latter was clearly an extension of the former.

[3] See generally *The Oxford History of the British Empire*, I: *The Origins of Empire*, ed. N. Canny (Oxford, 1998).

[4] See A. L. Rowse, *The England of Elizabeth* (1951), ch. 2: 'The Elizabethan Discovery of England'; and for a more recent (and less fervently patriotic) treatment, R. Helgerson, *Forms of Nationhood: The Elizabethan Writing of England* (Chicago and London, 1992).

[5] The literature on this theme is reviewed and extended in *The Myth of Elizabeth*, ed. S. Doran and T. S. Freeman (Basingstoke, 2003).

of Britain that did not necessarily sit comfortably with how the English viewed themselves and their role in the world.[6]

Needless to say, 1603 confronted the Scots too with challenges to their self-perceptions and esteem. The union of the crowns brought them into an uncomfortably close relationship with the 'auld enemy', while James VI and I's British agenda had implications for the northern kingdom that were, if anything, even more threatening to Scotland's historic identity than they were to England's. Yet the Scots were perhaps better prepared to meet these challenges. They had experience enough of being, as it were, in bed with an elephant; and, if the first half of the sixteenth century had taught them anything new about their relationship with England, it was that when the elephant got its act together, as it did briefly in the 'Rough Wooing' of the 1540s, its superior weight could be brought to bear on Scotland with devastating effect.[7] Neither Henry VIII nor Protector Somerset was able to bring the Scots to heel; nevertheless, they had made England's superiority in terms of manpower and money abundantly clear. At the same time, they had revitalised claims to feudal superiority over the Scottish kingdom – claims that relegated the Scottish crown to a mere dependency of its English counterpart – that the Scots had had to contend with for centuries. Indeed, it was precisely the belief that they owed no allegiance to the English crown – that they were not in any sense English – that lay at the heart of the Scots sense of themselves as Scots.[8] Part of the success of the Stewart dynasty – and, whatever their manifold individual inadequacies, as a dynasty the Stewarts were phenomenonally successful – lay in their willingness to identify themselves as the upholders and defenders of Scottish autonomy in the face of English aggression. It was no accident that a succession of Stewart monarchs, from James III to James V, sought to project an image of themselves as emperors within their own kingdom, wielding supreme jurisdiction within the bounds of their realm and, crucially, recognising the supremacy of no external jurisdiction.[9] When James IV married Margaret Tudor in 1503, he did so as an imperial monarch whose status, lineage and legitimacy – at least

[6] B. Galloway, *The Union of England and Scotland, 1603–1608* (Edinburgh, 1986); B. Levack, *The Formation of the British State: England, Scotland and the Union, 1603–1707* (Oxford, 1987); J. Wormald, 'James VI, James I and the Identity of Britain', in *The British Problem, c. 1534–1707: State Formation in the Atlantic Archipelago*, ed. B. Bradshaw and J. Morrill (Basingstoke, 1996), 148–71; A. I. Macinnes, 'Regal Union for Britain, 1603–38', in *The New British History: Founding a Modern State, 1603–1715*, ed. G. Burgess (London and New York, 1999), 33–64.

[7] M. Merriman, *The Rough Wooings: Mary Queen of Scots, 1542–1551* (East Linton, 2000).

[8] R. A. Mason, 'Scotching the Brut: Politics, History and National Myth in Sixteenth-Century Britain', in *Scotland and England, 1286–1815*, ed. R. A. Mason (Edinburgh, 1987), 60–84; Mason, *Kingship and the Commonweal*, 78–103.

[9] R. A. Mason, 'This Realm of Scotland Is an Empire? Imperial Ideas and Iconography in Early Renaissance Scotland', in *Church, Chronicle and Learning in Medieval and Early Renaissance Scotland*, ed. B. E. Crawford (Edinburgh, 1999), 73–91.

in his own estimation – far exceeded that of his upstart and usurping father-in-law. Stewart monarchs had a bad habit of over-estimating their power and authority; but historians must be wary of under-estimating their ambition. In James's eyes, in marrying Margaret Tudor he was doing Henry VII a favour (not vice versa), lending the Tudor monarchy further legitimacy while at the same time positioning the Stewart dynasty in the English succession. James IV might well have agreed with Henry VII's alleged comment on the possibility of dynastic union that the greater would draw the lesser, but he would have seen such a union as an extension of the Stewart not the Tudor *imperium*.[10]

But the imperial pretensions of the Scottish monarchy reached their high point, not under James IV, but in the latter half of the 1530s, in the reign of his son and successor, James V.[11] No doubt this was partly inspired by Henry VIII's break with Rome and the ringing assertion that 'this realm of England is an empire' on which Henrician caesaropapalism was founded. James V was as attracted as his uncle by the potential dividends to be derived from pursuing imperial ideas to their logical conclusion and asserting royal supremacy over the church. However, James was able to have his cake and eat it – at least temporarily. That is, he gained massive financial concessions from the papacy without having to break with Rome, while at the same time pulling off a stunning dynastic coup by marrying a Valois princess, thus simultaneously reaffirming both Scotland's 'auld alliance' with France and its independence of England. It was in this context, in the afterglow of a lengthy sojourn at the French court of Francis I, that James's almost obsessive interest in the iconography of empire flourished most luxuriantly. That the Stewart monarchy was an imperial monarchy – that the realm of Scotland was an empire – was proclaimed as never before in royal architecture, on royal seals, on the coinage and in the definitive reconstruction of the Scottish crown itself as an arched or closed imperial one. Such dizzying self-confidence was

---

[10] N. Macdougall, *James IV* (Edinburgh, 1989), 248ff. It is worth noting that, in October 1509, shortly after Henry VIII's accession to the English throne, Margaret Tudor bore James IV a son who was baptised Arthur – presumably a conscious recollection of the new English king's deceased elder brother, but surely also indicative of the Stewart king's British ambitions. The baby died within a year, but significantly James V was also to baptise his second legitimate male heir, Arthur, in April 1541 (he died the same month). *Handbook of British Chronology*, ed. E. B. Fryde *et al.*, 3rd edn (1986), 60–1.

[11] For what follows, see Mason, 'This Realm of Scotland Is an Empire?'. James V's reign is undergoing major scholarly revision and the views presented in standard works such as G. Donaldson, *Scotland: James V – James VII* (Edinburgh, 1965), ch. 4, are now largely untenable. See rather J. Cameron, *James V: The Personal Rule, 1528–42* (East Linton, 1998); C. Edington, *Court and Culture in Renaissance Scotland: Sir David Lindsay of the Mount* (Amherst, 1994); *Stewart Style, 1513–42: Essays on the Court of James V*, ed. J. H. Williams (East Linton, 1996); and A. Thomas, 'Renaissance Culture at the Court of James V' (Ph.D. thesis, Edinburgh University, 1997).

perhaps misplaced. Yet the death of James V, aged barely thirty, was no more the result of hubris than it was of a broken royal will or a broken royal heart. It was neither military defeat at the hands of the English at Solway Moss in November 1542 nor the death of his two legitimate male heirs the previous year that killed the young king. Much more prosaically, it was plague or cholera that took his life on 14 December 1542, leaving the Stewart dynasty hanging by the frail thread of his sole legitimate heir, Mary, born less than a week before.[12]

It hardly needs saying that, while the succession of an infant female precipitated a major and enduring crisis for the Stewart dynasty and the Scottish kingdom, it presented Henry VIII with an unexpected opportunity to solve England's Scottish 'problem' once and for all. The betrothal of the young Queen of Scots to his own son and heir, Prince Edward, promised to effect a dynastic union that would extend Tudor hegemony throughout the British mainland, while allowing Henry to pursue the far more interesting prospect of war with France.[13] Yet Henry's aggressive pursuit of his objectives served only to alienate even those Scots who were sympathetic to Anglo-Scottish friendship and unity. It is hard now to tell how strong the Scottish unionist lobby actually was, but the case for dynastic union had been powerfully articulated in 1521 by John Mair or Major of Haddington, best known as a highly influential Parisian theologian and philosopher, but also the author of a Latin *History of Greater Britain* that has the distinction of being the first printed work in which the case for Anglo-Scottish union was set out at any length.[14] Mair duly emphasised the geographical logic, as well as the commonality of language and custom, that made the existence of two separate kingdoms within one island seem so anomalous. At the same time, however, he argued that any union between them must be based on parity of status and esteem. Whatever the inequalities of wealth, population and resources, a union founded on English assumptions of feudal and cultural superiority would prove unacceptable to Scots who, like Mair himself, were intensely proud of their ancestors' successful struggle to maintain the Scottish kingdom's independence of England. To some extent, these preoccupations surface in the treaties of Greenwich of 1543 through which Henry's desire for union appeared on the point of being realised. The reiterated concern to preserve the Scottish kingdom's ancient laws and liberties may owe more to fear of intensive English government and heavy

---

[12] Cameron, *James V*, 324–5.

[13] D. M. Head, 'Henry VIII's Scottish Policy: A Reassessment', *Scottish Historical Review*, 61 (1982), 1–24; Merriman, *Rough Wooings*, esp. ch. 5.

[14] John Major, *A History of Greater Britain as well England as Scotland*, ed. and trans. A. Constable (Scottish History Society, X, 1892). For commentary, see Mason, *Kingship and the Commonweal*, ch. 2.

English taxation than to the theorising of John Mair. Nonetheless, the treaties looked forward to a union of the crowns, but not to a union of the kingdoms.[15]

In any event, the treaties proved a dead letter – neither side had any confidence in the other – and Scottish suspicions that Henry VIII was intent on subjugating their kingdom seemed to be amply confirmed by the brutal military campaigns that ensued and that left a trail of death and destruction throughout southern Scotland. The English crown's claim to feudal superiority over Scotland was once again invoked and the Scots reacted predictably, branding the English as heretic spawn of the devil, and reasserting the historic and continuing autonomy of their kingdom.[16] It was to all intents and purposes a replay of the Scottish resistance to Edward I, the only ideological difference – though a crucially important one – being the introduction of a potentially explosive religious dimension to the conflict. Oddly, this was not an issue that seemed to concern Henry VIII. Indeed, he seems never even to have recast his belief in English feudal superiority over Scotland in the imperial language that would have lent real weight and substance to the belief that, in breaking free of Rome, England had recovered its imperial status.[17] It was only following Henry's death in 1547, and the accession of Edward VI under the protection of the duke of Somerset, that religion became central to England's Scottish policy, and that the war effort was justified in terms of a providential opportunity to create an explicitly British kingdom that was both Protestant and imperial. Paradoxically, not only were Scots at the forefront of the propaganda campaign that first popularised the idea of a Protestant Britain, but in their enthusiasm for it they were prepared to jettison all the elaborate historical lore that had been developed to underpin Scottish freedom from English overlordship. Instead, they argued that from the earliest times the Scottish realm had been part of a greater English *imperium* – albeit an *imperium* that was more accurately named Britain or even Great Britain – and that the marriage of Mary Stewart to Edward Tudor heralded, not the creation, but the re-creation of an ancient British empire.[18] In the 1530s the alleged British origins of the

[15] Merriman, *Rough Wooings*, 118–21.

[16] The English claim had been fully set out on Henry VIII's behalf just prior to James V's death in *A Declaration, Conteynyng the Iust Causes and Consyderations of this Present Warre with the Scottis, wherin alsoo Appereth the Trew & Right Title that the Kinges Most Royall Maiesty Hath to the Souerayntue of Scotlande* (1542), reprinted in *The Complaynt of Scotlande*, ed. J. A. H. Murray (Early English Text Society, 1872), 191–206.

[17] For this and what follows, see Mason, *Kingship and the Commonweal*, 251–61; D. Armitage, *The Ideological Origins of the British Empire* (Cambridge, 2000), ch. 2.

[18] See in particular James Henrisoun (or Harryson), *An Exhortacion to the Scottes to Conforme Themselves to the Honourable, Expedient & Godly Union betweene the Realmes of England & Scotland* (1547), reprinted in *Complaynt of Scotlande*, ed. Murray, 207–36.

Emperor Constantine had been invoked to justify the claim that the realm of England was an empire. By the late 1540s, the first Christian emperor had become a symbolic precedent for an empire that was explicitly British – or, perhaps more accurately, Anglo-British – as well as emphatically Protestant.

Although the 'Edwardian Moment' proved fleeting enough, the Constantinian vision of a Protestant and imperial British kingdom survived it and would be reinvigorated, albeit in somewhat more muted form, in the early years of Elizabeth's reign.[19] Meanwhile, of course, in desperation the Scots entered into a dynastic alliance with France that effectively ceded to the Valois dynasty the sovereignty over their kingdom that they had consistently denied the Tudors,[20] while in England the accession of Mary and her marriage to Philip II promised a return to the Catholic fold under Habsburg dominance. Rather than being the seat of an impregnable Protestant and imperial monarchy, Britain in the 1550s looked set to be balkanised by Catholic superpowers with their own imperial agendas. In the event, as France and Spain fought each other to a standstill, Mary Tudor died in 1558 and the Valois king, Henry II, was accidentally killed the following year in a tournament held to celebrate the outbreak of peace with Spain. Just as Elizabeth now found herself queen of England, able to reassert the crown's imperial authority and impose a moderately Protestant religious settlement, so Mary Stewart suddenly found herself queen of France as well as Scotland, controlled by a Guise family network intent on pressing her Catholic claim to the English throne. In such a context, as discontent with French Catholic rule in Scotland flared into open rebellion, there was renewed hope for Protestantism throughout Britain.[21]

To be sure, in 1559, most English politicians were much more exercised by the loss of Calais to the French than they were by the ever more desperate pleas for assistance emanating from the north. Yet there were those, like Elizabeth's secretary, William Cecil, who were not only sympathetic to the Edwardian vision of a Protestant and imperial Britain – Cecil had actually accompanied Somerset on his later Scottish campaigns – but who saw amity and ultimately union with Scotland

[19] On the 'Edwardian Moment', and the subsequent influence of these ideas, see A. H. Williamson, *Scottish National Consciousness in the Age of James VI* (Edinburgh, 1979), ch. 1.

[20] P. Ritchie, *Mary of Guise in Scotland, 1548–1560: A Political Career* (East Linton, 2002), esp. chs. 1–2, on the significance of the 'protectoral' alliance established by the treaty of Haddington in 1548.

[21] For a brief recent analysis of the British dimension of the Scottish Reformation, see C. Kellar, *Scotland, England and the Reformation, 1534–1561* (Oxford, 2003), esp. ch. 6; see also J. E. A. Dawson, *The Politics of Religion in the Age of Mary Queen of Scots: The Earl of Argyll and the Struggle for Britain and Ireland* (Cambridge, 2002), ch. 3.

as fundamental to England's long-term security.[22] English foreign policy would thus be orientated away from the chimera of French conquests and concentrate instead on securing England's hegemony in Britain and Ireland. As in the late 1540s, moreover, strategic pragmatism might be couched in the language of Protestant apocalypticism. For what was unfolding in 1559–60 was surely the workings of divine providence, a God-given opportunity to effect the peaceful conjunction of the two realms that had been so foolishly spurned in the 1540s and that had reaped the divine retribution of the 1550s. Elizabeth, in short, might yet emerge in the 1560s as a British as well as an English Constantine. Yet, however urgent, providential and apocalyptic its significance, such a vision of a Protestant and imperial Britain was beset by problems that would continue to dog the cause of Anglo-Scottish union throughout the Elizabethan period and beyond. First, it was by no means clear in 1559–60 that Elizabeth was willing or able to play the key role assigned to her. Second, it was based on sweeping aside the claim of Mary Stewart not only to be the legitimate Queen of Scots but also to have a rightful place in the English succession. And third, this essentially Anglocentric vision of Britain's imperial destiny took little or no account of Scottish sensibilities. It is on these issues as they worked themselves out in Elizabeth's reign that the remainder of this paper is focused.

It perhaps hardly needs saying that the idea of Elizabeth acting out the role of a godly British Constantine, delivering the people of Scotland as well as England from the thraldom of popery, proved as spectacular a piece of miscasting as could be imagined. Elizabeth had no sympathy with the kind of apocalyptic scenarios that saw her leading British – or, still worse, European – Protestantism in a final showdown with the antichristian church of Rome. Constantine was a convenient enough means of legitimising royal authority over the English church, but Elizabeth betrayed no interest in extending her imperial remit to encompass her northern neighbour.[23] If she had a long-term Scottish policy, let alone a vision of Britain, it is remarkably hard to discern what it was. Certainly, Cecil was able to cajole her into embarking on what proved to be a decisive intervention on behalf of Scottish Protestantism in 1559–60, but it was reluctant and half-hearted – and was emphatically

    [22] J. E. A. Dawson, 'William Cecil and the British Dimension of Early Elizabethan Foreign Policy', *History*, 74 (1989), 196–216; S. Alford, *The Early Elizabethan Polity: William Cecil and the British Succession Crisis, 1558–1569* (Cambridge, 1998).

    [23] Significantly, the dedication of the 1563 edition of John Foxe's *Acts and Monuments*, in which Elizabeth is closely identified with the Emperor Constantine, is quietly dropped from subsequent editions – a measure of Foxe's own disenchantment with the queen's understanding of the limited nature of her religious role; see further T. S. Freeman, 'Providence and Prescription: The Account of Elizabeth in Foxe's "Book of Martyrs"', in *Myth of Elizabeth*, ed. Doran and Freeman, 27–55.

not born of an ideological commitment to a Protestant and imperial British kingdom. Elizabeth's reluctance is perhaps understandable: cash-strapped and insecure, she had no desire to embroil herself in a war with France such as had undermined and eventually destroyed Protector Somerset. Moreover, deeply conscious of her own sovereign rights, she had an evident distaste for interfering with those of another kingdom and sister queen. Thus Elizabeth remained unmoved by the claim to feudal superiority over Scotland which had so excited her father and which Cecil was not slow to resurrect. In so far as Elizabeth had a Scottish policy – and one is tempted to say that her policy was actually not to have a policy – it was limited to short-term measures, pursued at minimal expense, aimed at defending her own dynastic rights and securing England's northern frontier.

As a result, the hopes harboured by Cecil and at least some of his Scottish allies that Anglo-Scottish amity and union might be secured immediately by setting aside Mary Stewart's claim to the Scottish throne and marrying Elizabeth off to the Hamilton heirs presumptive, was little more than pie in the sky.[24] Elizabeth would have none of it. In any event, the death in December 1560 of Mary Stewart's husband, the French king Francis II, and the Scottish queen's decision to return to her native kingdom, put paid to the fevered marital speculations of the advocates of a Protestant Britain. Whoever else Elizabeth might marry, it would not be Mary. Yet, though dynastic union appeared to have reached an impasse, strenuous efforts continued to be made to find an accommodation between the two queens which would settle the English succession while advancing, or at least not prejudicing, the Protestant British cause. Once again, however, Elizabeth's unwillingness to discuss either the succession or her own marital plans ensured that these tortuous negotiations got nowhere. By July 1565, when Mary took matters into her own hands and married by Catholic rite Henry Stewart, Lord Darnley, heir to the earl of Lennox, grandson of Margaret Tudor and second only to Mary herself in the English succession, the proponents of Protestant union were in despair. Indeed, by the end of the following year, when Mary staged an elaborate Catholic baptism for her son and heir, Charles James, the future James VI and I, it was Britain's Catholic community that had reason to celebrate.[25] However, any hopes of a Catholic succession to the British thrones were quickly dashed by the bizarre and self-destructive acts that led within a matter of months to Mary's imprisonment and enforced abdication. Clearly, Mary's enemies in Scotland were not motivated solely or even primarily by the desire for Anglo-Scottish union. Nonetheless,

[24] Kellar, *Scotland, England and the Reformation*, 197–201.
[25] M. Lynch, 'Queen Mary's Triumph: The Baptismal Celebrations at Stirling in December 1566', *Scottish Historical Review*, 69 (1990), 1–21.

with Mary in prison and her son in the hands of a committed Protestant regent, it was possible once again to think in terms of the amity and ultimately union that were fundamental to the British agenda.[26]

It is perhaps not surprising that such an agenda was no more meaningfully pursued after 1567 than it had been in 1559–60. After all, Elizabeth's understanding of the matter had not substantially altered: she remained no more willing to play the British Constantine than she was to countenance the deposition of a fellow monarch. Mary's escape from prison and flight to England afforded Elizabeth the opportunity of furthering the cause of a united Protestant Britain simply by extinguishing Mary as the main focus of Catholic opposition to it. But while many of her subjects, as well as many Scots, bayed for the deposed queen's blood, Elizabeth refused to satisfy them. So unwilling was she to violate the rights of a fellow sovereign, that she would rather have had Mary restored than executed. The result was the uneasy compromise that saw Mary incarcerated in England while Elizabeth lent unenthusiastic support to the succession of Protestant regents who governed Scotland in the name of James VI. Even the earl of Morton, the most enthusiastically pro-English as well as the longest serving of those regents, was offered only minimal and grudging support – and refused a pension.[27] Elizabeth simply was not interested and the British strategy that had once so excited at least some of her councillors quietly slipped from the agenda. As a result, Morton's fall in 1578 caught the Elizabethan regime almost totally unawares, while the baronial factionalism that characterised the last years of James's minority remained an unfathomable – though occasionally threatening – mystery.

Commenting on this phase of Anglo-Scottish relations, Wallace MacCaffrey once wrote that Elizabeth's 'attitude to Scottish politicians was not very different from that of her later successors towards troublesome tribal neighbours on the fringes of empire'.[28] It is hard to disagree. Elizabeth treated the Scots with a cynical disdain that was born not just of personal prejudice but of assumptions that were deeply rooted in English culture. Just as the claim to English feudal superiority drew inspiration from Geoffrey of Monmouth's twelfth-century *History of the Kings of Britain*, so English attitudes to their neighbours were moulded by the ethnology of his close contemporary, Gerald of Wales.[29] On the cultural spectrum that lay between English civility and Irish barbarism,

---

[26] Alford, *Early Elizabethan Polity*, chs. 6–7; Dawson, *Politics of Religion*, ch. 5.

[27] K. M. Brown, 'The Price of Friendship: The "Well-affected" and English Economic Clientage in Scotland before 1603', in *Scotland and England*, ed. Mason, 139–62, at 144–5.

[28] W. MacCaffrey, *Elizabeth I* (1993), 435.

[29] See, for example, H. Morgan, 'Giraldus Cambrensis and the Tudor Conquest of Ireland', in *Political Ideology in Ireland, 1541–1641*, ed. H. Morgan (Dublin, 1999), 22–44.

the Scots were evidently closer to savagery than they were to civilisation. When, in 1577, William Harrison wrote the *Description of Britain* that prefaced Holinshed's *Chronicles*, he not only drew on the unionist literature of the 'Edwardian Moment' to substantiate the English claim to 'the souereigntie of this Ile', but also pilloried the (admittedly ancient) Scots as uncivilised barbarians 'who used to feed on the buttocks of boies and womens paps, as delicate dishes'.[30] It is fair enough to highlight the development of an Anglo-Scottish Protestant culture that served to promote British integration and unity in the later sixteenth century.[31] Nevertheless, it would be wrong to under-estimate the depth and enduring power of age-old ethnic prejudices. As King James was to discover after 1603, only a radical change of 'hearts and minds' would make possible his vision of a united British kingdom.

Meanwhile, in the early 1580s, James was emerging from a long and tumultuous minority. In August 1582 he was forcibly kidnapped by the Ruthven Raiders, a coalition of Protestant nobles who had seen the meteoric rise of Esmé Stuart, a cousin of Darnley whom James elevated to the dukedom of Lennox, both as a threat to their own power and as a potentially sinister re-grouping of a Catholic, pro-Marian alliance. The following year James made good his escape and, while it is remarkably difficult to determine exactly when his personal rule began, by the mid-1580s he was no longer simply a prisoner of factional interests.[32] In the so-called 'Black Acts' of 1584 he set out a legislative framework that was clearly intended as a reassertion of royal authority over both church and state. Indeed, as the archbishop of St Andrews, Patrick Adamson, made clear in his printed commentary on the acts, James was emperor in his own kingdom, a Scottish Constantine whose writ must run over ecclesiastical as well as civil affairs.[33] As he emerged from his minority, the young Scottish king was intent on reaffirming the imperial status claimed by his Stewart ancestors. At the same time, of course, he was acutely aware of his place in the English succession and intent on ingratiating himself with – or at least not alienating – potential supporters in the Elizabethan regime. For their part, Elizabeth and her councillors were rather slow to respond to James's emergence as a ruler in his own right. It was not so much the appearance on the political scene of an adult,

[30] Raphael Holinshed, *Chronicles of England, Scotland and Ireland* (London, 1807–8), I, pp. 10, 196.

[31] J. E. A. Dawson, 'Anglo-Scottish Protestant Culture and Integration in Sixteenth-Century Britain', in *Conquest and Union: Fashioning a British State, 1485–1725*, ed. S. G. Ellis and S. Barber (London and New York, 1995), 87–114.

[32] See J. Goodare, 'Scottish Politics in the Reign of James VI', in *The Reign of James VI*, ed. J. Goodare and M. Lynch (East Linton, 2000), 32–54.

[33] Patrick Adamson, *A Declaration of the Kings Maiesties Intentioun and Meaning toward the Lait Actis of Parliament* (Edinburgh, 1585); Mason, *Kingship and the Commonweal*, 205–7.

male and independent rival to Elizabeth's authority within Britain that concentrated the English mind. Rather it was the looming threat of war with Spain that led, in July 1586, to the drawing up of an Anglo-Scottish league that, while offering James no explicit recognition of his right as Elizabeth's successor, gave his cause tacit support in the form of an annual pension.[34] However, the real price of accommodation with the Elizabethan regime would only become apparent later that year when James's mother was finally tried and condemned for treason.

As a means of teasing out Scottish attitudes to Elizabeth and Elizabethan England, it is well worth dwelling on the events surrounding the execution of Mary Queen of Scots. Elizabeth's own agonising over the act, and subsequent denial that she was responsible for it, are well known and need not detain us further.[35] Less often remarked upon is the popular Scottish outrage at the deed. James himself, in a famous letter of protest against his mother's trial and sentence, not only reflected with a singular lack of diplomatic tact on Elizabeth's father's nasty habit of beheading his bedfellows, but went on to comment that he hardly dared to go outdoors 'for crieng oute of the whole people; and what ys spoken by them of the quene of England, yt greves me to heare, and yet [I] darre not fynd faulte with yt except I would dethrone myself, so ys whole Scotland incensed with this matter'.[36] James was no doubt exaggerating for effect. It is notable, for example, that when he ordered the Edinburgh ministers to pray for his mother, they 'obstenatlie refusit'.[37] The more radical of the Scots clergy evidently saw no reason to regret the passing of a daughter of Antichrist. Perhaps less predictably, however, the Scottish nobility was almost literally up in arms at what they construed as Mary's unlawful murder. At a convention in May 1587 and again at a parliament summoned in July, they begged James to revenge his mother's murder, vowing to assist with men and money, 'sa lang as ather blude or breath may last'. Whatever their view of Mary as a person, the nobility's pride was deeply hurt by what they saw as England's typically high-handed treatment of their exiled queen. Yet, as Elizabeth and her councillors had calculated, this atavistic response, symptomatic though it was of the deep distrust that lingered between the two kingdoms, proved short-lived. James thanked his nobility for their offer of arms

---

[34] H. G. Stafford, *James VI of Scotland and the Throne of England* (New York and London, 1940), 8–10, 293; J. Goodare, 'James VI's English Subsidy', in *Reign of James VI*, ed. Goodare and Lynch, 110–25.

[35] For a recent treatment, see J. Guy, *'My Heart is My Own': The Life of Mary Queen of Scots* (London and New York, 2004), 479–97.

[36] *King James's Secret: Negotiations between Elizabeth and James VI relating to the Execution of Mary Queen of Scots, from the Warrender Papers*, ed. R. S. Rait and A. I. Dunlop (1927), 60–2.

[37] *The Historie and Life of King James the Sext, 1566–1596*, ed. T. Thomson (Bannatyne Club, XIV, 1825), 225.

and men, but promised only 'to do tharein as tyme and occasioun sould permit'.[38]

Time and occasion, and the looming threat of Spanish invasion, ensured that the Scots never mounted their threatened invasion of England and that James remained true to the 1586 accord with Elizabeth. Like Elizabeth, James no doubt shared the view attributed to his envoy, the master of Gray – a view for which Gray was later banished – that 'the dead don't bite (*mortui non mordent*)'.[39] But neither James nor Elizabeth could openly admit that they had wilfully violated the sanctity of the royal office or tampered with the inviolable principle of indefeasible hereditary right. It was probably easier for James to square his conscience than for Elizabeth. He had had no direct hand in the murky business and, provided Mary's treason left no stain on his own honour and did not jeopardise his own place in the English succession, he had little reason to mourn a mother whom he had never known and whose very existence was a political and dynastic liability. In his *Memoirs*, Sir James Melville of Halhill commented that, on ripe consideration, James decided not to disturb the peace of the English kingdom by attempting to avenge an evil act perpetrated, not by Elizabeth, but by her misguided councillors. Instead, Melville added astutely, because Elizabeth was 'of good years and not like to live long', James might as well bide his time and wreak vengeance once he had come into his rightful inheritance.[40] In the summer of 1587, James turned twenty-one, while Elizabeth was nearing her fifty-fourth birthday. Elizabeth's grandfather, Henry VII, had died aged fifty-two; her father, Henry VIII, aged fifty-five; and her half-sister, Mary Tudor, aged forty-two. By any reasonable actuarial calculus, James's accession to the English throne was imminent. He was not to know that Elizabeth would defy all the actuarial odds and live not for five more years, nor even for ten, but for fifteen and more.

It was a long time to wait, and a tense and frustrating one too, for James could never be totally certain that his succession to the English throne would go unchallenged.[41] It is no surprise that, in the course of the 1590s, as this most literate and intelligent of kings reflected on the nature of kingship, he should develop a theory of divine right monarchy, based on indefeasible hereditary right and the free, absolute – and, by implication, imperial – authority vested in his person.[42] His thoughts were as much on

---

[38] *Ibid.*, 230, 234.

[39] *Ibid.*, 226–7; *King James's Secret*, ed. Rait and Dunlop, 154–5, 209–10.

[40] *Memoirs of Sir James Melville of Halhill, 1535–1617*, ed. A. F. Steuart (1929), 318.

[41] P. Croft, *King James* (Basingstoke, 2003), 43–50, summarises these concerns and details some of the king's clandestine correspondence over the succession with English courtiers ranging from Essex to Lord Henry Howard and Robert Cecil.

[42] Notably in his *The True Lawe of Free Monarchies* (1598), reprinted in *King James VI and I, the Political Writings*, ed. J. P. Sommerville (Cambridge, 1994), 62–84.

England, and on Catholic opposition to his succession there, as they were on Scotland. Meanwhile, as Elizabeth's last decade wore interminably on, it was in Scotland that some of the most interesting speculation on the future of Britain emerged. In 1594, for example, Andrew Melville, in the unlikely guise of a court poet, celebrated the birth and baptism of James's first male heir, Prince Henry, by articulating a vision of united Britain that openly challenged the imperial ideas of the king himself.[43] Melville was not only a Calvinist revolutionary, but also a civic humanist, the friend and in some respects the intellectual heir of James's former tutor and *bête noir*, George Buchanan. Like Buchanan, he was fiercely opposed to the idea of empire, not just on the presbyterian grounds that the royal supremacy was incompatible with the independence of the church, but also because it sapped the civic energy on which political participation depended, turning subjects into slaves rather than citizens.[44] Like that other Scottish presbyterian unionist, David Hume of Godscroft, Melville envisaged Britain, not as an empire, but as some sort of godly confederation whose constituent polities would be covenanted with each other as well as with God.[45]

Melville and Godscroft were hardly representative of broadly based Scottish opinion. Nevertheless, their views are worth noting because they indicate that, by the mid-1590s, some Scots were not just reconciled to the prospect of union, but were intellectually excited by its possibilities. To be sure, as the post-1603 unionist literature makes clear, they worried about Scotland's status within a united Britain – fearing, as the pro-union lawyer John Russell put it, that Scotland would become 'subalterne' to England and 'thairby ancienne Scotland to loss hir beauty for evir! God forbid!'[46] – and probably only a handful would have subscribed to Godscroft's Calvinist republican reconfiguration of its polity. But it was the Scots rather than the English who were exercised and even energised by the idea of Britain and it was Scots who led the way in developing a language and conceptual framework capable of articulating an understanding of Britain's multiple monarchy as something other than the product of a

[43] *Principis Scoti-Britannorum natalia*, printed in the original Latin with English translation in George Buchanan, *The Political Poetry*, ed. and trans. P. J. McGinnis and A. H. Williamson (Scottish History Society, fifth series, VIII, 1995), 276–81. The poem was not well received in England: M. Lynch, 'Court Ceremony and Ritual during the Personal Reign of James VI', in *Reign of James VI*, ed. Goodare and Lynch, 71–92, at 89.

[44] See Williamson's introduction to Buchanan, *Political Poetry*, 31–6.

[45] See *The British Union: A Critical Edition and Translation of David Hume of Godscroft's 'De Unione Insulae Britannicae'*, ed. and trans. P. J. McGinnis and A. H. Williamson (Aldershot, 2002).

[46] John Russell, 'A Treatise of the Happie and Blissed Unioun', in *The Jacobean Union: Six Tracts of 1604*, ed. B. R. Galloway and B. P. Levack (Scottish History Society, fourth series, XXI, 1985), 84.

dynastic lottery.[47] As a Scot, and the first British king, James VI and I not unnaturally shared this enthusiasm and was prepared to experiment with the governance of his multiple monarchy – so long as it reinforced rather than undermined his own authority. But his campaign for closer and more complete union, and for the fashioning of a new British identity, met with either stony English silence or vocal English resistance. As a result, he was inclined to fall back on variations of the Anglo-British imperial ideology first articulated in the late 1540s, an ideology that allowed the new Britain to be construed as little more than old England writ large.[48]

Yet one cannot help thinking that, when James gloried in his Constantinian and even Arthurian inheritance, he understood it to mean something different from Elizabeth's understanding of it: expansive, perhaps even transoceanic, rather than insular and introverted. Commenting on the view that Henry VIII was possessed of a grand British imperial vision, J. J. Scarisbrick expressed doubt that the English king was 'either guilty or capable of such high statesmanship'.[49] In this respect, as apparently in so many others, Elizabeth was entirely her father's daughter. In circumstances that were far more favourable to Anglo-Scottish concord and integration, when indeed the future of Britain was hers to shape, she chose to do as little as possible. For better or for worse, Britain and its empire owe far more to James Stewart than they do to Elizabeth Tudor.

[47] In addition to the works already cited, see in particular A. H. Williamson, 'Patterns of British Identity: "Britain" and its Rivals in the Sixteenth and Seventeenth Centuries', in *The New British History*, ed. Burgess, 138–73.

[48] Mason, *Kingship and the Commonweal*, 266–9; A. H. Williamson, 'Scotland, Antichrist and the Invention of Great Britain', in *New Perspectives on the Politics and Culture of Early Modern Scotland*, ed. J. Dwyer *et al.* (Edinburgh, 1982), 34–58.

[49] J. J. Scarisbrick, *Henry VIII* (1976), 548–50.

Transactions of the RHS 14 (2004), pp. 295–308 © 2004 Royal Historical Society
DOI: 10.1017/S0080440104000179   Printed in the United Kingdom

'NEVER ANY REALM WORSE GOVERNED': QUEEN ELIZABETH AND IRELAND

By Hiram Morgan

ABSTRACT. Elizabeth's reign was calamitous for Ireland and indeed the mis-management there was close to bringing disaster upon England as well. Why could she not have muddled through in Ireland with the sort of Tudor consensus and conciliation that worked for England and Wales? Elizabeth had good intentions towards Ireland and Irish but these were stymied by a range of historical, political, gender and personal issues. Unlike Wales, the subjugation of Ireland had not been completed during the middle ages. Henry VIII had embarked upon the integration of Ireland at a time of religious upheaval and strategic threat. This process – the so-called reformation of Ireland – was still ongoing when Elizabeth came to the throne and the international situation became more menacing both ideologically and militarily as her reign unfolded. Female monarchical rule was a difficult enough task in the home polity but the task of governing a subordinate kingdom through male proxies made the government of Ireland doubly difficult. This paper starts with the problems facing Elizabeth in Ireland, looks at the personalities and policies of those she governed through, examines the responses of the Irish elite and makes some conclusions.

The damning judgement in the article title is quoted by Wallace MacCaffrey from a passage where the queen blamed the misgovernment of Ireland in 1597 on her officials there from the highest to the lowest.[1] However, MacCaffrey's authoritative biography of the queen – the only one to treat Ireland as a part of the overall assessment of her reign – puts a good measure of the blame for the disasters in Ireland on Elizabeth herself. He says she was 'wholly unfitted' for the task confronting her there, that her lack of vision condemned her second kingdom to penny-pinching, short-term policies.[2] Much the same assessment could be attached to Elizabeth's management of metropolitan affairs. In fact there was nothing at all visionary in Elizabeth's rule. It was not about creating an empire in Ireland or elsewhere, despite many aspirations in that direction emerging from sections of the intelligentsia, gentry and merchant classes. Elizabeth was not a great monarch. She captained the English ship of state with a mixture of luck and canniness through very treacherous waters into a safe harbour but the jerry-built and increasingly mutinous Irish ship of state,

[1] Wallace MacCaffrey, *Elizabeth I* (1993), 430.
[2] *Ibid.*, 433.

to which she had to shout orders and send over vice-captains of varying competences, came close to sinking and pulling the attached English one down after it.

The completion of the medieval conquest of Ireland during Elizabeth's reign should not be regarded as one of her achievements. Indeed, one of her major problems was precisely the cultural and ideological heritage derived from that medieval conquest. To justify the 1169 invasion, Giraldus Cambrensis and other propagandists had configured the Irish, their language, customs and politics as barbarian. These ideas died hard in England and amongst the leaders of the English Pale in Ireland.[3] Elizabeth herself seems to have set out to depart from this English chauvinist mindset. One of the most remarkable documents surviving from her reign is the primer in the Irish language presented to the queen in 1562 by Christopher Nugent, baron of Delvin in Westmeath. She had specifically asked Delvin, then a student at the Inns of Court, to compose it. In its little preface he assured himself that the queen in the light of her great proficiency in languages would have no trouble learning Irish: 'For thereby your subiects shall receaue justice, ciuilitie planted, their loue towards your maiestie encreased, leauing to posteritie an example of vertue to follow your glorious acts and deedes.'[4] The Irish phrases in this book may have aided the queen in exchanging pleasantries with the many Irish suitors who came to court, including Grace O'Malley, the so-called pirate queen of Connacht, who visited Greenwich Palace in 1593.[5] Yet this was gesture politics. It never formed part of a wider policy to respect Irish culture and language. If the Elizabethan state in Ireland had spent a tenth of what it spent on the materiel of war on bibles and prayer books in Irish and on an Irish-preaching clergy, history might have been different. Unlike Wales where sensible cultural policies were pursued, Ireland was not completely under control.

Elizabeth's approach was also conditioned by the situation in which she currently found the country and by the policies already in place. She ruled about half of Ireland directly and the rest via great lords who acknowledged her sovereignty to varying degrees. Henry VIII in crushing the Kildare rebellion of 1534 had established a standing army in Ireland and installed an English lord deputy there as governor. In 1541 by statute of the Irish parliament he had exchanged the medieval title given by the pope as 'Lord of Ireland' for 'King of Ireland'. This envisaged establishing full sovereignty throughout Ireland with direct

---

[3] Hiram Morgan, 'Giraldus Cambrensis and the Tudor Conquest of Ireland', in *Political Ideology in Ireland, 1541–1641*, ed. Hiram Morgan (Dublin, 1999), 22–44.

[4] Queen Elizabeth's Irish Primer, Guinness Library, Farmleigh House, Dublin.

[5] For Grace O'Malley's visit to court, see Anne Chambers, *Granuile: Ireland's Pirate Queen, c. 1530–1603* (Dublin, 2003), ch. 8.

crown government and English law. To achieve this Henry had pursued mostly conciliatory policies but there was one overarching problem – Henry's break with Rome had made England an international pariah and in doing this Ireland became its strategic weak-spot. By the time Elizabeth came to the throne the confrontational policies of the conquest and colonisation of Ireland had already been set in train under Edward and Mary.[6] It is interesting to ponder why the conquest of Ireland took place during the reigns of a minor and two female monarchs! Did they lack the necessary control there to stop the juggernaut that was the Tudor conquest?

Thus as well as her responsibilities for the physical and spiritual well-being of her Irish subjects, Elizabeth had the inherited task of making a reality of the sovereign claims implicit in the title of 'Queen of Ireland'. This requirement was in conflict with her tight-fisted approach to finance. She demanded that the so-called 'reformation of Ireland' should pay for itself so that Ireland would not be a drain on the English exchequer. In matters of defence and foreign policy she had strategic threats in Ireland from France and later from Spain to take notice of. And just as Spanish monarchs were keen to maintain 'nuestra reputación' in overseas dependencies, so she worried about the public manifestation of her sovereignty in Ireland – what she referred to as 'our honour'.[7] A large number of letters drafted by the secretaries and signed by the queen about land grants, jobs and policies survive. Only rarely do you glimpse a personal reason showing through which may fairly be regarded as the queen's own opinion. Such opinions occur more in letters dealing with crisis situations or involving royal prerogative. There are a few letters and postscripts in her own hand. Some of these were obscure letters to lord deputies who were courtiers as well. Some of the most impassioned are scolding letters to lord deputies who had made calamitous decisions or who had exceeded their authority. The most obscure is the 'Harry' letter she sent to Sidney in 1565;[8] we have her extraordinary and increasingly exasperated correspondence with Essex as his government in Ireland collapsed in 1599[9] and then there is the note addressed 'Mistress Kitchenmaid' sent to Mountjoy in 1600 who was at last putting things right in her Irish kitchen. She reminded him with reference to his patron and predecessor Lord Essex: 'that no vainglory

---

[6] Brendan Bradshaw, *The Irish Constitutional Revolution of the Sixteenth Century* (Cambridge, 1979).

[7] Hiram Morgan, *Tyrone's Rebellion, the Outbreak of the Nine Years War in Tudor Ireland* (Woodbridge, 1993), 220.

[8] *Letters and Memorials of State*, ed. Arthur Collins (2 vols., 1746), I, 7–8.

[9] *Calendar of State Papers, Ireland, 1599–1600*, ed. E. G. Atkinson (1899), 98–101, 105–7, 114–16, 150–3.

or popular fawning can ever advance you forward, but true duty and reverence to your prince, which two afore your life I see you do prefer'.[10]

Her government of Ireland was assisted by a succession of secretaries of state in England – William Cecil, Thomas Smith, Francis Walsingham, Robert Cecil – and often by a sub-committee of the English privy council attended by Old Ireland hands such as former governors like Sir James Croft and Sir John Perrot. In Ireland itself there was the government in Dublin headed by the lord deputy and the Irish privy council and in the course of Elizabeth's reign presidents and provincial councils were established in Munster and Connacht. As the administration of Ireland increased in size, the patronage possibilities expanded also and as a result Irish jobs from that of lord deputy down became part of the power plays between the great court factions – Sussex, Burghley and Robert Cecil on the one hand and Leicester and subsequently Essex on the other. Above all, the queen was particularly reliant on the men she appointed lord deputy of Ireland. If having to govern through men was one of the problems of female monarchy, having to govern an overseas territory through a succession of ambitious, macho proxies was an even greater undertaking. William Camden, writing in 1610, described the lord deputy's authority as 'very large, ample and royal... And verily there is not (look throughout all Christendom againe) any other vice-roy that commeth nearer with the majestie of a king, whether you respect his jurisdiction and authority or his traine, furniture and provision'.[11] If anything the power of this official had grown during Elizabeth's reign – indeed it could be said that in suppressing 'overmighty subjects' of Ireland the crown made an 'overmighty officer' of the lord deputy.[12]

Elizabeth began her Irish government *in media res* and had inherited Thomas Radcliffe, the earl of Sussex, as her governor there. He had already begun the use of martial law to force the Irish into line and reorganised the Laois-Offaly plantation in the Midlands of Ireland. He was anxious to counter an alleged French threat from Scotland by making war to prevent the McDonnells intruding into Antrim from the Highlands and Islands. Subsequently he made war against Shane O'Neill claiming that he was making common cause with Scotland. Liquidating Shane O'Neill became the be-all and end-all of policy – 'if Shane is overthrown all is settled; if Shane settle, all is overthrown'.[13] What in fact Sussex was doing was forcing Shane into league with Mary Queen of Scots. This

[10] *Calendar of Carew Papers, 1589–1600*, ed. J. S. Brewer and William Bullen (1869), 480–1.

[11] William Camden, 'Ireland and the Smaller Islands in the British Ocean', 71, a separately paginated section of his *Britain* (1610).

[12] This argument is advanced in Hiram Morgan, 'Overmighty Officers: The Irish Lord Deputyship in the Early Modern British State', *History Ireland*, 3/4 (1999), 17–21.

[13] Quoted in Ciaran Brady, *The Chief Governors: The Rise and Fall of Reform Government in Ireland* (Cambridge, 1994), 78.

became a recurrent factor in English policy and Irish reaction as the frontier of crown government advanced. Allegations of foreign intrigues by the Irish were merely pretexts for English aggrandisement. And once the English took action on these grounds, their allegations quickly became self-fulfilling prophecies because the Irish lords were thereby forced into the hands of foreign potentates. With the expansion of military activity and the extension of government came the New English Protestants, a growing cadre of officials, soldiers, clergy and planters closely tied to the patronage of the lord deputy.[14]

Elizabeth replaced Sussex with Sir Henry Sidney, a gentleman-companion of Edward VI and Leicester ally who was already lord president of Wales, on the promise that he would reform Ireland and make it self-financing.[15] Elizabeth commended him into God's hands 'considering you are entrid into that realme as a large field or world overrun with brambles and replenished with ravening beasts'.[16] Sidney declared martial law nationwide and established the Court of Castle Chamber as an Irish Star Chamber jurisdiction.[17] He solved the problem of Shane O'Neill by having him assassinated by the McDonnells in 1567 but reform proved more difficult. Colonisation schemes in Munster provoked the first Desmond war (1568–72) led by James Fitzmaurice. Sidney was out of government by the time colonisation plans for Ulster came to fruition in the early 1570s. To save money the queen favoured private colonies under Sir Thomas Smith and the first earl of Essex but they went badly wrong. Smith's son was killed in 1573 and the earl of Essex in frustration perpetrated massacres at Belfast against the Clandeboye O'Neills and at Rathlin Island against the McDonnells. One might find fault with the queen for applauding these actions but she believed the first were rebels and the second to be alien intruders.[18] Sidney returned to government in 1575 with a new nationwide reform scheme. He would make the standing army in Ireland pay for itself by establishing a uniform tax called a composition in lieu of the various provisioning arrangements known as cess which had existed hitherto. This tax was to be imposed by prerogative rather than parliamentary sanction. The loyal Pale communities headed by Lord Delvin mounted a protest campaign and dispatched a delegation to court. With Fitzmaurice conspiring abroad, Sidney attempted to play the grand strategy card

[14] This argument is advanced in Hiram Morgan, 'British Policies before the British State', in *The British Problem, 1534–1707*, ed. B. Bradshaw and J. S. Morrill (1996), 66–88.

[15] Nicholas Canny, *The Elizabethan Conquest of Ireland: A Pattern Established, 1565–76* (Hassocks, 1976), chs. 2 and 3.

[16] *Sidney State Papers*, ed. Tomás Ó Laidhin (Dublin, 1962), 19.

[17] David Edwards, 'Beyond Reform: Martial Law and the Tudor Reconquest of Ireland', *History Ireland*, 5/2 (1997), 17–21.

[18] *Calendar of Carew Papers, 1575–88*, ed. J. S. Brewer and William Bullen (1868), 21.

claiming that it was cheaper to keep an army in Ireland than the cost of evicting a foreign one, which he estimated at £200,000.[19] The queen eventually opted for a cheap compromise with the Palesmen after Lord Chancellor Gerard deserted Sidney's camp.[20]

Most of Sidney's plans were ruinous or ended in ruins. Where he succeeded was in propaganda. Sussex may have put in place the policy of conquest and colonisation but it was Sir Henry Sidney who seized on the office and its viceregal status as a vehicle for self-promotion. He remodelled Dublin Castle, renovated the tomb of Strongbow the Norman conqueror of Ireland, set up inscriptions and even had places named after him. Sidney wrote long letters to court about his progresses round the country.[21] He brought Edmund Campion over to write up his less than successful experiment in parliamentary consultation with the political nation in 1568–71.[22] In the preamble to the attainder of O'Neill in the Irish Statutes, which he urged to be printed in 1572, he was portrayed as the new Strongbow come to complete the conquest.[23] In 1577 the Irish section of Holinshed's *Chronicles* was dedicated to Sidney.[24] Though he left the government of Ireland under a cloud not long afterwards, the propaganda continued. In 1581 John Derrick brought out his *Image of Irelande*. This work was dedicated to Sir Philip Sidney and in a set of amazing woodcuts portrayed Sir Henry Sidney commanding the army in Ireland and sitting under the cloth of state taking submissions.[25] In 1583 Sir Henry sent his long bombastic memoir of government to Secretary Walsingham.[26] Both the *Image* and the 'Memoir' were job applications – one public, the other private – for Sidney or his son to return to Ireland. In both the overwhelming representation of the governorship is a martial one wielding the sword of justice.

The queen had ignored Sidney's wish to send his son to deal with the second Desmond war (1579–83) which Fitzmaurice's return had sparked. Instead she sent Lord Grey who became the exemplary reform governor in the eyes of his secretary Edmund Spenser. The queen applauded his

[19] *Letters and Memorials of State*, ed. Collins, 183.

[20] Brady, *Chief Governors*, 140–58.

[21] Morgan, 'Overmighty Officers', 18–19.

[22] 'Campion's Historie of Ireland', 130–8, a separately paginated section of *The Historie of Ireland Collected by Three Learned Authors*, ed. James Ware (Dublin, 1633).

[23] *Statutes at Large Passed in the Parliaments Held in Ireland*, ed. W. Ball (21 vols., Dublin, 1786–1804), I, 322–38.

[24] *Holinshed's Irish Chronicle: The Historie of Irelande from the First Habitation Thereof, unto the Yeare 1509 Collected by Raphaell Holinshed, Continued till the Year 1545 by Richard Stanyhurst*, repr., ed. Liam Millar and Eileen Power (Dublin, 1979), 3–5.

[25] John Derricke, *The Image of Irelande* (1581), repr., ed. D. B. Quinn (Belfast, 1985), plates 6 and 12.

[26] For a recent edition, see Ciaran Brady, *A Viceroy's Vindication? Sir Henry Sidney's Memoir of Service in Ireland, 1556–78* (Cork, 2002).

massacre of the papal mercenary force which landed at Smerwick in 1580. She was exultant writing in her own hand

> The mighty hand of the Almightiest power hath shewed manifest the force of His strength in the weakness of the feeblest sex, and minds this year to make ashamed ever hereafter to disdain us. In which action I joy that you have been chosen the instrument of His glory, which I mean to give you no cause to forthink. Your loving sovereign, Elizabeth R.[27]

But God's chosen proceeded to go on a killing spree; during his government between September 1580 and August 1582 by his own admission he executed nearly 1,500 'chief men and gentlemen' by martial law, 'not accounting those of meaner sort . . . and killing of churls, which were innumerable'.[28] He even executed people in areas not in revolt. When he started executing Palesmen, including officials, for alleged conspiracy, he had to be recalled.

It was a further two years before another lord deputy was appointed – Sir John Perrot – a rich Welsh sheepfarmer with an expansive personality. Perrot declared that 'Her Highnesse equally balanceth her subiects according to their due deserts, without respect of Nation, as having interest in God from them all alike.'[29] Like Sussex, Essex and Sidney, he attempted to expel the Scots in rather pointless expeditions. At first the queen was all praise: 'I fynd well by the prosperous success of your honest services, that God favoureth the steppes of true intents and valiant myndes, and therefore should condempne my judgement yf I praised not souch a servant.'[30] Perrot pursued all the previous reform policies simultaneously and acted like a viceroy communicating directly with the king of Scotland and making independent overtures to the English parliament for money. When a treaty of Nonsuch was reached to intervene in the Netherlands and a treaty of amity was signed with Scotland, Elizabeth promptly called a halt to Perrot's adventures. In a clause added to a letter in her own hand she admonished Sir John:

> Let us have no more such rash unadvised journeys without good ground, as your last fond journey in the North. We marvel that you hanged not such saucy an advertiser as he that made you believe so general a company were coming. I know you do nothing but with a good intent for my service, but yet take better heed ere you use us so again.[31]

As a result the queen cut back Perrot's budget, his troop numbers and ordered him to take the advice of his senior privy councillors. She also ordered a restraint on the use of martial law and as a result only ten

---

[27] Quoted in Alfred O'Rahilly, *The Massacre at Smerwick (1580)* (Cork, 1938), 5–6.

[28] Quoted in Edwards, 'Beyond Reform', 20.

[29] E. C. S., *The Government of Ireland under the Honorable, Iust and Wise Governour, Sir John Perrot* (London, 1626), 49

[30] *Calendar of Patent and Close Rolls of Chancery in Ireland*, ed. J. Morrin (3 vols., 1861–4), II, 92.

[31] *Calendar of State Papers, Ireland, 1586–88*, ed. H. C. Hamilton (1877), 43.

martial law commissions were issued until it was abolished altogether in 1591. Perrot had left government in 1588 amid a fanfare of publicity. In the Armada crisis which followed shortly afterwards Ireland remained quiet, in spite of the number of Spanish sailors and soldiers shipwrecked there, because the year before Perrot had kidnapped any potential trouble-makers and imprisoned them in the dungeon of Dublin Castle.[32]

However, when Perrot angled to return to Ireland, his successor Fitzwilliam and Lord Burghley, Fitzwilliam's patron, concocted a huge conspiracy against him. It was claimed that Perrot had plotted with the king of Spain – the main evidence came from a priest already in jail for forging Perrot's signature. Notwithstanding the obviously trumped-up nature of the charges, the queen allowed the case to continue. Perrot was eventually tried and found guilty in Westminster Hall, but left unexecuted he died in the Tower.[33] Besides the treason charges, Perrot's opponents had brought to the queen's attention the many expletive statements which Sir John had uttered when the queen sent him countermanding orders:

> If she use men thus, she will have but cold service, for one day she will have need of me . . . Stick not so much upon her Majesty's letter, she will command what she will but we will do what we list . . . Ah now silly woman, now she will now curb me, she shall not rule me now . . . God's wounds, thus is to serve a base bastard piss-kitchen woman, if I had served any prince in Christendom, I had not been so dealt withal.[34]

The only reasonable explanation for the strange case of Sir John Perrot is that the queen wanted to teach him a lesson in humility and by extension all other governors of Ireland.

In fact a lot of Irish business was transacted at court with the representations made by the Irish to the queen acting as a restraint on the excesses or exuberances of the English administration in Ireland. For instance the compositions being demanded by Sidney and later by Perrot were settled by compromises at court negotiated over their heads and much to their chagrin by the Palesmen.[35] Though many Irish suitors visited court only the richest Irish nobles could afford prolonged and expensive residence required. One of the most famous visits was that of Shane O'Neill in 1562 organised by the rehabilitated earl of Kildare. Shane disliked the terms he had received and ultimately Kildare's influence was not strong enough either with the government or with Shane to avoid war. The Catholic Kildare quickly abandoned his Ulster relative and continued to benefit from queen's liberality, remaining high enough in her confidence to survive a conspiracy by Lord Deputy

[32] Morgan, *Tyrone's Rebellion*, ch. 3.
[33] Morgan, 'The fall of Sir John Perrot', in *The Reign of Queen Elizabeth: Court and Culture in the Last Decade*, ed. John Guy (Cambridge, 1995), 109–25.
[34] Quoted in *ibid.*, 221.
[35] Brady, *Chief Governors*, ch. 6.

Fitzwilliam in early 1570s. In 1579 he was commended by the queen for his good offices in sorting out the Pale demonstration over the composition only to end up in the Tower contaminated by the continental conspiracies of his more zealous followers.[36]

The most successful Irish courtier was Thomas Butler, the tenth earl of Ormond, known as Black Tom or Tom Duff and nicknamed 'Lucas' by the queen.[37] In fact Black Tom was in the first rank of courtiers and not far behind Leicester and Hatton in the queen's affections. Part of the Boleyn connection and a former companion of King Edward, Ormond attended many state functions and ceremonials with the queen and was believed, quite correctly, to have considerable influence with her. In the first few years of her reign, when his friend Sussex was lord deputy, he benefited from all manner of grants and perks from the queen. He received so much in the province of Munster, there are good grounds for believing that the royal favour towards him was a substantial cause of the alienation from the crown of his rival the decidedly uncourtly earl of Desmond. His reputation survived intact the battle of Affane with Desmond, the last private affray between feudal hosts in the Tudor dominions. The following year the queen demanded that Sidney actively support his causes since 'his former service and his truth always to us and our crowne is not lest unconsidered but preferred afore others, that have never at all times deserved the like'.[38] Ormond's influence with the queen was such that he could break the government of lord deputies. His influence was behind the recall of Sidney in 1571 (he held him responsible for his brothers' siding with Fitzmaurice) and again in 1578 after Sidney wanted the composition tax extended to his liberties. Ormond was critical of Lord Grey's terror tactics to suppress the second Desmond war and it was Ormond himself who stepped in to complete the campaign in a more conciliatory manner. By this stage he seemed a natural candidate for the lord deputyship but he had also become a hate figure for the New English. Perrot succeeded but he too fell foul of Ormond half way through his term in office. In August 1588 he helped organise the army at Tilbury and he carried the sword of state before the queen when she arrived there to rally the troops.[39] Ormond came into his own after Leicester's demise. He was given the garter in 1588 and between 1590 and 1592 served as earl marshal of England. It was during this time that the use

---

[36] Vincent Carey, *Surviving the Tudor: The Wizard Earl of Kildare and English Rule in Ireland* (Dublin, 2002); *Walsingham Letter-Book*, ed. James Hogan and N. McNeill O'Farrell (Dublin, 1959), 101–2.

[37] David Edwards, 'Butler, Thomas, 10th earl of Ormond', *Oxford Dictionary of National Biography* (Oxford, forthcoming), and *idem*, *The Ormond Lordship in County Kilkenny 1515–1642* (Dublin, 2003).

[38] *Sidney State Papers*, ed. Ó Laidhin, 23.

[39] *The Copie of a Letter Sent to Don Bernardin de Mendoza* (1588), 22.

of martial law was abolished in Ireland. Ormond also offset the worst effects of the plantation of Munster which followed the second Desmond War. He himself acquired confiscated rebel lands within his own liberty of Tipperary and assisted the law suits of other landowners whose estates had been wrongly or mischievously included by the New English surveyors.[40] Clearly Ormond was a man of extraordinary influence!

The alternative to lobbying at court was of course resistance at home and conspiracy abroad.[41] As New English officers and settlers pressed on local lords with long-standing property rights, customs and liberties, it was almost inevitable that these men would seek alliances with England's enemies abroad. Shane O'Neill solicited help from Mary Queen of Scots, and the Guise family in France. As England's relations deteriorated with Spain, James Fitzmaurice in Munster sought help from Philip II. Critically, circumstances changed in the midst of Fitzmaurice's first revolt. In 1570 Pope Pius V declared Elizabeth excommunicated and absolved her subjects from their allegiance. Henceforth Fitzmaurice was able to pose as a Catholic champion with the papal bull – *Regnans in exclesis* – as his legitimation. In 1574 he went into exile, ending up in Rome where he was given a mercenary army by the pope in 1578. However, most of this went off with Sir Thomas Stukley to fight in King Sebastian of Portugal's madcap crusade in Morocco and Fitzmaurice returned to Munster with only a handful of men. He distributed printed proclamations – probably written by Sanders the English Jesuit in his entourage – denouncing the queen as a heretical, female ruler born from an adulterous relationship. Though widely circulated, there was in fact little public response to this rhetoric and Fitzmaurice was killed in a skirmish soon afterwards. But over-reaction by local English officials provoked a widespread rebellion and of course the land confiscations and eventually the Munster plantation which they ultimately sought. However, militant Counter-Reformation ideals once embedded could not be wished away. There was a further dimension. Pope Adrian IV had granted Ireland to the kings of England by the 1155 bull *Laudabiliter* as a sort of medieval UN mandate with the objective of 'Christianising' and civilising the Irish. With the queen of England now an excommunicated heretic, was it not time that Ireland was given a new Catholic monarch? This idea would be developed further during the revolt of Hugh O'Neill, earl of Tyrone at the end of the century.

[40] These claims are dealt with in A. J. Sheehan, 'Official Reaction to Native Land Claims in the Plantation of Munster', *Irish Historical Studies*, 23/92 (1983), 297–317.

[41] Irish overtures to continental powers are summarised in J. J. Silke's pamphlet, *Ireland and Europe, 1559–1607* (Dublin, 1966).

Indeed, it is fair to say that Elizabeth's greatest challenge in Ireland came from the wily Hugh O'Neill.[42] He was a man of considerable personal charisma who plainly charmed the queen. Letters patent which he requested for one of his fosterbrothers refer to the earl as one 'to whom Her Majesty would not willing deny any favour, knowing his devotion to her'.[43] She was disgusted when he broke out into rebellion and, together with his son-in-law Red Hugh O'Donnell, began conspiring with Spain; after all she claimed that she had raised him from the dust to be the queen's O'Neill, her man in Ulster. The problem was that crown officials, most notably Sir Henry Bagenal the would-be provincial governor of Ulster backed by the increasingly corrupt Lord Deputy Fitzwilliam, were bent on undermining the traditional power of the O'Neills in Ulster. The earl of Ormond tried to keep Hugh loyal in the same way as Kildare had done for his uncle Shane O'Neill in the 1560s, but ultimately it was impossible to hold back the dogs of war.

It was difficult to contain the revolt in Ireland because of England's military commitments on the Continent. When the Dublin government attempted to negotiate with O'Neill, the queen denounced the actions of her commissioners Gardiner and Wallop as 'derogatory to our honour' and a 'disgrace to us in government'.[44] When a new lord deputy, Sir William Russell, was sent over, he summoned O'Neill to Dublin but having interviewed him allowed him to return home. Once again the queen flew into a rage denouncing it 'as foul an oversight as ever was committed in that kingdom'.[45] Interestingly, she said that such things were all 'too common in foreign service', as if governing the queen's own inheritance of Ireland was more to be likened to Leicester's proceedings in the Netherlands.[46] In 1595 Sir John Norris was brought back from the continent with a veteran force but this had little effect other than to endanger the whole mission by dividing the Irish command between him and Russell. Again the English were forced into negotiations. This time the queen was incensed that Gardiner and Wallop had addressed their letters to O'Neill 'Your very Good Lord' and had signed them 'Your Loving Friends' and again denounced their talks with a proclaimed rebel as 'utterly repugnant to all royal considerations'. His daring request for liberty of conscience was deemed 'a matter meet for no subject to require'.[47] Despite her fury, pacification was pursued and a fudged settlement reached at the spring of 1596. This peace process went awry when

[42] See Morgan, *Tyrone's rebellion*.
[43] *Cal. Patent Rolls, Ireland*, ed. Morrin, II, 125.
[44] Morgan, *Tyrone's rebellion*, 165.
[45] *Ibid.*, 172.
[46] Cambridge University Library, MS Kki 15, no. 61, fos. 126–7.
[47] Morgan, *Tyrone's Rebellion*, 201–2.

Spanish agents arrived in West Ulster and O'Neill agreed to fight on. Taking hold of the legitimacy conferred by *Laudabiliter* and by *Regnans in exclesis*, O'Neill and O'Donnell wrote to Philip II as follows in May 1596:

> Since, to our great and unspeakable detriment, we have experienced acts of injustice and wrongdoing on the part of the officials whom the ruler of England used to send to us, we pray and beseech Your Majesty to designate as king over this island someone who is close to you, a man who is completely honourable and gifted, for your majesty's own benefit and that of the commonwealth of Ireland, a man who will not in the least disdain to rule over us, but also to be among us and to rule and advise our people with kindness and wisdom.[48]

Unfortunately for the Ulster lords, the Spaniards did not arrive until five years later and then it was too little, too late. Nevertheless in the meantime they had seen off Lord Deputies Russell and Burgh and in 1598 O'Neill had crushed Bagenal at the Yellow Ford, the single greatest victory the Irish ever won over the English. This had led to a nationwide revolt and to the overthrow of the newly erected English plantation in Munster. It was the sort of outcome that the planter and poet Edmund Spenser had feared when he wrote his 'View of the Present State of Ireland' in 1596.[49] Now one of the settlers forced to flee, perhaps Spenser himself, penned 'A Supplication of the Blood of the English Most Lamentably Murdered in Ireland, Cryeng out of the Yearth for Revenge.' This was a direct challenge to government in England, and particularly Elizabeth herself, for not adequately defending the settlers or looking after their interests.[50]

The result of disasters at the Yellow Ford and in Munster was the dispatch of Robert Devereux, the second earl of Essex. On the face of it he was just the sort of governor Spenser yearned for – a Protestant military man. He came to Ireland with the largest English army yet brought to the country – some 19,000 – and with a more ample patent than any Irish governor before.[51] The problem was that Essex was no longer high in the queen's favour and he disliked being away from court with Robert Cecil there as principal secretary. His campaign was a disaster; the promised expedition to sail from England and to garrison itself at Lough Foyle behind Irish lines was never dispatched. Instead Essex made a disastrous march through the south of Ireland dispersing an army diminishing through desertion and disease into garrison. By the late summer of 1599 he had only 4,500 men as a field army – too small to confront the Irish confederates, let alone invade their northern stronghold. As a result he made the fateful mistake of negotiating alone with O'Neill at a river ford

[48] Quoted in *ibid.*, 210.
[49] For an online edition see http://celt.ucc.ie/published/E500000-001/index.html
[50] 'A Supplication of the Blood of the English Most Lamentably Murdered in Ireland, Cryeng out of the Yearth for Revenge' (1598), ed. Willy Maley, *Analecta Hibernica*, 36 (1995), 1–77.
[51] *Cal. Patent Rolls, Ireland*, ed. Morrin, II, 520–2.

on the Ulster borders. Piecing together the evidence, it seems certain that Essex did not conspire with O'Neill.[52] Instead he hoped to return to court and brow beat the queen into a peace agreement. Though victory in Ireland would have been better, even a satisfactory peace in Ireland relieving the worse effects of the Irish war on English society and economy would have been immensely popular. The queen would have none of it and arrested him. Not only had he overstepped his powers in Ireland by dabbling with prerogative matters there, he was plainly a would-be dictator with a large army in Ireland officered by his clients by which he would have controlled the succession in England if permitted to do so.

In the aftermath of Essex's arrest, O'Neill went for the full faith and fatherland approach. In an attempt to win over the Catholic loyalists he drew up the twenty-two articles which would have given Catholics control of the government of Ireland. Cecil marked this document with the single word – 'Ewtopia'.[53] In a simultaneous proclamation he threatened the Palesmen by invoking the spectre of excommunication if they did not support him. His rhetoric turned the language of the Tudor conquest on its head, assuring those who joined him that

> I will employ myself to the utmost of my power in their defence and for the extirpation of heresy, the planting of the Catholic religion, the delivery of our country of infinite murders, wicked and detestable policies by which this kingdom was hitherto governed, nourished in obscurity and ignorance, maintained in barbarity and incivility and consequently of infinite evils which are too lamentable to be rehearsed.[54]

Far from winning over the Palesmen these political manoeuvres only forced Elizabeth's hand and as a result Mountjoy was sent over to wage war to the finish. He was ably seconded by Sir Henry Docwra at Lough Foyle, Sir Arthur Chichester at Carrickfergus and by Sir George Carew in Munster. The English began to grind down the rebellious Irish with a series of close, mutually supporting garrisons which devastated the country and reduced the population to starvation. The showdown came at Kinsale where the Spaniards had finally landed to support their Irish co-religionists. They received little local support. Carew had captured and dispatched the local leaders – James FitzThomas Fitzgerald and Florence McCarthy – to the Tower of London. The recusant Catholics of the Towns – even though their dissatisfaction was evident as early as 1596 when the queen's style and title was discovered torn out of grammar books in their schools – stood neutral.[55] O'Neill and O'Donnell marched

[52] Hiram Morgan, 'By God I Will Beat Tyrone in the Field: Essex and Ireland', unpublished paper delivered at the Earl of Essex conference, Tower of London, 23 Feb. 2002.

[53] Hiram Morgan, 'Faith and Fatherland in Sixteenth-Century Ireland', *History Ireland*, 3/2 (1995), 17.

[54] Quoted in *ibid.*, 17.

[55] *Calendar of State Papers, Ireland, 1596–97*, ed. E. G. Atkinson (1893), 17.

the full length of Ireland only to be decisively and massively defeated at Kinsale. The propaganda published soon afterwards painted it as a double victory, a victory over the Irish and over the Spaniards.[56] The end of the Irish resistance and the Anglo-Spanish war was at last in sight. Eventually O'Neill surrendered to Mountjoy at Mellifont at the end of March 1603, the lord deputy having kept the queen's death a secret to avoid any last minute hitches.[57]

Whereas Elizabeth began her reign with the allegiance and goodwill of the majority of the inhabitants of Ireland, by the time of her death she was left with a sullen and forced obedience. In the first place it had been a bloody disaster; a conservative estimate would be 50,000 soldiers and civilians killed in wars in Ireland during her reign but the total might even exceed 100,000.[58] It was also a costly disaster – Irish wars cost far more than the Spanish Armada and the war in the Netherlands combined and the Nine Years War at the end of the reign cost almost £2,000,000.[59] This nearly brought disaster upon England itself. The final conflict with O'Neill put a terrible strain on English money and manpower but bankruptcy was avoided by the expedient of debasing the Irish currency by reducing its silver content by three-quarters.[60] There is no doubt that the bloody and costly conquest of Ireland which occurred during Elizabeth's reign has had serious consequences not just for the rest of Irish history, but also for the subsequent course of Anglo-Irish relations. Furthermore Ireland bore the consequences of Elizabeth's sins of omission. Because Elizabeth did not marry and bear children, her kingdoms passed to James of Scotland. This union of crowns had a far greater impact in Ireland than in England. In the early seventeenth century James's plantation of Ulster saw the mass arrival of lowland Presbyterian Scots in the north of Ireland. Formerly these people had been regarded as aliens. By the 1630s and the 1650s both Wentworth and Cromwell were regretting that they had been allowed to settle – they had changed the ethnic-religious mix in Ulster and the politics of Ireland for ever.

---

[56] For new perspectives on the end of the Nine Years War, see *The Battle of Kinsale*, ed. Hiram Morgan (Bray, 2004).

[57] Nicholas Canny, 'The Treaty of Mellifont and the Re-organisation of Ulster, 1603', *Irish Sword*, 9/37 (1970), 249–62.

[58] If we credit Sir Warham St Leger's claim of 30,000 dying from famine at the end of the second Desmond war alone, it is not hard to reach the higher figure, combining direct casualties of war and related diseases and famines, for the whole of Elizabeth's forty-five-year reign: Michael MacCarthy-Morrogh, *The Munster Plantation: English Migration to Southern Ireland, 1581–1641* (Oxford, 1986), 26.

[59] Historical Manuscripts Commission, *Salisbury Papers*, XV, ed. M. S. Giuseppi (1930), 1–2.

[60] See Joseph McLaughlin, 'What Base Coin Wrought', *in Battle of Kinsale*, ed. Morgan, ch. 10.

Transactions of the RHS 14 (2004), pp. 309–19 © 2004 Royal Historical Society
DOI: 10.1017/S0080440104000118   Printed in the United Kingdom

ELIZABETH I AND THE SOVEREIGNTY OF THE NETHERLANDS 1576–1585

By Simon Adams

ABSTRACT. Elizabeth I's apparent vacillation over the Dutch Revolt is possibly the most disputed aspect of her foreign policy. On two occasions she was formally offered sovereignty of the rebel provinces, of Holland and Zeeland in 1576 and of the United Provinces in 1585. The circumstances of both offers were very similar, however different the outcomes. The course of the negotiations reveals how Elizabeth's prevarication arose from a moral dilemma: how to reconcile her acceptance of the legitimacy of the Dutch cause with her conscientious objection to territorial expansion.

On 2 January 1576 an embassy from the States of Holland and Zeeland arrived at Gravesend. Composed of three leading supporters of the prince of Orange – Paulus Buys, *landsadvocaat* of Holland, Frans Maelson, *burgemeester* of the town of Enkhuisen, and Orange's lieutenant, Philip de Marnix, sieur de St Aldegonde – its purpose was to offer Elizabeth I election as countess of Holland. Nearly ten years later, at the end of June 1585, Buys and Maelson returned to England as members of a much larger embassy from the States General to offer Elizabeth the sovereignty of the United Provinces.[1] On this occasion Buys represented Utrecht, his native province, having resigned as *landsadvocaat* of Holland the previous autumn over the proposed offer of sovereignty to Henri III of France. St Aldegonde was then governor of the beleaguered city of Antwerp. In 1576 Elizabeth did not reject the Holland offer absolutely, but preferred to attempt mediation with Philip II first. In 1585 she agreed to aid the United Provinces under terms set out in the three agreements known collectively as the treaty of Nonsuch.

---

[1] Holland and Zeeland had been united under the count of Holland since 1323. In 1575–6 the States of Zeeland, which had only been reconstituted after the surrender of Middelburg in 1574, sat jointly with those of Holland, who had famously convened on their own authority in Dordrecht on 19 July 1572. 'United Provinces' was initially the designation of the provinces and towns who had signed the Union of Utrecht of January 1579, but in 1580 the States General of the Netherlands accepted the union as generally binding. In the procuration for the delegates of the States General in 1585 (printed in *Foedera, Conventiones, Litterae*, ed. Thomas Rymer (10 vols., The Hague, 1740), VI, 183), they are entitled 'Les Etatz Generaulx des Provinces Unies du Pais Bas assavoir Guelderes, Flandres, Holland [etc.].'

Despite the importance of Anglo-Dutch relations in Elizabeth's reign, neither of these negotiations has received the full treatment it deserves.[2] This is doubly unfortunate because a comparison of the two reveals a series of similarities so striking as to impart a distinct air of *déjà-vu* to those of 1585. Similarity in content has caused the mis-filing of a number of undated English memoranda.[3] Like Buys, Elizabeth's three leading councillors, Lord Burghley, the earl of Leicester and Sir Francis Walsingham, played prominent roles on both occasions. In 1585 they were joined by Sir Christopher Hatton and the new Lord Admiral, Charles, Lord Howard of Effingham, who took the places of the earl of Sussex and Sir Nicholas Bacon, deceased in the interval since 1576. In both 1576 and 1585 there were hopes that the Dutch cause would be taken up in parliament, although Elizabeth made sure it was not. Lastly, there were the activities of the 'busy' Welshman, William Herle. In July and August 1585 Herle and Burghley engaged in an extensive correspondence, in which Herle relayed criticisms of Burghley's apparent coldness towards the Dutch and Burghley in turn defended himself at length. It has been claimed that Herle was the instrument of either Walsingham or Leicester in a factional struggle over the Nonsuch treaty.[4] However, an almost identical correspondence survives from 1576. On the earlier occasion it is clear that if Herle was acting on behalf of anyone it was 'mi friend Pawll Buys'; this was probably also the case in 1585.[5]

1576 was not the first time Elizabeth had been offered the sovereignty of a continental Protestant community. In an obscure episode in November 1572, following the Massacre of St Bartholomew's Eve, the town of

---

[2] Conyers Read, *Mr. Secretary Walsingham and the Policy of Queen Elizabeth* (3 vols., Oxford, 1925), provides the fullest accounts of both negotiations; those in Wallace T. MacCaffrey, *Queen Elizabeth and the Making of Policy 1572–1588* (Princeton, 1981), are cursory. However, Read was not confident of his Dutch and his treatment of 1576 is heavily dependent on J. M. B. C. Kervijn de Lettenhove, *Les Huguenots et les Gueux* (6 vols., Brussels, 1883–5), whose hostility to both Orange and Elizabeth was notorious. For 1585 Read relied no less heavily on J. L. Motley, *History of the United Netherlands* (4 vol. edn, 1876), who derived his account from Jan Wagenaar, *Vaderlandsche Historie* (21 vols., Amsterdam, 1749–59). F. G. Oosterhoff, *Leicester and the Netherlands 1586–1587* (Utrecht, 1988), concentrates on the period after Nonsuch. A brief reappraisal of the background to Nonsuch can be found in Simon Adams, 'The Decision to Intervene: England and the United Provinces 1584–1585', in *Felipe II (1527–1598): Europa y la Monarquía Católica*, ed. José Martínez Millán (5 vols., Madrid, 1999), I, 19–31.

[3] In the *Calendar of State Papers, Foreign Series, Elizabeth, 1575–7* (1880) [hereafter *CSPF, 1575–7*], arts. 598–9 date from 1584/5, while art. 539 dates from 1578.

[4] Initially by Read, *Walsingham*, III, 116–19.

[5] British Library [hereafter BL], Lansdowne MS 43, fo. 124, Herle to Burghley, 29 July 1584. Charles Wilson detected Herle's closeness to Buys in 1575, but not in 1585: *Queen Elizabeth and the Revolt of the Netherlands*, rev. edn (The Hague, 1979), 37–9.

La Rochelle had offered to transfer allegiance to her. But the Dutch negotiations were of another order. On both occasions acceptance of the Dutch offer was understood to mean entering 'suddenly into a war with the kyng of Spayne', as Burghley put it in January 1576.[6] In 1585, although he again claimed 'that her majesty for this quarrell is to sustayn a greatar warr than ever in any memory of man it hath done', that challenge was accepted.[7] Elizabeth herself took a defiant tone when addressing the Dutch embassy after the main Nonsuch treaty was signed on 10 August: 'Messieurs, Vous voyez astheure que jay ouverte le porte et que je m'embarque de tout pour vous en une guerre contre le roy d'Espaigne. Eh bien, je ne m'en donne pas de peine.'[8]

The question why Elizabeth took ten years to reverse the position she took in 1576 has been the subject of an historiographical debate that stretches back to William Camden and his Dutch contemporary Pieter Bor.[9] It is also too large a subject to be addressed here. No less important, however, is what the substance of the negotiations reveals about Elizabeth I's approach to foreign relations. From the nineteenth century onwards there is an established – if not entirely coherent – image of Elizabeth: cold, avaricious, vacillating. Her own prevarication was the reason for the ten-year delay and a combination of events and the pressure of an interventionist party forced the final decision on her in 1585, following a factional struggle at her court.[10] Yet both Elizabeth and her government could move with impressive speed and efficiency when they wanted, and indeed as they did in the spring of 1585.[11] However, Elizabeth also read the fine print and defined her policies carefully, and the situations she faced were more complex than the clichés allow.

Both offers were made during emergencies, when the Dutch faced a major Spanish offensive, and as a result they had both a military and a political dimension. The summer of 1575 saw failure of a compromise settlement of the Revolt in the negotiations at Breda. The upshot was the effective repudiation of the sovereignty of Philip II by Holland and Zeeland, while Philip's governor-general, Don Luis de Requesens, attempted to split Holland from Zeeland by the capture of Oudewater

[6] The National Archives (Public Record Office), State Papers 70/137/25 [hereafter TNA (PRO), SP], 'To be answered to the Hollanders' (endorsed 15 Jan.), in Burghley's hand.

[7] TNA (PRO), SP 103/33/8, 13 July 1585.

[8] 'Rapport van de Nederlandsche Gezanten in 1585 naar Engeland gezonden', *Kronijk van het Historische Genootschap* (fifth series, II, 1866), 274.

[9] Thanks to Camden's hostility to the Dutch, his treatment of the Netherlands Intervention in the Annales is tendentious. Pieter Christianz Bor was given access to the archives of the States of Holland and Utrecht and his *Oorsprongh, begin ende vervolgh der Niederlantscher Oorlogen*, 2nd edn (5 vols., Amsterdam, 1679–84), is a valuable source for material that has not otherwise survived.

[10] Most recently in MacCaffrey, *Making of Policy*, 336–40.

[11] See Adams, 'Decision', 24–5.

and Schoonhaven and then the siege of Zierikzee, which lasted until
2 July 1576. The deaths of Orange and the duke of Anjou in the summer
of 1584 encouraged the duke of Parma to gamble on the great siege of
Antwerp over the winter of 1584–5. In both instances the Spaniards
in fact over-reached themselves. The expense of Requesens's 1575–6
campaign caused the financial crisis that triggered the decisive mutiny
of the Army of Flanders in the summer of 1576. In 1585 Parma lacked
the resources to advance beyond Antwerp in the face of English intervention.

The 1576 offer was rapidly overtaken by events: the death of Requesens
on 5 March, the subsequent collapse of the Brussels administration, the
mutiny and then the general revolt in the following autumn. There is
something of a dead end about it. Furthermore a number of important
aspects of the Holland proposals remain either unclear or disputed. The
surviving archives of the States of Holland for the sixteenth century are
limited to the Resolutions; the correspondence and memoranda files have
completely disappeared.[12] Moreover, both in 1575 and again in 1584 the
States voted to keep the negotiations with England secret.[13]

The repudiation of Philip II's sovereignty in 1575 did not take the form
of a formal *Acte van Verlating*, as was passed by the States General in 1581.
Instead on the analogy of the *Joyeuse Entré* of Brabant of 1356, Holland
and Zealand considered themselves empowered to take such measures as
they considered necessary to protect their privileges and liberties.[14] But
they also had to create a new government. This took the initial form of the
Union of Dordrecht under which the prince of Orange was recognised
as *Hoge Overheid* for the duration of the war, essentially a regularisation
of his 'dictatorship'. The union was agreed by Holland on 11 July 1575,
but not by Zeeland, and Orange considered that Zeeland's rejection
made the *Hoge Overheid* unworkable.[15] On 20 September he proposed its
abolition and the States responded that they were willing to accept his
government under any title he chose, 'ja als grave van Holland', the first
time the countship was offered to him publicly.[16] However, a fortnight later
(3 October), Orange informed the States that they should seek the help

---

[12] The Resolutions have been published: *Resolutiën van de Heeren Staten van Holland en
Westvriesland* (276 vols., The Hague, n.d., c. 1750–98) [hereafter *Res. Holland*].

[13] *Res. Holland, 1575*, 732. For 1584, The Hague, Algemeen Rijksarchief [hereafter ARA],
3.01.04. 01.337 (MS Resolutien, Staten van Holland, 1584), fos. 427v–8 (18/28 Aug.).

[14] This argument had been employed by Orange since 1567 and was developed most fully
by Johan Junius in his *Discourse* of 1574; see *Texts concerning the Revolt of the Netherlands*, ed. E. H.
Kossmann and A. F. Mellink (Cambridge, 1974), 15, and, in general, Martin van Gelderen,
The Political Thought of the Dutch Revolt 1555–1590 (Cambridge, 1992), 130–3.

[15] See J. W. Koopmans, *De Staten van Holland en de Opstand* (The Hague, 1990), 121–2, and
K. W. Swart, *Willem van Oranje en de Nederlandse Opstand 1572–1584* (The Hague, 1994), 99.

[16] *Res. Holland, 1575*, 649.

and protection of a foreign potentate. This proposal caused some debate, but on the 13th it was agreed in principle, with the precise choice of foreign prince left to Orange.

According to Bor, a committee of the States that included the count of Culemburg, Buys and Maelson addressed the issue of foreign assistance at Orange's instigation.[17] They discussed the form – whether 'protectie of bescherming' (protection or defence) – and ultimately settled on offering the countship. They also assessed the three main candidates, the Holy Roman Emperor Maximilian II, Henri III of France and Elizabeth. Maximilian was rejected because he had refused assistance heretofore and the empire was divided in religion. Henri III was written off owing to the civil war in France (the Fifth War of Religion). England offered both a shared religion and powerful maritime assistance. It was also noted that Elizabeth was of the blood of the counts of Holland of the Hainault dynasty, through John of Gaunt's mother, Philippa of Hainault. On 21 and 22 November Buys and Maelson were commissioned ambassadors to England. Their instructions followed on the 28th, but to keep them secret they were not registered, though it was understood that if Elizabeth refused election as countess, they were to obtain a substantial loan.[18] Offering Elizabeth the office of countess had distinct advantages; it was constitutionally straightforward, and as countess it would be difficult for her to abandon the provinces. 'Protection' was a novelty, and what it involved was not clear. When he considered it several months later, Burghley was not too sure what it meant either.[19]

Orange's own role in the offer has remained controversial. His over-riding concern was military assistance for the relief of Zerikzee, but he did not consider independence a viable option (whether he was count of Holland or not) and therefore sovereignty had to be transferred to a monarch powerful enough to defend the provinces. His choice was Henri III. Not only were the military resources of France superior, but he had been disillusioned by what he considered to be Elizabeth's hesitant attitude to the revolt since 1572. However, his confidence in France was not shared by a number of key figures in Holland, among them Buys and Culemburg, who distrusted France after 1572 and preferred England. Moreover, the Fifth War of Religion effectively removed France until its outcome was known. Therefore Orange gave his support to the embassy

---

[17] Bor, *Oorsprongh*, I, 641–3. The documents on which this account is based are not printed, and it is not clear if this committee met before or after 3 Oct. It is not always possible to reconcile Bor's account with the *Res. Holland*.

[18] *Res. Holland*, *1575*, 668–9, 692–3, 730–2.

[19] See his undated memoranda from the 1576 negotiations, *CSPF*, *1575–7*, art. 567, and BL, Additional MS [hereafter Add. MS] 48129, fo. 92.

to England despite his scepticism, because if it failed, opposition to a subsequent approach to France would be crippled.[20]

There had been earlier suggestions that Elizabeth take Holland and Zealand under protection, but her own response to Breda had been to revive her efforts for a ceasefire and a mediated settlement. Otherwise, she claimed, Orange would turn to France. This was not, given the Fifth War, a threat Requesens took seriously. In October Culemburg and two other members of the States of Holland secretly informed Elizabeth of the offer of the countship and urged her to accept it. Burghley brooded on this eventuality in late October.[21] Despite the States' secrecy, the purpose of the Holland embassy was widely known – even in Scotland – weeks before it arrived.[22] Elizabeth had plenty of time to consider her response, and, in the circumstances, her otherwise unexplained decision to recall the parliament of 1572 for a brief second session between 8 February and 15 March 1576 remains a curious one.

Shortly after the Holland embassy arrived, Requesens, worried that Elizabeth was going to summon parliament over assistance to Holland, sent an envoy of his own on a spoiling mission. His choice was the governor of Antwerp, Cardinal Granvelle's brother, Frederique de Perrenot, sieur de Champagny. Champagny's secret instructions (12 January) were specifically to delay an English commitment to Orange until the parliament was dismissed. Champagny's lengthy correspondence with Brussels has survived largely intact and has helped to skew the established account.[23] He gives the impression that when he arrived Elizabeth was on the verge of accepting the Holland offer, but with a mixture of charm and persuasion he caused her to hesitate.[24]

This account is in error on a number of grounds. Elizabeth informed the Hollanders on 15 January that she understood Philip II had consented to her mediation and that she wished to pursue this option first.[25] Champagny did not arrive in England until the 24th, and thanks in

---

[20] This argument is implied in Lettenhove, *Huguenots et Gueux*, III, 579–81, 586, although he obscures it by claiming at one point that Orange was demoralised in the autumn of 1575, but then later that he was clever enough to realise he should go with the flow of Dutch opinion. Its influence can also be found in Swart, *Oranje*, 102–5.

[21] *CSPF, 1575–7*, 152 (Daniel Rogers to Burghley, 9 Oct. 1575), 159 (Burghley memorandum, 17 Oct.), 171 (instructions for John Hastings, 29 Oct.).

[22] Edinburgh, National Library of Scotland, Advocates MS 1.2.2, art. 37, Walsingham to Morton, 27 Dec. 1575, denying the reports, though admitting 'very great and large offers' would be made.

[23] Brussels, Archives Générales du Royaume, Papiers d'Etat et de l'Audience, liasse 361, substantially printed in Kervijn de Lettenhove, *Relations politiques des Pays-Bas et de l'Angleterre sous le règne de Philippe II* (11 vols., Brussels, 1882–1900), VIII. For Champagny's instructions, see arts. 3039–40.

[24] Lettenhove, *Huguenots et Gueux*, IV, 602, derived in part from Champagny's own memoirs.

[25] TNA (PRO), SP 70/137/25–26v, 'to be answered to them of Holland'.

part to the opening of parliament he did not have his first audience until 5 February. He found Elizabeth angry because she assumed Requesens had sent him with his agreement to her mediation. There was, however, a further dimension to the embassy: Champagny's well-known antipathy to Spaniards. At the beginning of March he was subjected to a sustained charm offensive to win him over to supporting removal of the Spanish army. It was later claimed that he joined the revolt in the autumn of 1576 under Elizabeth's influence.

Both the Dutch negotiations and Champagny's embassy were brought to an end by the unexpected death of Requesens, news of which reached England by 10 March. However, five days earlier a report had come from Dover that an English ship carrying the fiancée of the Portuguese ambassador had been attacked by a Zeeland privateer in the harbour and that she had been taken to Flushing. Elizabeth was infuriated by this violation of her territory and Orange's initial refusal to apologise and make restitution caused a frost in their relations for several months. The Holland delegation eventually left under something of a cloud, but that was due more to Anglo-Dutch mutual bloody-mindedness over the Dover incident than Champagny's diplomatic skill.

Elizabeth's preference for mediation has generally been written off as either wishful thinking or an excuse for prevarication. Yet it deserves some reappraisal. Her desired outcome for the Netherlands crisis was what has been termed the 'Burgundian solution'. This involved the Netherlands remaining under Philip's sovereignty, but with its traditional liberties intact, a native governor, no Spanish troops and at least liberty of conscience. This was little different to Orange's position up to Breda. Almost without exception the various manifestos published in Orange's name or by his supporters between 1568 and Breda defined his aims as the defence of the king's subjects and their liberties against the oppression of his governor-general (the duke of Alba in the first instance) and the cruelty of the Spanish army.[26]

There are, however, further ramifications. Conventionally we are told that Elizabeth did not like rebels or supporting rebellion. But did she consider the Dutch rebels? Her response to the Holland offer on 15 January 1576 included the important admission that 'Being so hardly treated as they have been . . . there is appearance of reason in their defending themselves and seeking aid other ways.' If other circumstances dissuaded her from going to war with Spain at that point, rejection of her mediation would give her all the more cause to do so.[27] Moreover, the very fact

---

[26] *Texts*, ed. Kossmann and Mellink, 15. Gelderen, *Political Thought*, 123–6, notes that there was one exception: the *Libellus supplex Imperatoriae Majestati* (1570), now attributed to St Aldegonde, which held Philip directly responsible.

[27] TNA (PRO), SP/70/137/25.

that she received this embassy formally, as she had done earlier ones from Orange, was in itself a tacit admission that in her eyes the 'rebels' possessed a legitimate authority. Even before Nonsuch, in March 1584, she made an important treaty with Orange for naval cooperation.[28]

The justification for her policy was a diplomatic relationship with the Burgundian provinces that pre-dated the Habsburg inheritance. Burghley referred to being 'conjoincted with them in ancient amyty' in 1576, but the case was advanced most explicitly in 1585, when Sir Christopher Hatton drew up a summary of the earlier treaties.[29] It was given a public exposition in the *Declaration of the Causes Moving the Queen of England to Give Aid to the Defence of the People Afflicted and Oppressed in the Low Countries* of October 1585. In the *Declaration* the relationship was described in the delightful phrase: 'this our realme of England and those countries have bene by common language of long time resembled and termed as man and wife'. The Declaration also accepted the Orangeist reading of the *Joyeuse Entré*: that under the 'ancient lawes' of the Netherlands, 'in such cases of general injustice . . . they are free from their former homages and at libertie to make choise of any other prince to bee their prince and head'.[30]

It might be argued that there was a difference over religion. By 1576 the various French edicts of toleration had provided an effective working definition of liberty of conscience. It meant freedom from an inquisition or heresy proceedings, but not the exercise of an alternative religious service or *liberté de culte*. For Elizabeth this distinction was an essential justification of her treatment of English Catholics, especially in response to suggestions that they be granted liberty of worship similar to that enjoyed by French Protestants.[31] The Breda Conference had broken down because the furthest religious concession Philip would make was the right of emigration, while Holland and Zeeland would accept nothing less than continued full public exercise of the Reformed Church.

In 1576 Elizabeth effectively accepted the position in Holland and Zeeland. Walsingham drafted a statement in her name that she would take the provinces under protection if Philip refused to concede that

> sooche placards, inquisytyons and other devyses as may any waye seme to tende to the molestyng of them for the professyon of ther relygyon now publyckly receyved and exercysed in the countryes of hol. and zelande shall be taken away and abolyshed

[28] Adams, 'Decision,' 21.

[29] BL, Add. MS 48129, fo. 92; Cotton MS Galba C VIII, fos. 93r–v, 'Mr Vice-Chamberlains notes touching the treaty with the States Commissioners', 13 July 1585.

[30] Recently reprinted in *Elizabethan Backgrounds: Historical Documents from the Age of Elizabeth I*, ed. Arthur F. Kinney (Hamden, CT, 1990), see 201.

[31] See Elizabeth's answer to the request of the Emperor Ferdinand I, 3 Nov. 1563, *CSPF, 1563* (1869), 581.

[as also that by way of tolleratyon they be permytted to exercyse there relygyon pryvatly in ther howses *deleted*].[32]

The deletion of the clause in brackets suggests that someone appreciated that it was now redundant. In March Elizabeth told Champagny that, given the strength of the Reformed Church in Holland and Zeeland, Philip would have to proceed with moderation.[33] Thereafter she stood by public exercise in Holland and Zeeland and later in the United Provinces. The second article of the offer of sovereignty to her in 1585 stated that the public exercise of the Reformed religion was to be maintained 'provided allwayes that no man shalbe brought into question for his conscience'. This was answered, 'her majestie accordeth this article for the maintenance of the Relligion presentlie published and professed amongst them'.[34]

By 1585 the sovereignty question had been redefined by the Dutch negotiations with France, first the treaty of Plessis lès Tours with the duke of Anjou in September 1580, and then the treaty the States General proposed to Henri III in the winter of 1584–5. In the latter they offered to become fully his subjects. However, Holland and Zeeland had taken a strongly independent stand in the French negotiations. In order to calm hostility in the two provinces to the treaty with Anjou, which included another offer of the countship to him in 1579, Orange accepted the sovereignty of the provinces on a provisional basis in July 1580. Clause 13 of the Plessis lès Tours treaty granted a definite autonomy to Holland and Zealand, especially in religion. Although Anjou was styled count of Holland and Zeeland, he also agreed to recognise Orange as sovereign on a permanent basis, a concession proclaimed in August 1582.[35] In the winter of 1583–4, in a further gesture of hostility to Anjou, there were renewed proposals in the States of Holland to recognise Orange as count, but these had not transpired by his death.

During the negotiations with the States General over the offer of sovereignty to Henri III in August to October 1584, the French specifically demanded the full inclusion of Holland and Zeeland.[36] This was the subject of much unhappiness in Holland. In early September Elizabeth was invited to make a counter offer, but at that point she wished to cooperate with France. It was in the belief that Elizabeth would be a

---

[32] TNA (PRO), SP 70/136/226 (undated).

[33] Lettenhove, *Relations politiques*, VIII, 223, Champagny to Requesens, 3 Mar. 1576.

[34] TNA (PRO), SP 103/33/124 (English translation), and apostilles, fo. 130.

[35] See Frédéric Duquenne, *L'Entreprise du duc d'Anjou aux Pays-Bas de 1580 à 1584* (Lille, 1998), 78–9. He notes that Utrecht never recognised Anjou at all.

[36] Bor, *Oorsprongh*, III, 465, the addresses of the French agent, the sieur des Pruneaux, to both the States General and the States of Holland, Aug. 1584. The French text of the address to the States General can be found in Paris, Bibliothèque Nationale de France, ms. français 3290, fo. 36.

partner in the French treaty that Holland agreed to it.[37] However, not only did Henri III not respond to Elizabeth's proposal, but he finally declined the Dutch offer in late February 1585. The news reached London on 6 March 1585 and Elizabeth's government then moved rapidly. On the 9th the States General was informed that she 'is fullie resolved to take the protection of them so as she may have sufficient caution delivered her for the dewe performance of such articles as may be accorded betwene them'.[38] Cautions were cautionary towns, the most debated item of the Nonsuch treaties.

Precisely what protector meant was still vague, though a contemporary memorandum gave four reasons why Elizabeth should become protector rather than sovereign. The first was to demonstrate that she was not motivated by expansionist ambitions; the others were the analogy with her actions in Scotland in 1560, the avoiding of tension with France over French claims in the Low Countries and the avoiding of a long war with the heirs of Burgundy, for the protectorate would last only until a peaceful solution was found.[39] It was, however, deliberately left to the Dutch to formulate the precise terms. The States General actually drafted three different treaties. The first involved the transfer of sovereignty, the second was for a protectorate and the last simply for military assistance.[40] The sovereignty treaty was essentially the treaty offered to Henri III with a few necessary amendments, such as the discarding of safeguards for the Reformed Church. The main difference between the sovereignty and protectorate treaties was that the latter outlined the specific military assistance expected from Elizabeth, which would have been unnecessary if she were sovereign. Both took it for granted that Elizabeth would appoint an English lieutenant general who would have civil responsibilities. Neither treaty said anything about cautionary towns, though the military assistance treaty did. It was also agreed that if she did not like the titles sovereign or protector she could chose whatever she wanted.[41]

What Elizabeth did was decline the sovereignty formally on 14 July 1585, but then agree to take on the defence of the Netherlands until a settlement was made. She also accepted most of the rest of the sovereignty treaty, including a civil role for her lieutenant-general. The cautionary towns proved the most difficult part of the negotiations, for the Dutch

[37] Buys was still unhappy, the reason for his resignation as *landsadvocaat*. In 'Decision', I gave insufficient attention to the Holland proposals of Sept. 1584.

[38] BL, Harleian MS 285, fo. 123, drafted by Walsingham. For the reaction in the Netherlands, see 'Decision', 25.

[39] BL, Cotton MS Galba C VIII, fo. 194, 'The reasons why her majestie should rather accept the title of a protector then of a sovereign.'

[40] ARA, 1.01.06.11106 (SG 11106, Register Engelandt, 1584–5), fos. 43–9 (sovereignty), 59–61 (assistance), 66v–70v (protection). The register includes both Dutch and French texts.

[41] *Ibid.*, fo. 70v.

were determined to bargain hard over them.[42] What was to be the source of much future confusion, however, was that in the main treaty (10 August) the political role of her 'governor general' was summarised in a mere five articles (16–20) out of thirty.[43]

The 10 August treaty was hastily drafted and the third component of the Nonsuch agreement, the Act of Ampilation, which increased English military assistance following the surrender of Antwerp later in August, was even worse. It is also true that in practice Elizabeth expected a far greater degree of political influence within the United Provinces than the 10 August treaty allowed for and never fully accepted the ramifications of *de facto* independence. Nevertheless a consistency of approach is found in both negotiations. The Dutch case was accepted; the main issue was the consequences. Had Elizabeth made a treaty with Holland and Zeeland in 1576, it is doubtful, *mutatis mutandis*, that its terms would have been significantly different. What had changed was a wider perception in England by 1584–5 that war with Spain was inevitable whatever happened in the Netherlands.[44]

---

[42] As argued by C. G. Roelofsen, 'De onderhandlingen over een verdrag van bijstand tussen de Staten-Generaal en Engeland in 1585/6', *Bijdragen voor de Geschiedenis der Nederlanden*, 22 (1968–9), 138–48.

[43] There are no reliable printed texts of the 10 August treaty, the most convenient manuscript copy is TNA (PRO), SP 103/33/211v–214v.

[44] On this point, see Adams, 'Decision', 23, 27.

ROYAL HISTORICAL SOCIETY:
REPORT OF COUNCIL.
SESSION 2003–2004

Officers and Council

- At the Anniversary Meeting on 21st November 2003, Professor M.J. Daunton was elected to succeed Professor J.L. Nelson at President after the Anniversary Meeting on 26th November 2004; I.W. Archer, MA, DPhil, succeeded Professor A.D.M. Pettegree as Literary Director; the remaining Officers of the Society were re-elected.
- The Vice-Presidents retiring under By-law XVII were Professor C.D.H. Jones and Professor R.D. McKitterick. Professor D.R. Bates, PhD and W.R. Childs, MA, PhD were elected to replace them.
- The Members of Council retiring under By-law XX were Dr. J.E. Burton, Dr. W.R. Childs and Professor V.I.J. Flint. In accordance with By-law XXI, amended, Professor J.H. Ohlmeyer, MA, PhD., Professor M.E. Rubin, MA, PhD and E.M.C. van Houts, MA, LittD, PhD. were elected in their place.
- haysmacintyre were appointed auditors for the year 2003–2004 under By-law XXXIX.
- Cripps Portfolio continued to manage the Society's investment funds.

Activities of the Society during the Year

The Society remains actively involved in working with research bodies, funding councils and other Learned Societies to protect and promote the interests of our discipline and allied disciplines.

The President and Honorary Secretary had a profitable meeting with Professor Geoff Crossick, Chief Executive of the AHRB on 9 March. The discussion included the implications of the Board's imminent transformation into a Research Council, the creation of new funding streams, the future of research centres, prospects for international funding, monitoring of large-scale AHRB projects and the reduction in funding for trainee archivists. Outstanding issues have been subsequently pursued through further meetings and correspondence.

An invitation from the AHRB to nominate 'ring-fenced' doctoral awards in certain fields was taken up by the Society. The President submitted a bid for six doctoral awards in historical fields where languages other than English are required, but regrettably this was not successful. Following the establishment of the AHRB Peer Review College, six representatives of the Society were nominated for membership.

The Society has closely monitored the discussions about the form of the next Research Assessment Exercise, responding to the Roberts Report (which may be read on the Society's website), and submitting suggestions to HEFCE.

The Society has also responded to consultative documents circulated by national bodies, principally English Heritage's review of the future of the National Monument Record at Swindon; the Documentary Heritage Review undertaken by the Church Commissioners relating to the future of Lambeth Palace Library and the Church of England Record Centre; and the National Archives' proposed revision of national archives legislation.

The Society monitored threats to teaching and research provision in Higher Education Institutions, such as the restructuring of medieval history at the University of Kent, and the closure of East Asian Studies at Durham University. A joint letter with HUDG was sent to the Director of SOAS, expressing concern at the loss of posts during the year. In order to be better informed about the changing contours of teaching and research, the Teaching Policy Committee is undertaking a survey across HEIs, which should provide reliable rather than anecdotal information about the health of our discipline and the challenges facing it.

The Society has co-opted Fellows with particular expertise to strengthen the membership of three of its committees. Professor Eric Evans and Dr Andrew Foster have joined the Teaching Policy Committee, Professor Michael Lynch has accepted an invitation to join the Research Policy Committee, and Dr Jon Parry has agreed to serve on the Finance Committee.

Relations with HUDG remain close and cordial, with regular meetings and joint ventures. The Society, HUDG and the Institute of Historical Research are collaborating on a major conference on 'History in British Education', to be held in February 2005. One of its objectives is to close the gap between history teaching in the secondary and tertiary sectors. Along with its partner, the Historical Association, the Society remains committed to support the strengthening of history teaching in schools, and its representatives have attended meetings of the History Subject Group on the Qualifications and Curriculum Authority, and a group sponsored by OCR to consider the reform of 'A' Level history. The implications of 'citizenship' classes for history teaching in schools is also being considered by Council. The President and Professor Dickinson have attended meetings over the past year with the Secretary of State for Education at which history teaching at all levels have been discussed.

Council has been considering the latest developments surrounding the 'Bologna Process', a European intergovernmental initiative to establish a European-wide standard in Higher Education, and has expressed its concerns to the Quality Assurance Agency.

The Society is represented on the panel of judges for the National Awards for Teaching in Higher Education, now in its second year. The awards are organised by the Subject Centre for History, Classics and Archaeology at the University of Glasgow. Senior representatives for the Subject Centre gave a helpful presentation to Teaching Policy Committee on its work and the potential for close co-operation with the Society. The Society has backed the Centre for Excellence in Teaching and Learning bid from the history department at Lancaster University.

The Honorary Secretary represented the Society in an informal alliance of Learned Societies, set up in May 2003 to engage with the White Paper on 'The Future of Higher Education'. Membership increased during the summer and autumn, and several letters were published in national newspapers warning against plans to concentrate research funding in a small number of elite institutions.

The Society is developing closer links with other Learned Societies to exchange information and consider collaborative ventures. In May a successful meeting was held with representatives from the Bibliographical Society, and a similar meeting with representatives from the Royal Geographical Society is being planned.

The Society agreed to the transfer of the Library of Professor Sir Geoffrey Elton, housed after his death at the Borthwick Institute in York, to new premises within the University of York. The collection will remain on open access and can be consulted free of charge.

The British National Committee of the International Committee of Historical Sciences, administered by the Society, has helped to finalise the topics and contributors to the 20th Quinquennial Congress, which will be held in Sydney, Australia, on 3rd–9th July 2005. 40 scholars from the UK were intending to attend.

Council and the Officers record their debt of thanks to Joy McCarthy, the Executive Secretary, and Amy Warner, Administrative Assistant, for their expert and dedicated work on these and other activities throughout the past year.

Meetings of the Society

• Four papers were given in London this year and three papers were read at locations outside London. Welcome invitations were extended to the Society to visit the history departments at the University of

Newcastle upon Tyne, Royal Holloway University of London, the University of Kent at Canterbury and the German Historical Institute London. The trip to Newcastle would have included a tour of the new developments in the town, but was curtailed because of yet more national rail difficulties. However, the 'replacement' visit to the City Centre and Millennium Bridge by taxi at night proved to be very spectacular and well worth the day's wait. The visit to Royal Holloway included a special exhibition at the Bedford Centre for the History of Women, and the visit to the University of Kent at Canterbury included a conducted tour of the Cathedral Archives and Library. Members of Council met with members of the History Departments to discuss issues of interest to historians before the papers were delivered. The lecture given at the German Historical Institute London ensured adequate appreciation of the inspirational redecoration of the interior of the building. As always, the Society received a warm welcome and generous hospitality from the hosts concerned and is very grateful to them for their kindness. Future visits are planned to include the University of the West of England, together with the British Empire and Commonwealth Museum, Bristol, on the 22nd and 23rd October 2004, the University of Southampton on Tuesday 26th April 2005, and the Universities at Dublin on 21st–22nd October 2005.

- Conferences were held i) a joint conference with The National Maritime Museum on 'Elizabeth I and the Expansion of England: Britain, Europe and the Wider World' was held on 4th–6th September 2003; ii) two events took place in memory of the Society's former President Professor Gerald Aylmer: the first annual lecture was held at the University of York on 11th October 2003, when Professor Paul Slack spoke on 'Government and information in seventeenth-century England', and the Seminar 2003 was held at the Institute of Historical Research on 21st October 2003 on the topic 'What do historians want from archivists [and vice-versa]?'; iii) a one-day conference, 'What can historians contribute to public debate?', was held at Chancellor's Hall, Senate House, London on 22 November 2003; and iv) a study day, 'Can we construct a history of trust?', was held in the Society's rooms at University College London on 7th February 2004.

- The Colin Matthew Memorial Lecture for the Public Understanding of History – previously known as the Gresham Lecture – was given on 6th November 2003 to an enthralled audience by Professor Brian Harrison at The Guild Church of St. Andrew, Holborn, London on '"A slice of their lives": The DNB's editors 1882–1999'. These lectures continue to be given in memory of the late Professor Colin Matthew, a former Literary Director and Vice-President of the Society. The lecture in 2004 will be on Wednesday 3rd November when Dr. Gareth Griffiths, Director of the British Empire and Commonwealth Museum,

Bristol, will speak on 'Presenting unwanted histories: the project to establish the British and Commonwealth Museum'. The lecture in 2005 will be on Wednesday 2nd November by Michael Wood.

- Future conferences would include:
  - i) a joint conference was planned with the North American Conference on British Studies and the British Association for American Studies, 'Crosstown Traffic: Anglo-American Cultural Exchange since 1865', to be held at the University of Warwick on 4–6 July 2004;
  - ii) a further one day seminar to commemorate the Society's former President, Professor Gerald Alymer, on 'Recasting the Past: Digital Histories' to be held at The National Archives, Kew, on 27th November 2004;
  - iii) a conference on 'History and Music' to be held at CRASSH, Cambridge, on 19th–20th March 2005;
  - iv) a joint conference with the Centre for English Local History, University of Leicester to mark the 50th Anniversary of W.G. Hoskins' *Making of the English Landscape* to be held on 7th–10th July 2005;
  - v) a one day conference with the History of Parliament Trust to mark the 400th anniversary of the Gunpowder Plot, to be held at Westminster Hall on 4th November 2005;
  - vi) A one day conference on 'New Directions in British Historiography of China' to be held on 28th November 2005 at the Institute of Historical Research, London.
  - vii) a joint conference with the YMCA, 'Christian Movements', to be held in Birmingham on 17th–19th February 2006;
  - viii) a conference, 'Cultures of Political Counsel?', to be held on 7th–9th April 2006, at the University of Liverpool;
  - ix) a joint conference with the German Historical Institute London on 'How violent were the Middle Ages?', to be held in July 2006 at Cumberland Lodge, Windsor;
  - x) a joint conference with the National Maritime Museum, on the Seven Years War, in July 2006 at Greenwich, and
  - xi) a conference to mark the Tercentenary of the Union with Scotland is scheduled to be held in 2007.

- A joint conference with the Institute of Historical Research and the Historical Association on 'History in British Education' will be held at the IHR on 14th–15th February 2005.

Prizes

The Society's annual prizes were awarded as follows:

• The Alexander Prize was awarded in 2004 to Ian Mortimer, BA, MA, RMSA, FRHistS, for his essay 'The Triumph of the Doctors: Medical Assistance to the Dying, c. 1570–1720'. Friday 21st May 2004

The judge's citation read:

'The general quality of entries was high and the range of themes highly interesting. The winning essay combined new research data with a hypothesis to examine, in a lucid and scholarly style; and the overall argument addressed big questions of culture, belief systems, medicine, and the role of the professions, in an exhilarating way.'

• The David Berry Prize for 2003, for an essay on Scottish history, was awarded to Mr. Mike Lyon for his essay 'Better that bairns should weep than bearded men": the Raid of Ruthven (1582) and the Master of Glamis'.

The judge's citation read:

'The 2003 David Berry Prize attracted 10 entries, a number of which had already been published or were worthy of publication. The winning essay reconstructed the chronology of the raid, examined its participants and assessed its impact on James VI and, more generally, on Scottish politics. 'The New Lanark Highlanders: Migration, Community and Language, 1785-c.1850' by Ian Donnichie and Margaret Nicholson came *proxime accessit*. This essay appeared in Volume 6 (May 2003) of *Family and Community History* and examined Highland-Lowland migration in the early stages of industrialization.'

• The Whitfield Prize for a first book on British history attracted 29 entries. The generally high quality of the entries was again commended by the assessors.

The prize for 2003 was awarded to:

Christine Peters for her book *Patterns of Piety: Women, Gender and Religion in Late Medieval and Reformation England* [CUP].

Proxime accessit was Holger Hoock for his book *The King's Artists: the Royal Academy of Arts and the Politics of British Culture 1760–1840* [Clarendon Press].

The judges wrote:

'The Whitfield Prize for a first book on British history attracted 29 entries. Over half were of a high or very high quality, though some publishers might be reminded of the criteria: three were not their author's first solely written history book, while several others failed to qualify as original and scholarly books of historical research.

The judges had difficulty in reducing the short list to a winner, but after much consideration they awarded the prize to Christine Peters for her *Patterns of Piety*. She displays a mastery of a wide range of sources (visual as well as documentary and literary) over a long time-span, and has provided a lively, well-written and important study which has implications well beyond her chosen subtitle. She demonstrates originality, an ambitious sweep, depth as well as breadth, and an imaginative approach to her evidence.

They adjudged Holger Hoock's *The King's Artists* a close runner-up. It covers a wide range of material in a very accessible way, is impressive in its interdisciplinary scope, and has very important implications for the relationships between cultural patronage, nationalism and the state in a crucial period.'

- Thanks to the continuing generous donation from The Gladstone Memorial Trust, the Gladstone History Book Prize for a first book on a subject outside British history was again awarded. The number of entries this year was 20.

The Prize for 2003 was jointly awarded to:

Norbert Peabody for his book *Hindu Kingship and Polity in Precolonial India*, Cambridge Studies in Indian History and Society, 9 (Cambridge, CUP, 2003) and

Michael Rowe for his book *From Reich to State. The Rhineland in the Revolutionary Age 1780–1830*, New Studies in European History (Cambridge, CUP, 2003)

The judges wrote:

'The Gladstone prize for a first book on Non British History attracted 20 entries, of which one was disqualified because it was not published in 2003, while several others were not felt to represent the scholarly and original research as stipulated by the Prize's criteria. About one half of the submitted books, almost all based on PhD research, were studies of high quality.

Two books stood out for their originality, fresh methodology and exemplary take on their subject with the result that the judges considered it only fair to award the Gladstone prize to their authors jointly:

Norbert Peabody challenges established notions of kingship and the construction of memory in the Hindu kingdom of Kota in Rajasthan in the eighteenth and early nineteenth century. He argues persuasively and with great authority that pre-colonial polities could be disharmonious, energetic and eclectic well before the advent of colonial influence. His study is a breath of fresh air that will form a new and most welcome point of departure for historians of colonial encounters.

Michael Rowe studied the political transformation of the Rhineland area from a polity dominated by the French to its incorporation by the Prussian state. Using a vast array of unpublished archival sources his proposition that the local Rhinelanders exploited their (French) Napoleonic juridical administration in order to forge their own identity as part of the new German polity is original and convincing. His exceptional command of the modern French and German historiography is impressive.'

- In order to recognise the high quality of work now being produced at undergraduate level in the form of third-year dissertations, the Society continued, in association with *History Today* magazine, to award an annual prize for the best undergraduate dissertation. Departments are asked to nominate annually their best dissertation and a joint committee of the Society and *History Today* select in the autumn the national prizewinner from among these nominations. The prize also recognizes the Society's close relations with *History Today* and the important role the magazine has played in disseminating scholarly research to a wider audience. 50 submissions were made.

First prize was awarded jointly to Sami Abouzahr [UCL] for his essay 'the European Recovery Program, and American Policy Towards Indochina, 1947–1950'; and

Charmain Brownrigg [University of Central Lancashire] 'The Merchant Mariners of North Lancashire and Cumberland in the Mid-Eighteenth Century'.

Third prize was awarded to Andrew Syk [University of Derby] 'The 46th Division on the Western Front'.

Articles by all three prize-winners presenting their research have appeared or will appear shortly in *History Today* editions in 2004.

At the kind invitation of the Keeper, all entrants and their institutional contacts were invited to a celebratory lunch and a behind the scenes visit to The National Archives at Kew in January 2004.

- The German History Society, in association with the Society, agreed to award a prize to the winner of an essay competition. The essay, on any aspect of German history, including the history of German-speaking people both in within and beyond Europe, was open to any postgraduate registered for a degree in a university in either the United Kingdom or the Republic of Ireland. The prize was presented at the Annual General Meeting of the German History Society, and was considered for publication in *German History*.

The judges of the first year's prize emphasized that each of the ten essays submitted was of good quality, covering interesting subjects in a mature and capable manner.

The winning essay was by Simone Laqua [Balliol College, Oxford] entitled 'Convent Life in Early Modern Munster?'

Joint second place were Paul Brand [University of York] '"They had said nothing about rebaptism": the surprising birth of Swiss Anabaptism', and Maximillian Horster [St. Edmund's College, Cambridge] 'The trade in political prisoners between the two German states, 1962–1989'.

The judges also commended Alexander Watson [Jesus College, Oxford] for his essay 'For Emperor and Fatherland?: the identity and fate of the German volunteers, 1914–1918'.

- Frampton and Beazley Prizes for A-level performances were awarded following nominations from the examining bodies:

Frampton Prizes:

o AQA
  Matthew R. J. Neal, Leicester Grammar School
o Edexcel Foundation incorporating the London Examination Board:
  No award
o Oxford, Cambridge and RSA Board:
  Henry Ellis, Eton College, Windsor
o Welsh Joint Education Committee:
  Menna Chadha, Cardiff High School

Beazley Prizes:

o Northern Ireland Council for the Curriculum Examinations and Assessment: Brian D. Sloan, Our Lady and St. Patrick's College, Knock
o Scottish Examination Board:
  A. Jonathan Waterlow, The Royal High School, Edinburgh

- At the request of the Director of the Institute of Historical Research, the Pollard Prize, awarded annually to the best postgraduate student paper presented in a seminar at the IHR, will be announced at the Society's Annual Reception in July, commencing in 2004.

Publications

- *Transactions*, Sixth Series, Volume 13 was published during the session, and *Transactions*, Sixth Series, Volume 14 went to press, to be published in November 2004.
- In the Camden, Fifth Series, *Religion, Politics and Society in Sixteenth-Century England*, eds. S. Adams, I. Archer, G.W. Bernard, F. Kisby, M. Greengrass and P. Hammer (Vol. 22) New Style 'Miscellany XXVI', and *Lollards of Coventry, 1486–1522*, eds. S. McSheffrey and N. Tanner (vol. 23) were published during the year. *Appeasement and All Souls: A Portrait with Documents*, ed. Sidney Aster (vol. 24) and *Foreign Intelligence and information gathering in Elizabethan England: Two English Treatises on the State of France, 1580–1584*, ed. David Potter (vol. 25) went to press for publication in 2004–2005.
- The Society's *Annual Bibliography of British and Irish History, Publications of 2002*, was published by Oxford University Press during the session. This was the final printed volume.

The Royal Historical Society Bibliography on British History commenced a new AHRB award in January 2004 and welcomed Simon Baker as Assistant Project Editor. The database is being updated more regularly, and has been greatly enhanced by the integration of records from the sister project *Irish History OnLine* which was scheduled to go live in August 2004. *The Bibliography* has continued to benefit from collaboration with *London's Past OnLine*.

The *Studies in History* Editorial Board was saddened by the news of the death Dr. Simon Walker, one of its Advisory Editors since 1995.

- Professor John Morrill succeeded Professor David Eastwood as Convenor of the Editorial Board.
- The second series continued to produce exciting volumes. The following volumes were published, or went to press, during the session:

  ○ *English Public Opinion and the American Civil War: A Reconsideration* by Duncan A. Campbell;
  ○ *Franco-Irish relations: politics, migration and trade, 1500–1610* by Mary Ann Lyons;
  ○ *Managing the British Empire: The Crown Agents for the Colonies, 1833–1914* by David Sunderland;
  ○ *1659: The Crisis of the Commonwealth* by Ruth Mayers;
  ○ *Women's Bodies and Dangerous Trades in England, 1880–1914* by Carolyn Malone; and
  ○ *Dualist heresy in Aquitaine and the Agenais, c.1000–c.1249* by Claire Taylor.

- As in previous subscription years, volumes in *Studies in History* series were offered to the membership at a favourably discounted price. Many Fellows, Associates and Members accepted the offer for volumes published during the year, and the advance order for further copies of the volumes to be published in the year 2004–2005 was most encouraging.
- The Society acknowledges its gratitude for the continuing subventions from the Economic History Society and the Past and Present Society to the *Studies in History* series.
- The re-publication of the Presidential lectures of Sir Richard Southern, with an introduction by Rob Bartlett, was due to be published by Blackwells in the Autumn 2004.
- Papers from the conference, 'Churchill in the Twenty-First Century', with a new introduction by Professor David Cannadine, went into production with Cambridge University Press, for publication in the Autumn 2004.

Papers Read

- At the ordinary meetings of the Society the following papers were read:

  ○ 'The Literary Critic and the Village Labourer: "Culture" in Twentieth-Century Britain'
  Professor Stefan Collini (2nd July 2003: Prothero Lecture)
  ○ 'Queen Victoria and India, 1837–1876'
  Professor Miles Taylor (24th October 2003 at the University of Newcastle upon Tyne)
  ○ 'Modernisation as Social Evolution: the German case'
  Professor John Breuilly (23rd January 2004 at the German Historical Institute of London)
  ○ 'Marmoutier and its serfs in the eleventh century'
  Professor Paul Fouracre (12th March 2004)
  ○ '"A sinister and retrogressive proposal: Irish women's opposition to the 1937 draft constitution'
  Dr. Maria Luddy (26th March 2004 at Royal Holloway, University of London
  ○ 'Women, servants, and by-employment in English rural households, 1440–1650'
  Dr. Jane Whittle (30th April 2004 at the University of Kent at Canterbury)
  ○ The Alexander Essay Prize reading
  The Triumph of the Doctors: Medical Assistance to the Dying, c.1570–1720' Ian Mortimer (21st May 2004)

- At the Anniversary meeting on 21st November 2003, the President, Professor Janet L. Nelson, delivered an address on 'England the Continent in the Ninth Century: III. Rights and Rituals'.
- At the Conference entitled 'Elizabeth I and the Expansion of England: Britain, Europe and the Wider World' held at the National Maritime Museum, Greenwich on 4th–6th September 2003, the following papers were read:

'"Elizabeth I and the Spanish Armada": A Painting and its Afterlife' Karen Hearn
'A Century on: Pepys and the Elizabethan Navy' C. S. Knighton
'Queen Elizabeth and the Myth of Sea-power in English History' N. A . M. Rodger
'Mathematics and the Art of Navigation: The Advance of Scientific Seamanship in Elizabethan England' Susan Rose
'Was Elizabeth I Interested in Maps – and Did It Matter?' Peter Barber
'Bringing the World to England: The Politics of Translation in the Age of Hakluyt' William H. Sherman
'Gloriana Rules the Waves: Or, the Advantages of Being Excommunicated (and a Woman)' Lisa Jardine
'France and Elizabethan England' Charles Giry-Deloison

'The King (the Queen) and the Jesuit: James Stuart's *True Law of Free Monarchies* in context' Peter Lake
'Elizabeth I: A Sense of Place in Stone, Print and Paint' Maurice Howard
'The Elizabethan Idea of Empire' David Armitage
'Scotland, Elizabethan England and the Idea of Britain' Roger A. Mason
'"Never any Realm Worse Governed": Elizabeth and Ireland' Hiram Morgan
'Elizabeth I and the Sovereignty of the Netherlands 1576–1585' Simon Adams

Finance

- The Society's overall position hardly changed between 2002–3 and 2003–4, improving by about the rate of inflation. However, this is the first year since 1999–2000 when the overall position did not deteriorate. Hopefully a corner is being turned. This was achieved because a small recovery in the value of our investments counterbalanced a deficit of nearly £20,000 on the income and expenditure account. We have continued to bear down upon expenditure and are considering ways of increasing our income, but we do not anticipate a significant improvement in our financial position in the short term. Caution is the current watch word and is likely to have to remain so for at least a few years yet.
- Council records with gratitude the benefactions made to the Society by:
  - Mr. L.C. Alexander
  - The Reverend David Berry
  - Professor Andrew Browning
  - Professor C.D. Chandaman
  - Professor G. Donaldson
  - Professor Sir Geoffrey Elton
  - Mr. E.J. Erith
  - Mr. P.J.C. Firth
  - Mrs. W.M. Frampton
  - Mr. A.E.J. Hollaender
  - Professor C.J. Holdsworth
  - Miss V.C.M. London
  - Professor P.J. Marshall
  - Mr. E.L.C. Mullins
  - Sir George Prothero
  - Dr. L. Rausing
  - Professor T.F. Reddaway
  - Miss E.M. Robinson
  - Miss J.C. Sinar
  - Professor A.S. Whitfield

Membership

- Council was advised and recorded with regret the deaths of 6 Fellows, 1 Life Fellow, 15 Retired Fellows, 1 Corresponding Fellows, 1 Associate and 1 Member.

These included

Lord Blake – Retired Fellow
Professor R. Brentano – Fellow
Lord Bullock – Retired Fellow
Mr. William Y. Carman – Retired Fellow
The Rev. Dr. L.W. Cowie – Retired Fellow
Professor J.S. Cummins – Retired Fellow
The Right Rev. G.M. Dilworth – Retired Fellow
Mr. E.J. Erith – Life Fellow
Emeritus Professor Paul Hair – Retired Fellow
Mr. A. Hendrie – Associate
Professor J.Q. Hughes – Retired Fellow
Professor E. Kossman – Corresponding Fellow
Mr. Michael MacLagan – Fellow
Dr. D.H. Newsome – Fellow
Professor D.M. Nicol – Retired Fellow
Dr. Robert Philips – Fellow
Professor B.J. Pimlott – Fellow
Miss Marjorie Reeves – Retired Fellow
Professor P.M. Stell – Retired Fellow
Dr. J.L. Tanner, CBE – Fellow
Dr. S.K. Walker – Fellow and member of *Studies in History* Editorial Board
Professor D.E.R. Watt – Retired Fellow
Mr. Donald J. Withrington – Retired Fellow
Professor Philippe Wolff – Corresponding Fellow

- 84 Fellows and 31 Members were elected. 4 new Honorary Vice-Presidents and 4 Corresponding Fellows were invited to accept election. The membership of the Society on 30th June 2004 numbered 2779, comprising 1865 Fellows, 551 Retired Fellows, 17 Life Fellows, 16 Honorary Vice-Presidents, 93 Corresponding Fellows, 77 Associates and 160 Members.
- The Society exchanged publications with 15 Societies, British and Foreign.

Representatives of the Society

- Professor David Ganz succeeded Professor D. d'Avray as the Society's representative on the Anthony Panizzi Foundation;
- The representation of the Society upon other various bodies was as follows:
  - Dr. Julia Crick on the Joint Committee of the Society and the British Academy established to prepare an edition of Anglo-Saxon charters;
  - Professor N.P. Brooks on a committee to promote the publication of photographic records of the more significant collections of British Coins;
  - Professor G.H. Martin on the Council of the British Records Association;
  - Mr. P.M.H. Bell on the Editorial Advisory Board of the *Annual Register*.
  - Professor C.J. Holdsworth on the Court of the University of Exeter;
  - Professor M.C. Cross on the Council of the British Association for Local History; and on the British Sub-Commission of the Commission International d'Histoire Ecclesiastique Comparée;
  - Professor L.J. Jordanova on the Advisory Council of the reviewing committee on the Export of Works of Art;
  - Professor W. Davies on the Court of the University of Birmingham;
  - Professor R.D. McKitterick on a committee to regulate British co-operation in the preparation of a new repertory of medieval sources to replace Potthast's *Bibliotheca Historica Medii Aevi.*;
  - Dr. W.R. Childs at the Court at the University of Sheffield;
  - Dr. J. Winters on the History Data Service Advisory Committee;
  - Dr. R.A. Burns on the user panel of the RSLP Revelation project 'Unlocking research sources for 19th and 20th century church history and Christian theology';
  - Dr. M. Smith on the Court of Governors of the University of Wales, Swansea.
  - Dr. R. Mackenney on the University of Stirling Conference.
  - Professor N. Thompson on the Court of the University of Wales Swansea.
  - Dr. C.J. Kitching on the National Council on Archives.
- Council received reports from its representatives.

Grants

- The Royal Historical Society Centenary Fellowship for the academic year 2003–2004 was awarded to Alban Gauthier studying for a doctorate at the University Lille-III Charles De Gaulle and working on a thesis entitled 'Feasting in Anglo-Saxon England: Places, realities, rituals, 5th–11th centuries'.

- The Society's P.J. Marshall Fellowship for the academic year 2003–2004 was awarded jointly to Catriona Kennedy, studying at the University of York, and working on 'Gender, Politics and Irish National Identity in the 1790s', and Izabela Orlowska, at SOAS, working on 'The Unification of the Ethiopian Empire, 1872–1889'.

- The Society's Research Support Committee continued to provide grants to postgraduate students for attendance at training courses or conferences, and funding towards research within and outside the United Kingdom. Funding is also available to organizers of workshops and conferences to encourage the participation of junior researchers.

- A new scheme to enhance the impact of the Society's support by bringing postgraduate speakers already in receipt of the Society's Research Funds to speak at participating departments around the country was planned to be introduced from the beginning of the forthcoming financial year, on a trial basis.

- Grants during the year were made to the following:

Training Bursaries

○ Ariadna ACEVEDO-RODRIGO, University of Warwick
'Annual Conference of the Society for Latin American Studies', held at the University of Leiden, the Netherlands, 2nd–4th April 2004.

○ Joanne APPLIN, University College London
'The College Art Association Annual Conference for Art Historians', held in Seattle, USA, 18th–21st February 2004.

○ Catherine ARMSTRONG, University of Warwick
Conference, 'Inhabiting the Body', held in North Carolina, USA, 19th–20th March 2004.

○ Manuel BARCIA PAZ, University of Essex
Conference, 'Literary Manifestations of the African Diaspora', held at the University of Cape Coast, Ghana, 10th–14th November 2003.

○ Maitseo BOLAANE, University of Oxford
'"Dealing with Diversity" – 2nd International Conference of European Society for Environmental History', held at Charles University, Prague, Czech Republic, 3rd–7th September 2003.

○ Tatjana BUKLIJAS, University of Cambridge
'2004 Meeting of the American Association for the History of Medicine', held at the University of Wisconsin in Madison, USA, 28th April–2nd May 2004.

o Emma CAVELL, Oxford University
'The 39th International Congress of Medieval Studies', held in Kalamazoo, Michigan, USA, 6th–9th May 2004.

o Fabio CHISARI, De Montfort University, Leicester
'IX Congress of the European Committee for Sport History', to be held in Crotone, Italy, 23rd–26th September 2004.

o Sally CRUMPLIN, University of St Andrews
'International Medieval Congress: Power and Authority', held at the University of Leeds, 14th–17th July 2003 and
'International Medieval Congress', held in Leeds, July 2004.

o Androniki DIALETI, University of Glasgow
'Social History Annual Conference 2004', held at the University of Rouen, France, 8th–10th January 2004.

o Miriam DOBSON, University College London
'American Association for the Advancement of Slavic Studies' Annual Convention, held in Toronto, Canada 20th–23rd November 2003.

o Nicola FOOTE, University College London
'Segundo Ecnuentro Internacional de Estudios Ecuatorianos', held in Quito, Ecuador, 26th–28th June 2004.

o Andrea GALDY, Post Doctoral Fellow of the Henry Moore Foundation
'Annual Conference of the Social History Society' held in Rouen, 8th–10th January 2004.

o Rebecca GILL, University of Manchester
Conference, 'Disraeli et L'Europe: L'Homme D'Etat et L'Homme de Lettres', held at the University of Paris X (Nanterre), 17th–18th June 2004.

o Matthew HAMMOND, University of Glasgow
'International Medieval Congress', held in Leeds, 12th–15th July 2004.

o Elinor HARPER, University of Warwick
'UIUC Fifth Annual Graduate Symposium on Women's and Gender History', held in Chicago, USA, 11th–13th March 2004.

o Judith Ann HILL, University of Surrey, Roehampton
Conference, 'Reading the Immigrant Letter: Innovative Approaches and Interpretations', held at Carleton University, Ottawa, Canada, 7th–9th August 2003.

o Takashi ITO, Royal Holloway, University of London
'Annual Conference of the Japan Society for European and American History', held in Sendai, Japan, 21st–22nd May 2004.

o Vassiliki KARALI, University of Edinburgh
'British Society for Eighteenth-Century Studies Annual Conference', held at St Hugh's College, Oxford, 3rd–5th January 2004.

o Garyfallia KOUNENI, University of St Andrews

'The 39th International Congress of Medieval Studies', held in Kalamazoo, Michigan, USA, 6th–9th May 2004.

o Kieran McGOVERN, University of Birmingham
'26th Annual Warren Susman Graduate History Conference', held at Rutgers, the State University of New Jersey, USA, 17th April 2004.

o Malcolm McLAUGHLIN, University of Essex
'European Social Science History Conference', held at Humboldt University, Berlin, Germany, 24th–26th March 2004.

o Carmen MANGION, Birkbeck College
Conference, 'Crossing Boundaries', held in Atchison, Kansas, USA, 28th–30th June 2004.

o Georgios PLAKOTOS, University of Glasgow
Conference, 'Developing Cultural Identity in the Balkans: Convergence Versus Divergence' held at the University of Ghent, Belgium, 12th–13th December 2003.

o Caroline PROCTOR, University of St Andrews
'The 39th International Congress on Medieval Studies', held at the Western Michigan University, Kalamazoo, Michigan, USA, 6th–9th May 2004.

o Kent RAWLINSON, University of Durham
'An Introduction to Latin for Historical Research', held at the Institute of Historical Research, London, 1st–5th December 2003.

o Matteo RIZZO, School of Oriental and African Studies, University of London
'African Studies Association 46th Annual Meeting' held in Boston, USA, 30th October–2nd November 2003.

o Lucy ROBINSON, University of Sussex
Conference, 'Carnival of the Oppressed – the Angry Brigade and the Gay Liberation Front' held in Amsterdam, 3rd–4th October 2003.

o Joanna ROYLE, University of Glasgow
Conference, 'Christina of Markyate: a Typology of Female Sanctity?', held in St Albans, 2nd–3rd August 2003.

o Pedro RUIZ-CASTELL, University of Oxford
o 'XVI Encontro do Seminario Nacional de Historia da Matematica – XII Encontro Nacional de Astronomia e Astrofisica', held in Coimbra, Portugal, 26th–27th July 2003.

o Elizabeth SCHOALES, University of Wales, Lampeter
'12th International Congress of Celtic Studies' held at the University of Wales, Aberystwyth, 24th–30th August 2003.

o Natalia SOBREVILLA, Institute of Latin American Studies, University of London
Second International Congress of Peruvianists Abroad', held in Seville, Spain, 1st–4th June 2004.

○ Paula STILES, University of St Andrews
  Conference, 'Noble Ideals and Bloody Realities: Warfare in the Middle Ages' held at the University of British Colombia, Canada, 31st October–1st November 2003.
○ Ayako TOWATARI, Institute of Historical Research
○ 'Social History Society Annual Conference', held at the University of Rouen, France, 8th–10th January 2003.
○ Karine VARLEY, Royal Holloway, University of London
○ 'Society for French Historical Studies 50th Annual Conference', held in Paris, 17th–20th June 2004.

[36]

Research Fund: Research within the United Kingdom

○ Douglas BRINE, Courtauld Institute of Art
  Visits to Belgium and northern France, 19th April–30th May 2004.
○ Michael BURTSCHER, University of Oxford
  Visits to Arundel Castle, Sussex, 13th May–17th June 2003.
○ Sally CRUMPLIN, University of St Andrews
  Visits to libraries in England, April–May 2004.
○ Sumithra DAVID, University of St Andrews
  Visits to libraries in London and Cambridge, 17th July–19th August 2004.
○ Sanchari DUTTA, Wolfson College, Oxford
  Visits to the British Library, the Wellcome Institute Library and The National Archives, March–April 2004.
○ Jane EADE, Victoria and Albert Museum/Royal College of Art
  Visits to churches and houses in England, November 2003–March 2004.
○ Richard GLASS, Anglia Polytechnic University
  Visits to libraries and record offices in England, January 2004–April 2005.
○ Nicola GUY, University of Durham
  Visits to the National Archives, Kew, 15th–19th December 2003 and 5th–11th January 2004 and
  Visits to the School of Slavonic and East European Studies Library, the Maughlin Library, King's College London and The National Archives, 8th–12th June 2004.
○ Stephen JOYCE, Nottingham University
  Visits to Leicestershire Records Office, Wigston; Loughborough Central Library and the University of Nottingham, April 2003–October 2005
○ Paola MERLI, De Montfort University

Visits to the archives of the Royal Opera House and the Victoria and Albert Museum, London, 15th December 2002–11th June 2003.
- Emily PAYNE, University of Kent
  Visits to the British Library, London, September and October 2003.
- Kimberly PERKINS, University of Glasgow
  Visits to the National Library of Scotland and National Archives of Scotland, Edinburgh and the National Archives, Kew, September and October 2003.
- Fiona ROBINSON, University of Durham
  Visits to the Imperial War Museum, London, 7th–14th December 2003.
- Fiona ROBINSON, University of Durham
  Visits to libraries and record offices in London and Cambridge, 18th–25th April 2004.
- Colin SKELLY, University of York
  Visits to the Birmingham Central Library, 12th–21st January 2004.
- D. Alastair SMITH, Dundee University
  Visits to the National Archives, Edinburgh, April–August 2003.
- Jelmer VOS, School of Oriental and African Studies
  Visits to the Angus Library, Regent's Park College, Oxford and the Archives Générales de la Congération du Saint-Esprit, Chevilly-Larue, Paris, February 2004.
- David WILLCOX, University of Kent
  Visits to the University of Sussex, Marylebone Information Service, and the British Library, July and August 2003.
- Colin YARNLEY, University of Birmingham
  Visits to the National Archives, Kew, September 2003.

[20]

Research Fund: Research outside the United Kingdom

- Ariadna ACEVEDO-RODRIGO, University of Warwick
  Visits to archives in Mexico, 17th May to 21st July 2003.
- Metin BERKE, Queen's University Belfast
  Visits to libraries in Athens, Patmos, Paris, Vatican, El Escorial and Vienna, October 2003–March 2004.
- Daniel BRANCH, University of Oxford
  Visits to archives in Kenya, 5th July–14th September 2004.
- Stephanie BURGIS, University of Leeds
  Visits to the Austrian National Library, Music Collection, Austria, April 2004.
- Stephanie DECKER, University of Liverpool
  Visits to the National Archives of Ghana, Accra and interviews, 20th June–27th July 2004.

○ Larissa DOUGLASS, University of Oxford
Visits to archives in Prague and Vienna, July and August 2003.

○ Allen FROMHERZ, St Andrews University
Visits to sites in Morocco, mid-February–late-March 2004.

○ Shirley HAINES, University of Nottingham
Visits to the Archive of Frederick Kiesler, Vienna and the Guggenheim Museum, Venice, March and May 2004.

○ Mary HUNTER, University College London
Visits to archives in Paris and Toulouse, July and August 2003.

○ Ryo IKEDA, London School of Economics
Visits to archives in the United States of America, October and November 2003 and archives in France, April 2004.

○ Nancy IRESON, Courtauld Institute of Art, University of London
Visits to the home of Joy Weber, Santa Fe, USA, June–July 2004.

○ Joel ISAAC, University of Cambridge
Visits to archives in the USA, 24th May–9th July 2003.

○ Elizabeth KEANE, University of Cambridge
Visits to the Harry S. Truman Presidential Library, Missouri, USA, 2nd February–12th February 2004.

○ Xabier LAMIKIZ, Royal Holloway, University of London
Visits to the Archivo General de Indias in Seville, Spain, 22nd May–5th June 2004.

○ Gabrielle LYNCH, University of Oxford
Visits to the Kenyan National Archives, Nairobi, August 2004–June 2005.

○ Alexandra MELITA, Royal Holloway, University of London
Visits to libraries and archives in Venice, 7th–13th July 2003.

○ Tatsuya MITSUDA, University of Cambridge
Visits to archives in Vienna, Berlin and Paris, 18th August–26th September 2003 and
Visits to archives in Hanover and Lyon, March–April 2004.

○ James MORRISON, University of Birmingham
Visit to the National Archives of Canada, May 2003.

○ Diego MUSITELLI, University of Manchester
Visit to the Centre des Archives D'Outre Mer, Aix-en-Provence, France, July–September 2003.

○ Julie PHAM, University of Cambridge
Visits to archives in China, 18th July–30th December 2004.

○ Ivan POLANCEC, University College London
Visits to the Vatican Archives Rome, Italy and Bibliotheque Nationale, Paris, France, 1st April–15th April 2003.

○ Jason ROCHE, University of St Andrews
Visits to the Aegean Littoral and Central Plateau, Turkey, 5th–26th January 2004.

o Yael RONEN-RAK, University of Cambridge
   Visits to archives in South Africa and Namibia, February–March 2004.
o Eugenia RUSSELL, Royal Holloway, University of London
   Visits to libraries in Greece, Italy and Israel, September–April 2004.
o Asaf SINIVER, University of Nottingham
   Visits to the National Archives, the Library of Congress, the National
   Security Archives and the George Washington Library, Washington
   D.C., July–August 2003.
o Elke STOCKREITER, School of Oriental and African Studies,
   University of London
   Visits to Zanzibar National Archives, Zanzibar and the Tanzania
   National Archives, Dar es Salaam, Tanzania, The Public Record
   Office, London and the Bodleian Library, Oxford, July 2003–June
   2004.
o John STRACHAN, University of Manchester
   Visits to archives in France, 14th February–5th June 2004.
o Richard TAWS, University College London
   Visits to archives in Paris and Vizille, France, July 2003.
o Julia VON DANNENBERG, University of Oxford
   Visits to archives in Germany, February–March 2004.
o Benedikta VON SEHERR-THOSS, Worcester College, Oxford
   Visits to German State Archive, Koblenz, and Archive of the German
   Foreign Office, Berlin, Germany.
o Daniel VAN VOORHIS, University of St Andrews
   Visits to the Herzog August Bibliothek, Wolfenbuttel, Germany, June
   2004.
o Thomas WALES, University of Edinburgh
   Visits to archives in the United States of America, 21st–30th July 2003.
o David WATSON, University of Dundee
   Visits to the William L. Clements Library, Michigan, USA, during the
   summer – autumn 2004.
o Christopher WRIGHT, Royal Holloway, University of London
   Visits to archives in Italy, October 2003–April 2004.

[35]

Workshop Fund

o 'The Fifteenth Century Conference 2004: Medieval Lives: People and
   Places in the 15th Century', held at Royal Holloway and Bedford New
   College, University of London, 2nd–4th September 2004 (Caroline
   BARRON and Hannes KLEINEKE).
o Conference, 'Trade: Histories, Cultures and Economies', held at the
   University of Wolverhampton, 11th and 12th September 2003 (John
   BENSON).

o Conference, 'Rethinking Britain, 1918–1959', held at the Centre for Contemporary British History, School of Advanced Study, University of London, 18th–19th March 2004 (Adrian BINGHAM).

o Conference, 'Interrogating Hearsay: Rumours and Gossip in Historical Perspective, 1500–2003', held at the University of Essex, 26th July 2003 (D. BORG-MUSCAT, M. McLAUGHLIN, C. SCHRODER).

o Conference, 'Four Empires and Enlargement. States, Societies and Individuals: Transfiguring Perspectives and Images of Central and Eastern Europe', held at the School of Slavonic and East European Studies, UCL, 6th–8th November 2003 (Daniel BRETT).

o 'The Anglo-Saxon Chronicle: An Interdisciplinary Conference', held at the University of York, 28th–30th July 2004 (Alice COWEN).

o 'Multidisciplinary Conference on the History of Religion', held at University College London, 29th–30th April 2004 (Joanna CROW).

o Conference, 'The Creation of Individual and Collective Identities in the Middle Ages', held at the University of Edinburgh, 29th May 2004 (Elizabeth ELLIOTT).

o Conference, 'Recipes in Early Modern Europe: The Production of Food, Medicine and Knowledge', held at the Wellcome Unit for the History of Medicine, Oxford, 13th–14th February 2004 (Catherine FIELD).

o 'Tenth Thirteenth Century England Conference', held at the University of Durham, 1st–3rd September 2003 (Robin FRAME).

o Conference, 'The Mercenary Identity in the Middle-Ages', held at the University of Wales, Swansea, 7th–10th July 2005 (John FRANCE).

o Conference, 'Masculinity, Patriarchy and Power: Interdisciplinary Approaches', held at the University of Southampton, 5th–7th April 2004 (Julia GAMMON).

o Conference, 'Domestic Designs: 1400 to the Present, A Postgraduate Research Day', held at the Royal College of Art, 9th February 2004, (Hannah GREIG).

o Conference, 'Memory', held at the Institute of Historical Research, 11th July 2003 (Jane HAMLETT).

o 'British Society for the History of Science Postgraduate Conference', held at the University of Manchester, 6th–8th January 2004 (Vanessa HEGGIE).

o Conference, '"The Unforgivable Crime?: Child Murder in History', held at St Antony's College Oxford, Friday 19th and Saturday 20th September 2003 (Anne-Marie KILDAY).

o Conference, 'The Experience of Poverty in Modern Europe: Narrative and Context', held at Oxford Brookes University, 3rd–5th September 2004 (Steven KING).

o Conference, 'The Cromwellian Protectorate', held at the History of Parliament, London, 17th January 2004 (Patrick LITTLE).

o Conference, 'Consecrated Women: Towards the History of Women Religious in Britain and Ireland', held at the Margaret Beaufort Institute of Theology, University of Cambridge, 16th–17th September 2004 (Ruth MANNING).

o Conference, '"Nasty Brutish and Short": Cheap Print and the Scholar', held at the University of Warwick, 19th June 2004 (Angela McSHANE JONES).

o Conference, 'Queer Matters', held at King's College London, 28th–30th May 2004 (Robert MILLS).

o Conference, 'Understanding Urban Wales', held at the University of Wales, Swansea, 9th–10th September (Louise MISKELL).

o Conference, 'Bastardy: the British Experience. Illegitimacy in History from the Medieval to the Modern Age', held at the University of Cambridge, 6th January 2004 (Thomas NUTT).

o 'Religion, the Individual and Society in Russia', held at the University of Wales, Gregynog, 28th–30th March 2004 (Irina PAERT)

o Conference, 'Immigration, History and Memory in Britain', held at the University of Leicester, 6th–7th September 2003 (Panikos PANAYI).

o Conference, 'Sex: Medieval Perspectives', held at the University of St Andrews, 11th–12th June 2004 (Caroline PROCTOR).

o Conference, 'Women in the British Country House, 1650–1900', held at the University of York and Castle Howard, Yorkshire, 14th–16th May 2004 (Jane RENDALL).

o Conference, 'Outrageous Stories: Women, Scandal and Subversion in Britain, held at the University of Warwick, 24th April 2004 (Sarah RICHARDSON)

o 'Society for the Study of French History 18th Annual Conference. Theme: Belief and Dissent', held at the University of Warwick, 1st–2nd April 2004 (Penny ROBERTS).

o Conference, 'Meeting of Minds: Comparing Migrant Experiences Across Ethnic Groups', held at the Camden Irish Centre, London, 22nd November 2003 (Louise RYAN).

o Conference, 'Royalists and Royalism: politics, region and culture, 1640–1660', held at Clare College, Cambridge, 23rd–25th July 2004 (David L. SMITH).

○ Conference, 'The English Revolution and its Legacies', held at University College London, 20th–21st February 2004 (Nicholas TYACKE).

[32]

ORS Awards

○ Katherine CHAMBERS, St John's College, Cambridge.
○ Natalya CHERNYSHOVA, King's College London.

[2]

THE ROYAL HISTORICAL SOCIETY
FINANCIAL STATEMENTS
FOR THE YEAR ENDED 30 JUNE 2004

haysmacintyre
Chartered Accountants
Registered Auditors
London

THE ROYAL HISTORICAL SOCIETY
REPORT OF THE COUNCIL OF TRUSTEES
FOR THE YEAR ENDED 30 JUNE 2004

The members of Council present their report and audited accounts for the year ended 30 June 2004.

PRINCIPAL ACTIVITIES AND REVIEW OF THE YEAR

The Society exists for the promotion and support of historical scholarship and its dissemination to historians and a wider public. This year, as in previous years, it has pursued this objective by an ambitious programme of publications – a volume of Transactions, two volumes of edited texts in the Camden Series and further volumes in the Studies in History Series have appeared, by the holding of meetings in London and at universities outside London at which papers are delivered, by the sponsoring of the joint lecture for a wider public with Gresham College, by distributing over £20,000 in research support grants to 125 individuals, and by frequent representations to various official bodies where the interests of historical scholarship are involved. It is Council's intention that these activities should be sustained to the fullest extent in the future.

RESULTS

The Society began to recover from the difficult year in 2003 with total funds increasing from £1,941,366 in June 2003 to £1,999,895 in June 2004, an increase of £58,529. This was largely due to an improvement in the stock market since the Society incurred a deficit of £19,595 from operating activities (2003: surplus of £8,352), after providing for slow moving publications.

Membership subscriptions saw an increase of £13,214 due to subscription rate increases set at the Society's Anniversary Meeting on 22 November 2002. Investment income amounted to £98,536 compared to £138,092 in 2003 when a special dividend was received for £67,564 in respect of Royal Bank of Scotland shares.

Income from royalties increased from £20,584 to £25,148, income from conferences generated £1,220 and grants for awards increased from £4,113 to £6,601. Total costs increased from £219,208 to £228,142.

FIXED ASSETS

Information relating to changes in fixed assets is given in notes 5 and 6 to the accounts.

INVESTMENTS

The Society has adopted a "total return" approach to its investment policy. This means that the funds are invested solely on the basis of seeking to secure the best total level of economic return compatible with the duty to make safe investments, but regardless of the form the return takes.

The Society has adopted this approach to ensure even-handedness between current and future beneficiaries, as the focus of many investments moves away from producing income to maximising capital values. In the current investments climate, to maintain the level of income needed to fund the charity, would require an investment portfolio which would not achieve the optimal overall return, so effectively penalising future beneficiaries.

The total return strategy does not make distinctions between income and capital returns. It lumps together all forms of return on investment – dividends, interest, and capital gains etc, to produce a "total return". Some of the total return is then used to meet the needs of present beneficiaries, while the remainder is added to the existing investment portfolios to help meet the needs of future beneficiaries.

The Society's investments are managed by Cripps Portfolio, who report all transactions to the Honorary Treasurer and provide six monthly reports on the portfolios, which are considered by the Society's Finance Committee which meets three times a year. In turn the Finance Committee reports to Council.

The Society closely monitors its investments, with its main portfolio being assessed against a bespoke benchmark and its smaller Whitfield and Robinson portfolios against the FTSE APCIMS balanced benchmark.

During the year the general fund portfolio generated a total return of 8.1% compared with its customised benchmark return of 9.65% and the W M Charities constrained by Income Index return of 12.28%. The Whitfield and Robinson portfolios generated returns of 9.23% and 8.72% respectively against their benchmark of 11.55%.

RISK ASSESSMENT

The trustees are satisfied that they have considered the major risks to which the charity is exposed, that they have taken action to mitigate or manage those risks and that they have systems in place to monitor any change to those risks.

GRANT MAKING

The Society awards funds to assist advanced historical research. It operates several separate schemes, for each of which there is an application form. The Society's Research Support Committee considers applications at meetings held 6 times a year. In turn the Research Support Committee reports to Council. A list of awards made is provided in the Society's Annual Report.

RESERVES POLICY

The Council have reviewed the Society's need for reserves in line with the guidance issued by the Charity Commission. They believe that the Society requires approximately the current level of unrestricted general funds of £1.8m to generate sufficient total return, both income and capital, to cover the Society's expenditure in excess of the members' subscription income on an annual basis to ensure that the Society can run efficiently and meet the needs of beneficiaries.

The Society's restricted funds consist of a number of different funds where the donor has imposed restrictions on the use of the funds which are legally binding. The purposes of these funds are set out in note 13 to 15.

STATEMENT OF TRUSTEES' RESPONSIBILITIES

Law applicable to charities in England and Wales requires the Council to prepare accounts for each financial year which give a true and fair view of the state of affairs of the Society and of its financial activities for that year. In preparing these accounts, the Trustees are required to:

- select suitable accounting policies and apply them consistently;
- make judgements and estimates that are reasonable and prudent;
- state whether applicable accounting standards have been followed, subject to any material departures disclosed and explained in the accounts;
- prepare the accounts on the going concern basis unless it is inappropriate to presume that the Society will continue in business.

The Council is responsible for ensuring proper accounting records are kept which disclose, with reasonable accuracy at any time, the financial position of the Society and enable them to ensure that the financial statements comply with applicable law. They are also responsible for safeguarding the assets of the Society and hence for taking reasonable steps for the prevention and detection of error, fraud and other irregularities.

MEMBERS OF THE COUNCIL

At the Anniversary Meeting on 21 November 2003, the Officers of the Society were re-elected.

The Vice-Presidents retiring under By-law XVII were Professor C D H Jones and Professor R D McKitterick. Professor D Bates and Dr W R Childs were elected to replace them.

The Members of Council retiring under By-law XX were Dr. J.E. Burton, Dr. W.R. Childs and Professor V.I.J. Flint. In accordance with By-law XXI, amended, Professor M E Rubin, Professor J H Ohlmeyer and Dr E M C van Houts were elected in their place.

APPOINTMENT OF TRUSTEES

In accordance with By-law XVII, the Vice-Presidents shall hold office normally for a term of three years. Two of them shall retire by rotation, in order of seniority in office, at each Anniversary Meeting and shall not be eligible for re-election before the Anniversary Meeting of the next year. In accordance with By-law XIX, the Council of the Society shall consist of the President, the Vice-Presidents, the Treasurer, the Secretary, the Librarian, the Literary Directors and twelve Councillors. The President shall be *ex-officio* a member of all Committees appointed by the Council; and the Treasurer, the Secretary, the Librarian and the Literary Directors shall, unless the Council otherwise determine, also be *ex-officio* members of all such Committees. In accordance with By-law XX, the Councillors shall hold office normally for a term of four years. Three of them shall retire by rotation, in order of seniority in office, at each Anniversary Meeting and shall not be eligible for re-election before the Anniversary Meeting of the next year.

STANDING COMMITTEES 2004

The Society was operated through the following Committees during the year ended 30 June 2004:

Finance Committee	Dr M Finn	
	Mr P J C Firth	– non Council Member
	Professor P Mathias	– non Council Member
	Dr J P Parry	– non Council Member
	Professor F O'Gorman	
	The seven officers (President – Chair)	
Membership Committee	Professor R J A R Rathbone	– Chair
	Professor D M Palliser	
	Professor H E Meller	
Publications Committee	Professor D R Bates	– Chair
	Dr R S Mackenney	
	Professor H E Meller	
	Professor J H Ohlmeyer	
	The seven officers	
Research Support Committee	Professor P J Corfield	– Chair
	Dr M Finn	
	Professor F O'Gorman	
General Purposes Committee	Professor L J Jordanova	– Chair
	Professor D M Palliser	
	Professor R J A R Rathbone	
	Professor M E Rubin	
	The seven officers	
Teaching Policy Committee	Dr W R Childs	– joint Chair
	Professor H.T. Dickinson	– joint Chair
	Dr S R Ditchfield	
	Professor E J Evans	– non Council Member
	Dr A W Foster	– non Council Member
	Dr E M C Van Houts	
	The seven officers	
Research Policy Committee	Dr C J Kitching	– Chair
	Professor J A Green	
	Professor G A Hosking	
	Professor L J Jordanova	
	The seven officers	

Studies in History	Professor D S Eastwood	– Convenor
Editorial Board	Professor J S Morrill	– Convenor – elect
	Professor M Braddick	– nonCouncil Member
	Dr S Church	– non Council Member
	Professor J Hunter	– Economic History Society
	Professor M Mazower	– non Council Member
	Dr R Spang	– non Council Member
	Professor M Taylor	– non Council Member
	Dr A Walsham	– Past & Present Society
	A Literary Director	
	Honorary Treasurer	
Election of Officers:	Professor L J Jordanova	– Convenor
President and Literary	Dr M Finn	
Director Subcommittee:	A Literary Director	
	Honorary Secretary	
	Honorary Treasurer	
Election of Officers:	President	– Convenor
Executive Secretary Subcommittee:	President – elect	
	Honorary Secretary	
	Honorary Treasurer	

AUDITORS

A resolution proposing the appointment of auditors will be submitted at the Anniversary Meeting.

By Order of the Board

24 September 2004
Honorary Secretary

INDEPENDENT REPORT OF THE AUDITORS
FOR THE YEAR ENDED 30 JUNE 2004

We have audited the financial statements of The Royal Historical Society for the year ended 30 June 2004 which comprise the Statement of Financial Activities, the Balance Sheet, and the related notes. These financial statements have been prepared under the historical cost convention (as modified by the revaluation of certain fixed assets) and the accounting policies set out therein.

This report is made solely to the charity's trustees, as a body, in accordance with the regulations made under the Charities Act 1993. Our audit work has been undertaken so that we might state to the charity's trustees those matters we are required to state to them in an auditor's report and for no other purpose. To the fullest extent permitted by law, we do not accept or assume responsibility to anyone other than the charity and the charity's trustees as a body, for our audit work, for this report, or for the opinions we have formed.

RESPECTIVE RESPONSIBILITIES OF TRUSTEES AND AUDITORS

The trustees' responsibilities for preparing the Annual Report and the financial statements in accordance with applicable law and United Kingdom Accounting Standards are set out in the Statement of Trustees' Responsibilities.

We have been appointed as auditors under section 43 of the Charities Act 1993 and report in accordance with regulations made under section 44 of that Act. Our responsibility is to audit the financial statements in accordance with relevant legal and regulatory requirements and United Kingdom Auditing Standards.

We report to you our opinion as to whether the financial statements give a true and fair view and are properly prepared in accordance with the Charities Act 1993. We also report to you if, in our opinion, the Trustees' Report is not consistent with the financial statements, if the charity has not kept proper accounting records or if we have not received all the information and explanations we require for our audit.

We read the other information contained in the Trustees' Report and consider whether it is consistent with the audited financial statements. We consider the implications for our report if we become aware of any apparent misstatements or apparent material inconsistencies with the financial statements.

BASIS OF AUDIT OPINION

We conducted our audit in accordance with United Kingdom Auditing Standards issued by the Auditing Practices Board. An audit includes examination, on a test basis, of evidence relevant to the amounts and disclosures in the financial statements. It also includes an assessment of the significant estimates and judgements made by the Trustees in the preparation of the financial statements, and of whether the accounting policies are appropriate to the charity's circumstances, consistently applied and adequately disclosed.

We planned and performed our audit so as to obtain all the information and explanations which we considered necessary in order to provide us with sufficient evidence to give reasonable assurance that the financial statements are free from material misstatement, whether caused by fraud or other irregularity or error. In forming our opinion we also evaluated the overall adequacy of the presentation of information in the financial statements.

OPINION

In our opinion the financial statements give a true and fair view of the state of the charity's affairs as at 30 June 2004 and of its incoming resources and application of resources in the year then ended and have been properly prepared in accordance with the Charities Act 1993.

haysmacintyre
Chartered Accountants   Fairfax House
Registered Auditors   15 Fulwood Place
                                                                                    London
                                                                              WC1V 6AY

24 September 2004

THE ROYAL HISTORICAL SOCIETY

STATEMENT OF FINANCIAL ACTIVITIES
FOR THE YEAR ENDED 30 JUNE 2004

	Notes	Unrestricted Funds £	Endowment Funds £	Restricted Funds £	Total Funds 2004 £	Total Funds 2003 £
INCOMING RESOURCES						
Donations, legacies and similar incoming resources	2	5,167	–	–	5,167	6,161
Activities In Furtherance Of The Charity's Objects						
Grants for awards		6,000	–	601	6,601	4,113
Conferences		1,220	–	–	1,220	–
Subscriptions		70,860	–	–	70,860	57,646
Royalties		25,148	–	–	25,148	20,584
Activities To Generate Funds						
Investment income	6	96,754	–	1,782	98,536	138,092
Other		1,015	–	–	1,015	964
TOTAL INCOMING RESOURCES		206,164	–	2,383	208,547	227,560
RESOURCES EXPENDED						
Cost of Generating Funds						
Investment manager's fee		11,717	262	–	11,979	11,853
Charitable Expenditure						
Grants for awards	3	30,757	–	9,569	40,326	42,717
Conferences and Receptions		10,961	–	–	10,961	8,363
Publications		81,571	–	–	81,571	58,039
Library		4,294	–	–	4,294	11,219
Support costs		64,596	–	–	64,596	73,143
Management and administration		14,415	–	–	14,415	13,874
TOTAL RESOURCES EXPENDED	4	218,311	262	9,569	228,142	219,208
NET (OUTGOING)/INCOMING RESOURCES		(12,147)	(262)	(7,186)	(19,595)	8,352
Transfers	14	(699)	–	699	–	–
Other recognised gains and losses						
Net gain/(loss) on investments	6	68,047	10,077	–	78,124	(144,171)
NET MOVEMENT IN FUNDS		55,201	9,815	(6,487)	58,529	(135,819)
Balance at 1 July 2003		1,882,975	44,577	13,814	1,941,366	2,077,185
Balance at 30 June 2004		£1,938,176	£54,392	£7,327	£1,999,895	£1,941,366

THE ROYAL HISTORICAL SOCIETY

BALANCE SHEET AS AT 30 JUNE 2004

	Notes	2004 £	2004 £	2003 (restated) £	2003 £
FIXED ASSETS					
Tangible assets	5		308		463
Investments	6		1,982,297		1,906,197
			1,982,605		1,906,660
CURRENT ASSETS					
Stocks	7	12,921		30,430	
Debtors	8	13,827		7,506	
Cash at bank and in hand		38,207		25,671	
		64,955		63,607	
LESS: CREDITORS					
Amounts due within one year	9	(47,665)		(28,901)	
NET CURRENT ASSETS			17,290		34,706
NET ASSETS			£1,999,895		£1,941,366
REPRESENTED BY:					
Endowment Funds	13				
A S Whitfield Prize Fund			36,630		34,297
The David Berry Essay Trust			17,762		10,280
Restricted Funds	14				
A S Whitfield Prize Fund – Income			1,574		2,932
BHB Fund			5,534		6,792
P J Marshall Fellowship			–		3,768
The David Berry Essay Trust – Income			219		322
Unrestricted Funds					
Designated – E M Robinson Bequest	15		108,735		92,950
General Fund			1,829,441		1,790,025
			£1,999,895		£1,941,366

Approved by the Council on 2004

President   J. L. Nelson

Honorary Treasurer J. Hoppit

The attached notes form an integral part of these financial statements.

THE ROYAL HISTORICAL SOCIETY

Notes to the Accounts For The Year Ended 30 June 2004

1. Accounting Policies

  (a) *Basis of Preparation*

      The financial statements have been prepared in accordance with the Statement of Recommended Practice 2000 "Accounting and Reporting by Charities" and with applicable accounting standards issued by UK accountancy bodies. They are prepared on the historical cost basis of accounting as modified to include the revaluation of fixed assets including investments which are carried at market value.

  (b) *Depreciation*

      Depreciation is calculated by reference to the cost of fixed assets using a straight line basis at rates considered appropriate having regard to the expected lives of the fixed assets. The annual rates of depreciation in use are:

        Furniture and equipment   10%
        Computer equipment   25%

  (c) *Stock*

      Stock is valued at the lower of cost and net realisable value.

  (d) *Library and archives*

      The cost of additions to the library and archives is written off in the year of purchase.

  (e) *Subscription income*

      Subscription income is recognised in the year it became receivable with a provision against any subscription not received.

  (f) *Investments*

      Investments are stated at market value. Any surplus/deficit arising on revaluation is included in the Statement of Financial Activities. Dividend income is accounted for when the Society becomes entitled to such monies.

  (g) *Publication costs*

      Publication costs are transferred in stock and released to the Statement of Financial Activities as stocks are depleted.

  (h) *Donations and other voluntary income*

      Donations and other voluntary income is recognised when the Society becomes legally entitled to such monies.

  (i) *Grants payable*

      Grants payable are recognised in the year in which they are approved and notified to recipients.

  (j) *Funds*

      Unrestricted: these are funds which can be used in accordance with the charitable objects at the discretion of the trustees.

      Designated: these are unrestricted funds which have been set aside by the trustees for specific purposes.

      Restricted: these are funds that can only be used for particular restricted purposes defined by the benefactor and within the objects of the charity.

      Endowment: permanent endowment funds must be held permanently by the trustees and income arising is separately included in restricted funds for specific use as defined by the donors.

      The purpose and use of endowment, restricted and designated funds are disclosed in the notes to the accounts.

      During the year the classification of funds was reviewed and as a result certain funds were reclassified. The revised classification is shown in the balance sheet and notes 13 to 15. There is no effect on the total fund balances as at 30 June 2003 and 30 June 2004 or on the overall results for the years then ended.

  (k) *Allocations*

      Wages and salary costs are allocated on the basis of the work done by the Executive Secretary and the Administrative Secretary.

  (l) *Pensions*

      Pension costs are charged to the SOFA when payments fall due. The Society contributes 10% of gross salaries to the personal pension plans of one of the employees.

2. DONATIONS AND LEGACIES

	2003 £	2004 £
A Browning Bequest	–	180
G R Elton Bequest	2,857	4,342
Donations via membership	944	410
Gladstone Memorial Trust	600	600
Sundry income	766	629
	£5,167	£6,161

3. GRANTS FOR AWARDS

	Unrestricted Funds £	Restricted Funds £	Total 2004 £	Total 2003 £
Alexander Prize	268	–	268	253
Sundry Grants	200	–	200	700
Research support grants (see below)	20,886	–	20,886	26,227
Historical Association	–	–	–	2,000
Centenary fellowship	5,425	–	5,425	8,225
A-Level prizes	500	–	500	500
A S Whitfield prize	–	1,099	1,099	1,125
E M Robinson Bequest				
– Grant to Dulwich Picture Library	2,375	–	2,375	2,375
Gladstone history book prize	1,103	–	1,103	1,062
P J Marshall Fellowship	–	6,700	6,700	–
British History Bibliography project grant	–	1,258	1,258	–
David Berry Prize	–	512	512	250
	£30,757	£9,569	£40,326	£42,717

During the year Society awarded grants to a value of £20,886 (2003: £26,227) to 125 (2003: 98) individuals.

GRANTS PAYABLE

	2004 £	2003 £
Commitments at 1 July 2003	5,573	3,937
Commitments made in the year	40,326	42,717
Grants paid during the year	(43,049)	(41,081)
Commitments at 30 June 2004 (Note 9)	£2,850	£5,573

4. TOTAL RESOURCES EXPENDED

	Staff Costs £	Depreciation £	Other Costs £	Total £	2003 £
Cost of Generating Funds					
Investment manager's fee	–	–	11,979	11,979	11,853
Charitable Expenditure					
Grants for awards (Note 8)	–	–	40,326	40,326	42,717
Conferences	3,349	–	7,612	10,961	8,363
Publications	18,546	–	63,035	81,571	58,093
Library	1,302	–	2,992	4,294	11,219
Support costs	34,900	155	29,541	64,596	73,143
Management and administration	–	–	14,415	14,415	13,874
Total resources expended	£58,097	£155	£169,890	£228,142	£219,208

STAFF COSTS	2004 £	2003 £
Wages and salaries	49,230	46,528
Social Security costs	5,129	4,542
Other pension costs	3,738	3,649
	£58,097	£54,719

The average number of employees in the year was 2 (2003: 2). There were no employees whose emoluments exceeded £50,000 in the year.

During the year travel expenses were reimbursed to 30 Councillors attending Council meetings at a cost of £5,028 (2003: £5,565). No Councillor received any remuneration during the year (2003 nil).

Included in management and administration is the following:

	2003 £	2004 £
Audit fee	6,698	6,698
Other services	540	493

5. TANGIBLE FIXED ASSETS

	Computer Equipment £	Furniture and Equipment £	Total £
COST			
At 1 July 2003	30,360	1,173	31,533
At 30 June 2004	30,360	1,173	31,533
DEPRECIATION			
At 1 July 2003	29,897	1,173	31,070
Charge for the year	155	–	155
At 30 June 2004	30,052	1,173	31,225
NET BOOK VALUE			
At 30 June 2004	£308	£–	£308
At 30 June 2003	£463	£–	£463

All tangible fixed assets are used in the furtherance of the Society's objects.

6. INVESTMENTS

	General Fund £	Robinson Bequest £	Whitfield Prize Fund £	David Berry Essay Trust £	Total £
Market value at 1 July 2003	1,751,878	110,191	42,598	1,530	1,906,197
Additions	335,773	8,054	10,144	409	354,380
Disposals	(323,406)	(15,865)	(17,133)	–	(356,404)
Net gain/(loss) on investments	61,692	6,355	2,595	7,482	78,124
Market value at 30 June 2004	£1,825,937	£108,735	£38,204	£9,421	£1,982,297
Cost at 30 June 2004	£1,674,122	£78,878	£35,927	£1,530	£1,790,458

	2004 £	2003 £
U K Equities	1,092,060	931,917
U K Government Stock and Bonds	705,188	834,084
Overseas equities	75,993	17,398
Uninvested Cash	109,056	122,798
	£1,982,297	£1,906,197

	2004 £	2003 £
Dividends and interest on listed investments	97,980	137,880
Interest on cash deposits	556	212
	£98,536	£138,092

7. STOCK

	2004 £	2003 £
Transactions Sixth Series	819	3,617
Camden Fifth Series	8,611	14,284
Guides and Handbooks	–	1,281
Camden Classics Reprints	3,491	11,248
	£12,921	£30,430

8. DEBTORS

	2004 £	2003 £
Other debtors	8,619	5,209
Prepayments	5,208	2,297
	£13,827	£7,506

9. CREDITORS: Amounts due within one year

	2004 £	2003 £
Trade creditors	4,863	2,773
Sundry creditors (Note 3)	2,850	5,573
Subscriptions received in advance	11,238	11,452
Accruals and deferred income	28,714	9,103
	£47,665	£28,901

10. LEASE COMMITMENTS

The Society has the following annual commitments under non-cancellable operating leases which expire:

	2004 £	2003 £
Within 1–2 years	–	–
Within 2–5 years	12,615	7,281
	£12,615	£7,281

11. LIFE MEMBERS

The Society has ongoing commitments to provide membership services to 17 Life Members at a cost of approximately £50 each per year.

12. UNCAPITALISED ASSETS

The Society owns a library the cost of which is written off to the Statement of Financial Activities at the time of purchase. This library is insured for £150,000 and is used for reference purposes by the membership of the Society.

13. ENDOWMENT FUNDS	Balance at 1 July 03 £	Incoming resources £	Outgoing resources £	Investment gain £	Balance at 30 June 04 £
A S Whitfield Prize Fund	34,297	–	(262)	2,595	36,630
The David Berry Essay Trust	10,280	–	–	7,482	17,762
	£44,577	£ –	£(262)	£10,077	£54,392

A S Whitfield Prize Fund
The A S Whitfield Prize Fund is an endowment used to provide income for an annual prize for the best first monograph for British history published in the calendar year.

The David Berry Essay Trust
The David Berry Essay Trust is an endowment to provide income for an annual prize for the best essay on a subject dealing with Scottish history.

14. RESTRICTED FUNDS	Balance at 1 July 03 £	Incoming resources £	Outgoing resources £	Transfers £	Balance at 30 June 04 £
A S Whitfield Prize Fund Income	2,932	1,372	(1,099)	(1,632)	1,574
BHB Fund	6,792	–	(1,258)	–	5,534
P J Marshall Fellowship	3,768	601	(6,700)	2,331	–
The David Berry Essay Trust	322	409	(512)	–	219
	£13,814	£2,383	£(9,569)	£699	£7,327

A S Whitfield Prize Fund Income
Income from the A S Whitfield Prize Fund is used to provide an annual prize for the best first monograph for British history published in the calendar year. The transfer represents an amount to the General Fund to reimburse paid outgoings.

BHB Fund
The British History Bibliographies project funding is used to provide funding for the compilation of bibliographies in British and Irish History.

P J Marshall Fellowship
The P J Marshall Fellowship is used to provide a sum sufficient to cover the stipend for a one-year doctoral research fellowship alongside the existing Royal Historical Society Centenary Fellowship at the Institute of Historical Research in the academic year 2003–2004. The transfer is in respect of amounts received within the General Fund in respect of the Fund.

The David Berry Essay Trust Income
Income from the David Berry Trust is to provide an annual prize for the best essay on a subject dealing with Scottish history.

15. DESIGNATED FUNDS	Balance at 1 July 03 £	Incoming resources £	Outgoing resources £	Investment gain £	Transfers £	Balance at 30 June 04 £
E M Robinson Bequest	£92,950	£3,466	£(3,051)	£6,355	£9,015	£108,735

E M Robinson Bequest
Income from the E M Robinson bequest is to further the study of history and to date has been used to provide grants to the Dulwich Picture Gallery. The transfer results from the release of an amount due to the General Fund no longer required.

16. GENERAL FUND

	Balance at 1 July 03 £	Incoming resources £	Outgoing resources £	Investment gain £	Transfers £	Balance at 30 June 04 £
	£1,790,025	£202,698	£(215,260)	£61,692	£(9,714)	£1,829,441

17. ANALYSIS OF NET ASSETS BETWEEN FUNDS

	General Fund £	E. M. Robinson Bequest Fund £	A.S. Whitfield Prize Fund £	A.S. Whitfield Prize Income £	BHB Fund £	David Berry Essay Trust £	David Berry Essay Trust Income £	Total £
Fixed assets	308	–	–	–	–	–	–	308
Investments	1,825,937	108,735	36,630	1,574	–	9,421	–	1,982,297
	1,826,245	108,735	36,630	1,574	–	9,421	–	1,982,605
Current assets	50,861	–	–	–	5,534	8,341	219	64,955
Less: creditors	47,665	–	–	–	–	–	–	(47,665)
Net current assets	3,196	–	–	–	5,534	8,341	219	17,290
Net assets	£1,829,441	£108,735	£36,630	£1,574	£5,534	£17,762	£219	£1,999,895